Business Mathematics:
A Worktext

Milton C. Olson, Ed. D.
Professor Emeritus State University of New York at Albany

F. Barry Haber, Ph. D., C.P.A.
Sioux Falls College

Bobbs-Merrill Educational Publishing   Indianapolis

The Bobbs-Merrill Company, Inc.
4300 West 62nd Street
Indianapolis, Indiana 46206

First Edition

First Printing—1981

Design by Sandra Strother

Cover design by Gene Lacy

Library of Congress Cataloging in Publication Data

Olson, Milton C.
    Business mathematics.

    Includes index.
    1. Business mathematics. I. Haber, F. Barry, joint author. II. Title.
HF5691.049   513′.93   80-10799
ISBN 0-672-97327-8

Business Mathematics:
A Worktext

Contents

Preface

Business Mathematics is intended especially for those who have not majored in mathematics. Practical applications of mathematics to banking, insurance, taxes, pensions, social security, and investments are of interest to all students. As a consumer, everyone has dealings with the business community, and many persons become a part of it as employees and managers.

A diagnostic test is provided to assess the capabilities of students in handling the basic mathematical processes. Appendix A provides materials for working on any difficulties discovered in this pretest. The work here should probably be done individually, with the instructor providing encouragement and guidance.

No algebraic or other complicated formulas are introduced in the text; instead, emphasis is placed on understanding the situations involved. First a clear, concise statement is given, followed by a specific example, then problems to be completed by the students. Answers to odd-numbered problems are given in Appendix D, so students can tell immediately whether they are on the right track. Each chapter contains a series of problems which review and summarize the material. The even-numbered problems can be used for testing purposes, should the instructor so desire.

As indicated in Appendix B, the use of hand calculators is encouraged, once students have displayed sufficient understanding of and skill in the basic processes. However, calculators are not necessary to complete the work efficiently and accurately.

Foreign exchange problems, the metric system, and conventional measurements are included, with some attention to changing measurements from one system to the other.

Some students may be interested in the operation of computers. Appendix C gives an introduction to the binary and octonal systems commonly used in computer applications.

Most of the topics provide excellent opportunities for discussing principles and problems which are based on but go beyond the mathematics involved. The social security system, various types of taxes, different kinds of life insurance policies, the role of credit, and the place of stocks and bonds in our economy all open doors to further study and discussion.

The authors thank the many persons in banking, insurance, investments, public accounting, the Social Security Administration, the Internal Revenue Service, and other agencies, who have provided the help needed to ensure up-to-date and reliable information.

Although the principles remain the same, unpredictable changes occur in tax rates, social security deductions and payments, interest rates, prices, and in a number of other areas. Some business practices vary from one locality to another. Business and government employees are usually very cooperative in providing the information needed for local applications.

Business
Mathematics:
A Worktext

Diagnostic Test

As you study business mathematics, you will find that it is not like any other course in mathematics or business. Many of the topics will already be familiar to you, although unfamiliar to other students. You may have bank accounts, own stocks; you may be making payments on a car or other purchase, be collecting social security, or have worked in an insurance office. Others will have had different experiences. Everyone will profit by a sharing of each person's expertise, and everyone will find some topics unfamiliar.

Almost every aspect of business involves some mathematics, so that a course in business mathematics becomes a sampling of business subjects. As you move from topic to topic, be alert to stirrings of interest or curiosity that may point the way to later specialization. Is it banking that appeals to you? Accounting? Retailing? Insurance? Statistics? Some other topic, or a combination of interests?

Unlike these business topics, none of the mathematics will be really new to you. What is different is the practical application of familiar processes. You are no longer merely practicing; this is real, and accuracy is extremely important.

Using the right procedure is most important of all. The most careful calculation will not provide the correct result if you have added when you should have subtracted or multiplied. In many cases in business, specific procedures must be followed exactly. At other times, the best approach is thinking the problem through and then proceeding carefully step by step.

Every type of problem presented in this book is clearly and fully illustrated. Study these illustrations carefully, making sure you understand what is being done and why. The solutions to the problems you are asked to solve will then come naturally to you.

Some people enjoy adding, dividing and so on with pencil and paper; many others do not. Speed is desirable, but accuracy should never be sacrificed for speed. Whether the work is done on paper or with a calculator, errors must be avoided. There are certain good ways of ensuring accuracy.

First of all, before you start calculating, guess the result—not a detailed guess necessarily, perhaps just an estimate of the extreme limits. Will the answer be more or less than a thousand? What would be reasonable? Should it be about half some other figure, twice that figure, or ten times it?

One of the most common errors in business mathematics is misplacing the decimal point. Guessing at the result beforehand will make this type of error less likely, but it still must be watched for.

Another common error happens in copying figures, either on paper or on a calculator. Digits may be transposed, as in substituting 428 for 482. A number like 667 is often written 677 instead. Punching the next higher or lower key on a calculator is very easy to do. This sort of error is not easy to spot, except by careful checking. Appendix B gives some suggestions for checking calculator computations.

Anyone who uses paper-and-pencil calculation very often will have developed shortcuts and quick methods of checking. For instance, if a problem includes multiplying a certain number by 4 and also by 8, the result of multiplying by 8 should be twice that of multiplying by 4. Such a person is also usually aware of his or her own most frequent errors (8×3? $6 + 7$?) and will be especially careful when such combinations occur. Making tables, such as a list of the multiples of 365 for some interest problems, can save much time and many errors.

If you come to this course with a solid background in basic mathematics, you are off to a good start. On the other hand, if your math is spotty or rusty, you may need to review some topics before going on. The pretest that follows contains some examples from placement tests given by prospective employers, some from standardized tests, and some adapted from later chapters in this book. If you make no serious errors on these examples, you should be able to proceed with no trouble. (Turn to Appendix A for the answers and evaluation.)

If you make many errors, you will save yourself much time and frustration by referring to Appendix A to sharpen your skills where needed. When you are able to solve all types of examples quickly and correctly, you will find the applications to business situations both understandable and interesting.

BASIC MATHEMATICS TEST

1.
$1.29
2.36
27.88
3.63
+ 4.27

$ 39.43

2.
51.81
27.05
40.65
30.11
31.04
39.53
21.45
25.97
49.84
+ 41.84

359.29

3. $24.83 + 2.98 + 15.14 =$ 42.95

4. $4^3/_8 + 2^2/_3 + ^1/_{12} =$ 7 1/8

5. $\frac{\$104.00}{12} + \$.50 =$ $ 9.16 2/3

6. $226.50 + (.4 \times 226.50) =$ 317.100

7.
$821.88
− 679.91

$ 141.97

8. Subtract $2.85 from $10.00: $ 7.15

9. $^1/_4 + ^1/_8 =$ 3/8 ✓

10. $486 − (.05 \times 486) =$ 461.7

11.
$ .38
× 3

$ 1.14

12.
18.4
× .06

1.104

13.
.0272
× 70

1.9040

14.
.004371
× 29
39339
008742
.126759

15. $.0125 \times 100 =$ 01.2500

16. $1,000,000 \times 1,000 =$ 1,000,000,000

17. $.0001 \times .0001 =$ .00000001

18. $325 \times 4 \times .04 =$ 52

19. $\$300 \times {}^{85}/_{100} \times {}^3/_{12} =$ $ 63.75

20. $^5/_{12} \times ^3/_{10} =$ 1/8

21. $4 \frac{1}{2} \times 3 \frac{1}{3} =$ 15

22.
$$\begin{array}{r} \overset{3}{\$94.70} \\ \times\ \ \ \ 18 \end{array}$$
75760
$9470
1,704.60

23. $49,945.60
$$\times\ \ \ \ \ \ .09$$
$149509(40)

24. $100.86
$$\times\ \ .004613$$
$.46526718

25. $\frac{7}{20} \times \$135 =$ $47.25

26. $.08 \times 2,346.04 \times \frac{50}{360} =$ 26.0671/9

27. $\frac{5}{12} \times 3,000 =$ 1250

28. $7 \times \dfrac{7 + 1}{2} =$ 28

29. $(31,200/150,000) \times$
$(18,700 - 1,500) =$ 3577.6

Round results to three decimal places:

30. $365 \div 7 =$ 52.143   **31.** $6.5\overline{)\,.0272}$ .004   **32.** $3,164\overline{)5,458}$ 1.725

33. $\$922.50\overline{)\$78.80}$ .085   **34.** $6,216\overline{)556,848}$ 89.583

Reduce to lowest terms:

35. $75/3,000 =$ 1/40   **36.** $72/3 =$ 24   **37.** $62,500/207,500 =$

25/83

Arrange from smallest to largest:

38. $\frac{1}{5};\ \frac{1}{3};\ \frac{1}{2};\ \frac{1}{4}$ 1/5 1/4 1/3 1/2   **39.** $\frac{2}{5};\ \frac{3}{8};\ \frac{1}{3}$ 1/3 - 3/8 - 2/5   **40.** $\frac{7}{10};\ .71;\ .07;\ .107$ .07 - .107 - 7/10 - .71

41. Round to the nearest 1,000:   **42.** To the nearest 100:

53,571 _54000_   53,571 _53,570_

43. To the nearest 10:

53,571 _53,600_

How much would you charge for (to the next higher penny):

44. One item at the price of 2 for 39¢?   _20_

45. Two items at the price of 4 for 55¢?   _28_

46. One item at the price of 12 for 43¢?   _4_

47. Two items at the price of 3 for 20¢?   _14_

48. Three items at the price of 4 for 9¢?   _7_

49. If 20 bags of potatoes weigh 110 lbs. and each bag when empty weighs ½ lb., what is the total weight of the potatoes?

_100_

50. A case of 24 cans of peaches costs $7.20 by the case. If sold separately each can costs 32¢. How much will a customer save on *each can* by buying a case? _2¢_

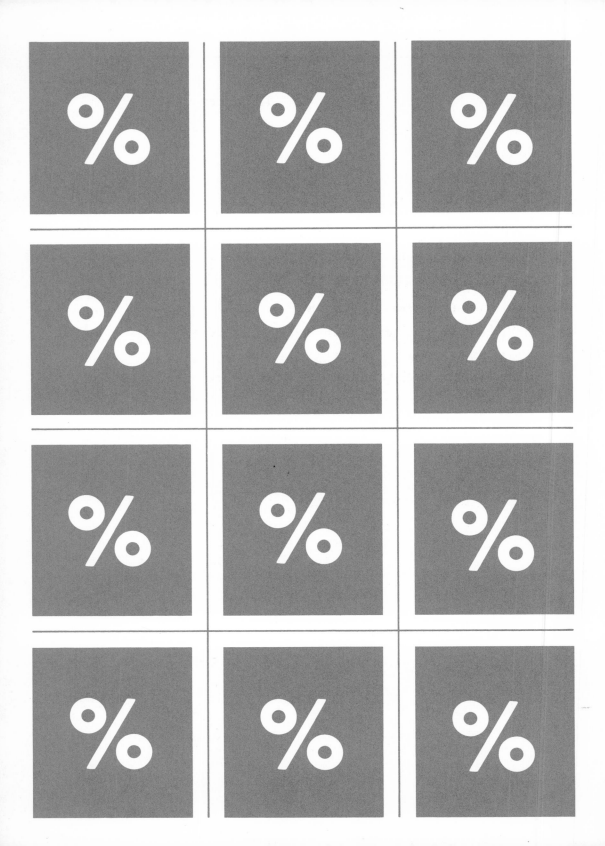

1

Percentage

1.1 MEANING OF PERCENT

To be able to deal intelligently with the many business and consumer problems that involve percentage, an understanding of percentage is essential.

Percentage is a special kind of fraction based on hundredths. The symbol "%," which is read "percent", means "hundredths" or "per hundred." Forty percent, for example, can be written as 40% and is the same as .40, or forty hundredths. This is also the same as 40/100, 4/10, or 2/5. In money terms, a percentage may be considered as cents on the dollar; for example, 8% of a dollar amount means 8 cents for each dollar.

A. To change a decimal to a percent, multiply the decimal by 100 (move the decimal point two places to the right) and add the percent sign.

Examples: .04 = 4%   3 = 300%   [i.e., 300% of 1]   .076 = 7.6%
              .0045 = .45%   4.8 = 480%

Problems

A. Express as percents:

1. .15 ___15___ %

2. .034 ___3.4___ %

3. .18 ___18___ %

4. .785 ___78.5___ %

5. .0753 ___7.53___ %

6. .002 ___.2___ %

7. .826 ___82.6___ %

8. 8.4 ___840___ %

9. .1526 ___15.26___ %

10. 2.57 ___257___ %

11. .51 ___51___ %

12. 6.00 ___600___ %

B. To change a fraction or a mixed number to a percent, first express the fraction as a decimal, then move the decimal point two places to the right and add the percent sign.

Examples: $^1/_5 = 1 \div 5 = .20 = 20\%$ $1^5/_8 = {}^{13}/_8 = 13 \div 8 = 1.625 =$
$$162.5\%$$

Problems

B. Write the following common fractions and mixed numbers as percents:

1. $14^1/_2$ _1450_ %   6. $4^3/_4$ _475_ %

2. $1^1/_4$ _125_ %   7. $2^1/_8$ _212.5_ %

3. $3^3/_8$ _337.5_ %   8. $^3/_{200}$ _1.5_ %

4. $3^1/_2$ _350_ %   9. $^7/_{10}$ _70_ %

5. $5^7/_8$ _587.5_ %   10. $^1/_{400}$ _.25_ %

C. To change a percent to a decimal, move the decimal point two places to the left and drop the percent sign.

Examples: $4\% = .04$ $85\% = .85$ $3.6\% = .036$
$$420\% = 4.20 \qquad 1/2\% = .005$$

Problems

C. Write the following percents as decimals:

1. 36% _.36_   7. .02% _.0002_

2. 7.4% _.074_   8. 6.97% _.0697_

3. 4.8% _.048_   9. .6% _.006_

4. $^1/_4$% _.004_   10. .85% _.0085_

5. 120% _1.20_   11. .268% _.00268_

6. .34% _.0034_   12. 6.3% _.0063_

1.2   FINDING A PERCENT OF A NUMBER

A percent may have little meaning by itself; you must know the number on which it is based. To find a certain percent of a number, express the percent as a decimal and multiply.

Example: 4% of 632 = .04 × 632 = 25.28

Sometimes it is more convenient to express a fractional part as a fraction. For example, to find $8\frac{1}{8}\%$ of $6,248, you might express $8\frac{1}{8}\%$ as 8.125% or as the decimal .08125, and then multiply. The result is $507.65. With the use of a calculator, this is easy, but you may find the following a simple means of checking your answer:

$$
\begin{array}{rcccl}
8\% \text{ of } \$6,248 & = & .08 \times & 6,248 & = & \$499.84 \\
\underline{\tfrac{1}{8}\% \text{ of } \$6,248} & = & \tfrac{1}{8} \times & 62.48 & = & \underline{+\quad 7.81} \\
8\tfrac{1}{8}\% \text{ of } \$6,248 & = & & & & \$507.65
\end{array}
$$

← Decimal   Percent →

Problems

Group 1

Find the given percent of the following numbers:

1. $2\frac{1}{2}\%$ of $600   *1500*
2. 3% of 30   *0.9*
3. 35% of 86   *30.1*
4. 8% of 800   *64*
5. 16% of 85   *13.6*
6. 15% of 325   *48.75*
7. 4.5% of 16.3   *0.7335*
8. $\frac{1}{2}\%$ of 90   *0.45*
9. 8.75% of 6,400   *560*
10. $4\frac{3}{4}\%$ of 625   *28.125*
11. .6% of 72   *0.432*
12. 22% of 164   *36.08*
13. $12\frac{1}{2}\%$ of 156   *19.5*
14. $7\frac{1}{2}\%$ of 48   *3.6*
15. 125% of 65   *81.25*

Group 2

1. A family found that 23% of their income went for food, 24% for housing, 8% for clothing, 5% for savings, 13% for car expenses, 5% for gifts and contributions, 4% for recreation and entertainment, and 18% for income taxes. If their annual income was $19,600, how much did they spend for each budget item?

    Food $ _4508_

    Housing $_4704_

    Clothing $_1568_

    Savings $_980_

    Car $_2548_

    Gifts and Contributions $_980_

    Recreation and Entertainment $_784_

    Income Taxes $_3528_

2. In a certain year, a single person with a taxable income of more than $20,200 but not more than $22,200 pays a federal income tax of $4,510 plus 36% of the taxable income over $20,200. How much income tax would a single person pay if the taxable income was $21,450? If the person was married and filed a joint return, the tax would be $3,260 plus 28% of the taxable income over $19,200. How much would be paid under these conditions?

    Single $_4960_

    Married $_3890_

3. One year, motor vehicles were 17.6% of all retail sales in the United States, home furnishings were 3.8%, groceries were 20.7%, and mail-order sales were .8%. If the total retail sales were $214,016,000,000, how much was spent for each of these items?

    Motor Vehicles $_37,666,816,000_

    Home Furnishings $_8,132,608,000_

    Groceries $_44,301,312,000_

    Mail-Order Sales $_1,712,128,000_

4. In one year, 73.8% of the $1,065,590,000,000 national income was earned in wages and salaries, 4.7% in farm income, and 11.5% in corporate profits. How much did each of these total?

    Wages and Salaries $ _78,640,542,000_

    Farm Income $ _5,008,273,000_

    Corporate Profits $ _12,254,285,000_

5. A salesperson made sales of $168,000 one year. The next year the sales increased 8%, and the third year 12%. How much were the sales in the third year?

    $ _203,212.80_

    13440
    35212.80

    168,000
    181440

1.3 EXPRESSING ONE NUMBER AS A PERCENT OF ANOTHER

To find the percent one number is of another, divide the first number by the second and express the result as a percent. For example, to find what percent 83 is of 620, divide 83 by 620 and round the answer to whatever degree of precision is needed. (Two decimal places in the final answer is usually sufficient.)

```
        .13387   =   13.39%
  620)83.0
       620
      2100
      1860
      2400
      1860
      5400
      4960
      4400
      4340
        60
```

Often, it is easier to show the relationship as a simple fraction and then express the fraction as a percent. For example, to find what percent 15 is of 75:

$$^{15}/_{75} = {}^1/_5 = .20 = 20\%$$

You can save time by learning the most common fractions as percents. Some of these are:

$\frac{1}{8} = 12\frac{1}{2}\%$ $\frac{3}{8} = 37\frac{1}{2}\%$ $\frac{2}{3} = 66\frac{2}{3}\%$

$\frac{1}{6} = 16\frac{2}{3}\%$ $\frac{2}{5} = 40\%$ $\frac{3}{4} = 75\%$

$\frac{1}{5} = 20\%$ $\frac{1}{2} = 50\%$ $\frac{4}{5} = 80\%$

$\frac{1}{4} = 25\%$ $\frac{3}{5} = 60\%$ $\frac{5}{6} = 83\frac{1}{3}\%$

$\frac{1}{3} = 33\frac{1}{3}\%$ $\frac{5}{8} = 62\frac{1}{2}\%$ $\frac{7}{8} = 87\frac{1}{2}\%$

Problems

Group 1

Find the following percents, to the nearest hundredth:

1. What percent of 66 is 22? _33.3_ %

2. 7 is what percent of 56? _12.5_ %

3. What percent of 72 is 12? _16.67_ %

4. 5 is what percent of 25? _20_ %

5. What percent of 20 is 12? _60_ %

6. 6 is what percent of 48? _12.5_ %

7. What percent of 12 is 4? _33.3_ %

8. 6 is what percent of 15? _40_ %

9. What percent of 36 is 18? _50_ %

10. 64 is what percent of 12? _533.33_ %

11. What percent of 45 is 16? _35.56_ %

12. 20 is what percent of 50? _40_ %

13. 68 is what percent of 232? _29.31_ %

14. What percent of 60 is 8? _13.33_ %

15. What percent of 264 is 64? _24.24_ %

16. 1.25 is what percent of 72.62? _1.72_ %

17. 9 is what percent of 50? _18_ %

18. 28 is what percent of 13? _2 15.38 %_

19. What percent of 9 is 50? _18_ %

20. 14 is what percent of 328? _4.27_ %

Group 2

1. After selling 1,100 copies of a book, a bookstore had 400 copies left. What percent of the books available for sale were sold?

_63.64_ %

2. A suite of furniture originally priced at $847.50 was sold at a discount of $67.80. What was the percent of discount?

_8_ %

3. A person deposited $4,500.00 in a savings account. A year later the total interest credit was $246.15. No additional deposits or withdrawals had been made. What was the simple interest percent for the year?

_5.47_ %

4. Mary Moore owns real estate assessed at $33,600 and pays property taxes of $1,890. What is the tax rate, expressed as a percent?

_5.63_ %

5. The buyer of a used car priced at $4,860 made a down payment of $1,200. What percent of the cost was still owed?

_24.69_ %

6. A salesperson sold $8,400 worth of furniture during a week and received a commission of $462. What percent of sales was the commission?

_5.5_ %

7. Anderson, Peterson, and Carlson form a partnership. Anderson invests $6,000; Peterson, $2,500; and Carlson, $4,000. What percent of the total has each person invested?

Anderson _48_ %

Peterson _20_ %

Carlson _32_ %

1.4   FINDING A NUMBER WHEN A CERTAIN PERCENT OF IT IS KNOWN

There are times when you know a certain percent of a number and want to know what the number is. For example, 256 is 8% of what number? If 8% of the number is 256, then 1% of the number must be $\frac{1}{8}$ of 256, or 32 ($256 \div 8 = 32$). The number we are trying to find is $100 \times 32 = 3,200$.

Sometimes you can make your work easier by using simple fractions. For instance, if you know that 60 is 25% of a number, you can also say that 60 is $\frac{1}{4}$ of that number. If $\frac{1}{4}$ of the number is 60, the number must be 4 times 60, or 240. Also, if you know that 75% of a number is 120, you know that $\frac{3}{4}$ of that number is 120. Then $\frac{1}{4}$ of the number is 120 divided by 3, or 40, and the number is 4 times 40, or 160. As you can see, you express the percent as a fraction and divide the number by the numerator and multiply it by the denominator.

Problems

Group 1

Find the missing number, to the nearest hundredth:

1. 120 is 35% of _342.86_
2. 33$\frac{1}{3}$% of _1332_ is 40.
3. 140 is 70% of _200_.
4. 5% of _375._ is 75.
5. 32 is $\frac{1}{2}$% of _640_.
6. $\frac{1}{5}$% of _160_ is 8.
7. 50 is 100% of _50_.
8. 62$\frac{1}{2}$% of _225,000_ is 3,600.
9. 60 is 300% of _20_.
10. 3% of _1200_ is 36.

11. 120 is 12$\frac{1}{2}$% of _960_.
12. 16$\frac{2}{3}$% of _6806_ is 410.
13. 40 is 8% of _500_.
14. 25% of _100_ is 400.
15. 240 is 37$\frac{1}{2}$% of _640_.
16. 40% of _2420_ is 60.5.
17. 75% of _30.1725_ is 40.23.
18. 545 is 2$\frac{1}{2}$% of _21800_.
19. 125% of _256 250_ is 2,050.
20. 87$\frac{1}{2}$% of _4287.5_ is 49.

Group 2

1. A salesperson received $4,300 in commissions for a year. If this was 15% of the salesperson's total income, what was the yearly income in dollars?

   $_64500_

2. A coat was reduced $15.60, which was 12% of its original price. For how much did the coat finally sell?

$ _130_

3. A person donated $30 to a particular charity. If this represented 2% of the total contributions, how much was the total?

$ _1500_

4. What is the full price of a refrigerator if a down payment of $48 is 16% of the price?

$ _768_

5. A manufacturer pays $10,400 for a machine, computing depreciation at 12½% a year. How much will be allowed for depreciation each year?

$ _1300_

1.5   FINDING THE PERCENT OF INCREASE OR DECREASE

In order to make proper comparisons and judgments, it is often necessary to find the percent of increase or decrease. To determine this, divide the amount of increase or decrease by the original number *before* the increase or decrease.

Example 1. If a family spent $1,765 for groceries one year and $1,882 the next year, what was the percent of increase?

Increase = $1,882 − $1,765 = $117

Percent of increase = $\dfrac{.06628}{1765\overline{)117.00}} = 6.63\%$

$$
\begin{array}{r}
.06628 = 6.63\% \\
1765\overline{)117.00} \\
105\ 90 \\
\hline
11\ 100 \\
10\ 590 \\
\hline
5100 \\
3530 \\
\hline
15700 \\
14120 \\
\hline
1580
\end{array}
$$

Example 2. If the property taxes on a piece of real estate were reduced from $2,340 to $1,895, what was the percent of decrease?

Decrease = $2,340 − $1,895 = $445

Percent of decrease =

$$\frac{.19017}{2,340)445.0000} = 19.02\%$$

```
       234 0
       211 00
       210 60
          4000
          2340
         16600
         16380
           220
```

Problems

Group 1

1. What is the percent of increase from 500 to 800? ___60___ %

2. A reduction from 400 to 300 is what percent of decrease? __25__ %

3. 480 is how many percent more than 360? __25__ %

4. An increase from $120 to $160 is an increase of what percent?
    __33⅓__%

5. A reduction of $50 from $250 is a reduction of what percent? __4__ %

Group 2

1. A toy was reduced from $15.00 to $11.25. What was the percent of
    decrease?
    __25__ %

2. Sales increased from $4,200 to $5,250 to $7,000. What were the percents
    of increase? The percent of increase for the third amount is based on the
    second amount.
    __2___ %   1050
    __25__ %   1750

3. After a discount, a bill that was originally $960 amounted to $840. What was the percent of discount?

_12.5_ %

4. A city of 70,000 increased 12% in each of two succeeding years. What was the total percent of increase for the two years?

_25.4_ %

70,000 | 8400.
          9408

5. Complete the following:

Dept.	Sales for May	Sales for June	Increase or Decrease	% of Increase or Decrease
A	$20,130.50	$18,540.60	$ 1589.90 - D	8 or 7.8
B	12,410.70	13,622.45	1211.75 - I	9 or 9.8
C	15,825.40	16,390.80	565.40 - I	3.6
D	14,270.30	11,604.20	2666.10 - D	19 or 18.7
E	7,802.00	13,624.50	5822.50 - I	74.6
F	9,061.50	9,452.00	390.50 - I	4.3
G	3,284.00	4,169.00	885 - I	26
Totals	$ 82784.40	$ 87403.55	$ 13131.15	

The Allways Discount Store
Comparisons of Departmental Sales

Chapter Review

Group 1
Express the following as percents:

1. .26 _26_ %   **3.** .4 _40_ %   **5.** .0461 _4.61_ %

2. 1.6 _160_ %   **4.** .003 _.3_ %   **6.** 1.923 _192.3_ %

Express the following percents as decimals:

7. 14% __.14__

8. 5.7% __.057__

9. 240% __2.40__

10. .0125% __.000125__

Change the following fractions to percents:

11. $^3/_8$ __37.5__ %

12. $^3/_{200}$ __1.5__ %

13. $^3/_{16}$ __18.75__ %

14. $^8/_{25}$ __32__ %

Complete the following:

15. 5% of __800__ is 40.

16. 16 is __12.5__ % of 128.

17. $^1/_4$% of 164 is __656__.

18. An increase from $20 to $25 is a __2__ % increase.

19. 140% of 48 is __34.29__.

20. A decrease from 248 to 124 is a __5__ % decrease.

21. __3__ % of 72 is 216.

22. 5.6% of $680 is $__12142.86__.

23. .6% of $18.40 is $__3066.67__

24. __20__ % of 114 is 23?

25. 40 is 4% of __1000__.

26. 12$^1/_2$% of __672__ is 84.

27. 106% of $250 is $__235.85__.

28. __4__ % of 160 is 64.

29. 3% of __80__ is 2.4.

30. An increase from 85 to 255 is an increase of __2__ %.

Group 2

1. A husband and wife file a joint income tax return, reporting a combined taxable income of $21,250. Their tax is $4,380 plus 32% of their taxable income over $20,000. How much tax must they pay? 1250

    $__4780__

2. An appliance dealer sold TV sets with a 20% down payment. How much should be paid

    On a $525 set? $__105__

    On a $345 set? $__69__

    On a $756 set? $__151.20__

3. One year, out of 84,409,000 workers in the United States, 3,027,000 were farm managers or workers, 8,644,000 were managers of other types of businesses, 14,548,000 were clerical workers, and 5,415,000 were sales workers. What percent of the total number of workers did each category have?

Farm Managers or Workers   _3.59_%   37.4

Other Managers _10.24_%   62.5

Clerical Workers _17.2_%   31634

Sales Workers _6.42_%   5284003.40

                                                                    5277500 00

                    484
                 =48.4% × X
4. One year, 32,446,000 women were employed in the United States. If this represented 48.4% of the total working population, what was the total working population?   32646676

   _66487,704_   67037,190

5. Find the amount of increase and the percent of increase in the population of the United States for each ten-year period:

Year	Population	Increase	Percent of Increase
1920	105,710,620	_____	_____
1930	122,775,046	17,064,426	16.1
1940	131,669,275	8,894,229	7.2
1950	150,697,361	19,028,086	14.4
1960	179,323,175	28,625,814	19
1970	203,235,298	23,912,123	13.3

2

Metrics, Measurements, and Foreign Exchange

2.1 CONVENTIONAL MEASUREMENTS

Measurements of size, weight, distance, time, temperature, direction, and money are part of our lives every day. Without standard units of measurement, the simplest transactions would involve hours of bargaining.

Over the centuries, many such standard units have been devised. In the United States, we have generally followed the conventional British system, with a few modifications, speaking of distance in feet or miles, of weight in pounds, and of volume in quarts or gallons. These terms are meaningful to us, but in order to use them we must either remember the relationships between them or refer to tables.

The most common conventional measurements of size are:

Length: 1 foot (ft.) = 12 inches (in.)
              1 yard (yd.) = 3 ft. = 36 in.
              1 mile (mi.) = 1,760 yd. = 5,280 ft.

Area: 1 sq. ft = 144 sq. in.
              1 sq. yd. = 9 sq. ft. = 1,296 sq. in.
              1 acre (A.) = 4,840 sq. yd. = 43,560 sq. ft.
              1 sq. mi. = 640 A.

Volume: 1 cu. ft. = 1,728 cu. in.
              1 cu. yd. = 27 cu. ft.

Problems

Group 1

1. 153 in. = _12_ ft. _9_ in.

2. 2 mi. = _3520_ yd.

3. 4 yd. 7 in. = _151_ in.

4. 81 sq. ft. = _9_ sq. yd.

5. 4 sq. yd. = _584_ sq. in.

6. 8 cu. yd. = _216_ cu. ft.

7. ½ A. = _21780_ sq. ft.

8. 10,368 cu. in. = _6_ cu. ft.

9. A hole on a golf course is 440 yd. from the tee. How many feet is that? How many miles?

    _1320_ ft.   _¼_ mi.

10. How many blocks an inch on a side could be packed in a box 1 ft. by 2 ft. by 6 in.?

    _1728_

Conventional measurements of
Capacity: 1 tablespoon (tbsp.) = 3 teaspoons (tsp.)
             1 ounce (oz.) = 2 tbsp.
             1 cup (c.) = 8 oz. = 16 tbsp.
             1 pint (pt.) = 2 c. = 16 oz.
             1 quart (qt.) = 2 pt. = 4 c.
             1 gallon (gal.) = 4 qt. = 8 pt.

Weight: 1 pound (lb.) = 16 ounces (oz.)
             1 hundredweight (cwt.) = 100 lb.
             1 ton (T.) = 20 cwt. = 2,000 lb.

Problems

Group 2

1. 17 pt. = __8 1/2__ qt.

2. 80 oz. = __5__ lb.

3. 250 cwt. = __25000__ lb.

4. 20,000 lb. = __10__ T.

5. 24 tsp. = __4__ oz.

6. 6 c. = __96__ tbsp.

7. 12 gal. = __48__ qt.

8. 18 lb. = __288__ oz.

9. How many 1/2-c. servings of ice cream are there in a half-gallon package?
    __16__

10. Nero Wolfe is described as weighing a seventh of a ton. How much is that
    in pounds?
    __1400__ lb.

2.2 METRIC MEASUREMENTS

The International System of Units, commonly called the metric system, is now
used in most countries in the world, and its use is increasing in this country. In
this system, all measurements of length, area, capacity, and mass (weight),* are
in multiples of ten: tenths, hundredths, and thousandths of a unit and tens,
hundreds, and thousands of units, for example.

*For most practical purposes, "mass" can be considered to mean the same thing as "weight."

The standard units are meters (length), grams (mass), and liters (capacity or volume). The symbols for the units are simply their initials, m, g, and L, with no period except at the end of a sentence. Note that the symbol for liter is capitalized in the United States, to avoid confusion with the numeral 1.

Commonly used prefixes are mega, meaning one million; kilo, one thousand; centi (c), one hundredth; and milli, one thousandth; these are also represented by their initials. Deci (d), for one tenth; deka (da), ten; and hecto (h), one hundred, are less frequently used.

Exponents are used to show square (^{2}) or cubic (^{3}) measure. In writing large numbers, a space is left instead of a comma.

Below are the most frequently used units in the metric system:

Length: 1 centimeter (cm) = 10 millimeters (mm)
1 meter (m) = 100 cm = 1 000 mm
1 kilometer (km) = 1 000 m

Area: 1 square meter (m²) = 10 000 square centimeters (cm²)
1 square kilometer (km²) = 1 000 000 m²

Volume: 1 cubic centimeter (cm³) = 1 000 cubic millimeters (mm³)
1 cubic meter (m³) = 1 000 000 cm³

Capacity: 1 liter (L) = 1 000 milliliters (mL)

Mass: 1 gram (g) = 1 000 milligrams (mg)
1 kilogram (kg) = 1 000 g
1 metric ton (t) = 1 000 kg

Note that metric measures of volume and capacity are interchangeable, since a liter is defined as a cubic decimeter (1L = 1 dm³). For example, the space within such objects as refrigerators and car trunks is usually expressed in liters, rather than cubic centimeters.

Problems

1.   1 g = _4 000_ mg = .001 kg

2.   1 L = 1 000 mL = _.01_ m³

3.   1 cm = _10_ mm = _.01_ m = .00001 km

4. 20 000 g = _20_ kg

5. 153 mL = _.153_ L

6. 1 t = 1 000 kg = _1,000,000_ g

7. 1 m = _100_ cm = _1000_ mm

8. 1 m² = 10 000 cm² = _____ mm²

9. 1 cm² = _.01_ m²

10. 1 m³ = _____ cm³ = 1 000 000 000 mm³

11. 1 km² = _1,000,000_ m²

12. 127 cm = _1.10_ m

13. 424 g = _.424_ kg

14. 53 132 mL = _____ L   _53,132.000_

15. 3 684 cm³ = _.003684_ m³

16. 5.000243 km² = _____ m²   _5 000 243_

2.3 ADDING AND SUBTRACTING MEASUREMENTS

In adding conventional measurements, it is usually easiest to add similar units separately and then simplify, if possible.

Example. Add 2 gal. 3 qt. 1 pt. and 2 qt. 1 pt.

$$\begin{array}{l} 2 \text{ gal. } 3 \text{ qt. } 1 \text{ pt.} \\ + \quad\quad 2 \text{ qt. } 1 \text{ pt.} \\ \hline 2 \text{ gal. } 5 \text{ qt. } 2 \text{ pt.} = 2 \text{ gal. } 6 \text{ qt.} = 3 \text{ gal. } 2 \text{ qt.} \end{array}$$

To subtract conventional measurements, it is sometimes necessary to express a larger unit in smaller units.

Example. Subtract 1 yd. 2 ft. 6 in. from 2 yd. 1 ft. 3 in.

$$\begin{array}{l} 2 \text{ yd. } 1 \text{ ft. } 3 \text{ in.} = 87 \text{ in.} \\ - \quad 1 \text{ yd. } 2 \text{ ft. } 6 \text{ in.} = 66 \text{ in.} \\ \hline \quad\quad\quad\quad\quad\quad\quad\quad 21 \text{ in.} = 1 \text{ ft. } 9 \text{ in.} \end{array}$$

Unlike conventional units, metric measurements can always be expressed as decimals.

Problems

1. Add 5 lb. 13 oz. and 6 lb. 5 oz.

   _____12_____ lb. _____2_____ oz.

2. Find how many feet of molding would be needed to finish the edge between the walls and ceiling of a room 12 ft. 9 in. by 18 ft. 9 in.

   _____63_____ ft.

3. One recipe calls for 3 c. 4 tbsp. of milk, another for 1 c. 12 tbsp., and a third for 2 c. 7 tbsp. How much milk will be needed to make all three recipes?

   _____8_____ c. _____6_____ tbsp.

4. From a 12-ft. board a carpenter cut one piece 3 ft. 7 in. long and another 5 ft. 10 in. How much was left?

   _____2_____ ft. _____7_____ in.

5. A football player kicks a 43-yd. punt from his own 26-yd. line; the receiver returns it 12 yd. Where is the ball put down?

   _____5 7_____

6. Add 5.07 m to 6.28 m.

   _____11.35_____ m

7. What is the total weight of four packages weighing 241 g, 193 g, 476 g, and 32 g?

   _____942_____ g

8. One container holds 2.000 751 m³, a second 4.000 203 m³, and a third 5.000 182 m³. How much will all three together hold?

   _____11.001136_____ m³

9. From a 2-liter carton, 23 cL of milk is measured out. How much is left in the carton?

   _____ cL

10. A truck when loaded weighs 5.45 t. The empty truck weighs 1.65 t. How heavy is the load?

_____3.8_____ t

153
225

2.4 MULTIPLYING MEASUREMENTS

When two measurements of length are multiplied together, the product is a measurement of area, or square measurement. When a square measurement is multiplied by a measurement of length, the product is a measurement of volume, or cubic measurement.

Example 1. Find the area of a rectangle 11 in. long and 5 in. wide.

11 in. × 5 in. = 55 sq. in.

Example 2. Find the volume of a box with a rectangular base 12 cm by 24 cm, and 8 cm high.

12 cm × 24 cm × 8 cm = 2 304 cm³

When multiplying a conventional measurement by a number, it is usually best to multiply each unit separately, and then simplify.

Example 3.   2 yd. 2 ft. 3 in.

$\underline{\qquad\qquad \times 3}$

6 yd. 6 ft. 9 in. = 8 yd. 9 in.

Problems

1. Multiply 9 gal. 3 pt. by 6.

_____56_____ gal. _____2_____ pt.

2. A room is 12 ft. 8 in. wide and 24 ft. long. How many sq. yd. of floor space does it have?

_____36⁴⁄₆_____ sq. yd.

$1.52 \overset{in}{} $
$\times 2 \,2 \overset{8\,in}{}$
$\times 43776$
$12\overline{\smash{)}43776}$

3. A machine weighs 8 lb. 2 oz. How much will 236 such machines weigh?

_____1917_____ lb. _____5_____ oz.

128
$\underline{+\ 2}$
$130\ oo$
$\times 236$
$16\overline{\smash{)}30680} = 1917.5$
30680

4. What is the total volume of 20 boxes, each holding 20 cu. ft. 120 cu. in.?

_____401_____ cu. ft. _____39_____ cu. in.

20 × 20 = 400   *1.3888*
120 × 20 = 2400 / 2400   *1.39*
1728

5. A school bus makes four trips a day, one of 5 mi. 723 yds., one of 7 mi. 328 yd., one of 9 mi. 924 yd., and one of 6 mi. 1029 yd. How far does it travel in five days?

143 / 190

_____118_____ mi. _____83_____ yd.

723
328
924
1024
3009

6.8272727
6.83

× 4
1760 / 12016

6. Multiply 9.28L by 6.

_____55.68_____ L

7. A room is 6.23 m wide and 10.48 m long. What is the area of the ceiling in m²?

_____65.2904_____ m²

8. Each of 236 identical packages weighs 2.324 kg. What is their total weight?

_____548.464_____ kg

9. What is the total volume of 20 boxes each holding 2.000 12 m³?

_____480000_____ m³

10. A school bus makes four trips a day, one of 9.723 km, one of 12.828 km, one of 16.924 km, and one of 18.029 km. How far does it travel in five days?

_____230.016_____ km

2.5 DIVIDING MEASUREMENTS

In dividing a conventional measurement, a remainder in a larger unit must be expressed in a smaller unit before you continue.

Example 1. Divide 15 lb. 4 oz. into 4 equal parts.

$$
\begin{array}{r}
3 \text{ lb. } 13 \text{ oz.} \\
4{\overline{)15 \text{ lb. } 4 \text{ oz.}}} \\
12 \text{ lb.} \\
\hline
3 \text{ lb. } 4 \text{ oz.} = 52 \text{ oz.} \\
52 \text{ oz.}
\end{array}
$$

To divide one measured quantity by another, it is easiest to express both quantities in the same unit.

Example 2. How many pieces of tape, each 13 in. long, can be cut from a tape 3 yd. long?

$$3 \text{ yd.} = 3 \times 36 \text{ in.} = 108 \text{ in.}$$

$$108 \text{ in.} \div 13 \text{ in.} = 8, \text{ with a remainder of 4 in.}$$

Problems

1. Divide 8 lb. 4 oz. by 2.

    _____4_____ lb. _____2_____ oz.

2. What is one-fourth of 3 qt. 2 c.?

    _____3/4_____ qt. _____1/2_____ c.

3. A board 11 ft. 6 in. long is to be divided into three equal parts. How long will each part be?

    _____ ft. _____ in.

4. What is the price per oz. for a 2-lb. package of chocolate mix costing $1.99?

    $_____.16_____

5. The heights of the five players on an American basketball team are 6 ft. 3 in., 6 ft. 8 in., 7 ft. 1 in., 6 ft. 5 in., and 5 ft. 11 in. What is their average height?

    _____6_____ft. _____1_____ in.

6. Divide 8.024 kg by 2.

    _____4.012_____ kg

7. What is one fourth of 3.24 L?

    _____.81_____ L

8. A ribbon 3 m long is to be divided into pieces 12 cm long. How many pieces will there be?

_____25_____

9. What is the price per gram for a 31-g box of cinnamon costing 55¢?

_.0177_ ¢

10. The heights of the five players on a European basketball team are 205 cm, 192 cm, 211 cm, 181 cm, and 199 cm. What is their average height?

_197.6_ cm

2.6   MEASUREMENTS OF TIME, CIRCLES, AND TEMPERATURE

Angle: 1 minute (′) = 60 seconds (″)
1 degree (°) = 60′
1 circle = 360°

Time: 1 minute (min.) = 60 seconds (sec.)
1 hour (hr.) = 60 min.
1 day (da.) = 24 hr.
1 week (wk.) = 7 da.
1 year (yr.) = 365 da., or 366 da. in a leap year
= 52 weeks 1 or 2 da.

Very short periods of time are measured in tenths of a second, hundredths of a second, etc.

Measures of temperature are different:

	Fahrenheit	Celsius
Freezing point of water	32°	0°
Boiling point of water	212°	100°

Problems

1. 125 min. = __2__ hr. __5__ min.

2. 4 days = __96__ hr.

3. 540″ = ___9___ ′

4. 75° 40′ = ___115___ ′

5. One morning the temperature was −3°C; during the day it rose 11°C. What was the later reading? _____°C If the earlier reading was −3°F and it rose 11°F, what was the later reading? _____°F

6. An artist colors in sections of a circle measuring 20° 30′, 50° 45′, and 38° 22′. How much has been colored altogether?

_____

7. A part-time worker works 3 hr. 40 min., 2 hr. 55 min., 4 hr. 10 min., 2 hr. 25 min., 3 hr. 45 min., and 5 hr. 30 min. What is the total for the week?

_____ hr. _____ min.

8. A class has 2 hr. 15 min. to complete a test. After 45 min., how much time is left?

_____ hr. _____ min.

9. A school is in session from 8:25 AM to 3:10 PM, Monday through Friday. How many hours a week is this?

_____ hr. _____ min.

10. A circle graph is to be divided into sections of $\frac{1}{2}$, $\frac{1}{4}$, $\frac{1}{7}$, and $\frac{3}{28}$. How many degrees and minutes would each contain, to the nearest whole minute?

_____   _____

_____   _____

2.7 INTERCHANGING MEASUREMENTS

A conventional measurement can be converted to a metric measurement, or vice-versa, by using a *table of equivalents:*

Conventional to Metric

1 in.	2.540 cm
1 ft.	30.480 cm
1 yd.	0.9144 m
1 mi.	1.609 km
1 sq. in.	6.452 cm^2
1 sq. ft.	0.093 m^2
1 sq. yd.	0.836 m^2
1 cu. in.	16.387 cm^3
1 qt.	0.946 L
1 gal.	3.785 L
1 oz.	28.350 g
1 lb.	453.592 g

Metric to Conventional

1 cm	0.3937 in.
1 m	1.094 yd. = 39.37 in.
1 km	0.621 mi.
1 cm^2	0.155 sq. in.
1 m^2	1.196 sq. yd. = 10.764 sq. ft.
1 cm^3	0.061 cu. in.
1 L	1.057 qt.
1 L	0.2642 gal.
1 g	0.035 oz.
1 kg	2.205 lb.

To convert °F to °C, subtract 32°, then divide by 1.8 (or multiply by 5, then divide by 9).

To convert °C to °F, multiply by 1.8 (or multiply by 9, then divide by 5), then add 32°.

Problems

1. 165 in. 4.191 m
2. 21 mi. = 33.785 km
3. 3 gal. = 0.7926 L
4. 45°F = ______ °C
5. 30 cm = ______ in.
6. 700 m = ______ yd. ______ ft. ______ in.
7. 30 kg = ______ oz.
8. 45°C = ______ °F
9. Is it easier to divide by 1.8 or to multiply by 5 and then divide by 9? Why are the results the same? ______________________________

____

10.   On the sideline of a football field, which is 100 yd. long, a 100-m running track is measured off. How much longer is the track than the football field, in meters and in yards?

_____ m

_____ yd.

11.   An Imperial gallon, used in Canada and Britain, is the equivalent of 1.201 U.S. gallons. How many U.S. gallons equal 13 Imperial gallons?

_____ gal.

12.   What is the equivalent in Imperial gallons of one U.S. gallon?

_____ Imp. gal.

2.8   FOREIGN EXCHANGE

Like metric measures, money is expressed in decimals, but the basic units (dollars, yen, marks, francs, rubles, pesos, kroner, pounds, etc.) vary from country to country.

Relative values change so frequently that rates of exchange are posted daily wherever one currency is exchanged for another; this is the ratio of the value of one currency to another. Many agencies, such as banks and hotels, collect a fee for making money exchanges.

Example 1. If the exchange rate is $1.7422 U.S. to a British pound (£), find the value in U.S. money of £100. Since each pound is worth $1.7422, *multiply* the *number* of pounds by the *value* of each pound.

$$100 \times \$1.7422 = \$174.22$$

Example 2. At the same rate of exchange, find the value in British money of $100 U.S. The ratio of the value of a dollar to a pound is 1/1.7422. To find the value in pounds of $100 U.S., *divide* the *number* of dollars by 1.7422.

$$100 \div 1.7422 = 57.399$$
$$\$100 = £57.39 \text{ (Fractions of pence are dropped.)}$$

Problems

1. What is the equivalent in U.S. currency of 1000 Japanese yen, if one yen is worth $.005125?

   $_____

2. If the exchange rate is one French franc to $.2202 U.S., how much should be exchanged for $100.00 U.S.?

   _____ FR

3. A U.S. resident traveling in Canada rents a motel room at an advertised rate of $22.00. If there is a 7% tax and a Canadian dollar is worth $1.03 U.S., how much must be paid in U.S. currency?

   $_____

4. A woman cashes a traveler's check for $50.00 U.S. in Copenhagen when the rate of exchange is 6.019 kroner to a dollar. If there is a charge of 2 kroner, how much money does she receive?

   _____ KR

5. If an air-mail letter from Scotland to the U.S. costs £.12 (12 pence) and one from the U.S. to Scotland costs $.31, which is more expensive when the rate of exchange is $1.731 to a pound?

   _____

   What is the difference in cents? $._____

   In pence?   £._____

Chapter Review

1. 48 gal. = __2__ qt.

2. 48 L = __48,000__ mL

3. 6 cu. ft. 24 cu. in. = __96__ cu. in.

4. 6.000024 m³ = _____ cm³

5. ³/₄ lb. = __4__ oz.

6. $^3/_4$ g = ——— mg

7. Add 5 T. 1,400 lb. to 6 T. 858 lb.

——— T. ——— lb.

8. Add 5.4 t to 6 858 kg.

——— kg

9. Brand A cola costs $.65 for a 2-qt. bottle; Brand B, $.95 for two 28-oz. bottles; Brand C, $1.59 for six 12-oz. cans. How much does each cost for an 8-oz serving?

A $———

B $———

C $———

10. A throat lozenge contains 6.25 mg of benzocaine. How much benzocaine is there in a package of 18 lozenges?

——— mg

11. A carton 18 in. × 16 in. × 12 in. contains how many cubic inches? How many cubic meters?

——— cu. in.

——— m³

12. What is the difference between 60° 25′ and 42° 38′?

——— ° ——— ′

13. When a clerk has worked 3 hr. 9 min. of a $7^1/_2$-hr. day, how much working time remains?

——— hr. ——— min.

14. When a Greek drachma is worth $.0272 U.S., how much should be exchanged in U.S. currency for 70.00 drachmas? How many drachmas for $70.00 U.S.?

$———

——— DR

3
Ratio, Proportion and Probability

3.1 RATIO

Some measures or quantities have very little meaning except in relationship to some other measure or quantity. For instance, if you read that in 1958 there were 160 deaths in commercial airline accidents in the United States and that in 1968 there were 351, you might think flying had become more dangerous. But if you also know that about $2\frac{1}{2}$ times as many miles were flown in 1968 as in 1958, you would see that flying had actually become safer.

Such a relationship between two or more quantities is shown as a *ratio*. If a school has 12 teachers and 228 students, the ratio of students to teachers is 228 to 12, which could be written using a colon, 228:12, or as a fraction, $^{228}/_{12}$. As with any other fraction, a ratio can be reduced to its simplest terms; the ratio of students to teachers in this case is seen to be 19:1.

Example 1. Three men form a partnership, the first investing $10,000, the second $25,000, and the third $35,000. What is the ratio of their investments?
$$10,000:25,000:35,000 = 10:25:35 = 2:5:7$$

A percentage may be thought of as a particular kind of ratio, always comparing part of a quantity to the whole quantity.

Example 2. What is the ratio of 1 yard to 3 inches? Since a yard is 36 inches, the ratio is 36:3, or 12:1.

As a percentage,
$$\frac{3 \text{ inches}}{1 \text{ yard}} = \frac{3}{36} = .0833 = 8.33\%$$

Problems

Reduce all ratios to lowest terms.

1. What is the ratio of 2 gal. to 1 qt.?

    _____8_____ to _____/_____

2. Find the ratio of $2.25 to $5.00.

    _____9_____ to __20__

3. Express the ratio of 4 cm to 2 m a. using a colon, b. as a fraction, c. as a decimal, d. as a percentage.

    a. __1:50__   c. ____.02____

    b. __1/50__   d. __2%__

4. A factory employs 325 laborers and 65 foremen. What is the ratio of foremen to laborers?

    _____/_____ to ___5___

5. A business has assets of $102,400 and liabilities of $12,800. What is the ratio of assets to liabilities?

    ___8___ to ___1___

6. In a recent year, the expenditure per pupil in the public schools of North Carolina was $880 and that in Rhode Island was $1,232. What was the ratio of North Carolina expenditures per pupil to that of Rhode Island?

    ___5___ to ___7___

7. According to the census of 1970, there were 322 farms in Alaska. Of these farms, 35 were 2,000 acres or more and 32 were of 10 to 49 acres. a. Find the ratio of large farms to the total number of farms; b. the ratio of small farms to the total number of farms; c. the ratio of small farms to large farms:

    a. ___5___ to __46__

    b. _____ to __10%__

    c. __32__ to __35__

8. A cheetah can travel at a speed of 70 m.p.h., a squirrel at 12 m.p.h., a giraffe at 32 m.p.h., a zebra at 40 m.p.h., and a garden snail at .03 m.p.h. Show the ratio of all five speeds, from slowest to fastest.

___.03___ : ___12___ : ___32___ : ___40___ : ___70___

9. a. What is the ratio of the snail's speed to the squirrel's? b. Of the zebra's speed to the giraffe's?

a. ___.0.3___ to ___1.2___   1 – 400

b. ___4___ to ___7___

10. In one year 105,060 men and 10,467 women earned bachelors' degrees in business; 25,506 men and 1,038 women, masters' degrees; and 787 men and 23 women, doctors' degrees. What was the ratio of women to men in each category? What was the ratio of bachelors' to masters' to doctors' degrees?

Bachelors' Degrees ___1___ to ___10___

Masters' Degrees ___1___ to ___25___

Doctors' Degrees ___1___ to ___34___

___143___ to ___33___ to ___1___

3.2 PROPORTION

A *proportion* is a way of saying that two ratios are equal. A proportion may be written in several ways:

$$6:18::1:3 \quad \text{or} \quad 6:18 = 1:3 \quad \text{or} \quad {}^{6}/_{18} = {}^{1}/_{3}$$

all of which are read, "Six is to eighteen as one is to three."

The first and fourth *terms* of a proportion, in this case 6 and 3, are called the *extremes*. The second and third terms, in this case 18 and 1, are called the *means*. It is always true that *the product of the extremes is equal to the product of the means*. In this case, $6 \times 3 = 18 \times 1$.

This rule is used to find the missing term in a proportion.

Example 1. Find the missing term in the proportion 14:7 = 98:? The product of the means is 7 × 98 = 686

$$14 \times ? = 686$$
$$? = 686 \div 14 = 49$$

The proportion is 14:7 = 98:49.

The computation is much easier if we first reduce a ratio to its simplest terms. The ratio 14:7 can be reduced to 2:1.

$$2:1 = 98:?$$
$$2 \times ? = 98 \times 1, \text{ or } 98$$
$$? = 98 \div 2 = 49$$

Example 2. A manufacturer has been purchasing a part needed for his product at three for $1.00. During six weeks, he paid $200.00 for these parts. He has an opportunity to purchase similar parts from another supplier at four for $1.00. How much could he expect to save in six weeks, at the same rate of production?

Since the price is quoted in fractions, that is, as so many for a dollar, the proportion is

$$\frac{1}{3} : \frac{1}{4} = 200 : ? \text{ or } \frac{\frac{1}{3}}{\frac{1}{4}} = \frac{200}{?}$$

$$\frac{\frac{1}{3}}{\frac{1}{4}} = \frac{1}{3} \times \frac{4}{1} = \frac{4}{3}$$

$$\frac{4}{3} = 200/? \text{ or } 4:3 = 200:?$$

$$4 \times ? = 200 \times 3 = 600$$

$$? = 600 \div 4 = 150$$

The new cost would be $150, so he would save $200 − $150, or $50.

Another way to solve this example is to express the present cost per part as $.33 $\frac{1}{3}$. Since he has paid $200, he has purchased $200 divided by $.33 $\frac{1}{3}$, or 600 parts. At the new price of four for a dollar, each costs $.25, so 600 parts would cost $150, for a saving of $50. This method is called the *unitary analysis method*.

Example 3. A car averages 16 miles to a gallon of gas and can travel a certain distance on $8\frac{1}{2}$ gallons. How many gallons will be needed to travel the same distance in a car which averages 25 miles to a gallon? Using the unitary analysis method, since the first car goes 16 miles on each gallon of gas, it will travel $8\frac{1}{2}$ times 16, or 136 miles, on $8\frac{1}{2}$ gallons. The second car will need 136 divided by 25, or $5\,\frac{11}{25}$ gallons, to travel 136 miles.

Using a proportion with fractional terms, since the cars go $\frac{1}{16}$ mile and $\frac{1}{25}$ mile on one gallon of gas,

$$\frac{1}{16} : \frac{1}{25} = 8\frac{1}{2} : ?$$

$$25 : 16 = 8\frac{1}{2} : ?$$

$$25 \times ? = 8\frac{1}{2} \times 16 = 136$$

$$? = 136 \div 25 = 5\frac{11}{25} \text{ gal.}$$

In either method, the actual arithmetic is the same.

Problems

1. Find the missing term in the proportion 12:5::60:?
    _____25_____

2. If pencils sell at 7 for 59¢, what should 4 pencils cost?
    _____34_____ ¢

3. A female teenager should have 1.3 g of calcium a day. One cup of skim milk provides 298 mg. How much skim milk would she need a day if that were the only source of calcium available?
    _____436_____ c

4. If two clerks can do a piece of work in eight days, how long should it take four clerks to do the work?
    _____|_____ days

5. A piece of beef weighing 5.56 lb. costs $9.34. How much can be bought for $6.00?

___357___ lb.

6. If 260 A. of land produces 9,100 bushels of grain, how many acres will be needed to produce 30,000 bushels?

_____ A.

7. A retailer who has been selling cording at 5 yd. for $1.00 increases the price to 3 yd. for $1.00. How much must a customer now pay for the amount that formerly cost $4.50?

$_____

8. A bus scheduled to travel at 55 m.p.h. is forced by weather conditions to slow down to 25 m.p.h. How much longer will it take to travel the distance usually covered in two hours?   *110 miles*

___2.4___

20
33 1/2

3.3 PARTITIVE PROPORTION

At times we may need to divide up a known total quantity according to some agreed-upon ratio. This requires three steps:

1. Add the terms of the ratio to find the total number of parts.
2. Divide the total quantity by the number of parts to find the amount of each part.
3. Multiply each term of the ratio by the amount of each part to find each share.

Example 1. Brown, Smith, and Jones are partners and agree to divide profits in the ratio of 3:1:2 respectively. How much should each receive if their total profit is $12,569.40?

Step 1: 3 + 1 + 2 = 6, the total number of parts
Step 2: $12,569.40 ÷ 6 = $2,094.90, value of each part
Step 3: 3 × $2,094.90 = $6,284.70, Brown's share
         1 × $2,094.90 = $2,094.90, Smith's share
         2 × $2,094.90 = $4,189.80, Jones's share

Note that adding the three shares totals $12,569.40, which provides a check for the computation.

Example 2. The 28 seats on a city council are allotted in proportion to the number of votes received by each party in an election. In one election, the Democrats received 8,496 votes; Republicans, 7,826; Independents, 2,923; and Conservatives, 2,057. How many seats will each party have?

Step 1:   8,496 + 7,826 + 2,923 + 2,057 = 21,302, total number

Step 2:   28 ÷ 21,302 = .0013, amount of each part

Step 3:   8,496 × .0013 = 11.0448; Democrats have 11 seats
          7,826 × .0013 = 10.1738; Republicans have 10 seats
          2,923 × .0013 = 3.7999; Independents have 4 seats
          2,057 × .0013 = 2.6741; Conservatives have 3 seats
          Check: 11 + 10 + 4 + 3 = 28

Note: Because the amount of each part (.0013) has been rounded, the amounts shown in Step 3 will total slightly less than 28.0000, but when these in turn are rounded, the total is 28.

Problems

1. Divide 36 into parts proportional to 1 and 2.

    _____ and _____

2. Elting, Fulton, and Gore formed a partnership with a cash investment of $54,000. How much did each partner invest if the capital ratio was 3:4:5 respectively?

    Elting $_____

    Fulton $_____

    Gore $_____

3. What was the share of each of the partners in Problem 2 in a profit of $3,780 if profits are divided in proportion to investment?

    Elting $_____

    Fulton $_____

    Gore $_____

4. A Booster Club starts a fund drive, promising to spend some of the money for awards, twice that much for uniforms, and twice as much for field improvements as for uniforms. If $1,358 is raised, how much will be spent for each purpose?

Awards $_____

Uniforms $_____

Field $_____

5. Jane, Jim, and June dig clams one day, agreeing to divide their catch according to the size of their families. If there are five in Jane's family, seven in Jim's, and three in June's, how many does each take from a total of 105?

Jane ___35___

Jim ___49___

June ___21___

3.4 PROBABILITY

One special use of ratio is in calculating probability, the likelihood that some particular event will happen.

The simplest illustration of probability is tossing a coin. There are only two ways it can come up, heads or tails. If we consider heads a win, then the probability of winning is the ratio between the number of ways the coin can come up heads (one) and the total number of ways it can come up (two), or 1:2, or $1/2$. The probability of losing is exactly the same: $1/2$.

If we throw a die, instead of tossing a coin, there are six possible outcomes instead of two, and the probability of throwing any particular number—four, for example—is the ratio between the number of ways that four can come up (one) and the total number of ways the die could come up (six), or 1:6, or $1/6$. The probability of losing is the ratio between the number of other ways the die could come up (five) and the total number of possibilities (six), or 5:6, or 5/6. Probabilities may also be expressed as decimals, in this case, .167 and .833.

If we tossed a coin twice, we would not be too surprised if it came up heads both times; even three times we could accept. But if it came up heads again and again, five or eight or twelve times, we would certainly suspect that the coin was weighted. If we were to toss an unweighted coin 1,000 times, the result would be close to 500 heads and 500 tails, or exactly half of the total each way. This is in agreement with the estimate of the probability of winning.

If there is no possibility that an event will happen, the probability is 0. If there is no possibility that it will *not* happen, the probability is 1. Any time a chance is taken (a coin tossed, a die thrown, or a lottery ticket bought, for instance), the probability that it will be a success plus the probability that it will not be a success is always 1.

Example 1. If one card is drawn from a full deck of 52 cards, what is the probability that it will be a queen? Since there are four queens in the deck, the probability is

$$^4/_{52} \; = \; ^1/_{13} \; = \; .0769$$

The probability that the card drawn will *not* be a queen is

$$^{48}/_{52} \; = \; ^{12}/_{13} \; = \; .9231$$
$$^1/_{13} \; + \; ^{12}/_{13} \; = \; .0769 \; + \; .9231 \; = \; 1$$

Example 2. A state lottery issues 74,880,000 tickets, of which 312 are jackpot winners. What is the probability that a particular ticket will be a jackpot winner?

$$\frac{312}{74{,}880{,}000} \; = \; \frac{1}{240{,}000} \; = \; .0000042$$

Problems

1. If a die is thrown, what is the probability of throwing a 2?

    1~6

2. What is the probability of throwing either a 2 or a 3 in one throw of a die?

    1~6

3. If a card is drawn from a deck and shown to be an ace, and if the card is then returned to the deck, the deck shuffled, and a card drawn, what is the probability that it will be an ace?

    _____ 4/52

4. If a card is drawn from a deck and shown to be an ace, and if that card is set aside and another card is drawn from the deck, what is the probability that it will also be an ace?

    _____ 3/51 _____

5. Nine co-workers form a pool on a baseball game, each one putting in 25¢ and drawing a number from 1 to 9. The one holding the number of the inning in which the greatest number of runs is scored takes all the money. a. What is the probability of winning? b.   How much money will the winner receive? c.   What is the ratio of the money received to the money the winner put in?

    a. _____ 1/9 _____

    b. $ _2.25_

    c. _____ to _____

6. In a pool like that in Problem 5, one person buys two chances at 25¢ each. a. What is the probability that she will win? b. If she does win, how much money does she receive? c. What is the ratio between money she spent and money she received?

    a. _____

    b. $_____

    c. _____ to _____

7. At a service club meeting, members may buy chances at $1.00 each. Half of the money taken in is put into a charity fund. The other half is divided evenly between two members whose numbers are drawn. a. If 14 members buy chances, what is the probability that any one of these will win? b. How much will each winning member receive? c. What is the ratio of the winnings to cost?

    a. _____ 1/7 _____

    b. $_3.50_

    c. _____ to _____

8. At the meeting described in Problem 7, what is the probability of winning, the amount won, and the ratio of winnings to cost, if 28 members buy chances? Which situation is the better bet?

Probability of Winning   _____

Amount Won $_____

Ratio of Winnings to Cost   _____ to _____

Better Bet   _____

1. The ratio of 75¢ to $30 is ____/____ to __40__.   75⟌30 40

2. The ratio of 10 minutes to 2 hours is ____/____ to __12__.

3. The ratio of 2 yds. to 3 in. is __24__ to ____/____.

4. The ratio of 3 mL to 7 L is __3__ to __7000__.

5. The ratio of 3¹/₃ to 10 is the same as __10__ to 30.

6. 12:5 = 6:? $x:y :: a:\boxed{b} = b = \frac{y \times a}{x}$ $x:y :: a:b$
   __2.5__ $x = \frac{y\,a}{b}$

7. ? :42 = 7:84 $b = \frac{y\,a}{x}$
   __3.5__

8. 16: ? = 4:24 $y = \frac{x\,b}{a}$
   __96__

9. 65:13 = ? :15 $a = \frac{x\,b}{y}$
   __75__

10. 10:40 = 50: ?
   __200__

11. Three workers earned a total of $3,000. If their shares were in the ratio of 4:3:5, how much did each receive? *12 ÷ 3000 = X 4335*

+ ÷ X

$ _____ *$1,000.⁰⁰*

$ _____ *$750.⁰⁰* *Page 42 3.3*

$ _____ *$1250.⁰⁰*

12. James invested $25,000 in a business, and his partner Steward invested $65,000. a. What is the ratio of their investments? b. If profits are to be divided in proportion to investment, what will each receive, from a profit of $19,863?

a. _____ *5* _____ to _____ *13* _____

b. James $ _____ *5517.5*

     Steward $ _____ *14345.5*

13. One person drives at 50 m.p.h., and another at 58 m.p.h. In how much less time will the second person drive a distance that takes the first driver 36 minutes?

58 36:50. ?= 31.03

_____ min.

14. If all the aces are removed from a deck of cards, what is the probability that the next card drawn will be a king?

_____ *1/12*

15. A circular target is marked off into sections of 30° each, numbered from 1 to 12. What is the probability that a dart thrown at the target will hit either the three or the seven?

_____ *1:6* *2 chances ÷ 12 posiblitis = 6*

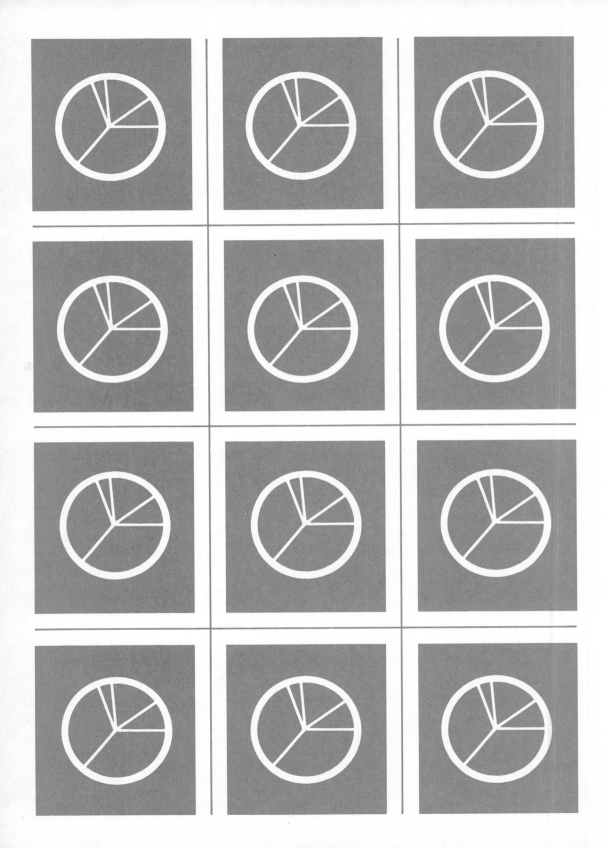

4

Graphs and Statistics

The quickest and clearest way to picture a set of figures or a relationship is to look at a graph. A graph will usually not show details, but trends and relative quantities are readily apparent.

There are several kinds of graphs. It is important to choose the kind that is best suited to the purpose at hand. In some cases, one set of figures may be shown in different kinds of graphs to emphasize different features.

4.1 BAR GRAPHS

One common type of graph is the bar graph. There are several guidelines for effective bar graphs:

Bars may be either horizontal or vertical.
Each bar must be the same width.
The graph will be easiest to read if the distance between bars is equal to the width of a bar.
Every graph should have a title.
Both vertical and horizontal axes should be labeled.
When time is represented, it is almost always shown on the horizontal axis.

Sometimes two or even three sets of figures may be shown on the same bar graph. They must be color-coded or otherwise distinguished to avoid confusion.

Example 1. In a bar graph, show the advertising expenditures in the United States in a recent year, in millions of dollars: newspapers, 7,595; magazines, 1,448; farm publications, 65; television, 4,493; radio, 1,690; direct mail, 3,698; business papers, 865; outdoor, 308; miscellaneous, 4,958.

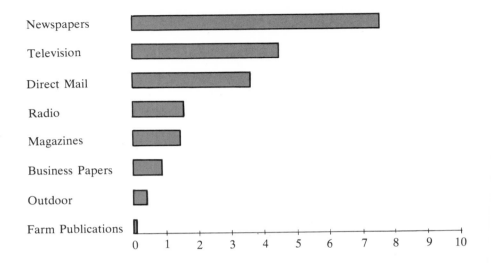

Fig. 4-1   19— U.S. Advertising Expenditures, in Billions of Dollars

These quantities will be more easily grasped if the different media are shown in order from largest to smallest. Since we only want to compare the media, the miscellaneous group may be disregarded. Fig. 4-1 pictures this example. Do you find any of the information pictured in the graph surprising?

Example 2. At 20-year intervals, the area and population of the contiguous United States from 1790 to 1970 have been:

	Area (sq. mi.)	*Population*
1790	888,881	3,929,214
1810	1,716,003	7,239,881
1830	1,788,006	12,866,020
1850	2,992,747	23,191,876
1870	3,022,387	39,818,449
1890	3,022,387	62,947,714
1910	3,022,387	91,972,266
1930	3,022,387	122,775,046
1950	3,615,211	151,325,798
1970	3,615,122	203,211,926

These figures are pictured in the bar graph shown in Fig. 4-2. Do you find any features of the graph particularly noticeable or interesting? What inference could you draw regarding density of population?

Problems

1. The Elections Research Center of the American Enterprise Institute estimates that voter turnouts in the latest national elections in eight countries were: Australia, 95%; Britain, 73%; Canada, 71%; France, 88%; Japan, 73%; Switzerland, 52%; United States, 54%; and West Germany, 91%. Show these percentages in a bar graph.

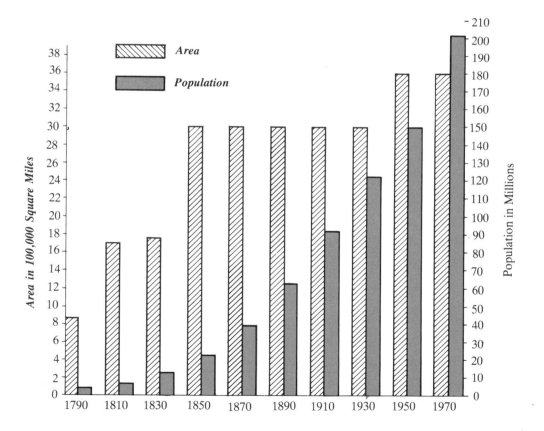

Fig. 4-2   Area and Population of the U.S. at 20-Year Intervals, 1790–1970

2. The Bureau of the Census reports that at 10-year intervals from 1790 to 1880, the population of Connecticut was 237,946; 251,002; 261,942; 275,248; 297,675; 309,978; 370,792; 460,147; 537,454; and 622,700. For the same years, Maine's population was 96,540; 151,719; 228,705; 298,335; 399,455; 501,793; 583,169; 628,279; 626,915; and 648,936. Show both these records on one bar graph.

3. According to the 1970 census, the population of the New England states included 9,043,517 urban and 2,798,146 rural residents; of the Middle Atlantic states, 30,406,301 urban and 6,792,793 rural; East North Central, 30,091,847 urban and 10,160,629 rural; West North Central, 10,388,913 urban and 5,930,274 rural; South Atlantic, 19,523,920 urban and 11,147,417 rural; East South Central, 6,987,943 urban and 5,815,527 rural; West South Central, 14,028,098 urban and 5,292,462 rural; Mountain, 6,054,979 urban and 2,226,583 rural; and Pacific, 22,799,412 urban and 3,723,219 rural. Show these figures, as well as the total population for each region, in a single bar graph.

4. The Motor Vehicle Manufacturers Association lists passenger car factory sales at 5-year intervals from 1900 to 1975 as follows: 4,192; 24,250; 181,000; 895,930; 1,905,560; 3,735,171; 2,787,456; 3,273,874; 3,717,385; 69,532; 6,665,836; 7,920,186; 6,674,796; 9,305,561; 6,546,817; and 6,712,852. Can you picture these figures on a bar graph? Explain.

_____

5. Find the population per square mile of the United States for each of the years listed in Example 2. Show these figures on a bar graph.

1790	_____	1890	_____
1810	_____	1910	_____
1830	_____	1930	_____
1850	_____	1950	_____
1870	_____	1970	_____

6. In preparing a bar graph do you prefer a ruler marked in inches or in centimeters? Why?

_____

4.2   CIRCLE GRAPHS

A circle graph (sometimes called a pie graph) is used for only one purpose: to show how a whole is divided into parts. To construct a circle graph, each part must be expressed as a percentage of the whole; that percentage of the 360° in a circle is found, and the appropriate angle is measured with the aid of a protractor. The percentage should always total 100% and the angles 360°, although allowance must be made for slight deviations caused by rounding off figures.

Example. The U.S. Treasury Department estimated its receipts in thousands of dollars for one year as: individual income taxes, $118,750,071; corporation income taxes, $38,664,197; social insurance taxes and contributions, $76,849,-353; excise taxes, $16,885,403; estate and gift taxes, $5,009,320; customs, $3,334,127; and miscellaneous, $5,355,013. Show these relationships on a circle graph.

The total collected is $264,847,474, and the percentages of the total and the number of degrees are:

	Percent	Degrees of Circle
Individual Income Taxes	44.84%	161.42°
Corporation Income Taxes	14.60	52.56
Social Insurance Taxes and Contributions	29.02	104.47
Excise Taxes	6.38	22.97
Estate and Gift Taxes	1.89	6.80
Customs	1.26	4.54
Miscellaneous	2.02	7.27
	100.01%	360.03°

Fig. 4-3 pictures the circle graph for these figures. What part of the total receipts are from corporation income taxes, social insurance, and excise taxes combined? Does this stand out on the graph? In the figures?

Problems

1. The Bureau of Labor Statistics reports that 20,705,000 men and 19,681,000 women are employed as white-collar workers; 24,625,000 men

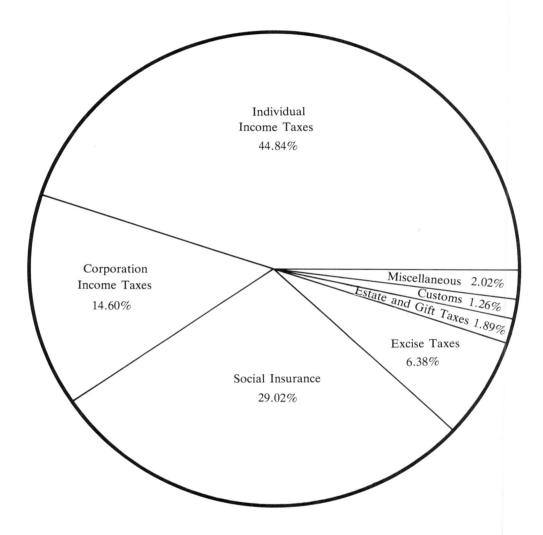

Fig. 4-3   U.S. Treasury Department Receipts, 19—

and 5,244,000 women as blue-collar workers; 4,120,000 men and 7,008,000 women as service workers; and 2,513,000 men and 514,000 women as farm workers. Construct a circle graph showing these figures for men, for women or for both combined.

2. Show the information on advertising expenditures in Fig. 4-1 in a circle graph. Which type of graph tells the most about the media?

3. According to the National Geographic Society, the area of Africa is 11,506,000 sq. mi.; Antarctica, 5,500,000 sq. mi.; Asia, 16,988,000 sq. mi.; Australia, 2,968,000 sq. mi.; Europe, 3,745,000 sq. mi.; North America, 9,390,000 sq. mi.; and South America, 6,795,000 sq. mi. Smaller pieces of land total 632,000 sq. mi. Show these parts of the earth's land area in a circle graph.

4. The U.S. Bureau of Economic Analysis reports expenditures for personal consumption in a recent year were, in billions of dollars: food, beverages, and tobacco, $203.1; clothing, accessories, and jewelry, $76.4; personal care, $13.4; housing, $136.0; household operations, $130.5; medical care, $75.8; personal business, $44.5; transportation, $115.3; recreation, $60.5; education and research, $13.5; and other (including religious and welfare contributions and foreign travel) $16.8. Show these relationships in a circle graph. How do your own living expenses compare with this report?

---

5. a.   Could you divide a circle into 100 "degrees" instead of 360°?
    b.   Would this make it easier to make a circle graph? Would it make it harder? c.   Could you express the parts of the whole in degrees without first expressing them in percentages?

    a.   _____

    b.   _____

    c.   _____

4.3   LINE GRAPHS

A very common type of graph is a line graph, usually showing time on the horizontal axis and some other quantity on the vertical axis.

The time on line graphs should be continuous. If there are gaps, as in Fig. 4-2, where the figures are shown at 10-year intervals, a bar graph should be used. Time periods may be grouped, perhaps into 10-year periods, but there should be no gaps. The line of the graph should not be extended in either direction beyond the time actually given.

Example. According to the Immigration and Naturalization Service, in the period 1821–1830, 143,439 immigrants were admitted to the United States; 1831–1840, 599,125 were admitted; 1841–50, 1,713,251; 1851–1860, 2,598,214; 1861–1870, 2,314,824; 1871–1880; 2,812,191; 1881–1890, 5,246,613; 1891–1900, 3,687,564; 1901–1910, 8,795,386; 1911–1920, 5,735,811; 1921–1930, 4,107,209; 1931–1940, 528,431; 1941–1950, 1,035,039; 1951–1960, 2,515,479; and 1961–1970, 3,321,677. Fig. 4-4 shows these figures in a line graph.

Can you think of reasons to explain why there are such high and low points? How different would you expect the graph to look if the figures were plotted for each year instead of for 10-year periods? What would you guess the figure for 1971–1980 might be?

Source: Immigration and Naturalization Service

Fig. 4-4   Immigrants Admitted to the U.S. in 10-Year Periods, 1821–1970

Problems

1. In 1961, there were 271,344 immigrants admitted to the United States; 1962, 283,763; 1963, 306,260; 1964, 292,248; 1965, 296,697; 1966, 323,040; 1967; 361,972; 1968, 454,448; 1969, 358,579; 1970; 373,326; 1971; 370,478; 1972, 384,685; 1973, 400,063; 1974, 394,861; 1975, 386,194; and 1976, 398,613. Construct a line graph to show this information. Is it as interesting as the graph in the example? Why?

2. The total assets of the Social Security Hospital Insurance Trust Fund from 1966 to 1974 have been: 1965–66, $851,204,000; 1966–67, $1,343,221,000; 1967–68, $1,430,636,000; 1968–69, $2,016,521,000; 1969–70, $2,677,401,-000; 1970–71, $3,103,106,000; 1971–72, $2,858,725,000; 1972–73, $4,368,-666,000; and 1973–74, $7,934,772,000. Show these figures in a line graph. Estimate what the assets would be in later years, then find these figures in an almanac or statistical abstract to see how close your estimates are.

3. On a line graph, show the winners' times in miles per hour at the Indianapolis 500 between 1946 and 1977: 1946, 114.820; 1947, 116.338; 1948, 119.814; 1949, 121.327; 1950, 124.002; 1951, 126.244; 1952, 128.922; 1953, 128.740; 1954, 130.840; 1955, 128.209; 1956, 128.490; 1957, 135.601; 1958, 133.791; 1959, 135.857; 1960, 138.767; 1961, 139.130; 1962, 140.293; 1963, 143.137; 1964, 147.350; 1965, 151.388; 1966, 144.317; 1967, 151.207; 1968, 152.822; 1969, 156.867; 1970, 155.749; 1971, 157.735; 1972, 163.465; 1973, 159.014; 1974, 158.589; 1975, 149.213; 1976, 148.725; and 1977, 161.331. (To avoid having a large empty space at the bottom of the graph, put a broken line above 0, leave out the lower speeds, and then start again with the lowest round number to allow room for all the speeds.)
   What is a reasonable grouping? Do you see a pattern? _____

4.4 MEASURES OF CENTRAL TENDENCY

Graphs are useful to show differences and changes; the opposite problem is finding a typical value for a set of figures.

The most familiar measure is the *average* or *mean,* found by adding all the figures and dividing by the number of figures. In many cases, the average gives a good idea of the makeup of the group.

For example if we were to find the average age of a class of beginning kindergarten children, the mean would almost certainly be between 5 and 6. In fact, the ages of all the children would be within a range of about 2 years. On the other hand, a class of beginning college students might include many recent high school graduates, ages 18–20, and a few students in their 40s or 50s. Suppose that in a class of 24 students, 6 students are 18 years old, 7 are 19, 8 are 20, 2 are 43 and 1 is 57. The average then is $22\frac{2}{3}$, although none of the students actually is 22 or 23. In fact, $\frac{7}{8}$ are younger than 22 and $\frac{1}{8}$ are older.

Another measure sometimes used is the *median,* or the middle value. As many individual measurements are more than the median as are less than the median. Out of 24 students in our imaginary college class, half are 19 or under and half are 19 or over, so the median is 19.

The third measure commonly used to describe a group is the *mode,* the most common single value. In this case, more students are 20 than are any other age, so the mode is 20. The choice of the most desirable measure is a matter of judgment in the particular situation.

In most actual work, finding the mean, mode, and median is not so simple as in our example. To make it easier, all the items in the list are arranged in order, usually from smallest to greatest. This is called an *array.*

Instead of showing each item separately, we may count the number of items of each particular value or within a range of values. The number of items in any category is called the frequency. The manner in which these frequencies occur is the frequency distribution. A special sort of graph called a histogram pictures the frequency distribution.

Example. On a September day, high and low temperatures in 66 United States cities were as shown in Table 4-1. Find the mean, mode, and median of the high readings. The first step is to arrange the listings in order, as in Fig. 4-5.

Table 4–1. High and Low Temperatures in 66 Cities

	High	Low		High	Low
Albany	60	30	Las Vegas	100	70
Albuquerque	79	50	Little Rock	87	61
Amarillo	73	53	Los Angeles	101	74
Anchorage	55	37	Louisville	79	57
Asheville	71	55	Memphis	80	65
Atlanta	78	62	Miami	85	75
Atlantic City	59	51	Milwaukee	73	59
Baltimore	68	46	Minneapolis	86	47
Bismarck	70	34	Nashville	84	63
Boise	91	56	New Orleans	86	75
Boston	54	33	New York	63	48
Brownsville	88	75	Norfolk	73	55
Buffalo	72	52	Oklahoma City	78	62
Charleston, SC	80	68	Omaha	78	53
Charleston, WV	76	53	Orlando	90	72
Chicago	76	54	Philadelphia	65	47
Cincinnati	76	49	Phoenix	99	78
Cleveland	73	51	Pittsburgh	67	47
Columbus	72	46	Portland ME	58	34
Dallas	75	67	Portland, OR	77	57
Denver	83	48	Rapid City	89	43
Des Moines	78	57	Reno	87	45
Detroit	71	46	Richmond	74	46
Duluth	73	39	St. Louis	77	55
Fairbanks	51	45	St. Petersburg	88	72
Hartford	60	30	Salt Lake City	81	52
Helena	84	45	San Diego	93	73
Honolulu	87	73	San Francisco	67	57
Houston	84	69	Sault Ste. Marie	63	49
Indianapolis	76	44	Seattle	67	57
Jacksonville	84	70	Spokane	84	54
Juneau	58	37	Tulsa	83	59
Kansas City MO	79	58	Washington	71	55

Since we are interested only in the temperatures as a group and not in the specific temperature for any certain city, the easiest way to do this is to use tick marks, as shown in Column A. Finding the average may be easier now: instead of adding each reading individually we can, if we wish, first multiply each reading by the frequency, that is, by the number of cities having that reading. The average high temperature is 5,047 ÷ 66 = 76.47.

The median is easy to find. Since 66 cities are listed, count 33 ticks from either end, then check your result by counting from the other end. In this case, the median is 77. If the middle point had turned out to be between two readings. 77 and 78, for example, the median would have been halfway between them, or 77$\frac{1}{2}$.

How do we find the mode? Two readings, 73 and 84, have frequencies of 5. We could call this a *bimodal distribution,* which sometimes happens, but another, better approach is to group the data, perhaps in 5-degree intervals, as shown in Column B. In this case, the mode is the group from 76–80, with a frequency of 15. We might designate the middle value, 78, as the mode.

A histogram makes the distribution clearer, as shown in Fig. 4-5. In this case, the mean, median, and mode all fall within the group from 76 to 80.

If, instead of being given the original or *raw* data, we had only the information in Column B, we could estimate the mean by multiplying each frequency by the midpoint of its group, and adding the products to find the sum of the readings:

$$
\begin{array}{rcl}
3 \times 53 &=& 159 \\
5 \times 58 &=& 290 \\
3 \times 63 &=& 189 \\
5 \times 68 &=& 340 \\
12 \times 73 &=& 876 \\
15 \times 78 &=& 1{,}170 \\
9 \times 83 &=& 747 \\
9 \times 88 &=& 792 \\
2 \times 93 &=& 186 \\
2 \times 98 &=& 196 \\
1 \times 103 &=& \underline{103} \\
 & & 5{,}048
\end{array}
$$

The total in this method, 5,048, is only 1 more than the total of the raw data, 5,047. The average, using the grouped data, is 76.48.

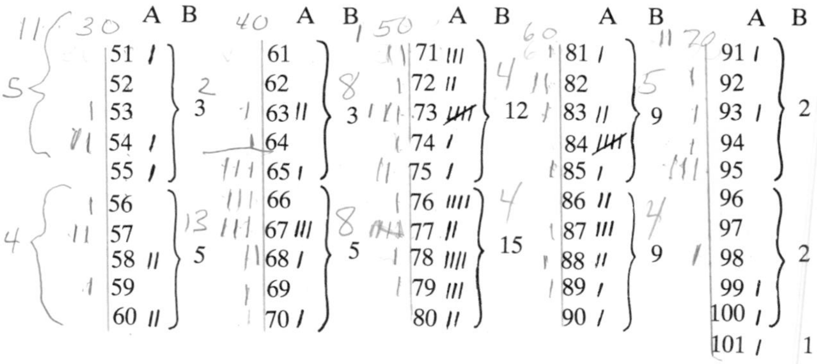

Fig. 4-5   Array of High Temperatures, 66 Cities

Problems

1. a. Find the mean, the median, and the mode of the data for low temperatures shown in Table 4-1.

   Mean 54.53   3599 ÷ 66

   Median 54.

   Mode 57

   b. Construct a histogram. Find the mean by using groupings. How does this mean compare with the true mean? How significant do you consider these data? How would the data for a day in July be different? A day in January?

   _____

   _____

   _____

2. Group the data in Table 4-1 in six to eight sections, not necessarily the same size, in some way that seems logical and meaningful to you. Find the average high and low temperatures for each section. Find the average of these averages. Is it the same as the average of all the data?

		Average High	Average Low
a.	————————————	————	————
b.	————————————	————	————
c.	————————————	————	————
d.	————————————	————	————
e.	————————————	————	————
f.	————————————	————	————
g.	————————————	————	————
h.	————————————	————	————
	Averages	————	————

3. Find the mean, the median, and the mode of the advertising expenditures for media shown in Example 1 in Unit 1 of this chapter, disregarding the miscellaneous figure.

Mean _____

Median _____

Mode _____

4. How would you describe a typical voter turnout of those shown in Problem 1, Unit 1? Would you use the mean, the mode, the median, or some other description?

_____

5. a.   What is the average area of the seven continents listed in Problem 3, Unit 2? b.   Which continent is closest to the average?

_____ sq. mi.

_____

6. a.   From 1821 to 1970, what was the average number of immigrants admitted to the United States per decade, as shown in Problem 1, Unit 3? b.   What is the median number? c.   How much difference is there between the mean and the median? d.   Which is greater? Why?

_____

a.   _____

b.   _____

c.   _____

d.   _____

_____

7. a.   Find the mean and median speeds of winners at the Indianapolis 500, as listed in Problem 3, Unit 3. After grouping, find the mode.

a.   Mean _____

Median _____

Mode _____

b.   Construct a histogram. Using the grouped frequencies, estimate the mean. How close is it to the true mean?

b.   _____

_____

4.5   INDEX NUMBERS

Some statistics have very little meaning except when compared to other figures. Are prices, sales, or enrollment going up or down? How do they compare with those of five or ten years ago? More important, is our income keeping pace with prices?

One way to show such a comparison is by *index numbers*. One particular value is taken as a standard, and each index number is expressed as a percentage of that standard.

For example, the Bureau of Labor Statistics, using 1967 prices as the standard, publishes monthly index numbers representing the prices of goods and services purchased by "average" families. Individuals can compare their incomes with these price indexes, and unions use them as a basis for wage contracts. By comparing the index for any year with that for the previous year, the *rate of inflation* can be shown. Indexes are also published for individual cities throughout the country.

Example 1. From the population statistics for the state of Connecticut in Problem 2, Unit 1, using 1790 as a base, find index numbers to represent the population in the later years shown.

$$237,946 \qquad\qquad 100 \text{ (base)} \qquad 1790$$
$$251,002 \div 2379.46 = 105.5 \text{ Index Number, } 1800$$
$$261,942 \div 2379.46 = 110.1 \qquad 1810$$
$$275,248 \div 2379.46 = 115.7 \qquad 1820$$
$$297,675 \div 2379.46 = 125.1 \qquad 1830$$
$$309,978 \div 2379.46 = 130.3 \qquad 1840$$
$$370,792 \div 2379.46 = 155.8 \qquad 1850$$
$$460,147 \div 2379.46 = 193.4 \qquad 1860$$
$$537,454 \div 2379.46 = 225.9 \qquad 1870$$
$$622,700 \div 2379.46 = 261.7 \qquad 1880$$

Example 2. Based on the year 1967, the consumer price index was 116.3 in 1970, 121.3 in 1971, 125.3 in 1972, 133.1 in 1973, 147.7 in 1974, 161.2 in 1975, and 170.5 in 1976. Find the percentage of increase for each period. What is the average percentage of increase? What is the percentage of increase for the whole period?

From 1970 to 1971, the difference was 5.0; the increase was 4.30%

1971 to 1972	4.0;	3.30%
1972 to 1973	7.8;	6.23%
1973 to 1974	14.6;	10.97%
1974 to 1975	13.5;	9.14%
1975 to 1976	9.3;	5.77%

Average percentage of increase = 39.71% ÷ 6 = 6.62%

Percentage of increase for whole period = 54.2 ÷ 116.3 = 46.60%

Why is the total percentage of increase more than the total of the yearly percentages?

Problems

1. Using 1790 as a base, find index numbers to represent the population in the years 1800–1880 in Maine as shown in Problem 2, Unit 1. How do they compare with the index numbers for Connecticut?

   1800 _157.16_   1810 _236.90_   1820 _309.03_

   1830 _413.77_   1840 _519.78_   1850 _604.07_

   1860 _650.80_   1870 _649.38_   1880 _672.82_

2. Based on the year 1967, the wholesale price index was 119.1 for 1972, 134.7 for 1973, 160.1 for 1974, 174.9 for 1975, and 183.0 for 1976. a. Find the percentages of increase for each period. b. Find the average percentage of increase. c. Find the percentage of increase for the whole period 1972–76. (Instead of dividing the difference by the earlier index in each case, try dividing the later index by the earlier index. What is the result?)

a. 1972–73 _____ %   1973–74 _____ %

1974–75 _____ %   1975–76 _____%

b. _____ %   c. _____ %

---

3. For two consecutive years, indexes for production of durable goods were 101.4 and 99.4; nondurable goods, 110.6 and 113.5; mining, 109.7 and 107.0; utilities, 128.3 and 133.7; residential construction, 115 and 163; other construction, 130 and 134; consumer prices, 116.3 and 121.3; wholesale prices, 110.4 and 113.9; and the total business index, 106.6 and 106.8. a.   Find the percentage of increase or decrease in each case.

	% of Increase	% of Decrease
Durable goods	_____	_1.97%_
Nondurable goods	_____	_____
Mining	_____	_2.46_
Utilities	_____	_____
Residential construction	_____	_____
Other construction	_____	_____
Consumer prices	_____	_____
Wholesale prices	_____	_____
Total business index	_____	_____

b. How do the indexes compare with each other and with the total?
c. What conclusions can you draw about the state of the economy in the year between these changes?

b. _____

c. _____

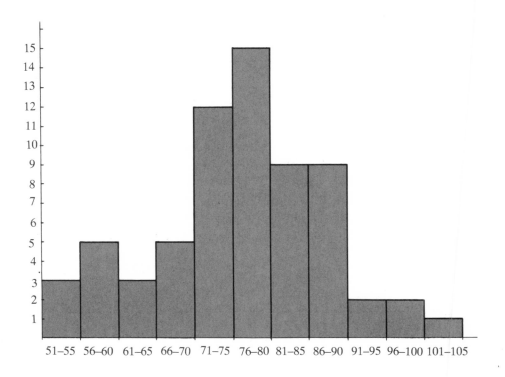

Fig. 4-6   Frequencies, High Temperatures in 66 U.S. Cities, September—, 19—

4.   Based on the 1910–14 average, indexes for wool prices received by U.S. farmers were 1920, 214; 1930, 119; 1940, 160; 1950, 341; 1960, 235; 1970, 194. If the average price received in 1930 was $.195 per pound, estimate the base price and the prices received in 1920, 1940, 1950, 1960, and 1970.

Base $_____

1920 $_____

1940 $_____

1950 $_____

1960 $_____

1970 $_____

5. Based on the prices in 1957–59, the 1967 index for all items of consumer goods was 116.3; for food, 115.2; housing, 114.3; transportation, 115.9; and medical care, 136.7. Based on the 1967 prices, the index for all items in 1973 was 133.1; food, 141.4; housing, 135.0; transportation, 123.8; and medical care, 137.7. What would the 1973 indexes have been had they been based on the 1957–59 prices?

1973

All Items ⎯⎯⎯⎯⎯⎯

Food ⎯⎯⎯⎯⎯⎯

Housing ⎯⎯⎯⎯⎯⎯

Transportation ⎯⎯⎯⎯⎯⎯

Medical Care ⎯⎯⎯⎯⎯⎯

6. In 1974 the U.N. Statistical Office compared the cost of living in various world cities, using New York City as a base. Some of the indexes were Bogota, Colombia, 64; Bonn, West Germany, 116; Cairo, Egypt, 77; Copenhagen, Denmark, 111; London, U.K., 83; Mexico City, Mexico, 89; Paris, France, 112; Sydney, Australia, 105; Tokyo, Japan, 121. If a New York family had an income of $22,500, how much income would they have needed to live comparably in each of the cities listed?

Bogota $14400.

Bonn $26,100.

Cairo $17,325

Copenhagen $24,975

London $18,625

Mexico City $20,025

Paris $25,200

Sydney $23,625

Tokyo $27,225

Chapter Review

1. Fifteen seas have these areas and average depths: Andaman Sea, 218,100 sq. mi., 3,667 ft.; Baltic Sea, 147,500 sq. mi., 331 ft.; Bering Sea, 873,000 sq. mi., 4,893 ft.; Black Sea, 196,100 sq. mi., 3,906 ft.; Caribbean Sea, 971,400 sq. mi., 8,448 ft.; East China Sea, 256,600 sq. mi., 1,539 ft.; Hudson Bay, 281,900 sq. mi., 305 ft.; Sea of Japan, 391,100 sq. mi., 5,468 ft.; Mediterranean Sea, 969,100 sq. mi., 4,926 ft.; Gulf of Mexico, 582,100 sq. mi., 5,297 ft.; North Sea, 164,900 sq. mi., 308 ft.; Sea of Ckhotsk, 537,500 sq. mi., 3,192 ft.; Red Sea, 174,900 sq. mi., 1,764 ft.; South China Sea, 1,148,500 sq. mi., 4,802 ft.; and Yellow Sea, 113,500 sq. mi., 121 ft. Picture both these sets of figures on one graph.

2. In a recent year, the U.S. had 51.81 telephones per 100 population and 667.0 telephone conversations per person; Australia had 27.05 and 198.7; Canada, 40.65 and 667.7; Denmark, 30.11 and 354.3; Iceland, 31.04 and 606.3; Liechtenstein, 39.53 and 299.5; the Netherlands, 21.45 and 176.1; Norway, 25.97 and 203.9; Sweden, 49.84 and 598.9; and Switzerland, 41.84 and 306.4. Show these statistics in a bar graph. a.   For these ten countries, what is the average number of telephones per 100 population? b.   Of conversations per person? c.   Using the U.S. as a base, find index numbers for each country.

a.   ﹘﹘﹘﹘﹘

b.   ﹘﹘﹘﹘﹘

	Telephones per 100 People	Calls per Person
c. Australia	﹘﹘﹘﹘	﹘﹘﹘﹘
Canada	﹘﹘﹘﹘	﹘﹘﹘﹘
Denmark	﹘﹘﹘﹘	﹘﹘﹘﹘
Iceland	﹘﹘﹘﹘	﹘﹘﹘﹘
Liechtenstein	﹘﹘﹘﹘	﹘﹘﹘﹘
Netherlands	﹘﹘﹘﹘	﹘﹘﹘﹘
Norway	﹘﹘﹘﹘	﹘﹘﹘﹘
Sweden	﹘﹘﹘﹘	﹘﹘﹘﹘
Switzerland	﹘﹘﹘﹘	﹘﹘﹘﹘

3. The approximate diameters of the nine planets of the solar system are Mercury, 3,100 mi.; Venus, 7,600 mi.; Earth, 7,900 mi.; Mars, 4,200 mi.; Jupiter, 87,000 mi.; Saturn, 72,000 mi.; Uranus, 31,000 mi.; Neptune, 33,000 mi.; and Pluto, 7,600 mi. a.   Show these relative sizes in a graph. b.   Is there a reason for showing the planets in the order shown or would another order be preferable? c.   Using the diameter of earth as a base, find an index number for each diameter. d.   What would a graph of the index numbers be like?

b. _in order of solar system_

c.   Mercury _39.24_   diameter × 7,900 or 79

    Venus _96.20_ base

    Earth   100

    Mars _53.16_

    Jupiter _1,101.27_

    Saturn _911.39_

    Uranus _392.41_

    Neptune _417.72_

    Pluto _96.20_

d. _____

4. In a recent year, according to the U.S. Office of Education, 666,700 bachelors' degrees, 176,749 masters' degrees, and 23,089 doctors' degrees were conferred. Ten years earlier, there were 362,554 bachelors' degrees, 64,487 masters' degrees, and 8,938 doctors' degrees. Construct a circle graph for each year. Do you find significant differences? _____

5. In 1967, according to the Federal Power Commission, production of electric energy from hydropower was 222.2 billion kilowatt-hours; from coal, 630.2; from nuclear energy, 7.3; from oil, 89.9; from gas, 264.7. It was estimated that in 1980 comparable figures would be from hydropower, 372.2; from coal, 1345.6; from nuclear energy, 544.0; from oil, 114.5; from gas, 486.7. Picture these relationships in two circle graphs.

6. The U.S. Department of Agriculture reported farm mortgages held by life insurance companies and by commercial and savings banks were, in millions of dollars, 1963, $3,391 and $2,053 respectively; 1964, $3,779 and $2,356; 1965, $4,285 and $2,662; 1966, $4,799 and $2,934; 1967, $5,211 and $3,164; 1968, $5,537 and $3,537; 1969, $5,761 and $3,851; 1970, $5,732 and $4,109; 1971, $5,608 and $4,441; 1972, $5,562 and $4,214; 1973, $5,643 and $4,792; and 1974, $5,992 and $5,458. Construct a graph to show these statistics. Using the 1967 figure as a base, find index numbers for each year.

	Insurance	*Banks*	*Total*
1963	_____	_____	_____
1964	_____	_____	_____
1965	_____	_____	_____
1966	_____	_____	_____
1967	100	100	100
1968	_____	_____	_____
1969	_____	_____	_____
1970	_____	_____	_____
1971	_____	_____	_____
1972	_____	_____	_____
1973	_____	_____	_____
1974	_____	_____	_____

7. Average monthly temperatures in °F from January to December are listed by the National Weather Records Center for Bismarck, ND as 9.9; 13.5; 26.2; 43.5; 55.9; 64.5; 71.7; 69.3; 58.7; 46.7; 28.9; and 17.8. For Honolulu: 72.5; 72.4; 72.8; 74.2; 75.9; 77.9; 78.8; 79.4; 79.2; 78.2; 75.9; and 73.6. For Nashville, Tennessee: 39.9; 42.0; 49.1; 59.6; 68.6; 77.4; 80.2; 79.2; 72.8; 61.5; 48.5; and 41.4. Show these data on one graph. What is the average temperature for each city?

Bismarck _____ °F

Honolulu _____ °F

Nashville _____ °F

8. Of registered scientists in the U.S., the National Register of Scientific and Technical Personnel reported that 9,759 were 24 years old or under; 51,661 were 25–29; 51,751 were 30–34; 47,199 were 35–39; 43,162 were 40–44, 35,336 were 45–49; 24,439 were 50–54; 15,971 were 55–59; 9,919 were 60–64; 4,748 were 65–69; and 3,050 were 70 or over. Show these frequencies in a histogram. Estimate the mean, median, and mode.

Mean   ————

Median   ————

Mode   ————

9. The ages of the justices of the U.S. Supreme Court at the time of their appointments have been 44, 55, 50, 45, 59, 56, 57, 55, 65, 63, 67, 68, 56, 62, 61, 57, 46, 47, 46, 61, 57, 62, 44, 56, 53, 62, 62, 52, 54, 60, 60, 57, 56, 54, 61, 53, 52, 65, 51, 53, 54, 52, 59, 59, 60, 56, 57, 55, 61, 51, 53, 56, 40, 49, 62, 49, 48, 57, 49, 58, 55, 50, 56, 43, 44, 54, 55, 59, 62, 62, 64, and 47. Show the frequency distribution, construct a histogram, and find the mean, mode, and median.

Mean   ————

Mode   ————

Median   ————

10. In a magazine article, a writer stated that the average salary paid to federal workers in Washington, D.C., in 1978 was more than $20,000. A union officer disputed this claim, saying that more than two-thirds of these workers earned less than $20,000 and that 80% of those earned less than $15,000. a. Could both writers be right? b. What sort of distribution do the figures suggest?

a.   ————

b.   ————

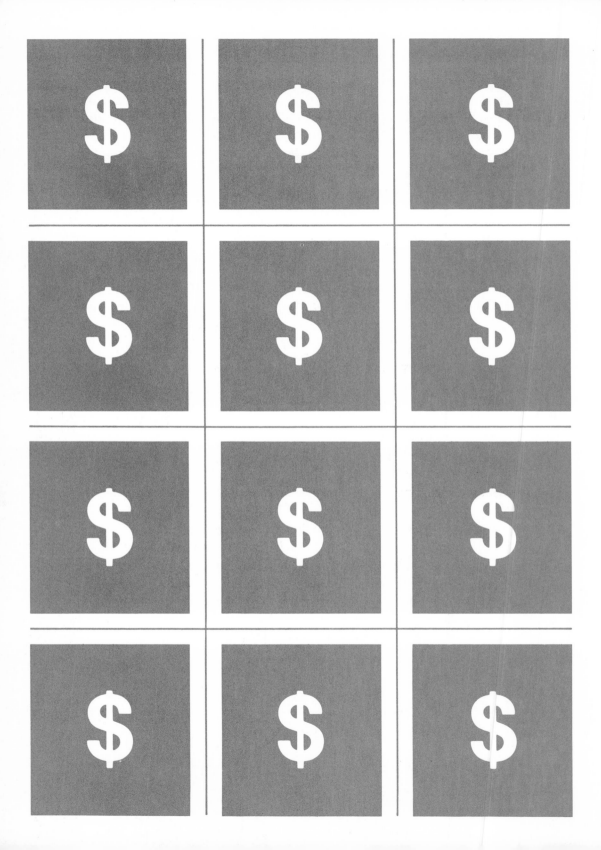

5

Simple Interest

5.1 COMPUTATION OF SIMPLE INTEREST

When money is borrowed, a charge is usually made for its use. The charge for the use of borrowed money is called *interest*. The borrowed money is called the *principal*. The number of years or parts of a year for which the money is borrowed is the *time*. The *rate,* usually expressed as a percentage, is the charge for each dollar each year. The *amount* is the sum of the principal and the interest, or the total to be paid back.

$$\text{Interest} = \text{Principal} \times \text{Rate} \times \text{Time}$$
$$\text{Amount} = \text{Principal} + \text{Interest}$$

Example. Mr. Jackson borrows $2,000 from Mr. Starr and agrees to pay it back, with interest at 5%, at the end of two years. The principal is $2,000, the rate is 5%, and the time is two years.

$$
\begin{aligned}
\text{Interest} &= \text{Principal} \times \text{Rate} \times \text{Time} \\
&= \$2,000 \quad \times .05 \times .2 \qquad = \$200 \\
\text{Amount} &= \text{Principal} + \text{Interest} \\
&= \$2,000 \quad + \$200 \qquad = \$2,200
\end{aligned}
$$

Problems

Group 1

In the following problems, the principal, rate, and time are given. Find the interest and the amount:

1. $2,500 for 3 years at 6%

   $ 450 $ 2950

2. $400 for 2 years at 8%

   $ 64 $ 464

3. $200 for 6 years at 5%

$___60___ $___260___

4. $250 for 3 years at 7%

$___52.50___ $___302.50___

5. $325 for 4 years at 4%

$___52___ $___377___

6. $900 for 1 year at 9%

$___81___ $___981___

7. $670 for 2 years at 6$^1/_2$%

$___87.10___ $___757.10___

8. $800 for 3 years at 5$^1/_2$%

$___932___ $___932___

9. $480 for 2$^1/_2$ years at 7%

$___84___ $___564___

10. $880 for 1$^1/_2$ years at 8%

$___105.60___ $___985.60___

11. $725 for 3$^1/_2$ years at 4$^1/_2$%

$___114.19___ $___839.19___

12. $4,000 for 4$^1/_2$ years at 6$^1/_2$%

$___1170___ $___5170___

13. $826.50 for 2 years at 6%

$___99.18___ $___925.68___

14. $894.50 for 1$^1/_2$ years at 5$^1/_2$%

$___73.80___ $___968.30___

15. $904.50 for 3$^1/_2$ years at 4$^1/_2$%

$___142.46___ $___1046.96___

16. $500 for 6 months at 8%

$___20___ $___520___

17. $700 for 6 months at 4%

$___14___ $___714___

18. $700 for 3 months at 6%

$___10.50___ $___710.50___

19. $80 for 3 months at 6%

$___1.20___ $___81.20___

20. $492.75 for 3 months at 5%

$___6.16___ $___498.91___

Group 2

1. Joseph Caster borrowed $1,200 and $1,500 for 1 year at 6% interest. How much interest did he pay on each loan? What was the total amount repaid?

$___72___

$___90___

$___2862___

2. If the loans in the previous problem had been made at 5%, what would the interest be?

$___60___

$___75___

$_2835_

3. Frances Sommer borrowed $880 for 2 years at 7%. What was the interest charge?

$_123.20_

4. Frank Strong borrowed $400 from his aunt for $1\frac{1}{2}$ years at 4%. How much did he pay his aunt?

$___424___

5. Janice Carr borrowed $300 for 2 years at $6\frac{1}{2}$% interest. How much did she repay when the loan became due?

$___339___

6. James Jones lent his friend Jack Rolf $700 for $2\frac{1}{2}$ years at 5%. How much must Jack Rolf pay altogether?

$_787.50_

7. Mary Smith loaned $2,250 to Ann Richards for $1\frac{1}{2}$ years at 6%. a. How much did Ann pay for interest at the end of that time? b. If the interest rate had been 5%, how much would the interest have been?

a. $_202.50_

b. $_168.75_

8. Louise Long made the following loans for $1\frac{1}{4}$ years. What interest should be charged in each case?

Emil Palm $1,750 at 6% $_131.25_

Jean Olson $2,400 at $6\frac{1}{2}$% $__180__

Joy Jilson $840 at 7% $_73.50_

Joseph Jay $2,300 at $6\frac{1}{2}$% $_186.88_

9. Donald Strum borrowed $5,200 from his brother John. He repaid him $4\frac{1}{2}$ years later, with $5\frac{1}{2}\%$ interest. How much did he pay?

$ _6487_

10. Alice Putney borrowed $3,650 from her father to open a coffeehouse. She promised to repay him as soon as possible and also to pay interest at the rate of $3\frac{1}{2}\%$. After $4\frac{1}{2}$ years, she found herself in a position to repay the loan. How much interest was owed at that time?

$ _574.88_

5.2   METHODS OF COMPUTING TIME

Sometimes only the dates of a loan and the payment are known. Before you can compute the interest, you must compute the time between these dates. To find the number of days between two dates, add up the number of days left in the month in which the loan was made. Add to this figure the number of days until the loan must be repaid. Count the due date, but not the day on which the loan was made.

Example. Find the exact number of days between June 11 and December 5 of the same year.

June 11–June 30	=	19 days
July	=	31
August	=	31
September	=	30
October	=	31
November	=	30
December 1–December 5	=	+5
		177 days

Problems

Group 1

Find the elapsed time; don't forget to consider the leap year when necessary:

1. August 9, 1982, to November 11 of the next year. _459_

2. February 14, 1980, to July 21, 1982. _889_

3. March 10, 1976, to December 22, 1979. _1382_

4. June 11, 1977, to October 29, 1979. _870_

5. July 6, 1979, to September 17, 1980. _439_

6. December 1, 1981, to January 10, 1983. _408_

7. November 16, 1982, to July 6, 1983. _134_

8. March 27, 1988, to January 2, 1990. _648_

9. August 28, 1989, to May 13, 1992. _989_

10. December 8, 1992, to December 11, 1994. _735_

Instead of adding each month separately, you can use a *table of days,* shown in Table 5-1. In a table of days, the days of the year are numbered from 1 (January 1) to 365 (December 31). For a leap year, add 1 to any date after February 28.

To find the elapsed time between two dates in the same year, look up the numbers of the two days and subtract. For example, to find the exact number of days between March 8 and November 26, find the numbers for November 26 (330) and March 8 (67) and subtract: 330 − 67 = 263 days, the elapsed time.

To find the elapsed time between days in successive years, find the number of days from the first date to the end of the year, and then add the number of days to the last date. For example, the elapsed time between June 2 and January 22 of the next year is computed:

$$December\ 31\ -\ June\ 2\ =\ 365\ -\ 153\ =\ \ \ \ 212\ days$$
$$January\ 22\ =\ +\ \ 22\ days$$
$$234\ days$$

Problems

Group 2
Find the elapsed time by using the table of days.

1. August 3, 1980, to January 5, 1981. _155_

2. February 5, 1984, to November 13, 1984. _281_

3. April 11, 1983, to December 1, 1983. _234_

4. September 9, 1979, to February 5, 1980. _149_

5. January 5, 1976, to April 6, 1976. _92_

6. March 22, 1982, to June 19, 1982. _89_

Table 5-1. The Number of Each Day of the Year
Counting from January 1

Day of month	Jan.	Feb.	Mar.	Apr.	May	June	July	Aug.	Sept.	Oct.	Nov.	Dec.	Day of month
1	1	32	60	91	121	152	182	213	244	274	305	335	1
2	2	33	61	92	122	153	183	214	245	275	306	336	2
3	3	34	62	93	123	154	184	215	246	276	307	337	3
4	4	35	63	94	124	155	185	216	247	277	308	338	4
5	5	36	64	95	125	156	186	217	248	278	309	339	5
6	6	37	65	96	126	157	187	218	249	279	310	340	6
7	7	38	66	97	127	158	188	219	250	280	311	341	7
8	8	39	67	98	128	159	189	220	251	281	312	342	8
9	9	40	68	99	129	160	190	221	252	282	313	343	9
10	10	41	69	100	130	161	191	222	253	283	314	344	10
11	11	42	70	101	131	162	192	223	254	284	315	345	11
12	12	43	71	102	132	163	193	224	255	285	316	346	12
13	13	44	72	103	133	164	194	225	256	286	317	347	13
14	14	45	73	104	134	165	195	226	257	287	318	348	14
15	15	46	74	105	135	166	196	227	258	288	319	349	15
16	16	47	75	106	136	167	197	228	259	289	320	350	16
17	17	48	76	107	137	168	198	229	260	290	321	351	17
18	18	49	77	108	138	169	199	230	261	291	322	352	18
19	19	50	78	109	139	170	200	231	262	292	323	353	19
20	20	51	79	110	140	171	201	232	263	293	324	354	20
21	21	52	80	111	141	172	202	233	264	294	325	355	21
22	22	53	81	112	142	173	203	234	265	295	326	356	22
23	23	54	82	113	143	174	204	235	266	296	327	357	23
24	24	55	83	114	144	175	205	236	267	297	328	358	24
25	25	56	84	115	145	176	206	237	268	298	329	359	25
26	26	57	85	116	146	177	207	238	269	299	330	360	26
27	27	58	86	117	147	178	208	239	270	300	331	361	27
28	28	59	87	118	148	179	209	240	271	301	332	362	28
29	29	...	88	119	149	180	210	241	272	302	333	363	29
30	30	...	89	120	150	181	211	242	273	303	334	364	30
31	31	...	90	...	151	...	212	243	...	304	...	365	31

NOTE: For leap years, after February 28, the number of the day is one greater than that given in the table.

7. June 2, 1977, to December 4, 1977. _185_

8. November 9, 1988, to November 2, 1989. _358_

9. July 5, 1980, to August 1, 1980. _27_

10. August 19, 1985, to December 21, 1985. _124_

5.3 COMPUTING THE RATE OF INTEREST

There are occasions when being able to compute the *rate of interest per annum* (per year) is important. For example, you may know that a bond costing $989.50 will pay interest of $36 for 6 months, whereas another bond costing $1,012.60 will pay $37 interest for 6 months. From the standpoint of return alone, which is the better investment? Knowing the rate earned on each will provide the answer. The rate of interest can be found by rearranging the basic formula to read

$$\text{Interest} = \text{Principal} \times \text{Rate} \times \text{Time}$$

$$\text{Rate} = \frac{\text{Interest}}{\text{Principal} \times \text{Time}}$$

In the first instance, $\text{Rate} = \dfrac{\$36}{\$989.50 \times \frac{1}{2}\,\text{yr.}} = .0728 = 7.28\%$ per year.

In the second instance, $\text{Rate} = \dfrac{\$37}{\$1,012.60 \times \frac{1}{2}\,\text{yr.}} = .0731 = 7.31\%$ per year.

Problems

Group 1

In the following problems, the principal, interest, and time are given. Express the rate as a percent to 2 decimal places, for each. (Notice that the loan "costs" or "earns" a certain amount of interest, depending on whether you are borrowing or lending.)

1. $3,000 for 2 years earns $360 interest.   _6_ %

2. $5,000 for 3 years earns $1,280 interest.   _8.5_ %

3. $2,000 for 1½ years earns $210 interest.   _7_ %

4. $6,500 for 4 years earns $2,000 interest.   _7.7_ %

5. $8,000 for 6 months earns $370.   _9.25_ %

6. $964.50 for 2½ years earns $212.20   _8.8_ %

7. $1,868.60 for ½ year earns $80.   _8.56_ %

8. $3,480 for 3 years costs $981.36.   _9.4_ %

9. $4,820 for 4 years costs $1,773.76.   _9.2_ %

10. $7,200 for 3½ years costs $2,595.60.   _1.03_ %

Group 2

1. You buy a bond for $999.49, including brokerage charges. If the bond pays you $34.56 each six months, what rate of interest are you earning?
    _6.92_ %

2. James Dill borrows $1,500 from a friend with the understanding that the loan will be repaid in two years with a total payment of $1,800. What is the rate of interest being charged?
    _10._ %

3. Janet Jones lends $1,200 to Karen Luff for a period of three months. If Karen pays Janet $1,225 in repayment of the loan in three months, what rate of interest has she paid?
    _8.33_ %

4. A bond costing $983.92 pays $7.20 each month. What rate of interest is being paid?
    _.7_ %

5. From the viewpoint of rate of interest earned, which is the better investment? a. $964 which pays $34.50 each 6 months, or b. $1,218 which pays $82.00 each year
    7.16   6.73

5.4   COMPUTING THE PRINCIPAL

On some occasions, the interest, the time, and the rate of interest are known and you need to know the principal. For example, how much will need to be invested at 8.4% for 6 months in order to earn $600? By rearranging the basic formula:

$$\text{Interest} = \text{Principal} \times \text{Rate} \times \text{Time}$$

to read:

$$\text{Principal} = \frac{\text{Interest}}{\text{Rate} \times \text{Time}}$$

$$\text{Principal} = \frac{\$600}{.084 \times \frac{1}{2}} = \$14{,}285.71$$

Problems

Group 1

In the following problems, the interest, time, and rate are given. Find the principal for each.

1. Rate of 7% earns $490 for 1 year. $_7,000_

2. Rate of 8% earns $1,500 for 2 years. $_9375_

3. Rate of 8.4% costs $2,400 for 3 years. $_9523.81_

4. Rate of 9.2% costs $1,840 for 2½ years. $_8000_

5. Rate of 7.8% costs $351 for 1½ years. $_3000_

6. Rate of 9.8% earns $1,820 for 3½ years. $_5306.12_

7. Rate of 10.3% costs $2,340 for 4½ years. $_5048.54_

8. Rate of 10.5% costs $4,725 for 5 years. $_9000_

9. Rate of 8.8% earns $216 for 6 months. $_4909.09_

10. Rate of 6.7% earns $172.80 for 6 months. $_5158.21_

Group 2

1. If you can buy bonds yielding 8%, how much will you need to invest in order to receive $480 each 6 months?

   $_12,000_

2. Mavis Jansen borrowed money at 8.8% interest and paid $800 for interest every 3 months. How much was the loan?

$ 36,363.64

3. Oscar Lopes wants to make an investment which will give him $200 a month in interest. If he can invest money at 9%, how much will he need to invest?

$_____

4. After 2½ years, a loan made at 7½% interest was repaid. The interest for the period amounted to $2,320. How much was the loan?

$_____

5. If a 9½% loan called for an interest payment of $1,860 for 1½ years, how much was the loan?

$_____

5.5   INTEREST FOR SHORT PERIODS

Interest rates are usually expressed as an *annual* or *per annum* rate. The basic formula for finding interest for short periods is the same as for longer periods, but the arithmetic may become more involved. For example, to find the interest on $900 for 44 days at 5%, your solution would be:

$$\text{Principal} \times \text{Rate} \times \text{Time} = \text{Interest}$$
$$\$900 \times .05 \times 44/365 = \$5.42$$

The time factor is the number of days interest is paid for (44) divided by the days in a year. (In a leap year, you would divide by 366.)

Tables of reciprocals give the interest amounts for one dollar for different numbers of days at varying rates of interest. The following is part of such a table for 5%:

Number of days	Reciprocal
40	.005479
41	.005616
42	.005753
43	.005890
44	.006027
45	.006164

You can determine the interest by multiplying the principal on which the interest is to be computed by the reciprocal. For example, the interest on $900 at 5% for 44 days can be found as follows:

$$\$900 \times .006027 = \$5.42$$

Problems

Find the interest. (Use the partial table of reciprocals where possible.)

1. $3,000 at 5% from November 1 to December 16. $_18.49_

2. $5,000 at 6% from July 3 to October 6. $_78.08_

3. $2,000 at 7% from August 7 to November 10. $_____

4. $1,000 at 5% from June 8 to July 20. $_____

5. $800 at 6% from January 6 to February 22. $_____

6. $1,500 at 5% from March 10 to April 19. $_____

7. $300 at 8% from April 20 to June 19. $_____

8. $400 at 7% from June 20 to July 20. $_____

9. $700 at 9% from July 21 to September 19. $_____

10. $500 at 6% from December 15 to February 3. $_____

5.6 ESTIMATING INTEREST BY USE OF 6% 60-DAY METHOD

With the introduction of computers and the adoption of truth in lending laws, the 6% 60-day method of calculating interest is rarely used for the actual computation of interest. However, the method can be used as a means of estimating what the interest should be.

The 6% 60-day method is based on the assumption that a year has 360 days. It is thus very simple to estimate the interest for 60 days at 6%, since $^{60}/_{360}$ is $^1/_6$ and $^1/_6$ of 6% is 1%, or .01. The interest for 60 days at 6% is therefore 1% of the principal. To estimate the interest on any sum for 60 days at 6%, simply move the decimal point two places to the left. For example, the estimated interest on $895 at 6% for 60 days is $8.95. Of course, the actual interest would be $895 $\times$ .06 $\times$ $^{60}/_{365}$ or $8.83. The estimate, in this case, is $.12 high. The estimate by this method will always be somewhat larger than the actual amount.

It is almost as easy to estimate the interest at 6% for other periods that are fractional parts of 60 days.

For 30 days, take $\frac{1}{2}$ of the interest for 60 days.

For 20 days, take $\frac{1}{3}$ of the interest for 60 days.

For 15 days, take $\frac{1}{4}$ of the interest for 60 days.

For 10 days, take $\frac{1}{6}$ of the interest for 60 days.

For 6 days, take $\frac{1}{10}$ of the interest for 60 days. (Move the decimal point a total of three places to the left.)

For 1 day, take $\frac{1}{6}$ of the interest for 6 days.
By using different combinations of these fractional parts of 60, it is possible to estimate interest for any number of days at 6%.

Example. Estimate the interest on $1,800 for 90 days at 6%.

Interest for 60 days at 6% = $18.00 (1% of $1,800)
+ Interest for 30 days at 6% = + 9.00
Interest for 90 days at 6% = $27.00

It is also possible to estimate interest at rates other than 6%.

At 3%, take $\frac{1}{2}$ of the interest at 6%.
At 4%, take $\frac{2}{3}$ of the interest at 6%.
At $4\frac{1}{2}$%, deduct $\frac{1}{4}$ of the interest at 6%.
At 5%, deduct $\frac{1}{6}$ of the interest at 6%.
At 7%, *add* $\frac{1}{6}$ of the interest at 6%.
At $7\frac{1}{2}$%, *add* $\frac{1}{4}$ of the interest at 6%.
At 8%, *add* $\frac{1}{3}$ of the interest at 6%.
At 9%, *add* $\frac{1}{2}$ of the interest at 6%.

Example. Estimate the interest for 60 days on $30,000 at 5%.

Interest for 60 days at 6% = $300 (1% of $30,000)
Less $\frac{1}{6}$ of 6% = − 50
Interest for 60 days at 5% = $250

Problems

Estimate the interest using the 6% 60-day method.

1. $325 for 60 days at 6%. $_____
2. $829.72 for 60 days at 6%. $_____
3. $425.60 for 30 days at 6%. $_____
4. $6,000 for 15 days at 6%. $_____
5. $692.60 for 15 days at 6%. $_____
6. $1,650 for 90 days at 6%. $_____
7. $2,800 for 45 days at 6%. $_____
8. $2,700 for 66 days at 6%. $_____
9. $1,200 for 75 days at 6%. $_____
10. $160 for 120 days at 6%. $_____
11. $2,400 for 60 days at 5%. $_____
12. $3,600 for 60 days at 4%. $_____
13. $3,000 for 60 days at 7%. $_____
14. $4,000 for 60 days at 8%. $_____
15. $2,500 for 60 days at 3%. $_____
16. $2,800 for 60 days at 9%. $_____
17. $2,040 for 40 days at 4%. $_____
18. $900 for 15 days at 3%. $_____
19. $1,200 for 66 days at 9% $_____
20. $312 for 129 days at 3%. $_____

Chapter Review

Group 1

Compute simple interest for each of the following:

1. $3,800 for 4 years at $8^1/_2$% $__1292__

2. $780 for $2^{1}/_{2}$ years at 9%. $_____

3. $640.60 for $1^{1}/_{4}$ years at 7%. $_56.05_

4. $920.40 for $1^{1}/_{2}$ years at $9^{1}/_{2}$%. $_____

5. $1,260 for $1^{3}/_{4}$ years at 8%. $_____

6. $2,420 for 2 years, three months at $7^{1}/_{2}$%. $_____

Find the number of days between:

7. September 10 and December 5 of the same year. ___86___

8. November 8 and December 22, 1983. ___336___

9. April 5, 1983, and March 6, 1984. _____

10. January 15 and October 21, 1983. _____

11. February 10 and June 4, 1984. _____

12. September 8, 1982, and March 6, 1984. _____

Find the rate for the following:

$$R = \frac{I}{P \times T}$$

13. $2,500 for 3 years earns $450 interest. ___6___%

14. $4,600 for 6 months earns $184 interest. _____%

15. $7,800 for 18 months costs $994.50. ___$8^{1}/_{2}$___%

16. $12,400 for 21 months costs $2007.25. _____%

17. $15,000 for 9 months earns $984.38. _____%

18. $3,690 for 3 months costs $78.80. _____%

Compute the principal needed to earn:

$$P = \frac{I}{R \times T}$$

19. $800 at 8% for 1 year. $_10,000_

20. $1,280 at $7^{1}/_{2}$% for 9 months. $_____

21. $2,650 at 8.8% for 3 years. $_10,03788_

22. $702 at 7.6% for $1^{1}/_{2}$ years. $_____

23. $1,860 at 9.2% for $2^{1}/_{4}$ years. $_____

24. $4,800 at 5.75% for 2 years. $_____

Compute the interest on:

25. $4,000 at 6% from September 6 to November 10. $_42.74_

26. $12,400 at 8$^1/_2$% from March 10 to June 6. $_____

27. $26,800 at 9% from April 20 to May 20. $_198.25_

28. $775 at 9$^1/_2$% from May 16 to July 22. $_____

29. $920 at 8$^3/_4$% from June 14 to September 5. $_____

30. $830 at 7.6% from July 3 to October 18. $_____

Estimate the interest, using the 6% 60-day method:

31. $890 for 30 days at 6%. $_4.45_

32. $3,260 for 90 days at 6%. $_____

33. $4,480 for 75 days at 9%. $_____

34. $6,200 for 40 days at 7$^1/_2$%. $_____

35. $624 for 126 days at 4%. $_____

36. $1,800 for 120 days at 8%. $_____

Group 2

1. Jerry Boles borrowed $3,200 for 18 months at 9.8% interest. What amount should he pay when the loan becomes due?

   $_____

2. Alice Perez loaned $840 to a friend, who is to repay the loan at the end of 15 months with interest at the rate of 5$^1/_2$% per annum. What is the amount to be repaid?

   $_____

3. A bond costing $1,002.52, including brokerage charges, pays you $44.61 every 6 months. What rate of interest are you earning?

   _____%

4. How much will you need to invest at 7.8% in order to receive $60 a month in interest?

   $_____

5. You are considering borrowing $920 for a period of 45 days. a. If you can borrow the money at $7^1/_2\%$, what would be the estimated interest cost, using the 6% method? b. What would be the actual cost?

a. $_____

b. $_____

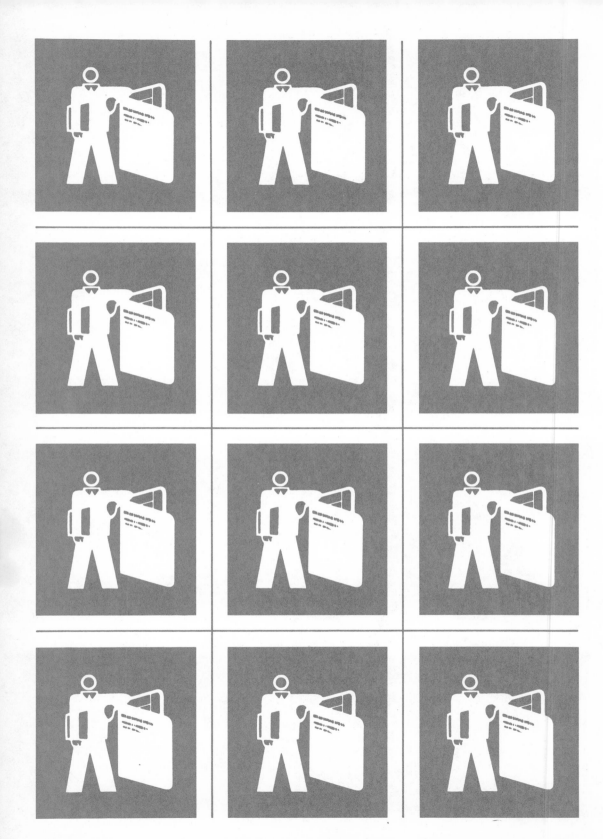

6

Compound Interest and Annuities

6.1 COMPOUND INTEREST—DETERMINING AMOUNT

If a person invests $2,000 in an account that pays 6% simple interest, at the end of a year the investment will have earned $120 ($2,000 × 6% × 1). If the interest is *compounded* quarterly, however, the earnings in one year will be $122.73. Here is the calculation:

Initial Investment	$2,000.00
Interest on $2,000 for 3 Months at 6% per Year	
(6% per Year = 1½% per Quarter)	+ 30.00
Amount of Investment at End of 3 Months	$2,030.00
Interest on $2,030 for Second Quarter	+ 30.45
Amount of Investment at End of 6 Months	$2,060.45
Interest on $2,060.45 for Third Quarter	+ 30.91
Amount of Investment at End of 9 Months	$2,091.36
Interest on $2,091.36 for Fourth Quarter	+ 31.37
Amount of Investment at End of Year	$2,122.73

The difference between the *amount* at the end of the year, $2,122.73, and the initial investment, $2,000, is the *compound interest:* $122.73. Compound interest is always more than simple interest, since it is computed on the interest earned as well as on the principal at the beginning.

Sometimes interest is compounded daily, quarterly, semiannually, or annually. The more frequently the interest is compounded, the greater the amount of interest will be.

Problems

Prepare a table showing the interest and the amount on deposit at the end of each period:

1. $2,400 for 3 years at 5%, compounded annually. _2 778.30_
2. $1,800 for 4 years at 6%, compounded annually.
3. $1,500 for 4 years at 8%, compounded annually.
4. $6,000 for 2 years at 10%, compounded semiannually.
5. $1,200 for 3 years at 9%, compounded semiannually.
6. $2,000 for 2 years at 16%, compounded quarterly.
7. $4,000 for 3 years at 4%, compounded quarterly.
8. $2,000 for 1 year at 12%, compounded monthly.
9. $1,500 for 4 years at 6%, compounded semiannually.
10. $500 for 4 years at 5%, compounded quarterly.

Table 6-1. Amount of $1 at Compound Interest for Specified Periods

Periods	1%	1½%	2%	2½%	4%	5%	6%
1.	1.010000	1.015000	1.020000	1.025000	1.040000	1.050000	1.060000
2.	1.020100	1.030225	1.040400	1.050625	1.081600	1.102500	1.123600
3.	1.030301	1.045678	1.061208	1.076891	1.124864	1.157625	1.191016
4.	1.040604	1.061364	1.082432	1.103813	1.169859	1.215506	1.262477
5.	1.051010	1.077284	1.104081	1.131408	1.216653	1.276282	1.338226
6.	1.061520	1.093443	1.126162	1.159693	1.265319	1.340096	1.418519
7.	1.072135	1.109845	1.148686	1.188686	1.315932	1.407100	1.503630
8.	1.082857	1.126493	1.171659	1.218403	1.368569	1.477455	1.593848
9.	1.093685	1.143390	1.195093	1.248863	1.423312	1.551328	1.689479
10.	1.104622	1.160541	1.218994	1.280085	1.480244	1.628895	1.790848
11.	1.115668	1.177949	1.243374	1.312087	1.539454	1.710339	1.898299
12.	1.126825	1.195618	1.268242	1.344889	1.601032	1.795856	2.012196
13.	1.138093	1.213552	1.293607	1.378511	1.665074	1.885649	2.132928
14.	1.149474	1.231756	1.319479	1.412974	1.731676	1.979932	2.260904
15.	1.160969	1.250232	1.345868	1.448298	1.800944	2.078928	2.396558

6.2   COMPOUND INTEREST—DETERMINING AMOUNT BY USE OF TABLE

Compound interest calculations can be simplified by the use of tables. Table 6-1, for example, shows the compound amount of $1 invested at varying rates of interest for specified periods of time. By reading down the proper column, you can see that $1 invested at 6%, compounded for 10 periods, will increase in value to $1.790848, one dollar invested at 2%, compounded for 15 periods, will be worth $1.345868 at the end of that time. Remember that the *period* could be a month, a quarter, a year or any other unit of time; the interest rate is given for that period.

You can determine the amount of any investment by multiplying the amount of $1, compounded for the designated number of periods, by the investment. Thus, the amount of $1,000 at 6%, compounded for 10 periods, is $1.790848 × $1,000, or $1,790.85. The amount of $2,000 at 2% for 15 periods is $1.345868 × $2,000, or $2,691.74.

Problems

Group 1

Using the appropriate compound interest table, find the amounts and the interest:

1. $4,000 at the end of 4 years at 6%, compounded annually.
   $5049.91 $1049.91

2. $9,000 at the end of 10 years at 5%, compounded annually.
   $_____ $_____

3. $2,000 at the end of 7 years at 4%, compounded semiannually.
   $2638.96 $638.96

4. $1,200 at the end of 5 years at 5%, compounded semiannually
   $_____ $_____

5. $6,000 at the end of 3 years at 4%, compounded quarterly.
   $6760.95 $760.95

6. $1,600 at the end of 6 years at 5%, compounded semiannually.
   $_____ $_____

7. $400 at the end of 2 years at 6%, compounded quarterly.
   $450.60 $50.60

8. $2,000 at the end of 15 years at 6%, compounded annually.

$_____ $_____

9. $2,000 at the end of 3 years at 8%, compounded quarterly. 4

$2536.48 $ 536.48

10. $2,000 at the end of 15 months at 12%, compounded monthly.

$_____ $_____

Group 2

1. What will $5,000 invested at 8%, compounded semiannually, amount to at the end of 5 years? How much will the compound interest be?

Amount $ 7401.22

Interest $ 2401.22

2. Janice Jones deposited $4,000 in the First Trust Company on her nineteenth birthday. The investment pays 6%, compounded quarterly. What amount was in her account on her twenty-first birthday?

$ _____

3. The Chase Trust Company pays 8% interest, compounded quarterly, to its investors. If Ralph Rowe deposits $3,000, how much will he have at the end of 3½ years?

$ 3958.44

4. Harold Hughes created a trust fund for his two children, Amelia and Arthur. He deposited $8,000 in the Alert Trust Company for Amelia and $8,000 in the Montreal Trust Company for Arthur. Each paid 6%, compounded quarterly. At the end of the third year, the Alert Trust Company increased its interest rate to 8%, compounded quarterly. How much more was in Amelia's trust fund than in Arthur's at the end of the sixth year?

Difference $ _____

5. Rachel Fox received an inheritance of $8,000, which she deposited in an account paying 6% interest, compounded quarterly. How much will be in the account at the end of three years? If the inflation rate is 5%, compounded annually, how much will she have gained in real purchasing power?

    1.5

    Amount in account $ *9564.94*

    Gain in Purchasing Power $ *9261*

6.3 COMPOUND INTEREST—USE OF COMPUTERS

By using computers, it is possible to compound interest daily with little difficulty. If the interest rate is 6% per year for a 365-day year, the interest on $1,000 for one day would be:

$$6\% \times \$1,000 \div 365 = \$.164383$$

If the interest is compounded daily, the interest for the second day would be:

$$6\% \times (\$1,000.00 + \$.164383) \div 365 =$$
$$6\% \times \$1,000.164383 \div 365 = \$.164411$$

Interest for the third day would be:

$$6\% \times (\$1,000.164383 + .164411) \div 365 =$$
$$6\% \times \$1,000.328794 \div 365 = \$.164438$$

As you can see, the interest increases slightly each day. Given the proper directions, computers can handle these computations quickly and accurately, so that interest compounded daily at any rate can be determined and recorded within less than a minute for any amount for any number of days.

6.4 COMPOUND INTEREST—DETERMINING PRESENT VALUE

An investment of $2,000 at the beginning of a year at 6% interest, compounded quarterly, is worth $2,122.73 at the end of the year. (See Unit 1.) Look at this situation from another angle. Suppose you know that the investment is worth $2,122.73 at the end of the year, but that you do not know its value at the beginning of the year. Here is how that value might be determined:

1. Determine the amount of $1 invested at 6%, compounded quarterly, for one year. Table 6-1 indicates that this value is $1.061364.

2. The ratio of the value of the investment at the beginning of the year to the value at the end of the year is

$$\frac{1}{1.061364} = .942184$$

The present value of $1 a year from now, if investments can be made at 6%, compounded quarterly, is $.942184. In the example given above, if the $2,122.73 is multiplied by .942184, the answer is $2,000, the original investment. Looking at the problem from this perspective, the difference between $2,122.73 and $2,000—$122.73—can be thought of as the *compound discount* rather than the compound interest.

Table 6-2 simplifies the computations a great deal. Note that the table indicates the present value of $1 compounded at varying rates of interest, from 1% to 6% *per period*. So if the rate is 6% per year, compounded quarterly, the rate per period is 6 ÷ 4 or 1¹/₂%. Looking at the table under 1¹/₂% for 4 periods, you will find the present value of .942184 we determined in our previous example.

Table 6-2. Present Value of $1 at Compound Interest for Specified Periods

Periods	1%	1¹/₂%	2%	3%	4%	6%
1.	0.990099	0.985222	0.980392	0.970874	0.961538	0.943396
2.	0.980296	0.970662	0.961169	0.942596	0.924556	0.889996
3.	0.970590	0.956317	0.942322	0.915142	0.888996	0.839619
4.	0.960980	0.942184	0.923845	0.888487	0.854804	0.792094
5.	0.951466	0.928260	0.905731	0.862609	0.821927	0.747258
6.	0.942045	0.914542	0.887971	0.837484	0.790315	0.704961
7.	0.932718	0.901027	0.870560	0.813092	0.759918	0.665057
8.	0.923483	0.887711	0.853490	0.789409	0.730690	0.627412
9.	0.914340	0.874592	0.836755	0.766417	0.702587	0.591898
10.	0.905287	0.861667	0.820348	0.744094	0.675564	0.558395
11.	0.896324	0.848933	0.804263	0.722421	0.649581	0.526788
12.	0.887449	0.836387	0.788493	0.701380	0.624597	0.496969
13.	0.878663	0.824027	0.773033	0.680951	0.600574	0.468839
14.	0.869963	0.811849	0.757875	0.661118	0.577475	0.442301
15.	0.861349	0.799852	0.743015	0.641862	0.555265	0.417265
16.	0.852821	0.788031	0.728446	0.623167	0.533908	0.393646
17.	0.844377	0.776385	0.714163	0.605016	0.513373	0.371364
18.	0.836017	0.764912	0.700159	0.587395	0.493628	0.350344
19.	0.827740	0.753607	0.686431	0.570286	0.474642	0.330513
20.	0.819544	0.742470	0.672971	0.553676	0.456387	0.311805
21.	0.811430	0.731498	0.659776	0.537549	0.438834	0.294155
22.	0.803396	0.720688	0.646839	0.521893	0.421955	0.277505
23.	0.795442	0.710037	0.634156	0.506692	0.405726	0.261797
24.	0.787566	0.699544	0.621721	0.491934	0.390121	0.246979

Problems

Group 1

Using Table 6-2, determine the present value and compound discount in each of the following situations:

1. $3,400 in 4 years at 8%, compounded semiannually.

$ _2484.35_

$ _915.65_

2. $6,600 in 5 years at 6%, compounded quarterly.

$ _____

$ _____

3. $8,200 in 18 periods of 1 month, at 1% per period.

$ _6855.34_

$ _1344.66_

4. $10,500 in 4 years at 12%, compounded quarterly.

$ _____

$ _____

5. $9,800 in 2 years at 18%, compounded monthly.

$ _6855.53_

$ _2944.47_

6. $1,870 in 4 years at 4%, compounded quarterly.

$ _____

$ _____

7. $2,360 in 5 years at 8%, compounded quarterly.

$ _1582.21_

$ _771.79_

8. $4,280 in 8 years at 6%, compounded semiannually.

$ _____

$ _____

9. $7,700 in 12 years at 6%, compounded annually.

$ _3826.66_

$ _3873.34_

10. $980 in 5 years at 16%, compounded quarterly.

$ _____

$ _____

Group 2

1. Jayne and Howard Daly wish to have $20,000 in 10 years so they can send their daughter to college. They have recently received a sizable inheritance. How much will they need to invest at 8%, compounded semiannually, in order to have the $20,000 in 10 years?

   $ _9127.74_

2. Alice and Ben plan to buy a house in 5 years. They have both been working and saving, and they have some funds to invest. How much will they need to invest at 6%, compounded quarterly, in order to have a down payment of $12,000 in 5 years?

   $ _8909.64_

6.5 ANNUITIES—DETERMINING AMOUNT

Systematic payment of a certain amount of money each period for a specified time may be referred to as an *annuity*. For example, you might deposit $100 each quarter in a savings account which pays 6% interest, compounded quarterly. How much would be on deposit at the end of the year? This would be the *amount* of the annuity. How much of this is interest?

Deposit at Beginning of Year	$100.00
Interest for 1st Quarter ($100 × .06 × ¹/₄)	1.50
Deposit at Beginning of 2nd Quarter	+ 100.00
	$201.50
Interest for 2nd Quarter ($201.50 × .06 × ¹/₄)	3.02
Deposit at Beginning of 3rd Quarter	+ 100.00
	$304.52
Interest for 3rd quarter ($304.52 × .06 × ¹/₄)	4.57
Deposit at Beginning of 4th Quarter	+ 100.00
	$409.09
Interest for 4th Quarter ($409.09 × .06 × ¹/₄)	+ 6.14
Amount of Annuity at End of Year	$415.23

The interest earned is $415.23 less the deposits of $400, or $15.23.

Problems

1. Compute the amount of an annuity of $250 per year at 8%, compounded annually, for 4 years. How much of this is interest?

   Amount of annuity $ _1216.65_

   Interest $ _216.65_

2. Eileen Jacobs deposits $300 every three months in a savings account paying 5½% interest, compounded quarterly. How much will she have in her account at the end of one year?

   $ _____

To simplify the work, annuity tables such as Table 6-3 have been prepared. The table is based on an annuity of $1 a period at the rate of interest *per period* specified for the prescribed number of periods. The interest is compounded each period. For example, the amount of an annuity of $1 per period at 4% compounded for 9 periods would be $11.006107. If you wish to know the amount of an annuity of $50 per period under the same conditions, all you need to do is multiply $11.006107 by 50. The answer is $550.30535, which rounds off to $550.31.

Be sure you are using the rate *per period*. Thus, 12% per annum, compounded monthly, is 1% per period; 8% per annum, compounded quarterly, is 2% per period.

Problems

Group 1

Using Table 6-3 determine the amounts of the following annuities:

1. $40 per month for 1½ years, at 12% per annum. $ _792.44_
2. $500 per year for 5 years, at 6% per annum. $ _____
3. $620 every six months for 10 years, at 8% per year. $ _1920091_
4. $380 every three months for 5 years, at 8% per year. $ _____
5. $60 per month for 5 years, at 18% per annum. $ _585947_   1.5

Group 2

1. Mary Moore agreed to make an investment of $75 a month for 20 months, at 12% per annum interest. What will the investment be worth at the end of that time? How much interest will be earned?

    Value of Investment $ *1667.94*

    Interest Earned $ *167.94*

2. Every year for 10 years, James Blake invested 10% of his annual salary of $18,000. He earned 6% interest on his investment, compounded annually. What was the value of his investment after 10 years? How much interest did he earn?

    Investment $ ─────────

    Interest $ ─────────

3. Sarah Adams plans to attend college in 5 years. To do so, she needs $8,000. She is going to invest $200 every 3 months at 8%, compounded quarterly. How much will she have at the end of 5 years?

    $ *4956.66*

Table 6-3. Amount of Annuity of $1 Per Period at Compound Interest

Period	1%	1½%	2%	4%	6%
1.	1.010000	1.015000	1.020000	1.040000	1.060000
2.	2.030100	2.045225	2.060400	2.121600	2.183600
3.	3.060401	3.090903	3.121608	3.246464	3.374616
4.	4.101005	4.152267	4.204040	4.416323	4.637093
5.	5.152015	5.229551	5.308121	5.632975	5.975319
6.	6.213535	6.322994	6.434283	6.898294	7.393838
7.	7.285671	7.432839	7.582969	8.214226	8.897468
8.	8.368527	8.559332	8.754628	9.582795	10.491316
9.	9.462213	9.702722	9.949721	11.006107	12.180795
10.	10.566835	10.863263	11.168715	12.486351	13.971643
11.	11.682503	12.041211	12.412090	14.025805	15.869941
12.	12.809328	13.236830	13.680332	15.626838	17.882138
13.	13.947421	14.450382	14.973938	17.291911	20.015066
14.	15.096896	15.682138	16.293417	19.023588	22.275970
15.	16.257864	16.932370	17.639285	20.824531	24.672538
16.	17.430443	18.201355	19.012071	22.697512	27.212880
17.	18.614748	19.489376	20.412312	24.645413	29.905653
18.	19.810895	20.796716	21.840559	26.671229	32.759992
19.	21.019004	22.123667	23.297370	28.778079	35.785591
20.	22.239194	23.470522	24.783317	30.969202	38.992727
60.	82.486367	97.657871	116.332570	247.510313	565.115872

6.6   ANNUITIES—DETERMINING PRESENT VALUE

Suppose you are interested in buying a financial plan which will pay you $1,000 every year for 6 years. If you can make an investment at 6%, compounded annually, to pay for this plan, how much will the plan cost? To find the answer, you need to compute the present value of the annuity. Here is how it can be done:

From Table 6-2, the following figures are available:

Present Value of $1

Due in 1 Year	$.943396
Due in 2 Years	.889996
Due in 3 Years	.839619
Due in 4 Years	.792094
Due in 5 Years	.747258
Due in 6 Years	+ .704961
	$4.917324

The total is the present value of an annuity of $1 for 6 years.

It will take 1,000 × $4.917324, or $4,917.32, to buy the plan suggested. To simplify computations, there are tables which indicate present values of annuities of $1 for different rates of interest for a variety of periods. A sample is given in Table 6-4. Check the present value of an annuity of $1 at 6% for six periods: $4.917324.

Problems

Group 1

Using the proper table, compute the present value of the following annuities:

1. $200 every 3 months for 5 years at 8%, compounded quarterly.

   $3 270,29

2. $100 every month for 5 years at 12%, compounded monthly.

   $4495,50

3. $1,500 a year for 20 years at 6%, compounded annually.

$_/7204.88_

4. $600 every 6 months for 10 years at 8%, compounded semiannually.

$_____

5. $800 every 3 months for 4 years at 6%, compounded quarterly.

$_11305.01_

6. $2,400 each year for 15 years at 4%, compounded annually.

$_____

7. $1,200 every 6 months for 10 years at 6%, compounded semiannually.

$_12,852.99_

Table 6-4. Present Value of Annuity of $1 Per Period

Periods	1%	1½%	2%	3%	4%	6%
1.	0.990099	0.985222	0.980392	0.970874	0.961538	0.943396
2.	1.970395	1.955883	1.941561	1.913470	1.886095	1.833393
3.	2.940985	2.912200	2.883883	2.828611	2.775091	2.673012
4.	3.901966	3.854385	3.807729	3.717098	3.629895	3.465106
5.	4.853431	4.782645	4.713460	4.579707	4.451822	4.212364
6.	5.795476	5.697187	5.601431	5.417191	5.242137	4.917324
7.	6.728195	6.598214	6.471991	6.230283	6.002055	5.582381
8.	7.651678	7.485925	7.325481	7.019692	6.732745	6.209794
9.	8.566018	8.360517	8.162237	7.786109	7.435332	6.801692
10.	9.471305	9.222185	8.982585	8.530203	8.110896	7.360087
11.	10.367628	10.071118	9.786848	9.252624	8.760477	7.886875
12.	11.255077	10.907505	10.575341	9.954004	9.385074	8.383844
13.	12.133740	11.731532	11.348374	10.634955	9.985648	8.852683
14.	13.003703	12.543382	12.106249	11.296073	10.563123	9.294984
15.	13.865053	13.343233	12.849264	11.937935	11.118387	9.712249
16.	14.717874	14.131264	13.577709	12.561102	11.652296	10.105895
17.	15.562251	14.907649	14.291872	13.166118	12.165669	10.477260
18.	16.398269	15.672561	14.992031	13.753513	12.659297	10.827603
19.	17.226009	16.426168	15.678462	14.323799	13.133939	11.158116
20.	18.045553	17.168639	16.351433	14.877475	13.590326	11.469921
60.	44.955038	39.380269	34.760887	27.675564	22.623490	16.161428

8. $3,400 every 3 months for 5 years at 4%, compounded quarterly.

   $_____

9. $2,800 every 6 months for 10 years at 12%, compounded semiannually.

   $ 32115.78

10. $4,200 every 3 months for 4 years at 12% compounded quarterly.

   $_____

Group 2

1. Jose is just starting his college career. The cost is estimated to be $6,000 a year for 4 years. If his parents can earn 8% a year, compounded quarterly, how much will they need to invest to provide half the costs to be paid at the end of each quarter?

   $ 10,193.28

2. A professional football player retired with the understanding that he would receive $30,000 from his club every 6 months for 10 years. How much will the club need to invest at 8%, compounded semiannually, to be able to guarantee these payments?

   $ _____

3. Out of her inheritance, Sylvia would like to buy an annuity which would pay her $5,000 a year for 15 years. What will the annuity cost if she invests her money at 6%, compounded annually?

   $ 48561.25

4. Bertha wishes to set aside enough funds to pay for the maintenance of her house for 10 years. She estimates that the cost will be $2,000 a year. How much will she need to invest at 6%, compounded semiannually, in order to provide the $2,000 a year?

   $ _____

5. Arnold Ackerman, in a divorce settlement, is given the choice of making a cash settlement of $20,000 to his former wife or paying her $1,200 every 6 months for 10 years. If money is worth 8%, compounded semiannually, which is the less costly arrangement for him? How much less?

$ _16308.39_

$ _3691.61_

6.7 SINKING FUNDS

The systematic accumulation of funds by investing a certain amount of money at the *end* of each period for a specified time may be thought of as a *sinking fund*. Sinking funds are used in business to provide money for such purposes as replacing old equipment, paying bond obligations, providing pension reserves, and launching building programs.

The question to be answered in sinking-fund problems is how much needs to be set aside at the end of each period at a certain rate of return in order to accumulate the desired amount by some specified future date. For example, how much will a business have to invest at the end of each year for 5 years, in order to have $40,000 to pay off bonds that will come due then? Table 6-5 simplifies the computation; in this example, it shows that to have $1 in 5 years, at 6%, $.177396 needs to be invested at the end of each year. To have $40,000, multiply $.177396 by 40,000; the answer is $7,095.84.

Table 6-5. Sinking-Fund Table Based on $1 at End of Each Period

Periods	1%	1½%	2%	3%	4%	6%
1.	1.000000	1.000000	1.000000	1.000000	1.000000	1.000000
5.	0.196040	0.194089	0.192158	0.188355	0.184627	0.177396
10.	0.095582	0.093434	0.091327	0.087231	0.083291	0.075868
20.	0.045415	0.043246	0.041157	0.037216	0.033582	0.027185
50.	0.015513	0.013572	0.011823	0.008866	0.006550	0.003444
60.	0.012244	0.010393	0.008768	0.006133	0.004202	0.001876
100.	0.005866	0.004371	0.003203	0.001647	0.000808	0.000177

A sinking-fund schedule shows the complete picture of the development of the fund. Here is the way the schedule might look for the $40,000 sinking fund discussed above:

Table 6-6. *Sinking Fund Accumulation Schedule*

End of	Interest for Year	Deposit	Increase in Fund	Amount in Fund
1st Year		$7,095.84	$7,095.84	$7,095.84
2nd Year	$425.75	7,095.84	7,521.59	14,617.43
3rd Year	877.05	7,095.84	7,972.89	22,590.32
4th Year	1,355.42	7,095.84	8,451.26	31,041.58
5th Year	1,862.49	7,095.93*	8,958.42	40,000.00

*Payment is larger by 9 cents to compensate for rounding fractions of cents earlier.

Problems

Group 1

How much will need to be invested at the end of each period, for the time specified, at the rate of return indicated, to build the sinking fund desired?

1. Sinking fund of $10,000 in 20 years with interest at 6%, compounded annually. Payments to the fund are made annually.

$ _271.85_

2. $30,000 in 30 years with interest compounded semiannually at 4% per annum. Payments made semiannually.

$ _____

3. $60,000 in 100 months with interest at 12% compounded monthly. Payments are made monthly.

$ _351.96_

4. $80,000 in 5 years with interest at 6%, compounded quarterly. Quarterly payments are made to the fund.

$ _____

5. $45,000 in 25 years at 8%, compounded semiannually. Payments are made semiannually.

$ _294.75_

Group 2

In $2\frac{1}{2}$ years a company will need to have $75,000 in an employees' pension fund. How much will the company need to invest at the end of each 6 months at 6%, compounded semiannually, in order to have the necessary funds available?

$ _14,126.63_

Prepare a sinking fund schedule similar to Table 6-6 to show how this fund is developed.

Chapter Review

Group 1

1. Prepare a table showing the interest and amount on deposit at the end of each period for $5,000 for 2 years at 8%, compounded quarterly.

   5858.30   Int. 858.30

2. Using the appropriate compound interest table, find the amount and the interest on $8,000 at the end of 6 years at 8%, compounded semiannually.

   Amount $ _12996.78_

   Interest $ _4996.78_

3. Using the appropriate table, compute the present value and the compound discount for $7,800 in 4 years at 12%, compounded quarterly.

   Present Value $ _4860.70_

   Compound Discount $ _2939.30_

4. Compute the amount of an annuity of $1,000 invested every three months for 3 years at 16%, compounded quarterly.

   $ _____   9385.07

5. Using the appropriate table, compute the amount of an annuity of $50 every 3 months for 4 years at 8%, compounded quarterly.

   $ _950.60_

6. What is the present value of an annuity of $300 every 3 months for 4 years at 6%, compounded quarterly?

   $ _4239.38_

7. How much will need to be placed in a sinking fund earning 6%, compounded annually, at the end of each year for 10 years in order to have $50,000 in the fund at the end of 10 years?

$ _3793.40_

8. How much interest will be earned on $10,000 for 3 days at 8% per year, compounded daily?

$ _6.58_

Group 2

1. Jamie Jolson deposited an inheritance of $12,000 in a savings account which paid 6%, compounded quarterly. a. How much would be in the account at the end of 3 years if no additions or withdrawals were made? b. If the interest were compounded daily, would there be more or less in the account?

    a. $ _14,347.42_   b. ___more___

2. In 4 years, Betty Ames will need $4,000 to take a trip she is planning. How much should she invest now at 8%, compounded quarterly, in order to have the $4,000 in 4 years?   2.

    $ _4684.64_

3. Julie Jones is planning to invest $500 every 6 months for 6 years. If she is able to earn 8%, compounded semiannually, how much will she have at the end of the 6 years?

    $ _7813.42_

4. John Barton needs to supplement his pension for the next 4 years until he becomes eligible for social security payments. How much will he need to invest at 8%, compounded quarterly, to receive $1,200 every 3 months for the next 4 years?

    $ _____

5. The Bertrand Company will need $100,000 in 5 years to buy back some stock. They plan to set up a sinking fund so that they will have the necessary funds to make the purchase. How much will they need to invest in the fund at the end of each year if they can earn 6%, compounded annually?

    $ _17739.60_

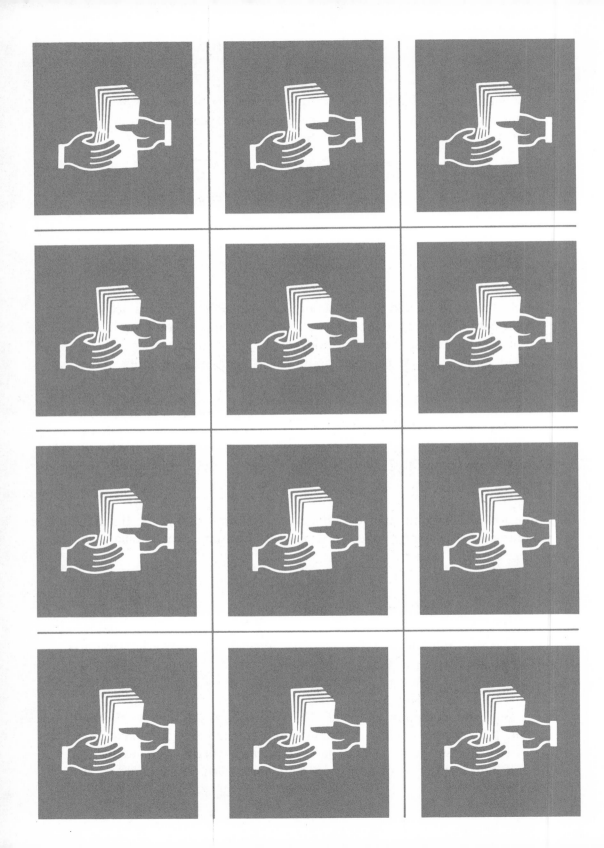

7

Banking Mathematics

While studying this chapter, collect all the information you can find, such as newspaper ads and bank literature, about the practices of banks, savings and loan associations, credit unions, and finance companies in your area.

7.1 CHECKING ACCOUNTS

There are many kinds of bank institutions (national, state, commercial, savings, and building and loan associations) and many kinds of bank accounts. Perhaps the most common is the *checking account,* where the customer deposits money and then writes checks to be paid from the money on deposit.

Checking accounts are a convenience for the depositor, who does not have to carry large amounts of money and can send money safely to distant places. Since checks are sent to the bank for payment, then canceled and returned to the depositor, these canceled checks serve as proof of payment.

Money deposited in a bank is safe. If a bank simply stored deposits in the vaults, the customers would have to be charged a fee to pay for salaries, buildings, and other expenses. Many banks do make some charges—for checkbooks, for small accounts with many transactions (deposits made and checks drawn), or for checks written with insufficient funds, for example—but most of a bank's expenses are met by lending money at interest. The Federal Deposit Insurance Corporation (FDIC) insures many bank deposits. Federal and state governments monitor banking practices.

It is important to write checks carefully and clearly and to keep a record (usually on the check stub) of each check drawn, each deposit made, and the balance in the account at all times.

At regular intervals, depositors are sent their canceled checks, along with a *bank statement* listing every transaction or charge and showing the balance after each day's business. These statements must be *reconciled* with the record on the check register. This is done by subtracting from the balance shown on the statement the amount of any outstanding checks (those written but not yet cashed) and adding any deposits not yet credited. The total of any checks or charges not yet entered is subtracted from the checkbook balance. The two balances should then be the same. If they are not, there must be an error in one or the other, and this error must be found and corrected. Depositors should never simply change their recorded balance to agree with that of the bank statement.

Example. M. Bourn's check register showed:

Date	Balance Forward	Checks	Deposits	Balance
10/3	$852.58	$32.00		$820.58
10/4	820.58	112.00		708.58
10/5	708.58	15.37		693.21
10/8	693.21	27.55		665.76
10/11	665.76	29.61	$148.30	784.45
10/13	784.45	40.00		744.45
10/26	744.45	15.39		729.06
10/29	729.06	22.94		706.12

Bourn's bank statement was:

Checks		Deposits	Date	Balance
			10/02	$852.58
$32.00	$112.00		10/05	708.58
15.37	Chg 3.00		10/06	690.21
27.55		$148.30	10/11	810.96
29.61	40.00		10/14	741.35
15.39			10/28	725.96

Reconciliation

Bank Statement Balance	$725.96	Checkbook Balance	$706.12
Plus Deposits Made Since Date	+ .00	Less Charge	− 3.00
Total	$725.96	Balance	$703.12
Less Outstanding Checks	− 22.94		
Balance	$703.02		

The two balances should be the same, but there is a difference of $.10. In checking the arithmetic, Bourn finds an error on the check register of 10/8 which accounts for the discrepancy. The correct balance is $703.02.

Problem

1. B. Rakstad's check register shows:

Date	Balance Forward	Checks	Deposits	Balance
3/1	$1,783.29	$51.75		$1,731.54
	1,731.54	20.00		1,711.54
3/2	1,711.54	273.80		1,437.74
3/3	1,437.74	29.56		1,408.18
3/5	1,408.18	87.90		1,320.28
3/6	1,320.28	2.75		1,317.53
3/12	1,317.53	489.26		828.27
	828.27	68.40		759.87
3/13	759.87	47.68		712.19
3/15	712.19	129.17	$728.49	1,311.41
3/17	1,311.41	18.75		1,292.66
3/20	1,292.66	78.50		1,214.16
3/28	1,214.16	237.80		976.36
3/30	976.36	56.38		919.98

Rakstad's bank statement shows:

Checks		Deposits	Date	Balance
			3/01	$1,783.29
$51.75	$20.00		3/02	1,711.54
237.80	29.56		3/05	1,444.18
Chg 10.83	87.90	$2.75	3/08	1,342.70
489.26			3/12	853.44
47.68	68.40	$728.49	3/15	1,465.85
18.75	78.50	129.17	3/21	1,239.43
237.80	5.98		3/31	995.65

Reconcile Rakstad's account:

Bank Statement Balance $————   Checkbook Balance $————

Plus Deposits Made Since Date ————   Less Charges   ————

Total ————   Balance   ————

Less Outstanding Checks ————

Balance ————

7.2 SAVINGS ACCOUNTS

Unlike checking accounts, most *savings accounts* are used primarily to set money aside for some future use. Such accounts draw interest. The money can be withdrawn whenever it is needed.

The interest on "regular" savings accounts is compounded sometimes daily and sometimes quarterly, either on the minimum amount or on the average amount on deposit during the quarter. In many cases, money deposited within 10 days after the beginning of a quarter, or money withdrawn within 5 days before the end of this period, draws interest for the whole period. Within regulatory limits, each bank sets its own rules, which are explained in the bank's literature and in the customers' passbook.

Interest on a "day-of-deposit to day-of-withdrawal" account is usually compounded daily for the exact number of days money is on deposit. Interest earned may be more or less than on a "regular" account, depending on the timing and the amounts of deposits and withdrawals. It is usually possible to transfer funds from one type of account to the other when desired.

Example 1. On April 9, $100 is deposited in a regular savings account at 6% interest, compounded quarterly; deposits made within 10 days of the beginning or withdrawn within 5 days of the end of a quarter are credited for the whole quarter. At the same time, $100 is deposited in a day-of-deposit to day-of-withdrawal account at 6%, compounded daily. If 6% compounded daily amounts to approximately .3458% for 21 days, and .4613% for 28 days, .5108% for 31 days, how much can be withdrawn from each account on June 28?

In the regular account, interest will be credited for $\frac{1}{4}$ year at 6% or
$$\$100 \times \frac{1}{4} \times \frac{6}{100} = \$1.50. \text{ Amount is } \$101.50$$

In the day-of-deposit to day-of-withdrawal account, interest and monthly amounts will be:

April: $100 × .003458 = $.35 Interest. Amount, April 30, $100.35
May: $100.35 × .005108 = $.51 Interest. Amount, May 31, $100.86
June: $100.86 × .004613 = $.47, Interest. Amount, June 28, $101.33

Example 2. If the accounts in Example 1 were opened on April 1, how much would be in each on July 1? (6% compounded daily for 30 days is approximately .4943%.)

In the regular account, the amount would be the same, $101.50.

In the day-of-deposit to day-of-withdrawal account, interest and monthly amounts would be:

April: $100 × .004943 = $.49 Interest. Amount, April 30, $100.49
May: $100.49 × .005108 = $.51 Interest. Amount, May 31, $101.00
June: $101.00 × .004943 = $.50 Interest. Amount, June 30, $101.50

Problems

1. If, in Examples 1 and 2, the regular account drew interest at the rate of $5\frac{1}{2}$%, compounded quarterly, with the same regulations, how much would be in the account on June 28 or July 1?

   $_____

   $_____

2. On January 1, a savings account drawing interest at 6%, compounded daily, amounts to $7,493.56. If no deposits or withdrawals are made, what will be the approximate amount in the account on April 1? On July 1? On the next January 1?

	Interest	Amount
January	_____	_____
February	_____	_____

March	————	———— April 1
April	————	————
May	————	————
June	————	———— July 1
July	————	————
August	————	————
September	————	————
October	————	————
November	————	————
December	————	———— January 1

3. If the account in Problem 2 drew interest at 6%, compounded quarterly, how much would be in the account on April 1? July 1? January 1?

$————

$————

$————

4. In Problems 2 and 3, what is the total interest earned for the year at 6%, compounded daily? At 6%, compounded quarterly? What is the effective interest rate (the equivalent simple interest rate) at 6%, compounded daily? At 6%, compounded quarterly?

$————   ———— %

$————   ———— %

7.3 SAVINGS CERTIFICATES

Savings institutions may pay higher rates of interest than the usual passbook rate when depositors buy *savings certificates*. Here, money is left in a special account for a specified length of time, commonly from six months to eight years.

The longer the period, the greater the interest rate will usually be. A minimum deposit is usually required.

If money is withdrawn from such a term account before maturity, the interest rate on the amount withdrawn is usually reduced to the passbook rate and 90 days' interest is forfeited.

Example. A 6-year savings certificate for $2,000 at 7.75%, compounded daily, is purchased from a savings bank where the passbook interest rate is 6%, compounded daily. After 2 years, $300 must be withdrawn. How much interest is lost? (7.75%, compounded daily, yields the equivalent of 8.0804%, compounded annually. 6%, compounded daily, yields the equivalent of 6.1830%, compounded annually, or 4.5723% for 275 days.)

At 7.75%, the interest on $300 for 1 year is $300 × .080804 = $24.24
Interest on $324.24 for 1 year is $324.24 × .080804 = $26.20
Two years' interest at 7.75% = $50.44
At 6%, the interest on $300 for 1 year is $300 × .06183 = $18.55
Interest on $318.55 for 275 days is $318.55 × .045723 = $14.57
Interest at 6% for 2 years less 90 days is $33.12
Loss of interest = $50.44 − $33.12 = $17.32

Problems

1. A 5-year savings certificate for $1,000 at 7.25%, compounded daily, is purchased from a bank where the passbook rate is 6%, compounded daily. After 4 years and 90 days, $250 is withdrawn. What is the penalty for early withdrawal? (7.25%, compounded daily, is approximately the equivalent of 7.5185% annually and 1.8036% for 90 days. 6%, compounded daily, is approximately equivalent to 6.1830% annually or 1.4903% for 90 days.)

    $_____

2. A savings bank offers 4-year savings certificates at 7.50%, for an effective annual rate of 7.90%, and 8-year certificates at 8.00%, for an effective annual rate of 8.45%. Assuming that a 4-year certificate could be renewed for another 4 years at the same rate, how much more would $1,000 in the 8-year account yield than in the two 4-year accounts? Under what circumstances would the 4-year account be preferable? $_____

3. In 1979 "Money Market Certificates" were available, paying interest at an annual rate of 9.774%, compounded daily, for a term of 6 months. If the depositor did not renew or redeem the certificate upon maturity, the account was converted to a day-of-deposit to day-of-withdrawal account at $5\frac{1}{2}$% annual interest, compounded daily. (9.774% annual interest, compounded daily, yields approximately 5.0263% in 6 months; $5\frac{1}{2}$% annual interest, compounded daily, yields approximately 2.7957% in 6 months.) a. If a $10,000 certificate was left on deposit after maturity, about how much would it be worth at the end of a year? b. About what would it have been worth if renewed at the same rate?

    a. $_____

    b. $_____

4. Instead of leaving the interest on a savings certificate to be compounded quarterly at 8%, the account holder may receive checks for the interest every three months. a. What would be the quarterly interest check on a $5,000 account? b. What would be the total interest for the year? c. How much interest would be credited the first year if it is left to be compounded?

    a. $_____

    b. $_____

    c. $_____

7.4   NEGOTIABLE ORDERS OF WITHDRAWAL (NOW) ACCOUNTS

Banks are not usually allowed to pay interest on checking accounts, but recently many banks have offered "NOW" accounts—savings accounts which draw interest but from which *negotiable orders of withdrawal,* exactly like checks, are paid.

Because banks compete for depositors, each bank interprets the regulations in the way expected to attract the most business. There is usually a minimum monthly balance ($500, $1,000, or $2,000) above which there is no charge for checks; sometimes this "monthly balance" is the smallest balance during the month, sometimes the average balance. For balances below the minimum, there may be a flat monthly fee, a charge for each check, or a combination of these.

Example 1. A NOW account had balances during December of $983.49, $903.45, $859.29, $834.04, $815.29, $720.19, $654.83, $592.34, and $497.26, with eight checks drawn. During January, with seven checks, the balances were $1,347.26, $1,012.79, $983.86, $857.31, $1,063.51, $1,012.63, $983.27, and $964.12. The bank pays 5% interest, compounded daily and credited on the last day of each month. According to the regulations of the bank, if the minimum monthly balance falls below $500, the charge is $2 a month and 20¢ per check. What are the charges for December and January? About how much interest was earned? (5% interest, compounded daily, for 31 days equals approximately .4225%.)

For December, with a minimum balance of $497.26, the charge is $2 plus 20¢ for each of eight checks, or $2 + $1.60 = $3.60.

For January, there is no charge, since the minimum balance is $857.31.

During December, the minimum balance is $497.26, on which the interest would be $497.26 × .004225 = $2.10

Interest on the maximum amount would be $983.49 × .004225 = $4.16

The actual amount of interest would be somewhere between these limits.

During January, interest would be between $2.10 and $5.69.

Example 2. Another bank makes no charge on NOW accounts if the average monthly balance is $1,000 or more. If the average is below $1,000, the monthly charge is 15¢ per check, with a minimum of $3. What would this bank charge the account in Example 1?

The average balance in December must be less than $1,000, since no balance is as much as $1,000; 8 × $.15 = $1.20, so the charge is the minimum, $3.

For January, it is impossible to compute the average, since there is no indication of the number of days each balance covered.

Problems

1. On the chart below, show the regulations of the banks in your area on NOW accounts:

Bank	Interest Rate and Method	Balance Required Without Charges		Charges if Below Requirement	Balance Required to Draw Interest	Other Features
		Minimum or Average?	Amount			

2. A third bank charges NOW accounts with a minimum monthly balance under $2,000 25¢ per check, with an additional $1 monthly fee if the balance falls below $500. What would be the charges in Example 1 under these conditions?

    December $_____

    January $_____

3. Suppose that, during a 30-day month, you make out a check for $39.35 every 5 days but make no deposits and write no other checks and that the balance in your NOW account was $1,183.85 at the beginning of the month. With the regulations in Examples 1 and 2 and in Problem 2, what would the monthly charges be?

    Example 1 $_____

    Example 2 $_____

    Problem 2 $_____

    Disregarding the interest earned, what would be the balance in the account at the end of the month in each case?

    Example 1 $_____

    Example 2 $_____

    Problem 2 $_____

About what would the interest be at 5%, compounded daily (.4118% for 30 days)?

$_____

4. In the circumstances described in Problem 3, what would be the charge and the balance in the account at the bank where you have an account or at the nearest bank to your home?

Charge $_____

Balance $_____

Chapter Review

1. In what ways are the banking practices in your area similar to those described in this chapter? In what ways are they different? What additional services do your local banks offer?

2. R. Herring's bank statement showed:

Checks		Deposits	Date	Balance
			5/01	$1023.76
$15.79	$25.00		5/07	
32.46		$283.55	5/08	
23.15	31.00		5/17	
5.95		10.00	5/25	
Bond	37.50		5/27	

Herring's check record showed:

Date	Balance Forwarded	Checks	Deposits	Balance
5/1				$1023.76
5/6		$15.79		
5/7		25.00		
		32.46		
5/8			$283.55	
5/15		23.15		
5/17		31.00		
5/25		5.95	10.00	
5/28		51.50		

Fill in the blanks on the bank statement and the check record; then reconcile the two on the form below.

Bank Statement Balance $_____   Check Record Balance $_____

Plus Additional Deposits   _____   Less Unrecorded Charges   _____

Balance $_____

Less Outstanding Checks   _____

Balance $_____

3. Suppose R. Herring's account in Problem 2 is a NOW account. The bank pays 5% interest, compounded daily, and charges nothing when the minimum monthly balance is $1,000 or more, charges 25¢ per check if the minimum balance falls below $1,000, with an additional $1.00 fee if the balance falls below $500. a. What charge would be made? b. About how much interest would be credited? (Allow .4225% interest.)

a. $_____

b. $_____

4. Suppose R. Herring's NOW account is with a bank which charges 15¢ per check, with a $3 minimum charge, if the average monthly balance falls below $1,000. What would the charge be?

$_____

5. A student inherits $5,000 and plans to save it in order to set up a business in 4 years. In a regular savings account at $5\frac{1}{4}$%, compounded daily, which is approximately equivalent to 5.42% annually, what would the amount be in 4 years?

$_____

6. a. Instead of using a regular savings account, the student in Problem 5 could buy a savings certificate paying 7.50%, compounded daily, for an annual equivalent of 7.78%. What would this amount to in 4 years?

$_____

b. If the student buys the savings certificate and then finds it necessary to withdraw $1,000 after 3 years, what will be the loss in interest, at the passbook rate of 5¼%, compounded daily, for an annual equivalent of 5.42% or 4.06% for 275 days?

$_____

7. A finance corporation offers a 4-year investment certificate at 8%, compounded quarterly. a. Would this provide more or less interest than the savings certificate? b. How much more or less? c. If this corporation is in a distant state and is not insured by the FDIC, would you recommend this investment?

   a.   _____

   b. $_____

   c.   _____

8. A credit corporation in another state offers insured 3-year certificates at 8.00%, 2-year certificates at 7.50%, and 1-year certificates at 7.25%, all compounded quarterly. (7.25%, compounded quarterly, is equivalent to 7.4496% annually. 7.50%, compounded quarterly, is equivalent to 7.7137% annually.) In case of early withdrawal, the rate is decreased to 6% for the whole period, but no additional penalty is imposed. Assuming that the same opportunities would be available later, would this be a good investment? Why?

   _____

   _____

   For a total of 4 years, would it be better to buy a. a 3-year and then a 1-year certificate, b. a 1-year and then a 3-year certificate, or c. two 2-year certificates? Why?_____

   _____

   If, like the student in Problem 6, you might have to withdraw $1,000 from a $5,000 investment after 3 years, would that affect your decision? In what way?_____

   _____

8

Short-Term Credit

One of the outstanding characteristics of our society is the extensive use of credit. People buy goods and services one day and pay for them later. Money may be borrowed from some source in order to buy goods and services for cash. In either case, the actual payment is made later. The use of credit of all types is even more common among business enterprises and among federal, state, and local governments. Our credit structure has become very complicated and subject to misuse. The federal and many state governments have enacted laws and regulations to protect consumers in the use of credit. For example, Regulation Z of the Federal Reserve Board requires that creditors must provide a written statement indicating the true annual rate of interest being charged. This regulation, more commonly known as the *truth-in-lending* regulation, applies to any business or individual who extends credit involving a finance charge for more than four installments. The act also requires the prompt correction of billing errors. The *Federal Equal Credit Opportunities Act* prohibits credit discrimination on the basis of sex or marital status.

The proper use of credit by both those giving and those receiving credit is important to the success of our business system and to our society in general.

8.1 CONSUMER USE OF CREDIT

Bills for electricity and gas used are prepared periodically (usually monthly or bimonthly) on the basis of meter readings. Payment of these bills is often encouraged by giving customers a discount if the bill (or invoice) is paid by a certain date.

Example. We received a bill on October 10 from the Central Power Company for the use of 566 kilowatt-hours of electricity, for a 59-day period ending October 5. The total bill is $31.09. If the bill is paid by November 2, the net amount (a smaller amount that will be accepted as full payment) is $29.61.

a. What is the amount of the discount?
b. What is the percent of discount?
c. If we paid the gross amount of the bill on November 12, what is the equivalent annual percent of discount for using the $29.61 for 10 days beyond the discount date?
a. $31.09 − $29.61 = $1.48 Amount of Discount
b. $1.48 ÷ $31.09 = 4.76% Discount
c. .0476 × $^{365}/_{10}$ = 173.74% Discount Annual Rate

The wise use of credit calls for the payment of the bill within the discount period.

Many stores extend credit to their customers in order to encourage purchases, to attract and maintain customers, and to meet competition. The credit terms should be understood by customers. Several large companies with stores in various parts of the country offer credit terms that call for the payment of bills within 30 days of the *billing date* if finance charges are to be avoided. The billing date might be the date of the purchase or a later date, depending on the time when the bill is prepared. Rather than all accounts becoming due at the end of the month, as the custom used to be, *cyclical billing* is often used. Cyclical billing refers to the practice of issuing statements throughout the month, so that the billing cycle for some customers will begin on the first day of the month, for some on the second, and so on. The billing activities and resultant jobs are thus spread throughout the month, without tremendous peaks and valleys of work.

If payment is not made within the 30 days, an additional charge may be added to the bill, usually at an *annual percentage rate* of 18% on the first $500 of the *average daily balance* and 12% on any part of the average daily balance higher than $500. State regulations on the maximum finance charges permitted and on the method of computing the charges vary somewhat. The computation in the following example is fairly typical.

Example. A statement received from the Beta Store shows that John and Marcia owe $620 for a purchase they made on April 18, which was billed on

April 25. To avoid a finance charge, they must pay for the purchase within 30 days of the billing date.

a. If they are to avoid the finance charge, what is the last date on which they can make payment?
b. If they paid $100 on June 4, what is the average daily balance for the billing period of 30 days, beginning on the due date?
c. If a charge is made at the rate of 18% per year on the first $500 and 12% per year on any amount above $500, what is the finance charge that would be made on June 24?

a. April 25 + 30 days = May 25
b. Balance of $620 from May 25 to June 4, a period of 10 days.
   Balance of $520 from June 4 to June 24, a period of 20 days.
   $620 × 10 = $ 6,200
   $520 × 20 = + 10,400
   _____
                $16,600
   $16,600 ÷ 30 = $553.33 Average Daily Balance
c. $500 × 18% × $^{30}/_{365}$ = $7.40
   $53.33 × 12% × $^{30}/_{365}$ = + .53
   _____
                $7.93 Finance Charge

Short-term consumer credit is also available under plans such as Master Charge or VISA, provided by banks. Many businesses use these plans to avoid the problems of making credit investigations and collections. The American Express Company offers a similar plan. In each case, the terms of credit are written out specifically to conform with federal and state regulations.

Problems

Group 1

What is the amount and percent of discount in the following?

1.	Gross $46.83	Net $39.90	$_____	_____ %
2.	Gross $54.17	Net $52.85	$_____	_____ %
3.	Gross $36.20	Net $32.50	$_____	_____ %
4.	Gross $29.84	Net $27.46	$_____	_____ %
5.	Gross $69.56	Net $65.08	$_____	_____ %

Find the comparable annual rate of interest for the following, if the discount for:

6.   10 days is 4.867% ———— %

7.   30 days is 5.216% ———— %

8.   20 days is 4.582% ———— %

9.   15 days is 2.794% ———— %

10.   12 days is 3.165% ———— %

What are the due dates in the following?

11.   15 days from billing date of January 22   ————

12.   30 days from billing date of February 28   ————

13.   20 days from billing date of April 25   ————

14.   25 days from billing date of May 16   ————

15.   40 days from billing date of October 14   ————

Group 2

1. Mavis Davis receives a bill from her power company for the gross amount of $54.85. If she pays the bill by May 1, she has to pay only $52.80. a. What is the percentage of the bill she will save if she pays it by that date? b.   Suppose she doesn't pay the bill until May 31. What annual rate of interest will she be paying?

a.   ———— %

b   %

2. Ben Barnes purchased $715 worth of furniture on July 8 from the Standex Furniture Company. The billing date was July 10. If Ben pays the bill within 25 days of the billing date, he will avoid any finance charge. After that, he will be charged at the annual rate of 18% on the first $500 of the average daily balance and 12% on any part of the average daily balance above $500. Ben pays $150 on August 15. He pays the remainder due plus finance charges on September 10. a. What is the average daily balance upon which the finance charges will be computed? b. What is the total finance charge?

c. What is the amount of the payment Ben needs to make on September 10 to pay his bill in full?

a. $_____

b. $_____

c. $_____

8.2   EXTENSION OF CREDIT

Any person or business selling merchandise or services must decide whether to extend credit. The decision probably will be based largely on whether it would be profitable to do so. Many companies operating supermarkets extend no credit and operate successfully, through the volume of business developed. Other companies, some operating nationally, offer short-term credit, using plastic credit cards as a convenient method for handling transactions. Still other persons and companies extend credit through banks that use Master Charge or VISA facilities or through such credit organizations as American Express or Diners Club.

Giving credit and handling credit transactions cost more than operating on a cash-only basis. Who should receive credit and for how much are important questions that can be properly answered only after careful investigation. Additional records need to be kept and bills or statements need to be sent out. In addition, some accounts will never be paid, for one reason or another. Only by careful control and a good credit system can these losses be kept to a minimum.

If the volume of business can be increased sufficiently, the additional gains may more than offset the additional costs of giving credit. What will happen in practice is not always easy to predict.

Example. Suppose you own a bookstore doing a cash business of $50,000 a year and that your net profit after deducting costs and expenses is 15% of the sales. You believe that if you grant short-term credit, your business will increase by 50% and your rate of net profit will decrease to 13%. Compare your present profit with the projected profit if you decide to give credit.

$$\text{Present Profit} = 15\% \text{ of } \$50,000 = \$7,500$$
$$\text{Projected Profit} = 13\% \text{ of } \$75,000 = \$9,750$$

Your confidence in this projection and the consideration of the extra work and worry involved will probably affect your decision about getting into the credit business. Some of the work and worry can be eliminated by using one of the bank systems for handling credit. If you do this, consider the bank charge of 8% of credit sales and the probability that your net profit rate will remain the same on cash sales, which are projected to be $30,000.

$$\text{Projected Profit} = 15\% \times \$30,000 = \$4,500$$
$$15\% - 8\% \quad = \quad 7\% \times \$45,000 = \underline{\quad 3,150}$$
$$\$7,650$$

Problems

1. Jacques Bekins owns and operates a retail store that does a cash business of $400,000 a year. His net profit is 6%. Jacques estimates that, by extending short-term credit, he will be able to increase his sales by 40%. He also estimates that uncollectible accounts will amount to $1/2$% of total sales and that his net profit rate, not counting uncollectible accounts, will decrease to 5%. a. What is his net profit in a cash-only business? b. If the projections are correct, what will his net profit be after he extends credit?

    a. $_____

    b. $_____

2. Jane Martin operates a small department store which does $250,000 in cash sales annually. The net profit is about 10% of sales. By extending short-term credit, Jane believes, she can double her business, with 50% of it still being for cash. By using one of the bank credit systems available, she can avoid most of the extra problems of operating the credit system, including the losses from uncollectible accounts. The bank will charge 8% of the credit sales for the services they render. a. What is the net profit now, when all business is for cash? b. What will the net profit be with short-term credit, using the bank system?

    a. $_____

    b. $_____

3. In Problem 2, suppose the net profit percentage on all sales decreases to 9%, with the 8% of credit sales charged by the bank still in effect. What will be the net profit?

    $_____

8.3 SHORT-TERM LOANS

By securing a loan, we may be able to purchase goods or services now and actually pay for them only when the loan is repaid. Banks and other lending institutions are in business to provide this kind of credit service. The use of money is purchased. A charge, usually called *interest,* is made for the use of money.

Example. In order to buy a new recorder, May Moore borrowed $300 from a credit association. She signed a promissory note promising to pay back the $300 in 3 months, plus interest at $8\frac{1}{2}\%$ per year.
   a. How much interest should she pay in 3 months?
   b. What is the total to be paid back?
   a. $300 \times 8\frac{1}{2}\% \times \frac{3}{12} = \$6.38$ Interest
   b. $300 + \$6.38 = \$306.38$, Amount to be Paid.

Problems

1. Adrian Wilson borrowed $175 to buy a wood stove to install in his fireplace. He signed a note promising to pay back the $175 in 2 months, plus interest at $8\frac{1}{4}\%$. How much will he have to pay when the note becomes due?

   $_____

2. Karna Kass borrowed $680 from a friend to buy a used car. She signed a note promising to pay the $680 at the end of 6 months, plus interest at the rate of $8\frac{1}{2}\%$ a year. How much will she have to pay at the end of 6 months?

   $_____

3. Jacob Green was able to borrow $1,250 from an uncle in anticipation of what he could earn during the summer, so he could pay some of his college debts. He promised to repay his uncle the $1,250 in 3 months, with interest at the rate of $6\frac{1}{2}\%$ per year. How much will he pay at the end of 3 months?

   $_____

4. If you lend $520 to a friend, with the understanding that you will be paid back in 90 days, plus interest at 8% per year, how much will you receive? (Count 365 days in a year.)

$_____

8.4 PARTIAL PAYMENTS

Sometimes promissory notes are paid in two or more partial payments. The problem is to determine the balance due when final settlement is to be made after one or more partial payments have been made. There are two principal methods used in this process, one called *the Merchants' Rule* and the second *the United States Rule.*

The Merchants' Rule
1. Interest is allowed on the total debt from its beginning to the day of settlement.
2. From the amount of principal plus interest, the partial payments and the interest on each from the day of the payment to the day of final settlement are subtracted.

The United States Rule
1. Each partial payment is applied against the interest due at the time of the payment.
2. The excess over the interest due is deducted from the principal. (If the payment is less than the interest due at the time of payment, no deduction is made until future payments added to the present one total more than the interest due.)

Example. An 8% promissory note for $3,800, dated March 1, is due 6 months from date. Partial payments were made as follows:

April 1	$750
June 1	10
August 1	1,000

What is the balance due when the note matures on September 1?

Merchants' Rule

March 1 Principal		$3,800.00
Interest March 1 to September 1 (6 months)		
8% × $3,800 × $^1/_2$ =		+ 152.00
Maturity Value of Note		$3,952.00
April 1 Payment	$750.00	
Interest April 1 to September 1 (5 months)		
8% × $750 × $^5/_{12}$ =	25.00	
June 1 Payment	10.00	
Interest June 1 to September 1 (3 months)		
8% × $10 × $^3/_{12}$ =	.20	
August 1 Payment	1,000.00	
Interest August 1 to September 1 (1 month)		
8% × $1,000 × $^1/_{12}$ =	6.67	
Total Credits		− 1,791.87
September 1 Balance Due		$2,160.13

United States Rule

March 1 Principal		$3,800.00
April 1 Payment	$750.00	
Less Interest on $3,800 from March 1 to April 1		
(1 month) 8% × $3,800 × $^1/_{12}$ =	− 25.33	
		724.67
April 1 Balance Due		$3,075.33
June 1 Payment	$10.00	
Interest on $3,075.33 from April 1 to June 1	41.00	
(As $41.00 interest is greater than $10 payment, nothing is done now.)		
August 1 Payment	1,000.00	
June 1 Payment	+ 10.00	
	$1,010.00	
Interest on $3,075.33 from April 1 to August 1		
$3,075.33 × 8% × $^4/_{12}$ =	82.01	
		927.99
August 1 Balance		$2,147.34
September 1. Interest on $2,147.34 from August 1 to September 1 (1 month) 8% × 2147.34 × $^1/_{12}$ =		+ 14.32
September 1 Balance Due		$2,161.66

Problems

Find the balance due on the settlement dates for each of the following debts, using the Merchants' Rule and United States Rule.

1. A $5,200 debt, due 6 months from March 1 with $8^1/_2\%$ interest has the following partial payments made: April 1, $500; June 1, $1,500; August 1, $2,000.

   Merchants' Rule $_____

   United States Rule $_____

2. A debt of $4,600 due in 4 months from June 10 with interest at 8% per year, had the following partial payments made: July 10, $1,500; August 10, $200; September 10, $800.

   Merchants' Rule $_____

   United States Rule $_____

3. A debt of $1,800 was due 5 months from August 18, with interest at 9% per year. Partial payments were made as follows: September 18, $400; October 18, $10; November 18, $500.

   Merchants' Rule $_____

   United States Rule $_____

Chapter Review

1. If the gross amount on a gas bill is $28.60 and the net amount is $27.10, what is the discount? What is the rate of discount?

   $_____   _____%

2. What date is 25 days from August 14?

   _____

3. A bill from the power company shows the gross amount due to be $63.80. If the bill is paid by June 5, only $61.70 needs to be paid. What percentage is saved if the bill is paid on June 5? If the bill is paid on June 25, what is the annual rate of interest?

   _____%   _____%

4. Merchandise valued at $840 was purchased on March 15, with the billing date of March 20. If payment is made more than 25 days from the billing date, there is a charge of 18% per year on the first $500 of the average daily balance and 12% per year on any part of the average daily balance over $500. If $200 is paid on May 1 and the remainder, including any finance charges, is paid on June 1, what is the average daily balance used as the basis for computing the finance charges? What is the amount of the payment on June 1?

$_____

$_____

5. Alfred Ayres owns a retail store doing a cash business of $80,000 a year. The net profit is 15% of sales. Mr. Ayres believes that by offering short-term credit to customers, he could increase his business by 40%. In the process, however, his rate of net profit would decrease to 10%. Compare his present profit with the projected profit if he extends credit.

Present Profit $_____

Projected Profit $_____

What considerations other than profit would you suggest ought to be considered before going into a credit business? _____

_____

6. How much will a loan of $1,800 for 3 months cost if the annual interest rate charged is 9%?

$_____

7. Find the balance due on the last payment date, using the Merchants' Rule and the United States Rule, for a debt of $6,400 due 5 months from April 1, with interest at the rate of 9% per year. Partial payments of $2,000 on May 1, $1,500 on July 1, and $1,200 on August 1 were made.

Merchants' Rule $_____

United States Rule $_____

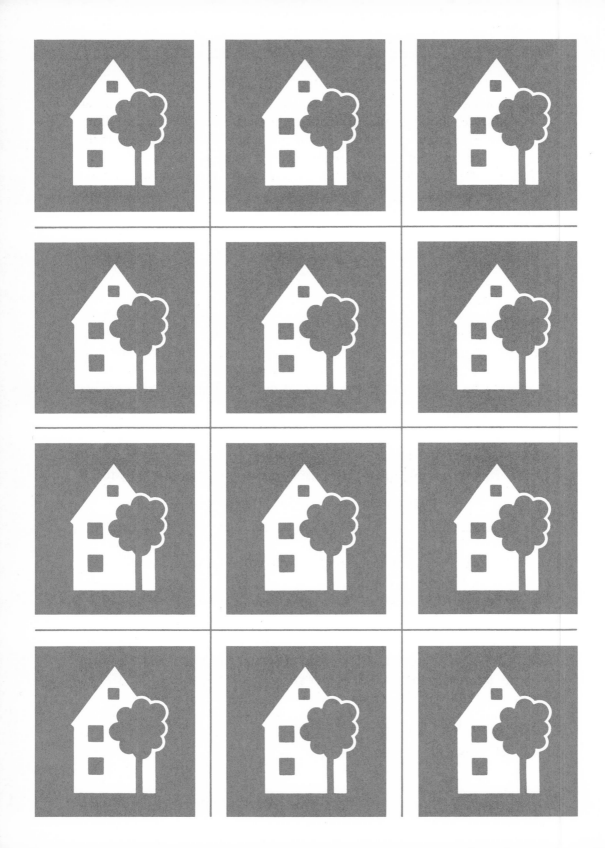

9

Intermediate and Long-Term Credit

Credit takes many forms. For the consumer, it might be the extension of credit for the relatively short time of 25 to 30 days by a department store or oil company, or a rather long-term 30-year loan on a house mortgage. It might also be credit for an intermediate length of time, such as 18 months or 3 years, for purchasing an appliance or a car on the installment plan. For corporations and governmental units, the same distinctions can be applied. Credit is involved in short-term loans based on notes and other commercial paper as well as in long-term bond issues sold in various ways.

9.I INSTALLMENT CREDIT

Installment credit involves debts which are repaid in periodic payments. The debts usually arise from the purchase of a major appliance or furniture, a car, or something else of substantial value. The debt may also be incurred by getting a loan.

Installment purchases usually require a down payment and then a series of payments to complete the transaction.

Example 1. You buy a television set priced at $560 by making a down payment of $56 and promising to pay $44.94 a month for 12 months. What is the total cost of the television set?

Down Payment	$ 56.00
12 × $44.94	+ 539.28
Total Cost	$595.28

What is the cost of the credit if the set could have been purchased for $560 in cash?

Total Cost	$595.28
Cash Price	− 560.00
Cost of Credit	$ 35.28

Example 2. A used car was priced at $2,450. It could be purchased on the installment plan for a down payment of 20%, and the balance in 18 monthly installments, with 8% a year for credit.

a. What is the amount of the down payment?
b. What is the balance owed?
c. What is the charge for credit?
d. What is the amount of each monthly payment?

    a.   20% × $2,450 = $490 Down Payment
    b. $2450 − $490 = $1,960.00 Balance Owed
    c.   8% × $1\frac{1}{2}$ × $1,960 = $235.20 Credit Charge
                   (18 months is $1\frac{1}{2}$ years)
    d. $1,960.00 + $235.20 = $2,195.20 Total Amount Owed
          $2,195.20 ÷ 18 = $121.96 Monthly Payment

Problems

The prices listed below were advertised in a sale of used cars. All taxes and fees are included in the prices. Fill in the "balance due" and "total paid" columns. All monthly payments are for 18 months.

	Price	Down Payment	Balance Due	Monthly Payment	Total Paid
1.	$2,550	$ 880.00	$ _____	$112.88	$ _____
2.	5,390	1,856.40	$ _____	232.44	$ _____
3.	1,850	370.00	$ _____	87.98	$ _____
4.	4,590	1,580.40	$ _____	198.32	$ _____
5.	3,768	1,319.00	$ _____	156.50	$ _____
6.	3,208	1,069.50	$ _____	136.66	$ _____

7. Thomas May purchased a stereo set for $280. He paid 25% of the price in cash and the balance in 12 payments of $18.42 each. How much did the stereo actually cost?

   $ _____

8. Jessie Jackson purchased a washer and dryer priced at $710 cash. She paid 15% with a check and financed the balance by promising to pay $29.04 a month for 24 months. How much more did the machine cost because it was paid for on the installment plan?

   $ _____

9. Mae Alpert purchased a living room suite for $680. She paid 20% down and promised to pay the balance in 12 equal monthly installments, along with finance charges of 8% per year. a. What was the down payment? b. What was the balance due? c. What was the finance charge? d. What was the monthly payment?

   a. $ _____

   b. $ _____

   c. $ _____

   d. $ _____

10. Jason Mason purchased a CB set for $460. He paid 15% down and agreed to pay the balance in 18 equal monthly payments. The finance charge was 7% per year. a. What was the down payment? b. What was the balance due? c. What was the monthly payment? d. If he had been able to pay cash, how much would he have saved?

   a. $ _____

   b. $ _____

   c. $ _____

   d. $ _____

9.2 BANK INSTALLMENT LOANS

Commercial banks make many loans to consumers which are repaid in installments. The usual method of computing the cost of a loan calls for deducting the interest in advance. Interest charges are figured on the face value of the note. The interest is then deducted from the face value to determine the amount actually received by the borrower. The borrower receives the smaller amount, but pays back the full face value in installments.

Example 1. Suppose you borrow money from a bank, signing a note for $250, payable in 12 monthly installments, with interest at 6% deducted in advance. a. How much would you receive? b. What are your monthly payments?
 a.   6% × $250 = $15
        $250 − $15 = $235 Amount Received
 b. $250 ÷ 12 = $20.83 Monthly Payment

Example 2. Suppose you wanted to borrow $250 (not $235) on a 12-month installment loan, with 6% interest deducted in advance. a. What will be the face value of the note representing what you promise to pay back? b. What will be the monthly payment?
 a. $250 is 94% of the amount of the note
        $250 ÷ .94 = $265.96 Face Value
 b. $265.96 ÷ 12 = $22.16 Monthly Payment

To facilitate the computation, banks use charts which show the monthly payments and the contract amounts (face value of note) at various rates for different installment periods. Table 9-1 shows part of such a chart for 6% interest deducted in advance. Note that the true rate of interest per year is also shown. This is required by truth-in-lending regulations.

The "amount to finance" shown in the first column is the amount actually received by the borrower, the "contract amount" is the face value of the note. On this chart, fractions of a cent have been dropped. This explains why the monthly payment for $1 for 12 months is $.08, while that for $10 is $.88, and for $100, $8.86. (A loan of $1 to be paid back in 12 installments would not actually be made, of course.) It also explains why the contract amount for $100 borrowed is $106.32, rather than $106.38 (100 ÷ .94).

The chart can be used to calculate the monthly payment with acceptable accuracy by combining figures.

Example. Suppose you borrowed $152 on a 12-month installment note at 6%, with interest deducted in advance. a. What is the face value of the note? b. What are the monthly payments?

Table 9-1. Monthly Payment Chart at 6% Deducted in Advance

Amount to Finance	12 Months		15 Months		18 Months	
	Monthly Payment	Contract Amount	Monthly Payment	Contract Amount	Monthly Payment	Contract Amount
$ 1	$ .08	$ .96	$ .07	$ 1.05	$ .06	$ 1.08
2	.17	2.04	.14	2.10	.12	2.16
3	.26	3.12	.21	3.15	.18	3.24
4	.35	4.20	.28	4.20	.24	4.32
5	.44	5.28	.36	5.40	.30	5.40
6	.53	6.36	.43	6.45	.36	6.48
7	.62	7.44	.50	7.50	.42	7.56
8	.70	8.40	.57	8.55	.48	8.64
9	.79	9.48	.64	9.60	.54	9.72
10	.88	10.56	.72	10.80	.61	10.98
20	1.77	21.24	1.44	21.60	1.22	21.96
30	2.65	31.80	2.16	32.40	1.83	32.94
40	3.54	42.48	2.88	43.20	2.44	43.92
50	4.43	53.16	3.60	54.00	3.05	54.90
60	5.31	63.72	4.32	64.80	3.66	65.88
70	6.20	74.40	5.04	75.60	4.27	76.86
80	7.09	85.08	5.76	86.40	4.88	87.84
90	7.97	95.64	6.48	97.20	5.49	98.82
100	8.86	106.32	7.20	108.00	6.10	109.80
Rate per Annum	11.58%		11.89		12.15%	

a. Amount to Finance $100   Contract Amount $106.32
                              50   53.16
                            + 2   + 2.04
   Amount to Finance $152   Contract Amount $161.52
b. Monthly Payment for $100 = $ 8.86
                              50   =   4.43
                            + 2   = + .17
   Monthly Payment for $152 = $13.46

If you did this problem without the chart, you would get:
   a. $152 ÷ .94 = $161.70
   b. $161.70 ÷ 12 = $13.48

By using the table, bank personnel can more easily and uniformly compute the monthly payments and stay within the established rates.

Problems

1. Frances Fowler borrows money from a bank and signs a note promising to pay back $400 in 18 equal monthly payments, with interest deducted in advance, at the rate of 7% a year. a. How much is deducted for interest? b. What is the amount received on the loan? c. What is the monthly payment?

    a. $ _____

    b. $ _____

    c. $ _____

2. John Adams borrows $500 and signs a note promising to pay the loan back in 12 equal monthly installments. Interest at the rate of 5% is deducted in advance. a. What is the total amount of the note? b. What is the monthly payment?

    a. $ _____

    b. $ _____

Use the monthly payment chart for the following:

3. Ophelia Baker borrows $188 on a 15-month installment contract, with 6% deducted from the face of the note in advance. a. What is the contract amount of the note? b. What is the monthly payment?

    a. $ _____

    b. $ _____

4. Carl Ingles borrowed $175 from his bank, promising to pay for the loan in 18 monthly installments. The interest rate is 6%, deducted in advance. a. What is the face value of the note? b. What is the monthly payment? c. If you did not use the chart, what would be the face of the note? d. What would be the monthly payment?

    a. $ _____

    b. $ _____

    c. $ _____

    d. $ _____

5. If you borrowed $90 and promised to repay the loan in monthly payments of $6.48, with interest at 6%, deducted in advance from the contract amount, how long would it take to repay the loan?

_____

9.3   PAYING INSTALLMENT CONTRACT IN FULL BEFORE MATURITY

There are times when a borrower or buyer on installment credit may find it possible and desirable to pay the debt completely before the maturity date of the loan. Under these conditions, it is customary for the borrower to receive at least a partial refund of the unearned interest. The federal truth-in-lending law requires that the methods of calculating this be disclosed at the time the agreement is initiated.

The *Rule of 78* prescribes a common method for calculating the refund. Under this rule, the numbers of the periods in an installment loan contract are totaled. For example, if it is a 12-month contract, the numbers 1 through 12 add up to 78, giving the name to the method, which is applicable to other periods as well. The periods in a 6-month contract total 21; in a 24-month contract, the total is 300.

Under the Rule of 78, the finance charge for the first month of a 12-month installment loan is $^{12}/_{78}$ of the total charge. The second month's charge is $^{11}/_{78}$ of the total, the third month's is $^{10}/_{78}$, and so on. The refund is computed by multiplying the total finance charge by a fraction whose denominator is the sum of the total number of periods in the contract and whose numerator is the sum of the numbers of the remaining periods, for which payment has not been made.

Example 1. After 6 payments, you find that you are able to pay a 12-month installment loan in full. If the finance charge was $120, how much should be refunded under the Rule of 78?
   a. The sum of the periods remaining is $1 + 2 + 3 + 4 + 5 \times 6 = 21$
   b. The sum of all the periods in the contract is $1 + 2 + 3 + 4 + 5 + 6 + 7 + 8 + 9 + 10 + 11 + 12 = 78$
   c. $^{21}/_{78} \times \$120 = \$32.31$

Example 2. Jennie Dow decided to pay off her 24-month installment loan after making 16 payments. The finance charge made for the loan was $284. Using the Rule of 78, what is the amount of the refund?

    a. The sum of the periods remaining is $1 + 2 + 3 + 4 + 5 + 6 + 7 + 8 = 36$

    b. The sum of all the periods in the contract is $1 + 2 + 3 + \ldots + 24 = 300$

    c. $^{36}/_{300} \times \$284 = \$34.08$

Problems

Calculate the amounts of unearned interest (refund) in the following, using the Rule of 78:

	Finance Charge	Number of Payments	Remaining Number of Payments	
1.	$ 84	12	7	$ _____
2.	162	6	2	$ _____
3.	76.50	10	3	$ _____
4.	312	24	9	$ _____
5.	312	12	6	$ _____

6. Ruth Rowan is making monthly payments on a 12-month installment loan contract. The finance charge for the loan is $93.80. After 5 payments, she decides to pay the loan in full. How much refund is she entitled to if the Rule of 78 is used?

    $_____

7. Ralph Rews paid off a 6-month installment loan with his second payment. If the finance charge for the loan is $64.20, how much refund should he receive under the Rule of 78?

    $_____

8. After making your first payment on a 10-month installment loan, you decide to pay the loan in full. If the finance charge for the loan was $126.80, how much refund should you receive under the Rule of 78?

9.4   APPROXIMATE TRUE ANNUAL RATE OF INTEREST

If you borrowed $480, to be paid back at the end of a year with 6% interest, you would pay $508.80. The "extra" $28.80 would represent 6% of $480, the amount of the loan. If the interest was deducted in advance, so that you actually received only $451.20 ($480 − $28.80), the true rate of interest on the amount received is $28.80 ÷ $451.20 = 6.4%.

If you pay back the loan with 12 monthly payments, you have the use of the total amount borrowed for only one month. What, then, is the actual interest rate you are paying?

Assume that you actually received $480, to be paid back in 12 monthly installments. Then consider that you are paying back 480 ÷ 12, or $40 of the loan itself, each month. The loan decreases each month, and the balances would total $480 + 440 + 400 + 360 + 320 + 280 + 240 + 200 + 160 + 120 + 80 + 40 = $3,120. The average debt is $3,120 ÷ 12 = $260. You can arrive at this figure more simply by averaging only the first and last monthly balances:

$$\frac{\$480 + \$40}{2} = \frac{\$520}{2} = \$260$$

If you paid $28.80 interest on this average debt of $260, the approximate true annual rate of interest is $28.80 ÷ $260 = 11.1%.

Example. What is the approximate true annual rate of interest on a loan of $100 to be repaid in 18 monthly installment payments of $6.10?
    $6.10 × 18 = $109.80 Total Amount Repaid
    $\frac{12}{18}$ × $9.80 = $6.53 Finance Charge per Year
    $100 ÷ 18 = $5.56 Part of Loan Repaid Each Month
    $\frac{\$100 + \$5.56}{2} = \frac{\$105.56}{2}$ = $52.78 Average Debt
    $6.53 ÷ $52.78 = 12.4% Approximate True Annual Rate of Interest

Problems

1. Find the approximate true annual rate of interest on a loan of $1,200 which is to be paid back in monthly payments of $107 for 12 months.

    _____%

2. What is the approximate true annual rate of interest on a loan of $640, payable at the rate of $47.50 a month for 15 months?

_____%

3. Maria Sanchez buys a refrigerator priced at $425. She pays $42.50 down and the rest in 12 equal monthly payments of $34.43. What is the approximate true annual rate of interest she is paying?

_____%

4. Manuel Lopez bought a stereo system for $870, with a down payment of 10%. He pays the balance in 18 monthly installments of $46.98. What is the approximate true annual rate of interest?

_____%

9.5 MORTGAGE LOANS

Banks and savings and loan associations lend money to home buyers, taking a mortgage note on the property as security for the loan. Interest is charged on the loan, which is usually paid in monthly installments over from 20 to 30 years.

Example. You buy a home for $60,000, paying $10,000 in cash and signing a mortgage note, by which you promise to pay the balance of $50,000 in equal monthly installments of $402.10. Interest at 9% on the unpaid balance is included in these payments. a. How much of the first three payments applies to interest and how much to repaying the principal of the loan? b. What is the balance of the loan after the three payments?

a. Amount of Mortgage Loan		$50,000.00
First Payment	$402.10	
Interest $\dfrac{9\% \times \$50,000}{12}=$	− 375.00	
	27.10	
Decrease in Principal		− 27.10
Balance of Loan		49,972.90
Second payment	402.10	
Interest $\dfrac{9\% \times \$49,972.90}{12}=$	− 374.80	
	27.30	
Decrease in Principal		− 27.30
Balance of Loan		49,945.60

$$
\begin{array}{lr}
\text{Third Payment} & 402.10 \\
\text{Interest } \dfrac{9\% \times \$49{,}945.60}{12} = & -\ 374.59 \\
& 27.51 \\
\text{Decrease in Principal} & -\ 27.51
\end{array}
$$

b. Balance of Loan After Three Payments $49,918.09

Note that the amount of payment applied to the balance of the loan increases with each payment and that the amount of interest each month decreases with the balance of the loan. This is an example of the *amortization* of a loan. In many instances, property taxes, fire insurance, and mortgage insurance costs become part of the payments.

Amortization tables are used to determine the monthly payment that will pay off $1,000 of a loan at a specified rate of interest over a certain number of years. Table 9-2 gives a portion of such a table.

Table 9-2. Partial Amortization Table

	Monthly Payment of Principal and Interest per $1,000			
Term	*8%*	*8½*	*9%*	*9½*
20 years	$8.37	$8.68	$9.00	$9.33
25 years	7.72	8.06	8.40	8.74
30 years	7.34	7.69	8.05	8.41

Example. You borrow $45,000 on a 9½% mortgage loan to extend over 30 years, with equal monthly payments made over that period. How much is the monthly payment?

$$45 \times \$8.41 = \$378.45$$

Suppose the loan is for 20 years. How much is the monthly payment?

$$45 \times \$9.33 = \$419.85$$

In this example, how much would be paid for principal and interest over the period of the loan in each case?

30-Year Mortgage: $378.45 \times 30 \times 12 = \$136,242$

20-Year Mortgage: $419.85 \times 20 \times 12 = \$100,764$

Other types of mortgage loan arrangements have been developed in recent years. A *graduated payment mortgage* loan, for example, provides for smaller payments at the beginning of the loan period, with the payments becoming larger later at a predetermined rate. This plan is attractive to young families buying their first home.

Example. Suppose you borrowed $35,000 on a 30-year graduated payment mortgage at 8% interest. The monthly payments for the first year are $212. Each year, through the first 10 years, the payments will increase 3% annually, according to the agreement. Compare this arrangement with a mortgage calling for level (equal) payments.

To the nearest dollar, payments would be:

Year	Level payments	Graduated payments	Difference
1	$257	$212	− $45
5	257	239	− 18
8	257	261	+ 4
11–30	257	285	+ 28

The *variable interest rate mortgage* provides for raising or lowering the rate charged, based on some reference index, such as the consumer price index. These changing rates can be accommodated with changes in the monthly payment, the maturity date of the loan, or a combination of both. Borrowers hope that rates will drop, and lenders' worries about increasing rates are minimized.

Problems

1. Joan and John Avelino buy a home for $70,000 by paying $15,000 in cash and signing a 20-year $9\frac{1}{2}$% mortgage note for $55,000. They promise to make monthly payments of $513.15 to pay for the debt. How much of the first three payments will apply to the principal of the loan?

   $ —————

2. In Problem 1, how much of the first three payments will be for interest?

   $ —————

3. Becky and Ben Ambrose are planning to buy a house and lot for $75,000, if they can finance the purchase. They have $10,000 for a down payment and believe they could pay no more than $525 a month on a mortgage note, even though they are both earning an income. If they can get a mortgage loan at 9% interest, for how many years will they need to finance the loan if they are to stay within the $525-a-month limit?

_____

Chapter Review

1. Mildred Myers purchases a used car priced at $3,640. She makes a down payment of $600 and promises to pay the balance in 18 equal monthly installments of $184.10 each. What will be the total amount she pays for the car?

    $ _____

2. Jim Joyce buys a sailboat priced at $1,880. He pays 20% down and promises to pay the balance in 12 monthly payments with 7% a year finance charges. What is the monthly payment?

    $ _____

3. Frank Foy borrows money from a bank and signs a note promising to pay back $600 in 24 equal monthly installments, with interest deducted in advance at the rate of 6% per year. a. What is the amount received on the loan? b. What is the monthly payment?

    $ _____

    $ _____

4. In Problem 3, suppose the actual amount received on the loan is $600. a. What would the face value of the note be? b. What would be the monthly payment?

    $ _____

    $ _____

5. Using the monthly payment chart in Table 9-1, which is based on 6% deducted in advance, what is the monthly payment for a loan of $150, to be repaid in 15 monthly payments? What is the face value (contract amount) of the note?

    $ _____

    $ _____

6. After 8 payments you decide to pay a 12-month installment loan in full. If the finance charge for the loan is $80.60, how much of this would be refunded under the Rule of 78?

    $ _____

7. You decide to pay off a 6-month installment loan after 3 payments. If the finance charge for the loan is $128.40, how much will you be refunded under the Rule of 78?

    $ _____

8. What is the approximate true annual rate of interest on a loan of $1,500, payable in 18 monthly payments of $94.70?

    _____%

9. How much per month will a $55,000 9% amortized mortgage loan cost if the term is 25 years? (Use Table 9-2.)

    $ _____

10. Albin and Dora Aldrich were trying to decide whether to buy a home on a 9% 30-year amortized mortgage or on a $9^1/_2$% 25-year mortgage. If the mortgage is for $40,000, what is the monthly payment for each? What is the total cost for each over the period of the mortgage?

    Monthly Payment 9% 30-year $ _____

    Monthly Payment $9^1/_2$% 25-year $ _____

    Total Cost 9% 30-Year $ _____

    Total Cost $9^1/_2$% 25-Year $ _____

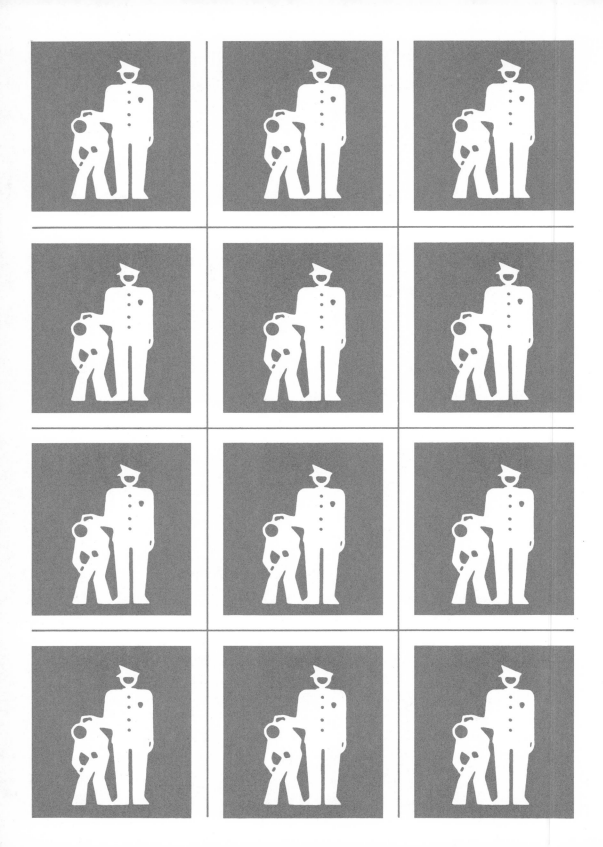

10

Casualty Insurance

An accident can happen to anyone. Physical injury may occur, but often the most serious result of an accident is the financial cost. To be protected against large financial losses from accidents, people buy insurance policies. In some states, this is required by law; in any case, it is a wise precaution. The person who buys a policy is called *the insured*. The company which sells it is *the insurer*. Most insurance is bought through a licensed insurance *agent* or *broker*.

10.I AUTOMOBILE INSURANCE

Every car owner should have—and often is required to have—*liability insurance,* that is, insurance that will pay for bodily injury to another person and for damage to another person's property. Liability insurance may also include protection against the cost of injury caused by uninsured motorists—drivers who are not insured or cannot be identified— and may include some other benefits for the insured as well.

Payments for insurance are called *premiums*. The cost of liability insurance varies, chiefly according to the amount of protection desired. The usual minimum policy is known as *10/20, 5,* which means that the insurer will pay up to $20,000 for injuries caused by any one accident, but not more than $10,000 to any one person injured in the accident, and up to $5,000 for property damage. Premiums for policies with higher limits do not increase proportionately. For example, the ratio of premiums might be as shown in Table 10-1. Premiums are usually rounded to the nearest dollar.

Table 10-1. Automobile Liability Insurance

Limit	Ratio of Premiums to 10/20, 5 Premium
	Percent of 10/20, 5 Rate
25/50, 10	119%
50/100, 25	130%
100/300, 50	141%

The premium charged a car owner is affected by the driving record (number of accidents and traffic arrests or citations), locale, the amount of driving done, and the age and sex of the driver—in other words, by factors that affect the statistical probability that an accident will occur.

"No-fault" insurance, which is in effect in some states, provides for the payment of only "medical" expenses incurred in an accident, without assigning the blame to any one person.

In addition to liability insurance, car owners may buy *collision* and *comprehensive* insurance, both of which pay for physical damage to the insured's car. As its name implies, collision insurance covers the damage caused by collision with another car, especially when fault is unclear, or with a fixed object such as a tree, building, or bridge abutment. Comprehensive insurance reimburses the owner for damage or loss from such causes as fire, theft, vandalism, earthquake, flood, or collision with a bird or animal.

Both collision and comprehensive insurance usually have a *deductible clause,* which provides that damage from any one incident up to a specified amount, commonly $200, will be paid for by the owner; the insurer will pay only for the damage over that amount.

Example 1. K.Dunn buys 50/100, 25 liability insurance, and collision and comprehensive insurance, both $200-deductible. The cost of a 10/20, 5 policy is $195; collision insurance is $83 and comprehensive insurance is $14 annually. Dunn chooses to pay quarterly, although there is an additional charge of $2 for each payment. According to Table 10-1, what will the annual premium be? What will each quarterly payment be?

$195 × 1.30 = $253.50, or $254 Liability Premium
$254 + $83 + $14 = $351 Total Annual Premium
$351 ÷ 4 = $88 Quarterly Share
$88 + $2 = $90 Quarterly Payment

Example 2. K. Dunn is responsible for an accident in which two people in the other car are injured, one with medical expenses of $53,425, the other with expenses of $5,280; damage to the other car is assessed at $7,890, and damage to Dunn's car is $548. How much will the insurer pay?

Since the limit is $50,000 for each injured person, the insurer will pay $50,000 for the first victim, $5,280 for the second victim, and the full $7,890 for the other car.

The collision insurance is $200-deductible, so the indemnity payment on Dunn's car will be $548 − $200, or $348.

Total paid by the company: $50,000
5,280
7,890
+   348
$63,518

Dunn must pay the remaining $3,425 due to the first victim, as well as the $200 deductible on the collision insurance.

Problems

1. H. Lee buys 25/50, 10 liability insurance (assume that the premium on 10/20, 5 would be $208). Lee also has $200-deductible collision insurance at $94 a year and $200-deductible comprehensive insurance at $21 a year. Lee pays quarterly, with an extra $2 charge for each payment. a. What will the quarterly bill be? b. How much will be paid in a year? c. Lee causes an accident in which two other cars are damaged, one to the amount of $1,568 and the other, $893; Lee's own car's damage is $1,250, and two other persons are injured, with medical bills of $960 and $1,350. How much will the insurance company pay? d. How much will Lee pay? e. How long a time would Lee pay the insurance premiums at that rate before the payments equal the cost to the insurance company for that accident?

   a. $ _____

   b. $ _____

   c. $ _____

   d. $ _____

   e. $ _____

2. If H. Lee in Problem 1 had bought 100/300, 50 liability insurance, as well as the collision and comprehensive insurance, a. What would quarterly payments be if a $2 charge were added to each payment? b. How much would be paid in a year? c. How much of the cost of the accident would the insurer pay? d. At that rate, how long would Lee pay before the premiums equal the cost to the company?

a. $ _____

b. $ _____

c. $ _____

d.   _____

3. If you buy $200-deductible comprehensive insurance and a tree falls on your car, damaging it to the extent of $558, how much will you collect? How much if a bird flies into the windshield, causing $198 damage?

$ _____

$ _____

4. If you have $200-deductible collision insurance, at a premium of $103, you may change to:

	Premium	Indemnity
a. $100-deductible, at an increase of 18%	$ _____	$ _____
b. $250-deductible, at a decrease of 6%	$ _____	$ _____
c. $500-deductible, at a decrease of 35%	$ _____	$ _____
d. $1,000-deductible, at a decrease of 71%	$ _____	$ _____

What would be the premium in each case? With each policy, what indemnity would the company pay on damages of $843? Which ratio of indemnity paid to premium cost would be most to your advantage? Which would be least to your advantage?

Most _____

Least _____

5. J. Chavez's total bill for automobile insurance is $442. If the bill is paid quarterly, $2 is added to each payment. a. What would the quarterly payment be? b. What would be paid in a year's quarterly payments? c. If, at the beginning of the year, Chavez paid one quarterly installment and then deposited $329 in a savings account at $5\frac{1}{2}\%$ interest, compounded monthly, what would be the amount in the account after three months? d. If the other three payments were made by withdrawing money from the savings account, would there be enough for the final payment after nine months?

   a. $ —————

   b. $ —————

   c. $ —————

   d. —————

6. Instead of making quarterly payments, as in Problem 5, Chavez could pay 40% down, 30% in 60 days, and the last 30% 60 days after that. a. What would the down payment be? b. What would each of the later payments be?

   a. $ —————

   b. $ —————

7. In the ten years from 1967 to 1977, the cost of auto repairs increased 104% and hospital services went up 200%. How much insurance would have been needed in 1977 to provide protection equivalent to that of 5/10, 5 in 1967.

   —————

10.2 FIRE INSURANCE

The cost of insurance against financial loss from fire depends upon the construction and condition of the building, the locale, and the availability of fire protection. Rates are expressed as the cost for each $100 of protection. An insured person can never collect more than the face of the policy, and if the amount of insurance coverage is less than 80% of the value of the building, the owner may not collect the full amount of a smaller loss. Premiums are usually rounded to the nearest dollar.

If the company cancels a policy before the end of the term, charges are *prorated:* the number of days the policy has been in effect is expressed as a fraction of 365. The charge is that fraction of the total premium, and the remainder is refunded to the formerly insured person.

If the insured cancels a policy, the charge is not prorated. Instead a "short-rate" table is used, parts of which are shown in Table 10-2.

Example. D. Wood buys fire insurance that covers 85% of the $128,500 cost of a four-family house, at the rate of $.48. If, after 152 days, the company cancels the policy, what will Wood's refund be? If Wood cancels the policy, what would the refund be?

$$.85 \times \$128,500 = \$109,225 \text{ Amount of policy}$$
$$1,092.25 \times \$.48 = \$524.28, \text{ or } \$524 \text{ Total Premium}$$
$$^{152}/_{365} \times \$524 = .4164 \times \$524 = \$218.19, \text{ or } \$218 \text{ Prorated Charge}$$
$$\$524 - \$218 = \$306 \text{ Refund}$$
$$.52 \times \$524 = \$272.48, \text{ or } \$272 \text{ Short-Rate Charge}$$
$$\$524 - \$272 = \$252 \text{ Refund}$$

Table 10-2. Fire Insurance

Short-Term Rate Table

Days in Force	Percentage of Annual Rate
30–32	19%
59–62	27%
88–91	35%
121–124	44%
150–153	52%
179–182	60%
210–214	67%
242–246	74%
270–273	80%
302–305	87%
333–337	94%
361–365	100%

Problems

Find a. the annual premium, b. the refund if the policy is canceled by the insured, and c. the refund if the policy is canceled by the insurer:

	Value of Property	Proportion Insured	Rate	Days in Effect	a.	b.	c.
1.	$ 68,000	80%	.59	123	$ ___	$ ___	$ ___
2.	$ 47,750	$4/5$	.63	242	$ ___	$ ___	$ ___
3.	$110,250	90%	.48	361	$ ___	$ ___	$ ___
4.	$ 89,300	100%	.82	31	$ ___	$ ___	$ ___
5.	$ 40,000	$5/8$	.76	182	$ ___	$ ___	$ ___
6.	$ 56,730	90%	.57	59	$ ___	$ ___	$ ___
7.	$ 72,680	80%	.61	151	$ ___	$ ___	$ ___
8.	$ 93,450	75%	.79	211	$ ___	$ ___	$ ___
9.	$ 42,500	80%	.81	89	$ ___	$ ___	$ ___
10.	$101,800	85%	.49	303	$ ___	$ ___	$ ___

10.3 HOMEOWNERS INSURANCE

People who own and live in a one- or two-family house may buy *homeowner's insurance;* which covers damage to the house and its contents, as well as losses from other causes such as wind, theft, or vandalism. It also provides liability insurance. People who rent can purchase *tenant's insurance.* These policies may also provide for extra living expenses if the insured home is temporarily uninhabitable.

Most such policies have a deductible clause. One company decreases the premium on a policy by 10% if it is $100-deductible, by 20% for $200-deductible, and by 25% for $250-deductible.

Housing costs are rising so rapidly that the cost of repairing or rebuilding a house often increases as much as 10% a year; insurance coverage should also increase, especially since 80% coverage is usually required for full protection.

Example. Homeowner's insurance was purchased for 85% of the cost of a $55,700 house built in 1978. The rate was .67, less a 20% reduction because of a $200-deductible clause. What was the annual premium? If houses in the area appreciate (increase in value) at a rate of 9% a year, what percent of the value will be covered by the policy after three years?

$$.85 \times \$55,700 = \$47,345 \text{ Coverage of Policy}$$
$$\$473.45 \times .67 = \$317 \text{ Total Premium}$$
$$\$317 - (.20 \times \$317) = \$317 - \$63 = \$254 \text{ Reduced Premium}$$
$$\text{Year 1} \quad \$55,700 \times 1.09 = \$60,713$$
$$\text{Year 2} \quad \$60,713 \times 1.09 = \$66,177$$
$$\text{Year 3} \quad \$66,177 \times 1.09 = \$72,133$$
$$\$47,345 \div \$72,133 = 66\% \text{ Coverage}$$

Problems

Find a. the amount of coverage; b. the annual premium allowing decreases of 10% for $100 deductible, 20% for $200 deductible, or 25% for $250 deductible amounts; c. the value of the property after three years; and d. the percent of coverage after three years:

	Beginning Value	Percent Covered	Coverage	Rate	Deductible Amount	Premium	Percent of Appreciation	Value after 3 Yrs	Percent of Coverage
1.	$ 85,700	90%	$ ———	.83	$100	$ ———	10%	$ ———	——— %
2.	58,350	80%	———	.74	200	———	8%	———	———
3.	64,980	85%	———	.69	250	———	9%	———	———
4.	101,600	95%	———	.65	250	———	$7\frac{1}{2}\%$	———	———
5.	89,600	80%	———	.58	100	———	$8\frac{1}{2}\%$	———	———
6.	93,550	100%	———	.71	200	———	10%	———	———
7.	49,800	85%	———	.63	100	———	9%	———	———
8.	51,650	80%	———	.55	250	———	7%	———	———
9.	60,700	85%	———	.76	100	———	8%	———	———
10.	75,600	80%	———	.62	250	———	9%	———	———

10.4 COLLECTING ON INSURANCE

Having an insurance policy does not necessarily mean that all the costs of a fire or accident will be recovered.

One problem is finding a fair evaluation of damaged or lost property. Is it the replacement value, the original cost less depreciation, or some other figure?

Example 1. A company evaluates items by estimating the useful life of the item, expressing the remaining life as a fraction of the total life, and finding that fraction of the original cost. What value would be put on a $135 camera expected to last 20 years and stolen after 13 years?

$$\frac{\text{Remaining Life}}{\text{Total Life}} = \frac{7}{20}$$

$$7/_{20} \times \$135 = \$47.25 \text{ Valuation}$$

A policyholder can never collect more than the face value of the policy. Many fire insurance policies carry an *80% clause,* which makes it the responsibility of the insured to have coverage equal to 80% of the value of the property. In case the coverage is less, damages will be reimbursed only in proportion to the ratio of the total coverage to 80%.

Example 2. After three years, a homeowner's insurance policy of $47,345 covers only part of the $72,133 value of the house. There is a fire, with damage assessed at $10,675. What will the insurance company pay?

.80 × $72,133 = $57,706 80% of Value
$47,345/$57,706 = 82.05% Ratio of Coverage to 80%
$10,675 × .8205 = $8,758.84 Payment, less deductible amount

If two or more policies are taken out on the same property, the owner cannot collect twice on the same loss. Instead, each policy pays in proportion to its share of the total insurance. The 80% clause also applies.

Example 3. A property valued at $81,500 is covered by two insurance policies, one for $40,000, the other for $15,000. What would each pay on a loss of $22,500?

$40,000 + $15,000 = $55,000 Total Coverage
.80 × $81,500 = $65,200 80% of Value
$55,000/$65,200 = 84.36% Ratio of Coverage to 80%
.8436 × $22,500 = $18,981.00 Total to Be Repaid
$40/_{55}$ × $18,981.00 = $13,804.36 Share of First Company
$15/_{55}$ × $18,981.00 = $5,176.64 Share of Second Company
(Check: $13,804.36 + $5,176.64 = $18,981.00)
Both shares are before deductions.

Problems

1. By the method of Example 1, what valuation would be placed on a watch purchased in 1975 for $198 and expected to run 18 years, if it is lost in 1980?

   $ ————

2. Another company evaluates items by taking the replacement cost and subtracting 6% for each year since the item was purchased. If a watch identical to the one in Problem 1 cost $225 in 1980, what valuation would this company put on the lost watch?

   $ ————

In Problems 3 to 10, find a. 80% of value; b. the ratio of coverage to 80%; c. the total to be repaid before deductions; and d., e., f. the share paid by each company before deductions.

	Value of Property	Co. A	Coverage Co. B	Co. C	Loss
3.	$ 48,000	$20,000	$15,000	———	$9,485
4.	73,050	30,000	20,000	———	1,278
5.	121,345	60,000	20,000	$10,000	25,431
6.	64,598	40,000	15,000	———	2,193
7.	114,445	40,000	40,000	8,000	12,857
8.	51,595	40,000	5,000	———	3,845
9.	84,151	50,000	10,000	1,000	7,680
10.	97,904	75,000	5,000	———	15,628

	a.	b.	c.	d.	e.	f.
3.	$ ————	————%	$ ————	$ ————	$ ————	$ ————
4.	$ ————	————%	$ ————	$ ————	$ ————	$ ————

5. $ _____ _____% $ _____ $ _____ $ _____ $ _____

6. $ _____ _____% $ _____ $ _____ $ _____ $ _____

7. $ _____ _____% $ _____ $ _____ $ _____ $ _____

8. $ _____ _____% $ _____ $ _____ $ _____ $ _____

9. $ _____ _____% $ _____ $ _____ $ _____ $ _____

10. $ _____ _____% $ _____ $ _____ $ _____ $ _____

Chapter Review

1. You have $200-deductible comprehensive automobile insurance, and your agent tells you that if you change to:

a.

$50-deductible, the premium would increase by 78% $ _____

$100-deductible, the premium would increase by 39% $ _____

$250-deductible, the premium would decrease by 11% $ _____

$500-deductible, the premium would decrease by 33% $ _____

$1,000-deductible, the premium would decrease by 44%$ _____

$200-deductible, with full coverage (0 deductible) on window-glass breakage, the premium would increase by 56% $ _____

a. If your present cost for comprehensive insurance is $31 annually, what would it be in each case above?

Which would prove the best buy if your only claim is:

b. for replacing a reflector at $45?   _____

c. for replacing a cracked windshield at $195?   _____

d. the car, valued at $4,225, which has been stolen and wrecked?   _____

2. G. Farkas buys 100/300, 50 car insurance, at 141% of the base rate of $201; $100-deductible collision insurance, at 118% of $97; and $100-deductible comprehensive insurance, at 139% of $27. a. What is the annual premium? b. If Farkas pays quarterly, with an extra $2 charge for each payment, what is the quarterly bill? What would the company pay on a claim of: c. $7,800 damage to another car? d. $14,000 medical bills for the other driver? e. $3,450 damage to Farkas's car in a collision? f. vandalism to Farkas's car causing $535 damage?

   a. $ _____

   b. $ _____

   c. $ _____

   d. $ _____

   e. $ _____

   f. $ _____

3. Find a. the annual premium; b. the refund if the policy is canceled by the insured; and c. the refund if the policy is canceled by the insurer, on a property insured for 85% of its $428,750 value, if the rate is .68 and the policy is canceled after 271 days. (Short-term rate is 80% of annual rate.)

   a. $ _____

   b. $ _____

   c. $ _____

4. A house valued at $57,895 is insured for 90% of its value. The rate is .58 less 10%, because the policy is $100-deductible; there is a further reduction of $9 because fire alarms are installed. Four years later, when the insurance is still the same, but house values have appreciated 8% a year, a fire causes $5,838 damage. a. What is the insurance coverage? b. What is the annual premium? c. What is the value of the house after four years? d. What is 80% of the house's value after four years? e. What is the ratio of coverage to 80%? f. What would the company pay?

   a. $ _____   d. $ _____

   b. $ _____   e.   _____%

   c. $ _____   f. $ _____

5. A building valued at \$339,570 is covered by three insurance policies: \$150,000 with A, \$50,000 with B, and \$65,000 with C; each policy is \$500–deductible. How much will each policy pay on damages costing \$37,895?

A   \$ _____

B   \$ _____

C   \$ _____

11

Life and Health Insurance

When a person dies—especially a person who has contributed to the support of a family—the survivors might be left in a very poor financial position, unless they have been protected by the purchase of life insurance.

There are different kinds of life insurance. What is the best policy at one time may be quite inappropriate at another time. A good insurance agent will plan a program that will provide the best protection when it is most needed, at a cost the customer can afford.

11.1 TERM INSURANCE

The type of life insurance policy that pays the greatest death benefits for the smallest premium is *term* insurance. Like casualty insurance, it is in force only for a certain time. The term may be as short as an airplane flight or as long as the thirty years of a mortgage, but a common term is five years. Often, a five-year term policy may be renewed or converted to another type of policy at a higher rate, but without a medical examination.

Since insurance premiums of any kind are based on statistical probabilities, the older an insured person is, the higher the rate will be. Premiums may usually be paid annually, semiannually, quarterly, or monthly; there are some extra charges for more frequent payments. Table 11-1 shows premiums that might be charged on a $30,000 five-year term policy.

Table 11-1. Premiums on $30,000 Five-Year Term Insurance

Age	Annual	Semiannual	Quarterly	Monthly
20	$ 84.00	$ 43.00	$21.80	$ 7.50
25	88.50	45.30	23.00	8.00
30	96.30	49.10	25.00	8.70
35	114.00	58.00	29.60	10.30
40	155.40	78.70	37.90	14.00
45	223.50	112.80	58.10	20.10

To find the annual premium for a $20,000 policy, take $2/3$ of the premium for a $30,000 policy. For a $10,000 policy, take $1/3$ of the premium for a $30,000 policy, and add $2.50. For a $5,000 policy, take $1/6$ of the premium for a $30,000 policy, and add $3.75.

Example 1. At age 25, George Luck buys a $30,000 5-year policy, paying quarterly premiums. If Luck were killed 2 years later, what would the beneficiary receive? How much would Luck have paid in? If Luck were killed 6 years later, how much would the beneficiary receive? How much would Luck have paid in?

Two years later, the beneficiary would receive the face value of the policy: $30,000.
Luck would have paid eight quarterly premiums of $23.00:
$$8 \times \$23.00 = \$184.00$$
After five years, the policy would no longer be in effect, so the beneficiary would receive nothing.
Luck would have paid $20 \times \$23.00 = \$460.00$.

A *decreasing-term* policy is intended to cover the cost of a mortgage or other loan which is being reduced by regular payments. The amount of the policy decreases as the amount of indebtedness decreases. In case of death, the loan is paid off completely.

Table 11-2. Annual Premiums on $20,000 Decreasing-Term Policies

Age	20-Year	25-Year	30-Year
20	$ 38.00	$ 41.00	$ 45.00
25	43.00	48.20	55.00
30	52.80	61.80	73.00
35	71.80	86.40	104.00
40	105.00	127.80	154.80
45	158.60	193.20	233.60

Table 11-2 shows one company's annual premiums for $20,000 decreasing term policies for 20, 25, or 30 years at different ages.

Example 2. Teresa Houser, age 35, has just purchased a house with a $20,000 20-year mortgage, to be paid in equal monthly installments, including life insurance. If there is an extra charge of 50¢ for each monthly premium, how much is each monthly payment for life insurance? What would the monthly premium be on a 30-year policy?

The annual premium is $71.80.
The monthly premium is ($71.80 ÷ 12) + $.50 = $6.48
On a 30-year policy, the premium would be ($104 ÷ 12) + $.50 = $9.17

Problems

1. How much more would be paid in monthly premiums than in semiannual premiums on a $30,000 five-year term policy taken out at age 35, according to Table 11-1?

    $_____

2. If you buy a $30,000 five-year term policy at age 20, paying annual premiums, and then renew it every five years until you reach 50, how much will you have paid in premiums?

    $_____

    What is the ratio of this amount to the amount your beneficiary would have received if you had died at any time during the 30 years?

    _____

3. a. What would the annual premium be on a $20,000 decreasing-term policy for 20 years, taken at age 30? b. How much would be paid in premiums during the term?

    a. $_____

    b. $_____

4. Premiums for decreasing-term policies for less than $20,000 are determined by finding the pro-rata fraction of the premium for $20,000 coverage and adding 75¢ per $1,000, for policies of less than $10,000, or 25¢ per $1,000, for policies of $10,000 to $19,999. What would the premium for a 20-year policy be at age 40 for a. $4,000, b. $12,000, c. $5,500?

a. $_____

b. $_____

c. $_____

11.2 STRAIGHT LIFE POLICIES

Straight life insurance, sometimes called *whole life* or *ordinary life,* gives protection throughout the insured's life. The insured may continue to pay premiums until death.

Because coverage will not stop after a few years, premiums for straight life policies begun before about age 55 are more than those for term insurance, but the premiums are the same for the whole life of the policy.

Premiums for straight life policies offered by one company are shown in Table 11-3.

Table 11-3. Annual Premiums on Straight Life Policies

Age	$2,000 Policy	$5,000 Policy	$10,000 Policy	$30,000 Policy
20	$26.78	$ 56.95	$108.90	$319.20
25	30.44	66.10	127.20	374.10
30	35.12	77.80	150.60	444.30
35	41.18	92.95	180.90	535.20
40	49.06	112.65	220.30	653.40
45	59.32	138.30	271.60	807.30

For a $1,000 policy, take $1/2$ of the $2,000 premium and add $2.
For a $20,000 policy, take $2/3$ of the $30,000 premium.

Because life insurance premiums are based on the likelihood that a person will die at a certain age and because women, on the average, live longer than men, the same company whose rates are shown in Table 11-3 has reduced rates as shown in Table 11-4.

Table 11-4. Annual Premiums on $10,000 Straight Life Policies

Age	Old Rate	New Rate, Men	New Rate, Women
20	$108.90	$ 97.40	$ 88.80
25	127.20	114.60	103.70
30	150.60	137.00	122.80
35	180.90	166.60	147.80
40	220.30	205.80	181.00

Example 1. According to Table 11-3, what was the premium on a $1,000 straight life policy taken out at age 40? On a $20,000 policy?

$1,000 Policy Premium ($49.06 ÷ 2) + $2 = $24.53 + $2 = $26.53

$20,000 Policy Premium $\frac{2}{3}$ × $653.40 = $435.60

Example 2. Comparing the old and new rates shown in Table 11-4, how much less in annual premiums will a 30-year-old man pay over the first five years a policy is in effect? A 30-year-old woman?

Man $150.60 − $137.00 = $13.60 Annual Saving

$13.60 × 5 = $68 Saving over 5 Years

Woman $150.60 − $122.80 = $27.80 Annual Saving

$27.80 × 5 = $139 Saving over 5 Years

Example 3. What is the ratio of the annual premium on a $30,000 straight life policy (Table 11-3) to that of a $30,000 5-year term policy, each taken at age 20? At age 45?

Age 20: $319.20 ÷ $84.00 = 3.800

Age 45: $807.30 ÷ $223.50 = 3.612

Problems

1. According to Table 11-3, what is the annual premium on a $1,000 straight life policy taken out at age 25? On a $20,000 policy?

$ 1,000 $_____

$20,000 $_____

2. If the quarterly premium is approximately 26% of the annual premium, estimate the quarterly premium for a. a $30,000 straight life policy taken at age 35, b. a $2,000 straight life policy taken at age 25, c. a $10,000 straight life policy taken at age 30 by a woman, at the new rate (Table 11-4), d. a $20,000 straight life policy taken at age 30.

    a. $_____

    b. $_____

    c. $_____

    d. $_____

3. What percent of the premium for a man is the premium for a woman for a $10,000 straight life policy taken a. at age 20? b. at age 25? c. at age 30? d. at age 35? e. at age 40?

    a. _____%

    b. _____%

    c. _____%

    d. _____%

    e. _____%

4. When the insured is 51, the annual premium on a $5,000 straight life policy is $179.95; the monthly premium is $16.20; and the quarterly premium is 26% of the annual premium. a. How much would be paid in a year? b. How much more than the annual premium is this?

    Monthly Premiums   a. $_____   b. $_____

    Quarterly Premiums   a. $_____   b. $_____

5. Over 5 years, how much more would a $30,000 straight life policy cost in annual premiums than a $30,000 5-year term policy, if both are taken out at age 30?

    $_____

11.3   LIMITED-PAYMENT LIFE POLICIES

Some life insurance policies call for the payment of premiums only for a limited time, such as twenty years, or until a certain age, usually 65. Premiums for these policies are higher than for straight life policies, since there will usually be fewer payments made, and the coverage remains in effect for life. Tables 11-5 and 11-6 show some rates for these types of insurance.

Table 11-5. Annual Premiums on 20-Payment Life Policies

Age	$2,000 Policy	$5,000 Policy	$10,000 Policy	$20,000 Policy
20	$ 41.16	$ 92.90	$180.80	$356.60
25	45.78	104.45	203.90	402.80
30	51.22	118.05	231.10	457.20
35	57.78	134.45	263.90	522.80
40	65.74	154.35	303.70	602.40
45	75.42	178.55	352.10	699.20
50	87.50	208.75	412.50	820.00
55	103.16	247.90	490.80	976.60

For a $1,000 policy, take ½ of the $2,000 premium and add $2.
For a $30,000 policy, multiply the $20,000 premium by 1.5.

Table 11-6. Annual Premiums on Life Paid-Up-at-65 Policies

Age	$2,000 Policy	$5,000 Policy	$10,000 Policy	$20,000 Policy
20	$ 28.40	$ 61.00	$117.00	$ 229.00
25	32.86	72.15	139.30	273.60
30	38.76	86.90	168.80	332.60
35	46.88	107.20	209.40	413.80
40	58.38	135.95	266.90	528.80
45	75.42	178.55	352.10	699.20
50	103.00	247.50	490.00	975.00
55	155.66	379.15	753.30	1,501.60

For a $1,000 policy, take ½ of the $2,000 premium and add $2.
For a $30,000 policy, multiply the $20,000 premium by 1.5

Compare the premiums for the two kinds of insurance at age 45 and at ages below and above 45. What are the relationships? How do you explain this?

Example 1. If the insured lives past the age of 65, how much will have been paid in annual premiums on a $20,000 paid-up-at-65 policy purchased at age 25? On a similar policy purchased at age 55?

$273.60 × 40 = $10,944 Purchased at Age 25
$1,501.60 × 10 = $15,016 Purchased at Age 55

Example 2. What would annual premiums total on a $30,000 20-payment life policy bought at age 35?

Premium $522.80 × 1.5 = $784.20
$784.20 × 20 = $15,684 Total

Example 3. At age 30, you must choose between a $10,000 20-payment life policy and a $10,000 life paid-up-at-65 policy. If you were to die at age 83, how much would you have paid on each? What would your beneficiary receive?

20-Payment Life Policy $231.10 × 20 = $4,622 Total Paid
Paid-Up-at-65 Policy $168.80 × 35 = $5,908 Total Paid

Either policy would pay the beneficiary $10,000.

Problems

1. In the circumstances described in Example 3, how much would you have paid if you were to die at age 52?

    $_____

2. a. At 26% of the annual premium, what would be the quarterly premium on a $30,000 20-payment life policy bought at age 40? b. What would be the total paid if the insured died at age 91? c. If the insured died at age 47?

    a. $_____

    b. $_____

    c. $_____

3.   a. For a person age 45, what is the ratio of the premiums on a $1,000 limited-payment life policy to those on a $2,000 policy? Express the ratio as a decimal also. b. Of premiums for a $5,000 to those for a $10,000 policy? c. Of premiums for a $10,000 to those for a $20,000 policy?

   a. —————— to —————, or .——————

   b. —————— to —————, or .——————

   c. —————— to —————, or .——————

4.   At age 50, about how large a paid-up-at-65 policy could you buy for the same annual premium for which you could buy a $30,000 20-payment life policy?

   $———————

5.   On $20,000 policies bought at age 20, how much would have been paid in annual premiums at age 70 on a   a. straight life policy? b. 20-payment life policy? c. life paid-up-at-65 policy?

   a. $———————

   b. $———————

   c. $———————

11.4 ENDOWMENT POLICIES

An *endowment policy* combines life insurance protection with a savings program for the insured. During the term of the policy, the face (amount) will be paid to the beneficiary at the death of the insured; but, if still living at the end of the term, the insured receives the proceeds of the policy (often including interest and dividends), either in cash (lump-sum payment) or as a life income (periodic payments). Because the face value must be paid by the end of the term, if not sooner, premiums are higher than for other types of insurance. Table 11-7 shows representative premiums for 20-year endowment and endowment-at-age-65 policies.

Table 11-7. Annual Premiums

20-Year Endowment			Endowment-at-Age-65	
$2,000 Policy	*$5,000 Policy*	*Age*	*$10,000 Policy*	*$20,000 Policy*
$ 84.12	$200.30	20	$141.30	$ 277.60
84.50	201.25	25	169.60	334.20
85.26	203.15	30	207.30	409.60
86.78	206.95	35	259.10	513.20
89.50	213.75	40	333.10	661.20
93.88	224.70	45	444.40	883.80
100.94	242.35	50	628.00	1,251.00

For a $1,000 policy, take $1/2$ of the $2,000 premium and add $2.

For a $10,000 policy, double the $5,000 premium and subtract $5.

For a $20,000 policy, multiply the $5,000 premium by 4 and subtract $15.

For a $30,000 policy, multiply the $5,000 premium by 6 and subtract $22.50.

For a $1,000 policy, divide the $10,000 premium by 10 and add $4.50

For a $2,000 policy, divide the $10,000 premium by 5 and add $5.

For a $5,000 policy, divide the $10,000 premium by 2 and add $2.50.

For a $30,000 policy, multiply the $10,000 premium by 3 and subtract $7.50.

Example. What is the ratio of the annual premium for a $30,000 20-year endowment policy bought at age 45 to that for a $30,000 endowment-at-age-65 policy?

20-Year Endowment Premium ($224.70 × 6) − $22.50
$$= \$1348.20 - \$22.50 = \$1,325.70$$
Endowment-at-Age-65 Premium ($444.40 × 3) − $7.50
$$= \$1,333.20 - \$7.50 = \$1,325.70$$

The ratio is 1:1. Since both policies will be paid in 20 years, this is to be expected.

Problems

Find the premiums for $30,000 20-year endowment policies and for $30,000 endowment-at-age-65 policies, for each age shown. Show the premium for the at-age-65 policy as a percentage of the 20-year policy premium.

	Age	20-Year Endowment	Endowment-at-Age-65	Ratio
1.	20	$_____	$_____	_____%
2.	25	$_____	$_____	_____%
3.	30	$_____	$_____	_____%
4.	35	$_____	$_____	_____%
5.	40	$_____	$_____	_____%
6.	45	$_____	$_____	_____%
7.	50	$_____	$_____	_____%

8. a. What is the annual premium for a $1,000 20-year endowment policy bought at age 25? b. For a $1,000 endowment-at-age-65 policy?

a. $_____
b. $_____

9. a. What is the annual premium at age 30 for a $10,000 20-year endowment policy? b. For a $20,000 10-year endowment policy?

a. $_____
b. $_____

10. a. What is the annual premium for a $5,000 endowment-at-age-65 policy taken at age 35? b. At age 40?

a. $_____
b. $_____

11.5 CASH VALUE OF LIFE INSURANCE

If a life insurance policy is canceled, except in the case of a term policy, some of the money that has been paid in premiums will be refunded. This amount is the *cash surrender value.*

Some insurance companies, called *mutual* or *participatory,* pay annual dividends on policies. The rate of the dividends varies from year to year.

Dividends may be applied to premiums, taken in cash, or used to buy additional insurance protection. In the case of an endowment policy, for example, the amount paid at the end of the term will be at least the face value, but may be considerably more.

A policyholder who is in need of cash but does not want to cancel a policy may borrow on it, up to a certain amount, at an interest rate specified in the policy. This rate is usually lower than the rates of other lending institutions. If an insured person dies before a loan has been repaid, the amount owed is deducted from the amount paid to the beneficiary.

Table 11-8 shows some cash surrender values allowed by one company on straight life policies.

Table 12-8. Cash Surrender Value per $1,000 of a Straight Life Policy

End of	Age When Policy Was Purchased				
Year:	20	30	40	50	60
5	$ 52.55	$ 70.66	$ 94.57	$124.70	$159.82
10	125.80	163.73	211.47	268.20	329.62
15	193.44	251.18	318.94	393.47	469.42
20	268.93	340.58	422.95	509.42	588.55

Example 1. Find the cash surrender value after 15 years of a $25,000 straight life policy purchased at age 30.

Cash Surrender Value $251.18 per $1,000
$251.18 × 25 = $6,279.50

Example 2. If the maximum loan is 95% of the cash surrender value, how much can a policyholder borrow at the age of 40 on a $35,000 policy purchased at age 20?

Cash Surrender Value $268.93 × 35 = $9,412.55
95% × $9,412.55 = $8,941.92 Maximum Loan

1. What is the cash surrender value after 15 years of a $30,000 straight life policy bought at age 50?

$_____

2. The maximum loan is 95% of the cash surrender value; how much can an insured borrow on a $10,000 policy taken out at age 40, when the insured is 45?

$_____

3. M. E. Brown bought a $30,000 straight life policy at age 30, paying annual premiums of $444.30. a. At age 50, how much had Brown paid in premiums? b. What was the cash surrender value? c. What percent of the total premiums paid was the cash surrender value? d. What was the maximum loan Brown could get, if it was 95% of cash surrender value?

a. $_____

b. $_____

c. _____%

d. $_____

4. After 20 years, D. Moto borrowed the maximum amount on a $15,000 straight life policy, purchased at age 50. If Moto died immediately after making the loan, what indemnity would be paid?

$_____

5. a. What indemnity would be paid on a $20,000 straight life policy purchased at age 60 if the insured died at age 70? b. What would the cash surrender value have been? c. What would have been paid in annual premiums of $1,092.60?

a. $_____

b. $_____

c. $_____

11.6 HEALTH INSURANCE

To protect themselves from the cost of treatment for illness or accidents, people buy *health insurance*. In many cases, *group health insurance* is paid for by an employer, often as part of a union contract. Medicare, which is available to persons 65 or over and to some others, is an example of health insurance. Blue Cross-Blue Shield, another provider of health insurance, and other similar programs are not limited to any age group.

Major medical insurance is designed to apply to expenses beyond the coverage of standard medical insurance policies.

Almost all health insurance policies have a deductible clause. Medicare hospital insurance will pay for most of the cost of a hospital stay, but the patient is responsible for part of the cost of a 60-day stay and for a larger part thereafter; Medicare medical insurance has $60-deductible provision. Other health insurance may cover these patient responsibilities, but will almost never duplicate Medicare insurance; a patient usually cannot collect twice for the same expense. Major medical insurance is usually $50 deductible.

Most health insurance policies also have maximum limits and may pay only a percentage of the costs. One major medical policy, for example, will pay 80% of the covered expenses not included in a standard health insurance policy, up to a maximum of $10,000 during a calendar year or $50,000 during a lifetime.

Problems

1. In 1980, Medicare hospital insurance paid for up to 60 days of a hospital stay, except for the first $180. If the hospital costs are $153.50 a day, how much of the bill for four days stay would Medicare pay?

   $_____

2. a. For premiums of $9.60 a month, Medicare will pay 80% of "reasonable" charges by doctors, after the first $60. How much of doctors' bills of $2,728 would Medicare pay in one year? b. How much would the patient pay in that year, in premiums and doctors' bills?

   a. $_____

   b. $_____

3. A major medical policy is offered, with $750 deductible, up to a maximum of $45,000 per person at these rates: age 20, $112.50; age 30, $121.00; age 40, $153.70; age 50, $210.40. A spouse may be covered at a premium of

80% of the insured's premium; one child for $35.60; two or more children for $61.60. What would be paid in premiums for a 40-year-old woman, her husband, and three children?

$_____

4. a. According to the rates shown in Problem 3, what premiums would be paid for a 30-year-old man, his wife, and one child? b. What would the company pay on medical bills for the child of $2,135?

a. $_____

b. $_____

5. A woman, age 67, was hospitalized for 403 days, at $139 a day. Medicare paid for 60 days, after the first $180; all but $45 a day for the next 30 days; and all but $90 a day for another 60 days. Her other health insurance paid the rest of the charges for the first 150 days and all the charges for the next 215 days. Her major medical insurance paid 80% of the remainder of the bill, except for the first $50, up to a limit of $20,000.

How much was paid by Medicare? $_____

How much by the other health insurance? $_____

How much by the major medical insurance? $_____

How much by the patient? $_____

What was the total bill? $_____

Chapter Review

1. Using Table 11-1, find the annual premiums for each policy at each age:

Age	$5,000	$10,000	$20,000	$30,000
20	$_____	$_____	$_____	$ 84.00
25	$_____	$_____	$_____	88.50
30	$_____	$_____	$_____	96.30
35	$_____	$_____	$_____	114.00
40	$_____	$_____	$_____	155.40
45	$_____	$_____	$_____	223.50

2. What is the premium for a $15,000 25-year decreasing-term policy a. at age 20? b. at age 30? c. at age 40? (See Unit 1, Problem 4.)

a. $_____

b. $_____

c. $_____

3. Show the annual premiums for $1,000 and $20,000 straight life policies, using Table 11-3:

Age	$1,000	$2,000	$20,000	$30,000
20	$_____	$26.78	$_____	$319.20
25	$_____	30.44	$_____	374.10
30	$_____	35.12	$_____	444.30
35	$_____	41.18	$_____	535.20
40	$_____	49.06	$_____	653.40
45	$_____	59.32	$_____	807.30

4. To the nearest whole percent, what is the reduction in premiums at the new rates in Table 11-4, for men and women, compared to the old rates?

Age	Men	Women
20	_____%	_____%
25	_____%	_____%
30	_____%	_____%
35	_____%	_____%
40	_____%	_____%

5. Find the premiums for $1,000 policies ($\frac{1}{2}$ the $2,000 premium + $2) and for $30,000 policies (1.5 × $20,000 premium) for a. the 20-payment life and b. the life paid-up-at-65 policies shown in Tables 11-5 and 11-6.

Age	$1,000 Policies		$30,000 Policies	
20	a. $_____	b. $_____	a. $_____	b. $_____
25	$_____	$_____	$_____	$_____

Age	$1,000 Policies		$30,000 Policies	
30	a. $_____	b. $_____	a. $_____	b. $_____
35	$_____	$_____	$_____	$_____
40	$_____	$_____	$_____	$_____
45	$_____	$_____	$_____	$_____
50	$_____	$_____	$_____	$_____
55	$_____	$_____	$_____	$_____

6. Find the premiums for $1,000 20-year endowment and $1,000 endowment-at-age-65 policies for each age from Table 11-7, and in each case show the premium for an endowment-at-age-65 policy as a percentage of that for the 20-year policy. How do these percentages compare with those in Problems 1–7 in Unit 4?

Age	a. 20-Year Endowment	b. Endowment at Age 65	Ratio b/a
20	$_____	$_____	_____%
25	$_____	$_____	_____%
30	$_____	$_____	_____%
35	$_____	$_____	_____%
40	$_____	$_____	_____%
45	$_____	$_____	_____%
50	$_____	$_____	_____%

7. From the information in the chapter, find the annual premium at age 25 for $20,000 policies of each kind: straight life (Table 11-3); life paid-up-at-65; endowment at age 65; 20-payment life; 20-year endowment; 5-year term; and 20-year decreasing-term. Arrange the premiums from smallest to largest, then estimate the quarterly premium (26% of the annual premium) and the monthly premium (9% of the annual premium) for each.

Kind of Policy	Annual Premium	Quarterly Premium	Monthly Premium
_____	$_____	$_____	$_____
_____	$_____	$_____	$_____

Kind of Policy	Annual Premium	Quarterly Premium	Monthly Premium
————	$————	$————	$————
————	$————	$————	$————
————	$————	$————	$————
————	$————	$————	$————
————	$————	$————	$————

8. A woman bought a $10,000 straight life policy at age 20, paying annual premiums of $88.80. At age 35, she considered canceling the policy and taking the cash surrender value. a. How much had she paid in premiums? b. What was the cash surrender value? c. How much more would the cash surrender value be in five more years? d. How much more would she have paid in premiums?

a. $————   b. $————   c. $————   d. $————

9. A man aged 60 bought a $5,000 straight life policy, paying annual premiums of $277.15. At the same time, his 30-year-old son also bought a $5,000 policy, paying quarterly premiums of $20.25. a. Ten years later, how much had each paid in premiums? b. What was the cash surrender value of each? c. How much could each have borrowed (95% of c.s.v.) d. If each had made the maximum loan, how much would the immediate indemnity have been in case of death?

	Father	Son
a.	$————	$————
b.	$————	$————
c.	$————	$————
d.	$————	$————

10. A patient with medical insurance paid $15.30 a month in premiums and had doctors' bills of $1,484.50 in one year. a. How much would the insurance pay, at 80% of costs after the first $50? b. How much would the patient have paid altogether?

a. $————
b. $————

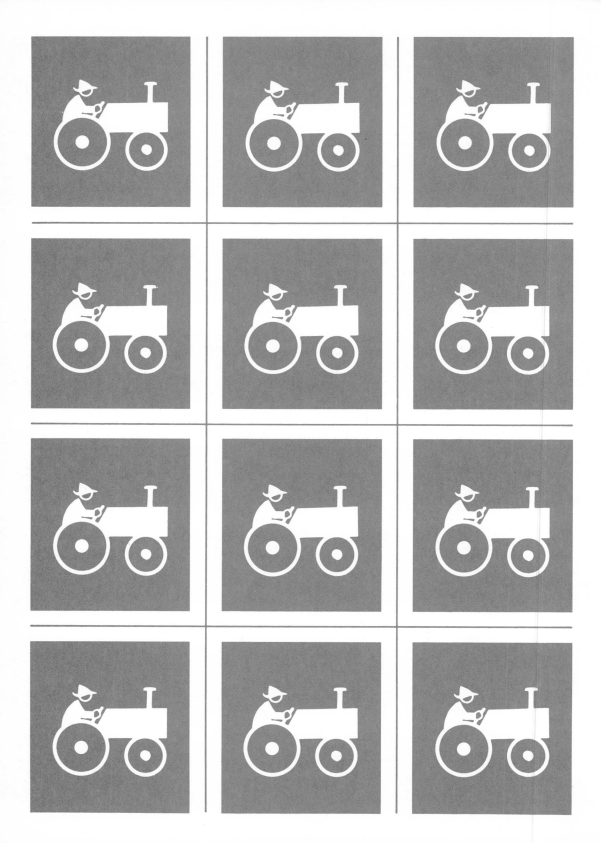

12
Taxes

Income taxes are levied against individuals, corporations, estates, and trusts by the United States government as well as by a majority of the states. Tax laws vary among the states but are generally patterned after the U.S. Internal Revenue Code.

An individual's income and filing status generally determine whether or not an annual income tax return must be filed.

An annual return must be filed if, for example:

You Were		Your Income Was at Least
Single (under 65)	and	$3,300
Married (filing joint return and both under 65)	and	5,400
Married (filing joint return and both over 65)	and	7,400
Self-Employed	and	400

Although your income may be less than the above amounts, you may still have to file. You must file, for example, if you owe Social Security taxes on tips you earned or if you owe no tax and you want a refund of the income tax that has been withheld from your pay.

Through the payroll-withholding taxes deducted from their wages, most employed persons will have already paid some, all, or more than their required annual income tax. The tax withheld is determined from federal withholding-tax tables similar to Table 12-1. The amount of tax withheld is based on the payroll period, filing status, wages earned, and number of withholding allowances claimed.

Table 12-1. *Partial Withholding Table for Federal Income Tax*
Weekly Payroll Period—Married Persons

If Wages Are		Number of Allowances Claimed Is					
At Least	But Less Than	0	1	2	3	4	5
		Amount Withheld					
$100	$105	$ 8.50	$ 5.60	$ 2.70	-0-	-0-	-0-
125	130	12.20	9.30	6.40	$ 3.50	$ .70	-0-
150	160	17.20	13.70	10.60	7.70	4.80	$ 1.90
200	210	26.20	22.70	19.20	15.80	12.30	9.40
300	310	47.50	43.00	39.00	34.90	30.90	26.90
400	410	73.00	67.60	62.30	57.70	53.10	48.50

Withholding allowances may be claimed as 0 (none) or for:
    a. Self (Taxpayer)   1
    b. Spouse (Taxpayer's)   1
    c. Dependents   1 each
    d. Blindness (of Self and/or Spouse)   1 extra
    e. Age (of Self and/or Spouse 65 or Over)   1 extra

If you have income such as interest or dividends in addition to your salary, you may wish to claim zero withholding allowances in order that a larger deduction will be made. Your deductions will then more nearly approximate the actual tax you will have to pay.

Example. Shelley Roe is married, and she and her husband care for one foster child. She earns $307.87 a week and claims three exemptions. How much is withheld from her paycheck each week for federal tax? How much has been withheld at the end of a year? (See Table 12-1.)
$307.87 is more than $300 but less than $310, so the deduction is $34.90 each week.
$34.90 × 52 = $1,814.80 Federal Tax Withheld for the Year

In addition to income taxes, Shelley is required to have social security taxes withheld (FICA Taxes).

1 Control number 321	ᘖᘖᘖ	2 Employer's State number 227	For Official Use Only

3 Employer's name, address, and ZIP code	4 Sub-total ☐ Cor-rection ☐ Void ☐	Make No Entry Here
Full River Stage 821 7th Street Anywhere, SD 57213	7 Employer's identification number 46-0348215	See Note on the Back of Copy D

10 Employee's social security number 081-72-9904	11 Federal income tax withheld $1,814.80	12 Wages, tips, other compensation $16,009.24	13 FICA tax withheld $981.24	14 Total FICA wages $16,009.24
15 Employee's name (first, middle, last) Shelley R. Roe		16 Pension plan coverage? Yes/No No	17 *	18 FICA tips -0-

21 East 49th
Anywhere, SD 57213

19 Employee's address and ZIP code

Wage and Tax Statement   **1978**   Copy A For Social Security Administration
*See Instructions for Forms W-2 and W-2P and back of Copy D

Form **W-2**   ▼   Department of the Treasury—Internal Revenue Service

Fig. 12-1   Wage and Tax Statement

At the end of the year, her employer prepares a *W-2 form,* reporting total wages and the federal and social security taxes withheld.

There are a number of terms that must be understood before an individual's federal tax can be determined:

a.   *Gross Income:* Every income tax return begins with gross income, a person's total income, which, except for some receipts specifically exempted, must be reported.

b.   *Deductions from Gross Income:* Business and certain other expenses may be deducted from gross income.

c.   *Adjusted Gross Income:* The amount after losses or business expenses are deducted is called adjusted gross income.

d.   *Zero Bracket Amount:* The lowest bracket in each of the tax-rate schedules has a tax rate of zero. For example, if you are married and file a joint return, the tax on $3,400 of taxable income is zero.

e.   *Excess Itemized Deductions:* Certain expenditures for such purposes as charity, interest, real-estate taxes, and medical expenses in excess of the zero bracket amount may be deducted from adjusted gross income.

f.   *Tax-Table Income:* Adjusted gross income less excess deductions.

g.   *Exemption Deduction:* A taxpayer is entitled to a $1,000 deduction from adjusted gross income for each exemption claimed.

h.   *Taxable Income:* Adjusted Gross Income − Excess Deductions − Exemption Deduction = Taxable Income

Computing the tax: The amount of tax may be determined from a *tax table,* if the tax-table income is less than $20,000 for a single person or $40,000 for a married couple filing jointly, or may be found by a tax computation, using a tax-rate *schedule.* The tax tables automatically allow for exemptions.

Table 12-2. Partial Tax Table for 1979
Single or Married, Three Exemptions

If Adjusted Gross Income Is		And You Are	
At Least	But Less Than	Single, Not Head of Household	Married, Filing Joint Return
$ 7,400	$ 7,450	$ 319	$ 144
9,600	9,650	716	474
11,550	11,600	1,088	806
12,800	12,850	1,561	1,031
16,000	16,050	2,092	1,640
18,800	18,850	2,853	2,228

Example. What is Shelley Roe's total tax, if her adjusted gross income is the same as her total income and she has no excess deductions? (Her husband has no income, and they file a joint return.) Will she pay more or receive a refund? How much?

$$\$307.87 \times 52 = \$16,009.24 \text{ Total Income}$$

$16,009.24 is more than $16,000 but less than $16,050, so the tax is $1,640.

$$\$1,814.80 - \$1,640 = \$174.80 \text{ Refund}$$

The tax computation calls for subtracting the excess itemized deductions and the total exemptions amount from the adjusted gross income to find the taxable income. The tax is then found from the tax-rate schedule shown in Table 12-3.

Table 12-3. Partial Tax-Rate Schedule for 1979
When Tax Tables Are Not Used
Married Taxpayers Filing Joint Return

Taxable Income		Tax on Column 1	Percent on Excess
Over	But Not Over		
$ 3,400	$ 5,500	-0-	14
5,500	7,600	$ 294	16
7,600	11,900	630	18
11,900	16,000	1,404	21
16,000	20,200	2,265	24
20,200	24,600	3,273	28
24,600	29,900	4,505	32
29,900	35,200	6,201	37

Example. If Shelley Roe has excess itemized deductions of $2,590, what tax should she pay for the year?

Adjusted Gross Income	$16,009.24
− Excess Itemized Deductions	− 2,590.00
Tax-Table Income	$13,419.24
− Personal Exemptions (3 × $1,000)	− 3,000.00
Taxable Income	$10,419.24
Tax on $7,600	$630.00
+ 18% of $2,819.24 ($10,419.24 − $7,600)	+ 507.46
Tax	$1,137.46

If Shelley lives in Delaware and her and her husband's taxable income is the same for state as for federal purposes, they would pay a state income tax based on the following tax-rate schedule:

Tax Rate Schedule for Delaware
Married and Filing Joint Return

If Taxable Income Is:

Over	But Not Over	Your Tax Is
$5,000	$ 6,000	$170 + 6.6% of Amount Over $5,000
$6,000	$ 8,000	$236 + 7.7% of Amount Over $6,000
$8,000	$20,000	$390 + 8.8% of Amount Over $8,000

Example.

Taxable Income	$10,419	
Tax on $8,000		$390.00
Tax on Excess ($2,419 × .088)		+ 212.87
State Tax		$602.87

If, however, they live in Georgia and their state taxable income is the same as their federal taxable income, the state tax would be based on the schedule below:

Tax Rate Schedule for Georgia
Married and Filing Joint Return

If Taxable Income Is:

Over	But Not Over	Your Tax Is
$ 5,000	$ 7,000	$110 + 4% on Amount Over $5,000
$ 7,000	$10,000	$190 + 5% on Amount Over $7,000
$10,000	—	$340 + 6% on Amount Over $10,000

Example.   Taxable Income $10,419

Tax on $10,000 $340.00

Tax on Excess ($419 × .06)   + 25.14

State Tax $365.14

Problems

1. Find the amount withheld for Social Security, at 6.13%, and the amount withheld for federal tax:

Weekly Wage		Withheld for Fed. Tax	Withheld for Soc. Sec.
a. $127.15	Wife, Claiming 0 Exemptions	$_____	$_____
b. $401.28	Married Man, 3 Exemptions	$_____	$_____
c. $307.60	Married Woman, 4 Exemptions	$_____	$_____
d. $156.30	Married Man, 5 Exemptions	$_____	$_____

2. How many total exemptions are allowed on the joint return of Jon Sampson, aged 68, and his wife, 67, who is blind?

_____

3. How many exemptions may be claimed by a married couple, both under 65, with whom two children and a dependent father live?

_____

4. Mr. and Mrs. Walter May, both under 65, have an adjusted gross income of $22,810.50. They have two children. What is their tax, if filed jointly?

$_____

5. Mr. and Mrs. Leopold Olson have $25,312.50 income from their business. They also earned $2,321 in interest, $3,350 in rent, and $2,900 in book royalties. They have business expenses of $7,233 and excess itemized deductions of $2,750. They claim four exemptions and file a joint return. a. What is their adjusted gross income? b. What is their taxable income? c. What is their tax?

a. $_____

b. $_____

c. $_____

6. Mr. and Mrs. Hasegawa have wages of $28,233.50 and itemize their deductions as follows:

Contributions	$780
Mortgage Interest	$2,320
Real Estate Tax	$1,150
Other	$300

They have three children; one child is blind. a. What is their total deduction? b. What is the total of their excess itemized deductions? c. What is the dollar amount of their exemption? do. What is their taxable income on a joint return? e. What is their tax (Use Table 12-3.)?

a. $_____

b. $_____

c. $_____

d. $_____

e. $_____

7. Mr. and Mrs. Martinez Rodriquez, who live in Delaware, have an adjusted gross income of $20,970 and excess itemized deductions of $2,133. A dependent sister lives with them. a. If $3,000.40 was withheld from their paychecks for the year, what is their tax-table income? b. What is their taxable income? c. What is their federal income tax liability on a joint return? d. Will they receive a refund or owe additional federal tax? How much? e. If the Delaware tax is based upon federal taxable income and $1,200 was withheld from their paychecks for state taxes, how much would they get back from or owe to the State of Delaware?

a. $_____

b. $_____

c. $_____

d. _____ $_____

e. $_____

8. Edward Kerrigan is married and earns $400.25 a week; his wife is blind. a. If they live in Georgia, how much income tax will be withheld from Ed's paycheck each week? b. How much social security tax will be withheld from his paycheck each week, at 6.13%? c. What will be the total federal

income tax withheld for the year? d. How much social security tax will be withheld for the year? e. How much will he take home each week? f. How many weeks' pay is withheld from his paycheck for federal tax? g. For social security? h. For all purposes?

a. $_____

b. $_____

c. $_____

d. $_____

e. $_____

f.   _____

g.   _____

h.   _____

9.   a. Using the data from Problem 8, determine Edward Kerrigan's taxable income. He has $700 excess itemized deductions. b. What would his state tax liability be?

a. $_____

b. $_____

10.   How many exemptions are allowed for a divorced woman with three children who provides all the income for the household, if they all live with her mother?

_____

12.2   PROPERTY TAXES

Such governmental units as counties, towns, and cities use the funds received from taxes levied on *real* and *personal* property as a major revenue source. In return for taxes paid, the local resident receives many valuable services. Schools, parks, swimming pools, police and fire protection, and other public services are provided from the tax dollars collected.

The dollar amount of tax revenue needed each year by a governmental unit depends on the planned expenditures. A plan setting forth the projected expenditures is called a *budget.* Once the budget is completed and approved, the tax dollars to be collected are known. Determining the tax to be paid by each individual property owner generally requires that:

a.   An *assessor* visit and inspect the property for the purpose of comparing it with other property of a similar nature and value.

b.   An *assessed value,* usually a percentage of the fair market value, be assigned to the property.

c.   The *tax budget,* after reduction for revenue from other sources, be divided by the total of all assessed values to find the *tax rate.*

Example.

Assessment List of Real Property City of Sioux Falls, South Dakota Appraised Value—Tax Not Calculated on This Value Below		
Residence Structure	Land Only	Total Real Property
$45,000	$7,500	$52,500

What is the assessed value for tax purposes if real estate is assessed at 48% of its appraised value?

$$\$52,500 \times 48\% = \$25,200$$

Example. What is the *tax rate* if the tax budget is $8,159,593, other revenues are estimated at $478, 251, and total assessed value on property is $225,921,800?

$$\begin{array}{ll} \text{Total Tax Budget} & \$8,159,593 \\ - \text{ Other Revenue} & - \ \ 478,251 \\ \text{Balance} & \$7,681,342 \end{array}$$

$$\$7,681,342 \div \$225,921,800 = .034 \text{ per Dollar}$$

Many times, tax rates are expressed in other ways. The .034 tax rate may be expressed as:

a.   Percentage   3.4% of Assessed Value
b.   Mills   34 Mills per Dollar (1 mill = $\frac{1}{10}$ cent)
c.   Cents   3.4 Cents per Dollar
d.   Dollars $3.40 per Hundred Dollars
e.   Dollars $34.00 per Thousand Dollars

After the tax rate has been announced, the property owner can determine the property tax by multiplying the tax rate by the assessed value.

Example.

Real-Estate Tax for 1979

Tax Receipt#	Mill Rate	Valuation	Total	First Installment	Second Installment
3,188	34	$25,200	$856.80	$428.40	$428.40

Valuation	$25,200
× Per Dollar	× .034
Tax	$856.80

(34 mills = 3.4 cents = .034 dollar)

Problems

Group 1

Find the assessed value and property tax for each of the following:

	True Value	Percentage of Valuation	Assessed Value	Tax Rate	Annual Tax
1.	$ 35,000	37%	$_____	24 Mills	$_____
2.	29,000	29%	$_____	$2.60 per Hundred	$_____
3.	85,000	34%	$_____	23.8 Mills	$_____
4.	120,000	66%	$_____	2.01 Percent	$_____
5.	250,000	45%	$_____	$23.80 per Thousand	$_____
6.	84,000	37%	$_____	36 Mills	$_____
7.	91,000	100%	$_____	1.05 Percent	$_____
8.	150,000	56%	$_____	27.83 Mills	$_____
9.	350,000	28%	$_____	$2.50 per Hundred	$_____
10.	700,500	31%	$_____	42 Mills	$_____

Group 2

1. The taxable property in a city is assessed at $51,482,000. The tax budget is $1,582,000. Other revenue is expected to be $228,000. a. What amount

must be collected from property tax? b. What is the tax rate, to 5 places? c. What is the rate per $1,000? d. What is the property tax on real estate valued at $75,300 and assessed at 53% of value?

a. $_____

b. _____

c. $_____

d. $_____

2. The total tax budget for the city of Canton is $3,253,200. If the tax rate is 34.5 mills, what is the total assessed value of Canton taxable property?

$_____

3. The school-tax rate is $2.84 per hundred. If property is valued at $87,000 and assessed at 37%, what will be the amount of school tax?

$_____

4. The Jones family paid a tax bill of $872.80 in their city. The tax rate was $3.16 per $100 of assessed value. What is the assessed value of their property?

$_____

5. If the county requires $893,000 of tax revenue from property assessed at $14,000,000, what should the tax rate per $100 be?

$_____

6. The assessed value of property is $25,300. If the tax assessor uses a 23% assessment, what is the assumed full and true value of the property?

$_____

12.3 SALES TAX

Governmental units use the *sales tax* as another major source of revenue. The items covered and the sales-tax rates vary, but generally, each time consumers make purchases, they pay a sales tax. For ease and accuracy, a sales-tax rate chart is used to help the clerk determine the tax to be collected. Many stores have cash registers that calculate the sales tax on each purchase electronically. An example of a partial 4% sales-tax rate chart is presented below. The rate chart shows the correct amount of tax to charge when the purchase is a fraction of a dollar.

Example.

4% Sales Tax

Amount	Tax	Amount	Tax	Amount	Tax
.13–.37	.01	1.13–1.37	.05	2.13–2.37	.09
.38–.62	.02	1.38–1.62	.06	2.38–2.62	.10
.63–.87	.03	1.63–1.87	.07	2.63–2.87	.11
.88–1.12	.04	1.88–2.12	.08	2.88–3.12	.12

On a purchase amounting to $0.67, the tax is rounded up to 3¢; on a purchase of $2.40, the tax is 10¢; and on $2.90, the tax is 12¢. Taxes are calculated on the total dollar value of each sale, not on each separate item of merchandise.

Problems

1. Calculate the sales tax and total cost for each of the following:

	Retail Price	Tax Rate	Tax	Total Cost
a.	$ 5.88	4%	$_____	$_____
b.	10.75	5%	$_____	$_____
c.	27.34	6%	$_____	$_____
d.	60.18	4%	$_____	$_____
e.	7.10	5%	$_____	$_____

2. If a city collects 4% sales tax on all purchases except food, what is the sales tax on this purchase?

Sugar	$1.10	Paper Towels	$ .87
Meat	4.23	Shoelaces	.25
Greeting Card	.50	Cheese	1.33

   $_____

3. What would be the sales tax in Problem #2 if a 6% sales tax were collected on all items?

   $_____

4. What is the sales tax at 6% on the purchase of the following?

Desk	$279.42	Light Bulbs	$ 0.94
Lamp	79.83	Blotter	4.83
Desk Set	31.93	Chair	29.42

$_____

5. A city levies a sales tax of 2¢ on purchases up to $.34, 3¢ on purchases between $.35 and $.69, and 4¢ on purchases of $.70 to $.99, with 5¢ on each whole dollar. What is the sales tax on each of the following purchases:

Amount of Purchases	Sales Tax
$ .83	$_____
1.29	$_____
3.47	$_____
2.50	$_____
7.21	$_____

12.4 OTHER TAXES

In addition to real estate, sales, and income taxes, there are federal, state, and sometimes local *excise taxes* on purchases of certain goods and services, such as tobacco, liquor, gasoline, room occupancy in hotels and motels, air transportation, telephone service, and stock transfers, in addition to special licenses and customs duties on imports.

A tax used in Europe, which has been the subject of discussion recently in the United States, is a *value-added tax*. The following shows how a 1% value-added tax is calculated for one specific item:

Production Level	Selling Price	Value Added	1% Tax
a. Ore in Ground	-0-	-0-	-0-
b. Mining Ore	$20	$20	.20
c. Processing Ore	35	15	.15
d. Pan for Cooking	45	10	.10
e. Distribution	50	5	.05
f. Consumer Price	55	5	.05
Totals		$55	$0.55

A value-added tax becomes similar in effect to a general sales tax. Notice that a sales tax on the consumer price of $55 at 1% would generate the identical 55¢ in tax revenue.

Problems

1. Your telephone bill of $18.93 is subject to a federal tax of 4% and a sales tax of 5%. What is your final bill?

    $_____

2. Your gasoline cost is $1.899 a gallon, including 15% taxes. What is the cost before taxes?

    $_____

3. Calculate the value-added tax based on the following production levels and prices:

	Production Level	Selling Price	Value Added	1% Tax
a.	Iron Ore in Ground	-0-	$_____	$_____
b.	Mining of Ore	$15	$_____	$_____
c.	Processing	35	$_____	$_____
d.	Delivery	40	$_____	$_____
e.	Metal Chair	75	$_____	$_____
f.	Distribution	85	$_____	$_____
g.	Consumer Price	97.50	$_____	$_____
	Totals		$_____	$_____

4. A telephone bill totals $21.75, including a sales tax of 5% and excise tax of 9%. What was the amount before taxes?

    $_____

5. Make a list of all the items you purchased in the past year that include some form of tax in the purchase price.

Chapter Review

1. Mary White is single, claims three exemptions, and has an adjusted gross income of $12,811. If she had $1,500 withheld from her paycheck for federal tax, would she owe tax or receive a refund? How much?

    $_____

2. If the tax rate is 45 mills on the dollar, what is the tax rate per $100?

$_____

3. Mr. and Mrs. Nate Millet have property assessed at 48% of its true value of $58,000. The area tax-rate schedule includes: county, $20.15; school, $13.81; city, $11.89; and water, $1.37. The rates are based on each $1,000 of assessed valuation. What is the Millets' total tax?

$_____

4. Walter Schneeman operates a business with a gross income of $87,940. His business expenses amount to $53,173. He has other income in the form of interest and rent of $13,500. Rental expenses were $7,941. His excess itemized deductions were $8,391, and he claims five exemptions, including himself. Use the tax-rate schedule, Table 12-3, to find his tax liability for the year.

$_____

5. Ruth and Jack Martin have a total income of $21,343, claim three exemptions, and have excess itemized deductions of $127. a. What will their federal tax be if they file a joint return? b. If they live in Delaware, what will their state tax be?

a. $_____

b. $_____

6. If a city requires a tax revenue of $956,160 from property in the city with an assessed valuation of $19,920,000, what tax rate per $100 should be established?

$_____

7. What are the total exemptions for Wayne Poppenga, aged 68, his wife, 66, who is blind, and his dependent sister, aged 67?

$_____

8. Federal excise taxes collected on automobiles amounted to $2,100 million. If total excise taxes collected amounted to $14,510 million, what percentage of the total were the automobile excise taxes?

_____%

9. Joyce Sikorski, a widow, lives in Georgia with her five children. She earns $401.12 per week, and her excess deductions amount to $483. a. What is her taxable income? b. What is her Georgia state tax?

   a. $_____

   b. $_____

10. If a city charges a sales tax of 1¢ on purchases of $.09 to $.24, 2¢ on purchases of $.25 to $.41, 3¢ on purchases of $.42 to $.58, 4¢ on purchases of $.59 to $.74, 5¢ on purchases of $.75 to $.91, and 6¢ on purchases of $.92 to $1.08, what would be the sales tax on a purchase of $.89. b. Of $4.29? c. Of $2.03? d. What is the tax rate?

   a. $_____

   b. $_____

   c. $_____

   d. _____%

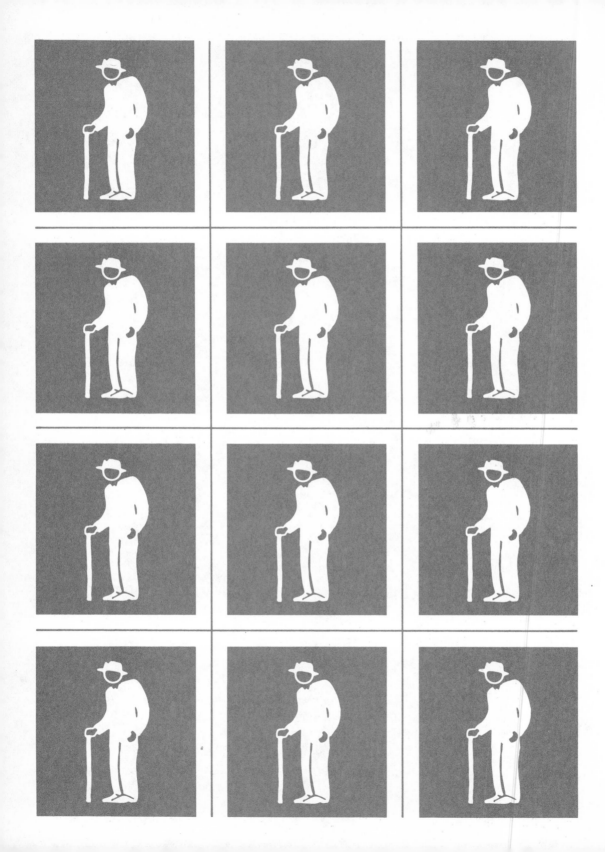

13

Pensions and Social Security

When a person retires or becomes disabled, it is important that provisions have been made for meeting the costs of living, including especially housing, food, clothing, and medical expenses. Insurance programs like those in Chapter 11 are often involved in these plans. Pension plans and Social Security provisions will be discussed in this chapter.

13.1 DEVELOPING A PENSION FUND

Corporations, unions, cities, states, the federal government, associations of professional workers, and other organizations develop pension plans for their employees or members. These plans vary a great deal, some requiring contributions from the employees or members, others not. Any good plan requires that funds be set aside and invested prudently to build an amount sufficient to pay pension obligations to eligible persons.

If you are not covered by a company or organization pension plan, you can plan to fund or supplement your retirement income by setting up an *Income Retirement Account* (IRA). The part of your income which you deposit in your IRA will be free of immediate income taxes up to $1,500 or 15% of your income each year, whichever is smaller. One advantage in having the special retirement account is that you will pay income taxes during your retirement years, when you get this money back. Your income taxes then will probably be less, because you will have more exemptions (2 instead of 1 after age 65) and because your total income will be less, qualifying you for lower income-tax rates.

If you are self-employed, you can set up a retirement plan for yourself under the Keough Act. Under this plan, you can contribute 15% of your earned income for a year, but not more than $7,500 in any taxable year, to a retirement account. Again, the amounts contributed plus the interest accumulated are not taxable until the payments are received later, usually in the form of a pension.

Table 13-1. Amount of Annuity of $1 per Period at Compound Interest

Periods	1¹/₂%	3%	4%	6%
25	30.063024	36.459264	41.645908	54.864512
50	73.682828	112.796867	152.667084	290.335905
70	122.363753	230.594064	364.290459	967.932170
100	228.803043	607.287733	1237.623705	5638.368059

Example. Suppose at age 40 you started to deposit $300 a quarter in an IRA carrying interest at 6%, compounded quarterly. How much would you have in the account at the end of 25 years, when you reach 65? This is a problem of determining the amount of an annuity of $300 per period at 1¹/₂% (6% ÷ 4) interest per period. Table 13-1 shows that the amount of an annuity of $1 per period for 100 periods (25 × 4) at 1¹/₂% per period is $228.803043. The total amount of $300 per quarter for 100 quarters at 6% per year compounded quarterly would be:

$$300 \times \$228.803043 = \$68,640.91$$

Problems

1. Janet Burns plans to deposit $750 every six months in an IRA for 25 years, after which she plans to retire. If she can earn interest at the rate of 6%, compounded semiannually, how much will be in the account after 25 years?

   $ _____

2. James Cass sets up a Keough plan which calls for a deposit of $7,500 a year until he retires, 25 years later. How much will be available to him at that time if he can earn 6%, compounded annually?

   $ _____

3. Suppose you plan to retire in 35 years and wish to develop your own pension plan. How much would you have available for your pension if you deposited $500 in an IRA every six months, if you could earn 8% per year, compounded semiannually?

   $ _____

13.2   DETERMINING PERIODIC PENSION RECEIPTS

After you build a fund to be used for a pension, the question becomes, "How much of a pension will it buy?" In the example given in Unit 1, the pension fund amounted to $68,640.91. Let us assume that you wish to receive a fixed amount every month for 10 years, at which time the fund will be depleted. Let us also assume that the rate of interest now available on the fund is 6% per year, compounded monthly: 6% per year ÷ 12 = $\frac{1}{2}$% per month. Table 13-2 tells us how much $1 will buy per month for 10 years, or 120 periods. You can see that $1 will buy $0.011102 per month for 120 months at $\frac{1}{2}$%, compounded monthly. Your arithmetic problem is simply:

$$\$68,640.91 \times .011102 = \$762.05 \text{ Monthly Pension Receipt}$$

Table 13-2. Periodical Payment of Annuity When Present Value Is $1

Periods	$\frac{1}{2}$%	$\frac{7}{12}$%	$\frac{3}{4}$%	1%
96	0.013141	0.013634	0.014650	0.016253
100	0.012732	0.013227	0.014250	0.015866
120	0.011102	0.011611	0.012668	0.014347
144	0.009759	0.010284	0.011380	0.013134
150	0.009492	0.010022	0.011128	0.012900

No payments would be made beyond 10 years. If you died before the 10 years elapsed, your beneficiaries would continue to receive the pension payments until the end of the 10 years.

The pension plan could also be set up to provide pension receipts each month until death. The computations involve life-expectancy tables. The formulas are more complicated than we can deal with here, but the amount that can be received each month per $1,000 of present value in a pension fund can be determined by questioning those who administer the fund. One retirement plan, for example, pays $94 annually per $1,000 in the pension fund for men and $83 per $1,000 for women who retire at the age of 65; the difference is accounted for by the fact that women, on the average, live longer than men. In the example, each year $68,640.91 would return:

$$\frac{\$68,640}{\$\ 1,000} \times \$94 = 68.640 \times \$94 = \$6,452.16 \text{ for Men}$$

$$\frac{\$68,640}{\$\ 1,000} \times \$83 = 68.640 \times \$83 = \$5,697.12 \text{ for Women}$$

Dividing each figure by 12 gives the approximate monthly receipt:

$6,452.16 ÷ 12 = $537.68 for Men

$5,697.12 ÷ 12 = $474.76 for Women

These amounts will vary, depending on which of several life-expectancy tables is used.

Problems

1. Suppose that at the time of your retirement you have accumulated $82,000 in a retirement account. a. How much will you receive per month for 12 years, if you are able to buy a retirement annuity at the rate of 7% per year, compounded monthly? b. Over the 12 years, how much will you actually receive? c. How much of this represents interest.

    a. $ _____

    b. $ _____

    c. $ _____

2. Sam Davis has accumulated $94,000 in a Keough-plan retirement account. How much can he expect to receive per month for 150 months, if the account earns 9% interest per year, compounded monthly?

    $ _____

3. Approximately how much per month will Sam Davis in Problem 2 receive for life, if he can buy a life annuity which will pay $88 per $1,000 for each year until he dies?

    $ _____

4. Nancy Barth has $58,000 in an IRA to supplement her retirement income. How much can she expect to receive per month for 8 years, if the account earns interest at the rate of 12% per year, compounded monthly?

    $ _____

5. Approximately how much per month would Nancy in Problem 4 receive for life, if she can buy a life annuity for $86 per $1,000 for each year until death?

    $ _____

13.3   FINANCING SOCIAL SECURITY

The funding of Social Security retirement and other benefits is not the same as building an IRA or Keough plan fund. During the years they work, employees, their employers, and self-employed persons make Social Security contributions at rates prescribed by Congress. These funds are used only to pay the benefits to the more than 33 million eligible people and to pay the administrative costs of the program. When today's workers' earnings stop or are reduced because of retirement, death, or disability, benefits will be paid to them from contributions by people in covered employment and self-employment at that time.

Part of the contributions goes for hospital insurance under Medicare, so workers will have help in paying their hospital bills when they become eligible. The Medicare medical insurance is financed by premiums paid by the people who have enrolled for this protection and by amounts contributed by the federal government.

Employed people's Social Security contribution is deducted each payday and sent, with an equal contribution from their employers, to the Internal Revenue Service. When people are self-employed and earn more than $400 a year, they pay their Social Security tax along with their income tax. In 1978, rates on earnings up to a maximum of $17,700 for 1978, $22,900 for 1979, $25,900 for 1980, and $29,700 for 1981 were set, with the rates shown on this schedule:

Years	Employees & Employers (Each)			Self-Employed People		
	A	B	Total	A	B	Total
1978	5.05%	1.00%	6.05%	7.10%	1.00%	8.10%
1979–1980	5.08%	1.05%	6.13%	7.05%	1.05%	8.10%
1981	5.35%	1.30%	6.65%	8.00%	1.30%	9.30%
1982–1984	5.40%	1.30%	6.70%	8.05%	1.30%	9.35%
1985	5.70%	1.35%	7.05%	8.55%	1.35%	9.90%

"A" denotes contributions for retirement, survivors, and disability insurance; "B" is for hospital insurance.

Example. During each quarter of 1979, R. Burns earned $6,500. How much should Burns have contributed to Social Security during the first quarter? How much should his employer have contributed? How much should each have contributed for the other quarters of 1979? What part of the total was for hospital insurance?

The first-quarter tax was $6,500 × .0613 = $398.45. The employer paid the same amount.

The contributions for the second and third quarters were the same: $398.45 each. During the fourth quarter, however, the maximum of $22,900 was reached. Therefore, fourth-quarter payments were on:

$22,900 − (3 × $6,500) = $22,900 − $19,500 = $3,400
Fourth-quarter payments were $3,400 × .0613 = $208.42
(3 × $398.45) + $208.42 = $1,195.35 + $208.42 = $1,403.77 Total
$22,900 × .0105 = $240.45 for Hospital Insurance

Problems

1. Mary Garcia's salary for each quarter of 1980 was $7,240. How much should have been deducted from her pay for Social Security during the fourth quarter?

   $ _____

2. The Moore Distributing Company has a $268,520 payroll covered by Social Security for the first quarter of 1981. How much should the company contribute to the government as its share of Social Security taxes?

   $ _____

3. Robert Benson earned $6,280.80 in the first quarter of 1980 while self-employed. How much should he have paid in Social Security taxes?

   $ _____

4. In one quarter of 1980, the Maynard Company paid $14,648.20 to the federal government for the Social Security tax. How much of this was for hospital insurance?

   $ _____

5. a. If Robert Benson earns $6,280.80 in the first quarter of 1981 as a self-employed person, what should he pay for hospital insurance? b. What total amount should he pay for Social Security?

   a. $ _____

   b. $ _____

13.4   DETERMINING "AVERAGE YEARLY EARNINGS"

The monthly benefits received from Social Security depend on the *"average yearly earnings"* during the period covered. Persons born in 1930 or later will need to count 35 years of service in determining the average, even though in some years, they may have had no earnings. A person who has more than 35 years of covered work would count only the highest 35 years in earnings.

Persons born before 1930 need to count fewer years in their average. For example:

Year of Birth	Years needed	Year of Birth	Years Needed
1915	21	1920	26
1916	22	1925	31
1918	24	1930 and later	35

The maximum earnings per year that can be counted are:

1951–1954	$3,600	1972	$ 9,000	1977	$16,500
1955–1958	4,200	1973	10,800	1978	17,700
1959–1965	4,800	1974	13,200	1979	22,900
1966–1967	6,600	1975	14,100	1980	25,900
1968–1971	7,800	1976	15,300	1981	29,700

To find your "average yearly earnings":

1. Add your earnings up to the maximum allowed for each year, beginning with 1951.

2. Divide by 35, if your birthday is 1930 or later; if you were born before 1930, divide by the number of years given for your year of birth. If you have more than the needed years of coverage when you retire, eliminate the lowest-paid years until you have the correct total.

    If you become disabled and are qualified, you will receive the same monthly payment that you would get if you were retiring at 65. If you become disabled before you are 24, you need credit for $1\frac{1}{2}$ years of work before you became disabled. If you are between 24 and 31, you must have credit for half the years between your 21st birthday and the time you became disabled. At 31 or later, you generally need credit for at least 5 out of the 10 preceding years.

"Average yearly earnings" are rounded to the nearest dollar.

Example 1. John Jacobs retired at age 62 in 1980. His annual covered earnings since 1951 were:

1951–1955	$5,000 annually	1971–1972	$10,400 annually
1956–1960	6,000	1973	11,400
1961	3,000 (part-time)	1974–1978	12,600 annually
1962–1965	7,400	1979–1980	18,000
1966–1970	8,500		

What are his "average yearly earnings" for social security purposes? Since Mr. Jacobs was born in 1918, he needs to count only 24 years in his average. The 24 years of highest earnings and maximum earnings to be counted are:

1979–1980	2 ×	$18,000	=	$36,000
1974–1978	5 ×	12,600	=	63,000
1973	1 ×	10,800	=	10,800
1971–1972	1 ×	9,000		
	1 ×	7,800	=	16,800
1966–1970	3 ×	7,800		
	2 ×	6,600	=	36,600
1962–1965	4 ×	4,800	=	19,200
1956–1960	2 ×	4,800		
	3 ×	4,200	=	+ 22,200
24 Years				$204,600

The "average yearly earnings" are $204,600 ÷ 24 = $8,525

Example 2. Marjorie Owens, aged 29, became disabled in 1980. Her earnings since 1972 (the year she became 21) were: 1973, $7,500; 1974, $8,500; 1975, $10,200; 1976, $14,500; 1977, $16,800; 1978, $17,200; 1979, $18,000. (The year in which the disability occurs is not counted.) What were her "average yearly earnings"?

Year	Amount Credited
1973	$ 7,500
1974	8,500
1975	10,200
1976	14,500
1977	16,500
1978	17,200
1979	18,000
7 Years	$92,400

"Average yearly earnings," to the nearest dollar:

$92,400 ÷ 7 = $13,200

Problems

1. O. Otis, born in 1918, retired at the end of 1980. His earnings since 1951 were never less than $26,000 a year. Find his "average yearly earnings."

   $ _____

2. J. Mazzaro, aged 62, applied for Social Security benefits in 1980. Since 1950, her annual salary had been $8,400. Determine her "average yearly earnings," using 24 years for the coverage and not counting 1980.

   $ _____

3. G. Reid was disabled in 1980 at the age of 30. If his salary had increased $800 each year, from $7,500 in 1971, find his "average yearly earnings."

   $ _____

4. What are W. Lawrence's "average yearly earnings" if he retires in 1980 after the following record of annual income: 1951–1953, $5,600; 1954–1957, $6,300; 1958–1962, $7,800; 1963–1966, $8,500; 1967–1970, $9,800; 1971–1975, $10,700; 1976–1979, $15,800. Use 24 years for the average.

   $ _____

5. a. Which years are *not* used in determining the "average yearly earnings" of R. Moore, who retired in 1980 with the following annual income record? 1951–1956, $4,490; 1957, $5,010; 1958, $4,556; 1959, $5,224; 1960, $6,220; 1961–1966, $7,430; 1967-1972, $8,200; 1973–1979, $8,460. Use the best 22 years. b. Find her "average yearly earnings."

   a. _____

   b. $ _____

13.5 ESTIMATING SOCIAL SECURITY RETIREMENT AND DISABILITY BENEFITS

Once you know the "average yearly earnings," you can estimate the amount of the monthly cash payments you will receive when you retire under certain conditions or when you are disabled. The exact amount will be determined by Social Security employees. Note from the examples given that a qualified disabled worker is entitled to the same payment as a qualified retired worker at 65 or over. If you retire at 62, you will receive smaller monthly payments, since you will probably get more of them and have paid for three years fewer.

When a worker receives retirement benefits, some of the worker's dependents, including those who are college students, may also be eligible for payment. In case of the death of an eligible worker, certain members of the family may receive monthly benefits. In addition, a single lump-sum payment, usually $255, is made.

The amounts given in the examples below are increased periodically in an attempt to keep up with inflation:

Examples of Monthly Cash Payments

"Average Yearly Earnings"	$923 or Less	$3,000	$4,000	$5,000	$6,000	$8,000
Retired Worker at 65 or Disabled Under 65	$114.30	$236.40	$278.10	$322.50	$364.50	$453.10
Retired Worker at 62	91.50	189.20	222.50	258.00	291.60	362.50
Wife or Husband at 65	57.20	118.20	139.10	161.30	182.30	226.60
Wife or Husband at 62	42.90	88.70	104.40	121.00	136.80	170.00
Wife Under 65, 1 Child	57.20	125.00	197.20	272.60	304.20	339.80
Widow or Widower at 65	114.30	236.40	278.10	322.50	364.50	453.10
Widow or Widower at 60	81.80	169.10	198.90	230.60	260.70	324.00
Maximum Family Benefit	171.50	361.40	475.30	595.10	668.60	792.90

Example 1. Martha Jackson retired at age 62; her husband was also 62. What did the family receive each month if her "average yearly earnings" were $6,000?

$291.60   Martha Jackson's Benefit
$136.80   Husband's Benefit

$291.60 + $136.80 = $428.40, which is less than the maximum of $668.60, so they will receive $428.40.

Example 2. If Martha Jackson died, what lump-sum payment would Mr. Jackson receive? What would his monthly benefits be?

$255 Lump-Sum Death Benefit
$260.70 Monthly Widower's Benefit

Example 3. James Otice retired at 65 with "average yearly earnings" of $7,200. Estimate his monthly benefit.

$7,200 is $^3/_5$ of the way between $6,000 and $8,000, so his benefit would be about $^3/_5$ of the way between $364.50 and $453.10, or about $364.50 + $\dfrac{3(\$453.10 - \$364.50)}{5}$, or about $417.70.

Problems

1. Nancy Cole retired at 65 with "average yearly earnings" of $5,000. Her husband was 62 years of age. What was the total family benefit?

   $ _____

2. Alan Gordon became totally disabled at 37. He had a wife and one child. What were the family benefits if he qualified for Social Security benefits and his "average yearly earnings" were $6,000?

   $ _____

3. Herbert Hooper retired at 65, and his wife was 65. If his "average yearly earnings" were $4,500, about how much would each receive?

   Hooper $ _____

   Wife $ _____

4. Using the figures for "average yearly earnings" of $5,000 and $8,000, estimate the benefits at $6,000. How do these compare with the amounts shown for "average yearly earnings" of $6,000?

   _____

5. a. What is the relationship between the benefit for a worker retiring at age 65 and that for his wife, also 65? b. Is it the same at all levels? c. Is it the same as the corresponding relationship when both are aged 62?

   a. _____

   b. _____

   c. _____

6. Saul Chamsky is 62 and has "average yearly earnings" of $8,000. His wife is 59, and they have no dependent children. What monthly benefit would they receive if he retires now? What can they expect to receive if he retires in 3 years? In 6 years? During the next 10 years, how much would they receive under each plan, assuming that Mrs. Chamsky applies for her benefits as soon as possible? If both live, how much would they receive during the next 20 years, under each plan?

Benefit Now $ ⸺⸺⸺⸺

Benefit in 3 Years $ ⸺⸺⸺⸺

Benefit in 6 Years $ ⸺⸺⸺⸺

Amount Received in 10 Years

Retiring Now $ ⸺⸺⸺⸺

Retiring in 3 Years $ ⸺⸺⸺⸺

Retiring in 6 Years $ ⸺⸺⸺⸺

Amount Received in 20 Years

Retiring Now $ ⸺⸺⸺⸺

Retiring in 3 Years $ ⸺⸺⸺⸺

Retiring in 6 Years $ ⸺⸺⸺⸺

7. Edna Paulsen retires at age 65 with "average yearly earnings" of $6,000. Her husband, Karl, also 65, has "average yearly earnings" of $5,000. He must choose between receiving benefits on his own account or on hers. How much would he receive monthly on each?

His Account $ ⸺⸺⸺⸺

Her Account $ ⸺⸺⸺⸺

If Edna Paulsen should die at age 67, Karl might then apply to receive benefits on his wife's account. If this were granted, how much would he then receive monthly?

$ ⸺⸺⸺⸺

Chapter Review

1. In planning for his future retirement, Charles Evans decides to deposit $250 quarterly in an IRA paying interest at the rate of 6%, compounded quarterly. If he is able to follow through on this plan, how much will be in the account at the end of 25 years? Use Table 13-1.

   $ _____

2. Over the years, Bernice Booth has been able to accumulate $50,000 in a retirement account. If the $50,000 can be invested at 9%, compounded monthly, how much per month can Bernice expect to receive for 12 years? See Table 13-2.

   $ _____

3. In Problem 2, approximately how much would Bernice receive per month for life, if a life annuity paid her $88 per $1,000 each year until she died?

   $ _____

4. If your quarterly salary is $7,500, how much is deducted each quarter in 1980 for Social Security?

   1st Quarter $ _____

   2nd Quarter $ _____

   3rd Quarter $ _____

   4th Quarter $ _____

   How much will the company for which you work contribute for the year?

   $ _____

5. As a self-employed person, how much would you contribute to Social Security in 1980, if you earned $30,000 during the year?

   $ _____

6. If you contribute $2,097.90 in 1980 to Social Security as a self-employed person, how much of this is for hospital insurance?

   $ _____

7. Suppose you are disabled at the age of 27 in March, 1981, after working for 6 years and that you qualify for Social Security benefits. What would your "average annual earnings" be for Social Security purposes, if you earned $10,000 in 1975, $12,000 in 1976, $14,000 in 1977, $15,000 in 1978, $17,000 in 1979, and $18,500 in 1980?

    $ _____

8. If your father retired in 1980 at age 65 and had "average yearly earnings" of $6,500, approximately how much would he receive per month from Social Security? b. If he was 62, what would the amount be?

    a. $ _____

    b. $ _____

9. In 1980, Angela, who was 62 and had "average yearly earnings" of $3,500, planned to retire with her husband, who was 65 and had "average yearly earnings" of $8,000. a. Would it be better for her to use her own account or to qualify for benefits as his wife on her husband's account? b. How much per month is the difference?

    _____

    $ _____

10. Carol Paton has invested $750 every 6 months for 25 years in an IRA paying 8%, compounded semiannually. a. How much is in her account at the end of 25 years? b. Carol also qualifies for Social Security in 1980 at the age of 65. If her "average yearly earnings" are $8,000, how much will she get per month from Social Security? c. If Carol can get $87 per $1,000 per year from her IRA, what is the total amount per month, including Social Security, that she can expect to receive?

    a. $ _____

    b. $ _____

    c. $ _____

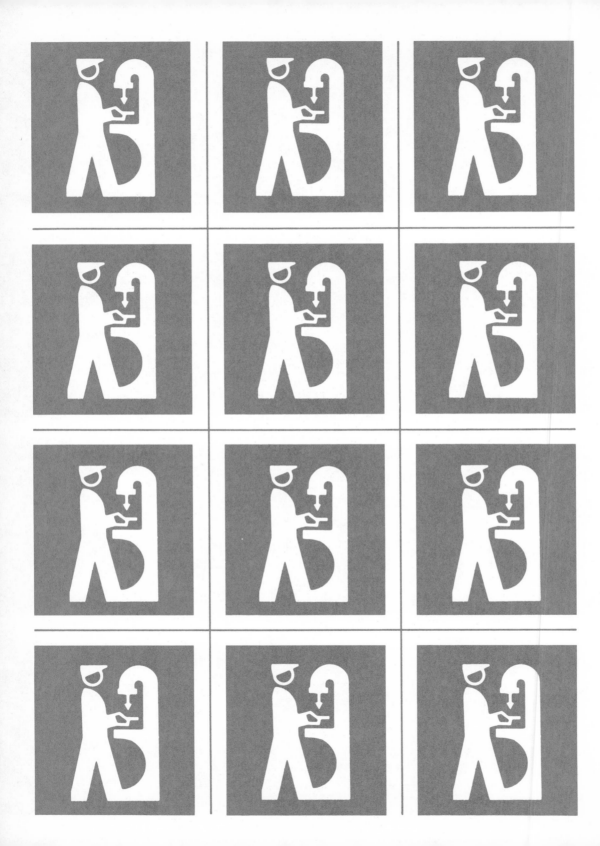

14

Payroll Mathematics

People are paid for the work they do on the bases of how long they work, what they produce, or how much they produce. If the basic element in the computation of pay is time worked, an hour, a day, a week, two weeks, a month, or even a year may be the unit of time used. Payment is made usually on a weekly, biweekly, or monthly basis. For hourly and piecework pay, the term *wages* is used. When the basic unit of time is a week or longer, the term *salary* is more common.

Pay for piecework or commission work is based on what is produced, whether a product or service. Additional incentives to produce are sometimes provided by increasing the piecework or commission rate on production or sales above a certain level. Intangibles, such as insurance, are included in this consideration.

In computing the amount of pay, mandatory and other deductions also must be considered in determining the actual *take-home pay*. Social Security taxes and income-tax withholdings are examples of mandatory deductions. Subtractions for insurance fees or for savings bonds are examples of "other" deductions, that is, voluntary deductions.

Accurate records of all payroll transactions must be kept so that proper reports can be made to the Internal Revenue Service and other agencies of government.

14.1 COMPUTING WAGES ON BASIS OF TIME

The most common basis for determining pay is the number of hours worked. A set number of hours per day or week is considered to be the *regular hours* of work, with any time worked over that period considered to be *overtime*. The regular hours are usually 7 to 8 hours a day or 35 to 40 hours a week.

A record of the number of hours worked may be made by having an employee punch a time clock when reporting for work and when leaving. The employee's time card records these times, showing the number of hours worked.

Example 1. As specified in the contract with the union, wages in the Model Manufacturing Company were to be computed on the basis of a $37\frac{1}{2}$-hour workweek, with any overtime to be paid at $1\frac{1}{2}$ times the regular hourly rate. M. Moore worked 8 hours on Monday, 7 hours on Tuesday, 6 hours on Wednesday, 9 hours on Thursday, and 10 hours on Friday. If the rate of pay was $5.80 an hour, what is Moore's gross pay for the week?

Monday	8
Tuesday	7
Wednesday	6
Thursday	9
+ Friday	+ 10
Hours Worked	40
− Regular Hours	− $37\frac{1}{2}$
Overtime Hours	$2\frac{1}{2}$

Regular Pay	$37\frac{1}{2} \times \$5.80 =$	$217.50
+ Overtime Pay	$2\frac{1}{2} \times 1\frac{1}{2} \times \$5.80 =$	+ 21.75
Gross Pay		$239.25

Example 2. If the union contract with the Model Manufacturing Company had specified that the regular hours of work were $7\frac{1}{2}$ hours per day and that any time over that was to be considered overtime, what would be M. Moore's gross wages for the week?

Monday	$7\frac{1}{2}$ hours
Tuesday	7
Wednesday	6
Thursday	$7\frac{1}{2}$
+ Friday	$7\frac{1}{2}$
Regular Time	$35\frac{1}{2}$ hours

Monday	$\frac{1}{2}$ hour
Thursday	$1\frac{1}{2}$
+ Friday	$2\frac{1}{2}$
Overtime	$4\frac{1}{2}$ hours

Regular Pay	$35\frac{1}{2} \times \$5.80 =$	$205.90
+ Overtime Pay	$4\frac{1}{2} \times 1\frac{1}{2} \times \$5.80 =$	+ 39.15
Gross pay		$245.05

What is the average pay per hour?

$$\$245.05 \div 40 = \$6.13$$

Problems

Group 1

a. Find the gross pay for the following persons on the basis of a 35-hour week, with $1\frac{1}{2}$ times the regular rate for overtime.

b. Then make the computations on the basis of a 7-hour day, with $1\frac{1}{2}$ times the regular rate for overtime on any one day.

		Mon.	Tue.	Wed.	Thu.	Fri.	Rate
1.	B. Benito	5	8	7	9	$7\frac{1}{2}$	$6.20
2.	S. Angus	8	4	–	10	8	$7.40
3.	M. Petri	$3\frac{1}{2}$	7	$8\frac{1}{2}$	$9\frac{1}{4}$	7	$7.20
4.	N. Layton	7	$8\frac{1}{4}$	$7\frac{1}{2}$	$8\frac{3}{4}$	$3\frac{1}{2}$	$6.70
5.	F. Farmer	$7\frac{1}{2}$	7	7	10	$8\frac{1}{4}$	$6.90

		a.	b.
1.	B. Benito	$_217_	$_13.95_
2.	S. Angus	$_2_	$_____
3.	M. Petri	$_252_	$_2.70_
4.	N. Layton	$_____	$_____
5.	F. Farmer	$_24.56_	$_38.8_

Group 2

1. The Nylon Company paid its employees on the basis of a $37\frac{1}{2}$ hour week, with time and a half for overtime. What gross pay would an employee earn who worked in one week as follows? Monday, $6\frac{1}{2}$ hours; Tuesday, 7 hours; Wednesday, 9 hours; Thursday, 8 hours; Friday, 10 hours. The rate of pay is $4.90 per hour.

$_____

2. Compute the gross pay in Problem 1 if the regular time is $7\frac{1}{2}$ hours a day.

    $_____

3. What is the average pay per hour received by the employee in Problem 2?

    $_____

4. The Rebel Corporation paid its workers on the basis of a 40-hour week, with overtime paid at $1\frac{1}{2}$ times the regular rate, except for work on holidays, when the rate was double the regular rate. Suppose you worked 9 hours on Monday, 10 hours on Tuesday, 8 hours on Wednesday, $9\frac{1}{2}$ hours on Thursday, $10\frac{1}{4}$ hours on Friday, and 6 hours on Saturday, which is a national holiday. What is your gross pay, if your regular rate was $6.10 an hour?

    $_____

5. What is the average rate per hour you would have received in Problem 4?

    $_____

14.2   COMPUTING WAGES ON BASIS OF UNITS PRODUCED (PIECEWORK)

In factories, numbering devices on machines give the count of the number of times the machine has been operated to produce a unit or part. The number of bushels of apples picked can be determined by a simple count. Knowing the count, the gross pay for such work can be determined by multiplying the number by the rate.

Example 1. M. Mason operates a knitting machine in a factory. She is paid at the rate of 58¢ for each item produced. Her record for one week showed the following numbers of units produced: Monday, 110; Tuesday, 121; Wednesday, 116; Thursday, 124; and Friday, 108. What are her gross earnings for the week?

$$110 + 121 + 116 + 124 + 108 = 579 \text{ Items}$$
$$579 \times \$.58 = \$335.82 \text{ Gross Earnings}$$

Sometimes workers are given an incentive to produce more, by being paid a higher rate above a set amount, sometimes referred to as a *standard* or *quota*.

Example 2. Suppose that the rate in Example 1 for any units produced above 500 was 68¢ rather than 58¢. What would be the gross earnings?

$$500 \times \$.58 = \$290.00$$
$$79 \times \$.68 = \underline{+\ 53.72}$$
$$\text{Gross Earnings} \qquad \$343.72$$

A variation of this incentive plan is to apply a certain rate up to the standard amount and then, if the standard is exceeded, to introduce a higher rate for *all* units produced. This is sometimes referred to as a *differential rate.*

Example 3. Suppose that, in Example 2, the rate of 58¢ applies if 500, the standard, is not reached. Once the production standard is reached, however, the 68¢ rate applies to the *total* number of units produced. What would the gross earnings be?

$$579 \times \$.68 = \$393.72 \text{ Gross Earnings}$$

Problems

1. A drill-press operator is paid 56¢ for each item drilled. In one week, the daily totals were 110, 128, 132, 108, and 104. What are the employee's gross wages?

   $_____

2. A machine operator receives 47¢ for each finished piece that passes inspection. During one week, the finished daily totals showed 102, 94, 118, 119, and 102. If 41 pieces were rejected, what were the operator's gross earnings?

   $_____

3. An assembly-line worker receives $9\frac{1}{2}$¢ for each process completed on the line, up to 1,500 a week. For each process completed above 1,500, the rate goes up to $10\frac{3}{4}$¢. The production in one week is 425, 605, 450, 510, and 485. What is the worker's gross pay for the week?

   $_____

4. If the arrangement in Problem 3 provided that, once the standard of 1,500 was reached, the rate of $10\frac{3}{4}$¢ would apply to *all* of the items produced, what would be the gross pay?

   $_____

5. The XRay Corporation paid its workers at rates for weekly production, as follows:

Under 1,000 Units	7.5¢
1,000–1,999 Units	8.0¢
2,000–2,499 Units	8.75¢
Over 2,499 Units	9.25¢

What would an employee who produced 2,600 units in a week receive as gross pay?

$_____

14.3 PAYING ON COMMISSION

Salespersons are often paid by a commission based on what they sell. A percentage of the total dollar value or a set amount for each unit sold may be used. Various modifications of a *straight-commission* plan are frequently used. Two examples are a *salary-plus-commission* plan and a *graduated scale;* the second provides for an increase in the commission rate when sales exceed a certain amount.

Example 1. Benjamin Barnes works for a straight 6% commission. If his sales for a certain week are $5,500, what is his gross pay?
$$\$5,500 \times .06 = \$330 \text{ Gross Pay}$$

Example 2. Myrna Jackson sells 11 sets of encyclopedias in a week. If her commission is $38.50 per set, what is her gross pay?
$$11 \times \$38.50 = \$423.50 \text{ Gross Pay}$$

Example 3. Molly Maxfield works for a salary plus commission, receiving a salary of $200 a week and a 4% commission on sales. During a four-week period, her sales amounted to $8,680. What was her gross pay for the four weeks?
$$4 \times \$200 = \$800.00 \text{ Salary}$$
$$.04 \times \$8,680 = \underline{+\ 347.20} \text{ Commission}$$
$$\$1,147.20 \text{ Gross Pay}$$

Example 4. Robert Ryan works on a 9% commission on all sales and an additional 3% commission on sales of over $10,000 a month. What is his monthly commission for a month in which he sells $14,500 worth of goods?

$$.09 \times \$14,500 = \$1,305.00$$
$$\$14,500 - \$10,000 = \$4,500; .03 \times \quad \$4500 = \underline{+ \ 135.00}$$
$$\$1,440.00 \text{ Total Commission}$$

Example 5. A salesperson with a quota of $1,800 a week receives a salary of $220 plus a commission of 8% on all sales and an additional $2\frac{1}{2}\%$ of sales over the quota. If the sales for a week are $2,250, how much is earned?

Salary	$220.00
$.08 \times \$2,250 =$	180.00
$\$2,250 - \$1,800 = \$450;$	
$.025 \times \$450 =$	+ 11.25
Total Earnings	$411.25

Problems

1. Jane Stewart sold $3,200 worth of women's dresses. How much did she earn if she was working on a commission of $8\frac{1}{2}\%$?

   $_____

2. A salesperson sold 75 items at $62 each in a month. What is the gross pay if the person is working on a commission of $33\frac{1}{3}\%$?

   $_____

3. In a four-month period, a real-estate salesman made sales amounting to:

1st Month	$80,000
2nd Month	0
3rd Month	45,000
4th Month	75,000

   a. If the commission received is 4%, what is the salesman's total commission for the four months? b. What is the average commission per month?

   a. $_____

   b. $_____

4. An automobile salesman receives a salary of $185 a week and a commission of 2% on all sales. During a 34-week period, he sold $258,500 worth of cars. What are his average weekly earnings?

   $_____

5. Priscilla Price is paid a commission of 7% on all sales she makes and an additional commission of 3% on sales over $12,000 a month. What is her gross pay for a month when her sales amount to $16,800?

   $_____

6. A piece of real estate was sold for $82,000. If the agent was paid a commission of $4,920, what was the rate of commission?

   _____%

14.4 PAYROLL DEDUCTIONS

Take-home pay, the actual amount an employee receives, is the gross pay less deductions. Some deductions are mandatory, others voluntary. Amounts withheld for the federal withholding income tax and for the Social Security (FICA) tax are mandatory deductions. Voluntary deductions include subtractions for insurance, for union dues, and for the purchase of savings bonds. The deduction of union dues is mandatory, however, if the contract between the union and the company specifies this.

Withholding Tax Deductions. Federal withholding income taxes are collected from workers every pay period. Some states also have a withholding income tax. The amount withheld is based on gross pay, marital status, and the number of withholding allowances claimed. The maximum number of allowances you can normally claim is one for yourself, one for your spouse, and one for each dependent. The Internal Revenue Service carefully defines the term "dependent" in its income tax publications.

Table 14-1 gives deductions to be made at various weekly salaries for a single person. Table 14-2 does the same for a married person. Tables are available from Internal Revenue Service offices for other pay periods.

Table 14-1. *Withholding Tax Deductions for Single Person, Weekly Payroll Period*

Wages Are—		The Number of Withholding Allowances Claimed Is—						
At least	But Less Than	0	1	2	3	4	5	6
		The Amount of Income Tax to Be Withheld Shall Be—						
$100	$105	$12.50	$9.00	$5.50	$2.60	0	0	0
105	110	13.40	9.90	6.40	3.40	$.50	0	0
110	115	14.30	10.80	7.30	4.10	1.20	0	0
115	120	15.20	11.70	8.20	4.90	2.00	0	0
120	125	16.10	12.60	9.10	5.70	2.70	0	0
125	130	17.00	13.50	10.00	6.60	3.50	$.60	0
130	135	17.90	14.40	10.90	7.50	4.20	1.40	0
150	160	22.60	18.60	15.00	11.50	8.10	4.70	$1.80
170	180	26.80	22.80	18.80	15.10	11.70	8.20	4.80
200	210	33.60	29.10	25.10	21.00	17.10	13.60	10.10
250	260	46.60	41.60	36.60	31.60	27.50	23.40	19.40
300	310	60.80	55.10	49.60	44.60	39.60	34.60	29.90
350	360	76.80	70.30	64.30	58.50	52.80	47.60	42.60
400	410	93.80	87.30	80.70	74.20	67.80	62.00	56.20
450	460	111.90	104.40	97.70	91.20	84.70	78.10	71.60
500	510	131.40	123.90	116.40	108.90	101.70	95.10	88.60

Table 14-2. *Withholding Tax Deductions for Married Persons, Weekly Payroll Period*

Wages Are—		The Number of Withholding Allowances Claimed Is—						
At Least	But Less Than	0	1	2	3	4	5	6
		The Amount of Income Tax to Be Withheld Shall Be—						
$100	$105	$8.50	$5.60	$2.70	0	0	0	0
105	110	9.20	6.30	3.40	$.50	0	0	0
110	115	10.00	7.10	4.20	1.30	0	0	0
115	120	10.70	7.80	4.90	2.00	0	0	0
120	125	11.50	8.60	5.70	2.80	0	0	0
125	130	12.20	9.30	6.40	3.50	$.70	0	0
130	135	13.10	10.10	7.20	4.30	1.40	0	0
150	160	17.20	13.70	10.60	7.70	4.80	$1.90	0
170	180	20.80	17.30	13.80	10.70	7.80	4.90	$2.00
200	210	26.20	22.70	19.20	15.80	12.30	9.40	6.50
250	260	36.50	32.50	28.50	24.80	21.30	17.90	14.40
300	310	47.50	43.00	39.00	34.90	30.90	26.90	23.40
350	360	59.50	54.90	50.30	45.70	41.40	37.30	33.30
400	410	73.00	67.60	62.30	57.70	53.10	48.50	43.80
450	460	87.00	81.60	76.20	70.80	65.40	60.50	55.80
500	510	103.00	96.90	90.70	84.80	79.40	74.00	68.70

Example 1. S. Rice earned $305 in one week. Rice is single and claims only one withholding allowance. What amount will be withheld for income taxes?

Look in the $300–$310 row and the 1 column of Table 14-1; this indicates that $55.10 will be withheld each week.

Example 2. P. Fleming is married and has two children. He claims four withholding allowances. How much should be withheld if his weekly salary is $308?

Table 14-2 shows that $30.90 will be withheld.

Problems

Find the amount to be withheld from weekly salaries for these people:

		Salary	Married	Allowance	
1.	A. Avellino	$209	No	1	$_____
2.	B. Berry	356	Yes	5	$_____
3.	C. Corts	175	No	2	$_____
4.	D. Ditzel	255	Yes	0	$_____
5.	E. Eckert	455	Yes	6	$_____
6.	F. Flint	123	No	3	$_____
7.	G. Green	306	No	4	$_____
8.	H. Helm	502	Yes	1	$_____
9.	I. Ingles	407	Yes	2	$_____
10.	J. Job	134	No	5	$_____

Social Security Taxes. Social Security legislation, which in this country originated in 1937 with the passage of the Federal Insurance Contribution Act (FICA), provides pensions after retirement. Disability payments, survivors' benefits, and medical and hospital benefits (Medicare and Medicaid) are also covered. To pay for these benefits, employees and employers pay a certain percentage of wages up to a maximum each year. In 1979 the percentage was 6.13% of wages, up to $22,900, for the employer and for the employee, a total of 12.26%. The employee's share is withheld from wages. Self-employed persons paid 8.10%. The percentages and maximum figures are set by congressional action and are subject to change.

Example 1. O. Orr earned $350 a week in 1979. How much of this was withheld for Social Security (FICA)?

$$.0613 \times \$350 = \$21.46$$

Example 2. P. Peabody, a salesperson, earned $21,500 during the period from January 1 through October 31. In November, Peabody's gross pay was $2,500. How much should be deducted for social security?

Maximum Subject to Tax	$22,900
Earnings Already Taxed	− 21,500
Amount Subject to Tax in November	$1,400

$$.0613 \times \$1,400 = \$85.82$$

Problems

Compute the amount to be deducted from gross pay for Social Security taxes at 6.13%, with a maximum of $22,900, for the following:

1. $128 $_____   6. $15,300 $_____

2. $624 $_____   7. $5,750 $_____

3. $24,800 $_____   8. $31,400 $_____

4. $378 $_____   9. $275 $_____

5. $22,900 $_____   10. $10,200 $_____

14.5 PAYROLL REGISTER

Computers are used extensively for the handling of payroll procedures, including computing and recording gross pay, deductions, and net pay. When the process is done by hand, a payroll register provides the means for providing the payroll information. Table 14-3 shows an example of a simplified payroll register.

Table 14-3. Payroll Register

Name	Gross Pay	Deductions				Net Pay
		FICA	Withholding	Other	Total	
N. Nels	$405.00	$24.83	$80.70	$37.50	$143.03	$261.97
O. Oakes	360.00	22.07	50.30	22.80	95.17	264.83
P. Price	456.00	27.95	91.20	41.60	160.75	295.25
Totals	$1,221.00	$74.85	$222.20	$101.90	$398.95	$822.05

Problem

Prepare a payroll register similar to Table 14-3. Use Tables 14-1 and 14-2 to determine the withholding tax and use 6.13% for the FICA tax.

P. Peters: married, with 4 allowances; gross pay, $404.50; other deductions, $18.20.

C. Cambria: single, with no claimed allowances; gross pay, $307.60; other deductions, $24.30.

Q. Quincy: single, with 1 allowance; gross pay, $354.80; other deductions, $19.60.

R. Ray: married, with 2 allowances; gross pay, $258.10; other deductions, $26.10.

S. Soles: single, with 2 allowances; gross pay, $176.20; other deductions, $14.50.

Payroll Register

Name	Gross Pay	Deductions				Net Pay
		FICA	Withholding	Other	Total	
Peters						
Cambria						
Quincy						
Ray						
Soles						
Totals						

Check your work by determining the totals of all columns. The totals of the three separate deduction columns should add up to that of the total deductions column. Subtracting this figure from the total of the gross pay column should give the total of the net pay column.

14.6   PAYING EMPLOYEES

The most common method of paying wages or salaries is by individual checks. An increasing number of companies offer the option of payments made directly to banks designated by the employees. In either case, employees are given an accounting of their gross wages and the deductions made to arrive at their take-home pay.

Sometimes payments are made in paper currency and coins. This is common when sailors are paid in ports away from their homes and in other situations where it might be difficult or inconvenient to cash checks. Paying in currency requires the employer to get money from the bank divided in such a way that there will be the proper number of bills and coins so that each employee can be paid the exact amount of net pay due.

The *change memorandum* illustrated in Table 14-4 provides the needed information.

Table 14-4. Change Memorandum

Name	Net Pay	$20	$10	$5	$1	50¢	25¢	10¢	5¢	1¢
Abrams	$334.17	16	1		4			1	1	2
Baker	265.27	13		1			1			2
Camp	192.18	9	1		2			1	1	3
Dolan	276.76	13	1	1	1	1	1			1
Early	425.87	21		1		1	1	1		2
Fink	258.27	12	1	1	3		1			2
Garcia	318.30	15	1	1	3		1		1	
Cioffi	516.22	25	1	1	1			2		2
Croll	351.56	17	1		1	1			1	1
Totals	$2,938.60	141	7	6	15	3	5	5	4	15

The employer prepares a check to be cashed at the bank for the total of the net pay column. A simple payroll slip, illustrated in Table 14-5, shows the bank teller the number of the various bills and coins needed.

Table 14-5. Payroll Slip

Denominations	Number	Amount
Twenties	141	$2,820.00
Tens	7	70.00
Fives	6	30.00
Ones	15	15.00
Half-Dollars	3	1.50
Quarters	5	1.25
Dimes	5	.50
Nickels	4	.20
Pennies	15	.15
Total		$2,938.60

Problem

Prepare a change memorandum and a payroll slip similar to Tables 14-4 and 14-5 from the following net-pay information: G. Gray, $265.82; H. Hewitt, $310.18; L. Lane, $382.16; M. Mack, $289.15; N. Needles, $332.47; S. Sam, $276.25; T. Thomas, $316.77; and L. Lopez, $322.46.

Change Memorandum

Name	Net Pay	$20	$10	$5	$1	50¢	25¢	10¢	5¢	1¢
Gray										
Hewitt										
Lane										
Mack										
Needles										
Sam										
Thomas										
Lopez										
Totals										

Payroll Slip

Denominations	Number	Amount
Twenties		
Tens		
Fives		
Ones		
Half-Dollars		
Quarters		
Dimes		
Nickels		
Pennies		
Total		

Chapter Review

1. Compute the gross pay for F. Fine, who works a regular 35-hour week at $4.95 an hour, with time and one-half for overtime. He works 9 hours on Monday, 7 hours on Tuesday, 10 hours on Wednesday, 5 hours on Thursday, and 7 hours on Friday.

    $_____

2. Suppose that in Problem 1 Fine worked on the basis of a 7-hour day, with time and one-half for overtime on any time worked over 7 hours. Compute his gross pay.

$_____

3. A corporation paid its workers on the basis of parts produced, as follows:

Under 500 Units	16.5¢
500–999 Units	18.0¢
1,000–1,499 Units	19.25¢
Over 1,499 Units	20.0¢

What does an employee who produces 1,800 units earn?

$_____

4. If you are paid a commission of 4% on all sales you make and an additional 3% on all sales above $80,000, what is your gross pay if you sell $115,000 worth of goods?

$_____

5. If you are single and claim one withholding allowance, how much should be deducted from your weekly salary of $256.50 for income taxes? (See Table 14-1.)

$_____

6. In Problem 5, how much should be deducted for Social Security taxes if the rate is 6.13%?

$_____

7. If the FICA tax is 6.13% of gross pay up to $22,900, what should be deducted from your gross pay of $26,800 for Social Security?

$_____

8. Complete the payroll register for the following employees: T. May: single, with 1 allowance; gross pay, $352; other deductions, $14.75. F. Day: married, with 6 allowances; gross pay, $407.50; no other deductions. E. Eve: single, with 3 allowances; gross pay, $206.80; other deductions, $10.15.

Payroll Register

Name	Gross Pay	Deductions				Net Pay
		FICA	Withholding	Other	Total	
T. May F. Day E. Eve						
Totals						

9. Prepare a change memorandum and a payroll slip from the following net-pay information: B. Turly, $216.85; C. Carl, $318.78; and M. Haines, $222.42.

Change Memorandum

Name	Net Pay	$20	$10	$5	$1	50¢	25¢	10¢	5¢	1¢
Turly Carl Haines										
Totals										

Payroll Slip

Denominations	Number	Amount
Twenties Tens Fives Ones Half-Dollars Quarters Dimes Nickels Pennies		
Total		

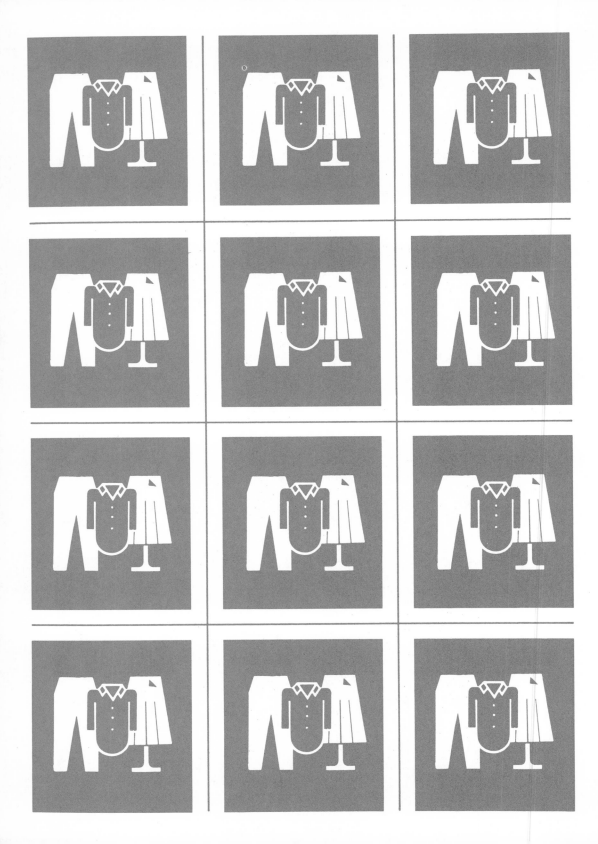

15

Pricing Mathematics

The *selling price* of a product must be high enough to cover the cost of buying or manufacturing the product, the expenses of operating the business, and a net profit. The profit is necessary if the business enterprise is to continue operating. At the same time, the price must be low enough to attract customers.

The amount added to the cost for expenses and profit is called *markup*. Any reduction in the original selling price is called *markdown*. The markup percent needed for successful operation varies considerably among types of businesses. A high-volume business, such as a supermarket, operates on a much lower markup percent than does a jewelry store, with a much lower volume of business, for example.

15.1 MARKUP BASED ON COST

Example 1. From experience in a certain business, the manager knows that the markup must be 25% of cost to cover the expenses of the operation and to provide a reasonable profit. Find the selling price of an article which costs $48.

$$\begin{array}{lr} \text{Cost} & \$48 \\ \text{Markup } .25 \times \$48 = & \underline{+\ 12} \\ \text{Selling Price} & \$60 \end{array}$$

Example 2. Find the cost of an article you plan to sell for $60, if you must realize a markup of 25%, based on cost. If markup is based on cost, then cost is the base, or 100%.

$$\begin{array}{lr} \text{Cost} & 100\% \\ \text{Markup} & \underline{+\ 25\%} \\ \text{Selling Price} & 125\% \end{array}$$

$$\text{Selling Price } \$60 = 1.25 \times \text{Cost}$$
$$\$60 \div 1.25 = \$48 \text{ Cost}$$
$$\text{Check: } \$48 + (25\% \times \$48) = \$48 + \$12 = \$60$$

The computation can be done by changing the 125% to an improper fraction:

$$125\% = 1.25 = 1\tfrac{1}{4} = \tfrac{5}{4}$$
$$\tfrac{5}{4} \times \text{Cost} = \$60$$
$$\text{Cost} = \$60 \times \tfrac{4}{5}$$
$$\text{Cost} = \$48$$

Example 3. Find the cost of an article which will provide a markup of $16, which is 25% of cost.

$$.25 \times \text{Cost} = \$16$$
$$\text{Cost} = \$16 \div .25 = \$64$$

Problems

Find the selling prices for the following, if the markup percent is based on cost:

1.	Cost	$18	Markup	20%	$ _____
2.	Cost	124	Markup	30%	$ _____
3.	Cost	8.60	Markup	22%	$ _____
4.	Cost	35.70	Markup	10%	$ _____
5.	Cost	326.80	Markup	40%	$ _____

Compute the cost of the following, if the markup percent is based on cost:

6.	Selling Price	$24	Markup	20%	$ _____
7.	Selling Price	118	Markup	30%	$ _____
8.	Selling Price	7.80	Markup	15%	$ _____
9.	Selling Price	226.50	Markup	40%	$ _____
10.	Selling Price	.95	Markup	12%	$ _____
11.	Markup	12	Markup	20%	$ _____
12.	Markup	7.50	Markup	15%	$ _____

15.2   MARKUP BASED ON SELLING PRICE

Most retail stores base their markup on the selling price. Suppose, for example, that in a certain type of business, you must have a markup of 30% based on selling price if you are going to operate successfully. How do you determine the selling price? If the markup is based on selling price, then the selling price should be considered to be 100%, or the base. The selling price is the cost plus markup. If the markup is 30% of the selling price, the cost must be 100% − 30% = 70% of the selling price.

Example 1. What must be the selling price if the markup is 30% of the selling price and the article you sell costs $15?

$$
\begin{aligned}
&\text{Selling Price} && 100\% \text{ (base)} \\
&\text{Markup} && \underline{-\ \ 30\%} \\
&\text{Cost} && 70\%
\end{aligned}
$$

$.70 \times$ Selling Price $= \$15$
Selling Price $= \$15 \div .70 = \$21.43$
Check: $\$21.43 - (.30 \times \$21.43) = \$15$

Example 2. At what price must you buy an article which is to be sold for $2.80, if your markup is to be 30% of the selling price?

$$
\begin{aligned}
&\text{Selling Price} && \$2.80 \\
&\text{Markup } (.30 \times \$2.80) = && \underline{-\ .84} \\
&\text{Cost} && \$1.96 \\
&\text{Check: } \$1.96 + \$.84 = && \$2.80
\end{aligned}
$$

Example 3. Find the selling price of an article if $20 represents a 25% markup, based on selling price.

$.25 \times$ Selling Price $= \$20$
Selling Price $= \$20 \div .25 = \$80$

Problems

Determine the selling price if the markup is based on the selling price:

1.	Cost	$144	Markup 25%	$ _____
2.	Cost	22	Markup 30%	$ _____
3.	Cost	8.20	Markup 13%	$ _____
4.	Cost	420	Markup 40%	$ _____
5.	Cost	3.80	Markup 10%	$ _____
6.	Markup	12	Markup 22%	$ _____
7.	Markup	4.80	Markup 15%	$ _____

Find the cost if the markup is based on the selling price:

8.	Selling Price $ 24	Markup 20%	$ _____
9.	Selling Price 260	Markup 30%	$ _____
10.	Selling Price 7.50	Markup 18%	$ _____
11.	Selling Price 575	Markup 35%	$ _____
12.	Selling Price 2.30	Markup $16\frac{1}{2}$%	$ _____

15.3 EQUIVALENT RATES OF MARKUP

In order to make accurate comparisons, it is sometimes necessary to express a markup percent based on the selling price as a percent based on the cost. The reverse is also true: a markup percent based on the cost may be expressed as a percent based on the selling price. In the process of making such changes, an *equivalent rate* is determined.

Knowing the percentage base is the key to determining equivalent rates. If the markup is based on the selling price, then the selling price is the base: 100%. If the markup is based on the cost, the cost is the base, or 100%. The relationship of selling price, markup, and cost must also be understood. Selling price is equal to cost plus markup, and cost is equal to selling price minus markup.

Example 1. The markup percent based on the selling price of an article is 25%. What is the equivalent rate based on cost?

Selling Price   100%
Markup   − 25%
Cost   75%
Markup Based on Cost 25% ÷ 75% = .25 ÷ .75 = $\frac{1}{3}$ = $33\frac{1}{3}$%

Example 2. The markup percent based on cost is 25%. What is the equivalent markup based on selling price?

Cost   100%
Markup   + 25%
Selling Price   125%
Markup Based on Selling Price 25% ÷ 125% = .25 ÷ 1.25 = .20 = 20%

10,183.28
48,561.25
16,308.39
+13,691.61

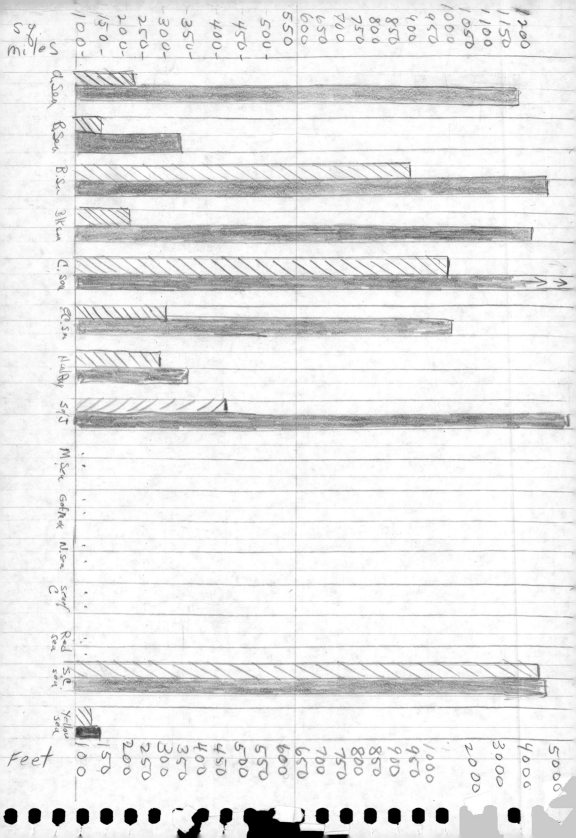

Problems

Group 1
Find the equivalent rates of markup based on cost for the following rates based on selling price:

1.	50%	_____ %		**4.**	30%	_____ %
2.	40%	_____ %		**5.**	12%	_____ %
3.	20%	_____ %				

Compute the equivalent rates of markup based on selling price for the following rates based on cost:

6.	20%	_____ %		**9.**	30%	_____ %
7.	10%	_____ %		**10.**	12%	_____ %
8.	40%	_____ %				

When the markup can be readily expressed as a common fraction, there is a shorter method of shifting the base from selling price to cost or from cost to selling price.

Example 1. Change a 25% markup based on cost to the equivalent markup based on selling price.

$$25\% = \frac{1}{4}$$

Add the numerator of the fraction (1) to the denominator (4) to determine the denominator of the markup based on selling price.

$$\frac{1}{4} \times Cost = \frac{1}{(4 + 1)} = \frac{1}{5} \times Selling\ Price$$
$$\frac{1}{5} = 20\% \text{ of Selling Price}$$

Example 2. Change a 20% markup based on selling price to the equivalent markup based on cost.

$$20\% = \frac{1}{5}$$

Subtract the numerator (1) from the denominator (5) to determine the denominator of the markup based on cost.

$$\frac{1}{5} \times Selling\ Price = \frac{1}{(5 - 1)} = \frac{1}{4} \times Cost$$
$$\frac{1}{4} = 25\% \text{ of Cost}$$

The numerator remains the same.

Problems

Group 2

Convert the following from markup based on cost to markup based on selling price:

1. 20% of Cost _____ %   **4.** 66 $^2/_3$% of Cost _____ %

2. 50% of Cost _____ %   **5.** 40% of Cost _____ %

3. 33$^1/_3$% of Cost _____ %

Convert the following from markup based on sales to markup based on cost:

6. 33$^1/_3$% of Selling Price ___ %   **9.** 10% of Selling Price ___ %

7. 40% of Selling Price ___ %   **10.** 66$^2/_3$% of Selling Price ___%

8. 20% of Selling Price ___ %

15.4 AVERAGING MARKUPS

The problem of pricing becomes more complicated when a variety of products are sold by one enterprise. In a supermarket, for example, the markup percents for fresh fruits and vegetables, meats, baked goods, and canned goods will vary a great deal. It is important to maintain an *overall* or *average markup* to meet the expenses of operation and to provide an adequate profit. How can this average markup be determined?

Example 1. The Main Store has 4 departments. Department A operates on a markup percent on sales of 25%; Department B, on 20%; Department C, on 15%; and Department D, on 40%. Sales for one month are A, $42,000; B, $53,000; C, $62,000; and D, $18,000. What is the average markup percent on sales?

	Sales	Gross Profit (Markup)	
A	$ 42,000	.25 × $42,000 =	$10,500
B	53,000	.20 × $53,000 =	10,600
C	62,000	.15 × $62,000 =	9,300
D	+ 18,000	.40 × $18,000 =	+ 7,200
	$175,000		$37,600

$37,600 ÷ $175,000 = 21.49% Average Markup on Sales

Sometimes the original selling price of goods needs to be changed. An *additional markup* may be added to cover expenses and provide an adequate profit, or the original selling price may be decreased by means of a *markdown* to attract buyers.

Example 2. A company sold $18,000 worth of a product at a markup of 30% of sales; then, after reducing the price by 5%, the company had additional sales of $56,000. What was the average markup on sales?

After the price was reduced 5%, the markup on each item was 25% of the original price. Since the reduced price was 95% of the original price, the markup percent based on sales was then $^{25}/_{95}$, or 26.3%.

	Sales		Gross Profit (Markup)
At Original Price	$18,000	.30 × $18,000	$ 5,400
After Markdown	+ 56,000	.263 × $56,000 =	+ 14,728
	$74,000		$20,128
		$20,128 ÷ $74,000 = 27.2%	

Problems

1. The departments of the Union Department Store had the following sales for the month of December: Shoes, $15,000; Men's Wear, $85,000; Women's Wear, $160,000; and Toys, $42,000. The markup percents on sales were: Shoes, 30%; Men's Wear, 25%; Women's Wear, 20%; and Toys, 40%. What was the average markup on sales for the store?

    _____ %

2. Fred's Sporting Goods Store sold fishing equipment and supplies, costing $38,000, at a markup of 30% based on cost; hunting equipment and supplies, costing $62,000, at a markup of 24% based on cost; and other sporting goods, costing $74,000, at a markup of 38% based on cost. a. What was the average markup percent based on cost? b. What was the average markup percent based on sales?

    a. _____ %

    b. _____ %

3. The Hadley Hosiery Store sold $15,000 worth of merchandise at a markup of 35% based on sales. After marking down the merchandise by 10%, the store sold $60,000 worth of merchandise. What is the average markup percent based on sales?

_____ %

4. A store had $50,000 worth of sales in Department X and $100,000 in Department Y, using a markup based on sales of 20% in Department X. What markup based on sales was used in Department Y if both departments had an average markup of 25%?

_____ %

15.5   MARKING GOODS IN CODE

The selling prices of goods in a retail store are usually marked clearly, so prospective customers can make their decisions readily. Many stores also mark goods with the cost prices. Knowing the costs without having to refer back to the original records, helps in computing markdowns for sales, taking inventory, and placing reorders.

Since the cost price is not meant for the prospective customer's information, it is written in a *code* that can be understood only by the people responsible for setting, marking, and recording prices.

Any word or phrase with ten different letters may be used as a code. For example:

H A R V E S T I N G	N I G H T M A R E S
1 2 3 4 5 6 7 8 9 0	1 2 3 4 5 6 7 8 9 0
Repeater X	Repeater Y

A *repeater* is a letter used when two figures coming together in a price are the same.

Example 1. A retailer marks items for sale using the HARVESTING code as follows:

  a. <u>EA.GX</u>
        $64.00

  b. <u>RH.XS</u>
        $38.75

What are the costs?

a. E = 5	b. R = 3
A = 2	H = 1
G = 0	X = 1
X = 0	S = 6
Cost = $52.00	Cost = $31.16

Example 2. Using the NIGHTMARES code, with Y for the repeater, how would a retailer mark articles that cost a. $19.00 and b. $26.62?

a. 1 = N	b. 2 = I
9 = E	6 = M
0 = S	6 = Y
0 = Y	2 = I

The code marking would be a. NE.SY and b. IM.YI.

Problems

Write the coded costs using the code word COMPLAINTS, with Z as a repeater, for the following cost prices:

1.	$24.00 _____	6.	$240.00 _____
2.	$38.92 _____	7.	$4.40 _____
3.	$1.30 _____	8.	$5.82 _____
4.	$364.00 _____	9.	$49.00 _____
5.	$17.50 _____	10.	$16.50 _____

The following prices have been coded with the word AUTHORIZED, with Y as a repeater; express them in figures:

11.	AT.ZE	$ _____	14.	OZ.DY	$ _____
12.	UO.YA	$ _____	15.	TZ.RD	$ _____
13.	HID.YT	$ _____			

Chapter Review

1. The Ray Retail Store marked up an article costing $7.60 at the rate of 23%, based on cost. What was the selling price?

   $ _____

2. To meet competition, the Ray Retail Store prices an article to sell for $18.80. What should the product cost if the markup is to be 23%, based on cost?

$ _____

3. If the Ray Retail Store decided to mark up an article costing $7.60 at the rate of 23%, based on selling price, what was the selling price?

$ _____

4. The Ray Retail Store markup on a certain article is $8.20. This represents 23% of the selling price. What is the selling price?

$ _____

5. The Ray Retail Store sold an item for $83.60. What did the store pay for this item if the markup was 23%, based on the selling price?

$ _____

6. The Moore Map Company decided to change its markup base from the selling price to the cost. If the rate of markup is 15%, based on the selling price, what is the equivalent rate, based on cost?

_____%

7. The Ribco Stationery Store shifted its $16\frac{2}{3}$% rate of markup, based on cost, to an equivalent rate based on selling price. What was the equivalent rate?

_____%

8. A retail store with three departments had sales of $24,000 in Department A, with a 21% markup, based on sales; Department B sold $38,000 worth of goods, at a markup of 18%, based on sales; and Department C had sales of $76,000, with a markup of 15%, based on sales. What was the average markup on sales of the three departments?

_____%

9. After $28,000 worth of merchandise is sold at a markup of 28%, based on sales, $45,000 is sold, with a markdown of 4%. What is the average markup percent, based on sales?

_____%

10. The Triangle Tie Company wanted to show the cost of its ties without the customers' knowledge. The code word EIGHTY-FOUR, with X for the repeater, was used for this purpose. a. How would you show $4.88? b. How would you show T.FT in figures?

a. _____

b. $ _____

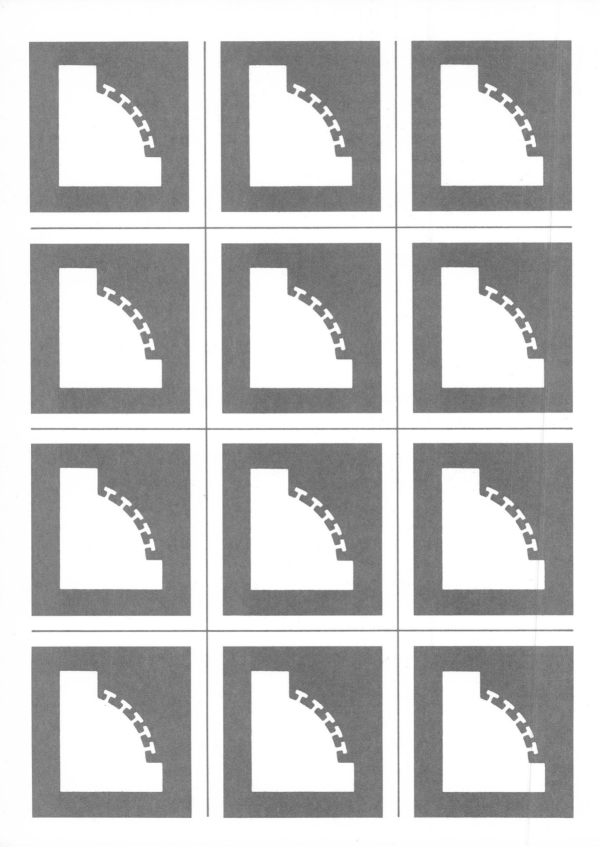

16

Trade and Cash Discounts

Discounts are given to buyers for a variety of reasons. If a company publishes a catalog with the actual selling prices indicated, the catalog is out of date when those prices change. In some parts of the economy, prices change rapidly. In these business activities, it would be almost impossibly expensive to publish new catalogs every time the prices change. To meet this problem, a *list price* or *catalog price,* which is somewhat more than the expected selling price, is given; a *trade discount* is subtracted from this to arrive at the actual selling price. By changing the percent of discount, the company can change the selling price readily for some or all of the items listed. Trade discounts may be given for quantity buying, to promote new business, or simply as a convenient way of indicating selling prices to prospective customers.

Cash discounts are given to encourage prompt payment for goods purchased. These discounts are based on the actual selling price and have nothing to do with the list price.

16.1 TRADE DISCOUNTS—FINDING SELLING PRICES

Trade discounts are based on the list or catalog price. Sometimes two or more discounts, known as *chain discounts,* are given. This makes it possible to give additional discounts to preferred customers or to encourage quantity sales, without changing the original basic discount.

Example 1. Find the selling price of a television set listed at $540, for which a trade discount of 15% is given.

$$.15 \times \$540 = \$81 \text{ Trade Discount}$$
$$\$540 - \$81 = \$459 \text{ Selling Price}$$

Example 2. Find the selling price of the television set listed at $540, if trade discounts of 10% and 5% are given.

$$.10 \times \$540 = \$54 \text{ First Discount}$$
$$\$540 - \$54 = \$486 \text{ First Reduced Price}$$
$$.05 \times \$486 = \$24.30 \text{ Second Discount}$$
$$\$486 - \$24.30 = \$461.70 \text{ Selling Price}$$

Note that the chain discounts of 10%–5% are not the same as a 15% discount. The base for the second discount is less than the base for the first one.

Example 3. Find the selling price of the television set listed at $540, if the trade discounts allowed are 5%–10%

$$.05 \times \$540 = \$27 \text{ First Discount}$$
$$\$540 - \$27 = \$513 \text{ First Reduced Price}$$
$$.10 \times \$513 = \$51.30 \text{ Second Discount}$$
$$\$513 - \$51.30 = \$461.70 \text{ Selling Price}$$

Note that the order in which the chain discounts are applied makes no difference in arriving at the selling price.

If the chain has a third discount, the same procedure is continued by applying the third discount percentage to the new base after subtracting the second discount.

Problems

Group 1

Compute the selling price for each of the following catalog prices:

1. $12 less 18% $ _9.84_
2. $3.50 less 32% $ _2.38_
3. $171.80 less 20% $_____
4. $960 less 33¹/₃% $_____
5. $79.60 less 25% $_____
6. $1,000 less 20% and 10% $_____
7. $1,200 less 25% and 20% $_____

8. $720 less 40% and 10% $_____

9. $400 less 10%, 10%, and 5% $_____

10. $1,600 less 20%, 10%, and 12½% $_____

Group 2

1. The Howes Hardware Store ordered merchandise listed at $2,840 from a distributor, with trade discounts of 30% and 8%. For how much should the store be billed?

    $_____

2. The Major Company, a mail-order house, listed a rocking chair in its catalog at $78.18. If they gave a 16⅔% trade discount to their retail customers, what was the selling price of two chairs?

    $_____

3. Carlos operates an automobile repair shop. He can buy parts from Supply Company A or from Company B, both of whose catalogs show the same list prices. Company A offers trade discounts of 25% and 10%, and Company B gives discounts of 30% and 5%. If Carlos needs parts listed at $90, compute the price each company would charge.

    A $_____

    B $_____

4. In Problem 3, Company A reduces its list prices by offering an additional 5% discount, so its chain discounts become 25%–10%–5%. What is the price of the parts listed at $90 now?

    $_____

5. A jobber buys electric stoves listed at $450 from a manufacturer. Trade discounts of 5%, 10%, and 25% are allowed. a. What is the cost to the jobber? The jobber discovers that he can buy the same type of stove from another manufacturer, who gives the same list price, with discounts of 25%, 10%, and 5%. b. What would be his net cost from this manufacturer?

    a. $_____

    b. $_____

16.2   COMPUTING EQUIVALENT SINGLE DISCOUNTS

By reducing a series of discounts to a *single equivalent discount,* you can readily compare the value of one series with that of another series. Using a single equivalent discount rather than a series also reduces the amount of computation and thus improves the chances of being accurate.

By using 100% as the list price, you can determine your single equivalent discount by following the procedure given in Unit 1.

Example 1. Find the single equivalent discount for chain discounts of 30% and 10%.

100%	List Price
$.30 \times 100\% = 30\%$	First Discount
$100\% - 30\% = 70\%$	First Reduced Percentage
$.10 \times 70\% = 7\%$	Second Discount
$70\% - 7\% = 63\%$	Selling Price
$100\% - 63\% = 37\%$	Single Equivalent Discount

Example 2. Find the single equivalent discount for chain discounts of 20%–10%–5%.

100%	List Price
$.20 \times 100\% = 20\%$	First Discount
$100\% - 20\% = 80\%$	First Reduced Percentage
$.10 \times 80\% = 8\%$	Second Discount
$80\% - 8\% = 72\%$	Second Reduced Percentage
$.05 \times 72\% = 3.6\%$	Third Discount
$72\% - 3.6\% = 68.4\%$	Selling Price
$100\% - 68.4\% = 31.6\%$	Single Equivalent Discount

Problems

Group 1

Compute the single equivalent discount for each of the following chain discounts:

1.	30%–5%	_____%	**6.**	30%–10%–5%	_____%
2.	5%–10%	_____%	**7.**	40%–15%–10%	_____%
3.	40%–10%	_____%	**8.**	25%–10%–5%	_____%
4.	20%–5%	_____%	**9.**	30%–5%–5%	_____%
5.	25%–20%	_____%	**10.**	5%–10%–10%	_____%

Group 2

A wholesale furniture company decides to quote single discounts rather than chain discounts on its merchandise. Find the single equivalent discount for the following:

1. Dressers: 25%–5%   —%   **5.** Refrigerators: 32%–8%–5%   —%

2. Dining sets: 35%–5%   —%   **6.** Bookcases: 25%–10%–6%   —%

3. Rugs: 40%–6%   —%   **7.** Coffee tables: 5%–8%–10%   —%

4. Ranges: 20%–8%   —%   **8.** Recorders: 22%–10%–5%   —%

16.3   NET SELLING PRICE EQUIVALENT

If your only interest is in the net selling price, it may be more convenient to work directly with the *net selling price equivalent* percentage. The net selling price is what the goods cost the buyer, except for taxes. The process for finding the selling price equivalent is the same as for finding the single equivalent discount, with the exception of the last step.

Example 1. Find the selling price equivalent, if the discounts offered are 25%–20%–10%.

100%	List Price
.25 × 100% = 25%	First Discount
100% − 25% = 75%	First Reduced Percentage
.20 × 75% = 15%	Second Discount
75% − 15% = 60%	Second Reduced Percentage
.10 × 60% = 6%	Third Discount
60% − 6% = 54%	Selling Price Equivalent Percentage

If you know the selling price equivalent, you need not bother with the discounts to determine the selling price. Multiply the list price by the selling price equivalent percentage.

Example 2. A suite of furniture is listed at $1,540, less 25%–20%–10%. How much will the buyer have to pay for the suite? By using the selling price equivalent computed in Example 1, all you need to do is multiply:

$$\$1,540 \times 54\% = \$1,540 \times .54 = \$831.60$$

If you are working with a large number of computations involving determining selling or purchasing prices, it might be wise to set up a table of selling price equivalents, such as that shown in Table 16-1.

Table 16-1. Selling Price Equivalents

Chain Discount	Selling Price Equivalent	Chain Discount	Selling Price Equivalent
10%–5%	85.5%	10%–10%–5%	76.95%
20%–10%	72.0%	20%–10%–5%	68.4%
25%–10%	67.5%	25%–10%–5%	64.125%
30%–10%	63.0%	30%–20%–10%	50.4%
30%–20%	56.0%	30%–10%–5%	59.85%

Problems

Compute the selling price equivalents for the following series of trade discounts.

1. 15%–10% _____%
2. 10%–10%–5% _____%
3. 20%–15% _____%
4. 25%–10%-10% _____%
5. 18%–10% _____%

6. 30%–8% _____%
7. 40%–10%–5% _____%
8. 24%–12%–5% _____%
9. 16%–10%–8% _____%
10. 26%–5%–10% _____%

Using Table 16.1, compute the selling prices for the following:

11. $280, less 20%–10% $_____
12. $1,860, less 30%–20% $_____
13. $875, less 20%–10%–5% $_____
14. $3,690, less 30%–20%–10% $_____
15. $5,940, less 10%–10%–5% $_____

16.4   COMPUTING LIST PRICE

When a dealer knows the cost price and the desired percent of discounts, based on list price, the problem is to find the list price.

Example 1. A wholesaler wishes to offer a 20% trade discount to customers and, at the same time, be able to sell the product for $36. What list price should he set?

$$
\begin{aligned}
100\% \quad &\text{List Price} \\
-\ 20\% \quad &\text{Discount} \\
\hline
80\% \quad &\text{Selling Price}
\end{aligned}
$$

$$.80 \times \text{List Price} = \$36$$
$$\text{List Price} = \$36 \div .8 = \$45$$
$$\text{Check:} \quad .20 \times \$45 = \$9 \text{ Discount}$$
$$\$45 - \$9 = \$36 \text{ Selling Price}$$

Example 2. The list price of an article is to be set at an amount which will permit trade discounts of 20%–10% and allow a selling price of $48. What is the list price?

$$
\begin{aligned}
100\% \quad &\text{List Price} \\
-\ 20\% \quad &\text{First Discount} \\
\hline
80\% \quad &\text{First Reduced Percentage} \\
.10 \times 80\% = -\ 8\% \quad &\text{Second Discount} \\
\hline
72\% \quad &\text{Selling Price Equivalent}
\end{aligned}
$$

$$.72 \times \text{List Price} = \$48$$
$$\$48 \div .72 = \$66.67 \quad \text{List Price}$$
$$\text{Check: } \$66.67 \times .72 = \$48$$

Table 16-1 could have been used to find the selling price equivalent.

Example 3. A dealer believes that, to meet competition, a discount of $80 must be given. This discount is to be 25% of the list price. What is the list price, and what is the selling price?

$$100\% \text{ List Price}$$
$$.25 \times \text{List Price} = \$80 \text{ Discount}$$
$$\$80 \div .25 = \$320 \text{ List Price}$$
$$\$320 - \$80 = \$240 \text{ Selling Price}$$
$$\text{Check:} \quad .25 \times \$320 = \$80$$
$$\$240 + \$80 = \$320$$

Problems

Group 1

Compute the list price for each of the following:

	Net Price	Discount			Net Price	Discount	
1.	$360	10%	$_____	**6.**	$290	20% – 10%	$_____
2.	$960	25%	$_____	**7.**	$2,490	10% – 10%	$_____
3.	$840	33⅓%	$_____	**8.**	$1,820	30% – 10%	$_____
4.	$3,000	25% – 20%	$_____	**9.**	$1,440	20% – 10% – 10%	$_____
5.	$4,896	15% – 10%	$_____	**10.**	$720	25% – 10% – 5%	$_____

Find the list and the net price for each of the following:

	Rate of Discount	Amount of Discount	List Price	Net Price
11.	20%	$18	$_____	$_____
12.	15%	$180	$_____	$_____
13.	10%	$270	$_____	$_____
14.	20%-10%	$560	$_____	$_____
15.	30%–20%–10%	$992	$_____	$_____

Group 2

1. A company paid $4,856.40 for goods purchased with a 10%–5% discount on the list price. What was the list price?

   $_____

2. The discount on the list price of merchandise was $788.48. If discounts of 20%–3% were given, what was the list price?

   $_____

3. Coats which had been marked to sell at $202.50 were marked down to $135. What was the discount rate on the original price?

   _____%

4. Find the list price of an end table which sells for $31.90 after discounts of 20% and 20%.

$_____

5. The discount given on the list price of merchandise is $159.80. If discounts of 15%–10% have been given, what is the selling price of the merchandise?

$_____

16.5   CHANGING PRICES BY CHANGING DISCOUNTS

One of the major advantages of using trade discounts is that you can change prices readily, merely by changing the discounts. The problem then becomes how you change discounts to give the desired results.

Example 1. An article is listed at $48 with a discount of 25%, so it is selling for $48 − (.25 × $48) = $36. To meet competition, the selling price needs to be decreased to $32. What should the discount rate be?

$48 − $32 = $16 New Discount

$16 ÷ $48 = $\frac{1}{3}$ = 33$\frac{1}{3}$% New Discount Rate

Example 2. If for some reason the price in Example 1 is to be increased to $40, the calculation would be

$48 − $40 = $8 New Discount

$8 ÷ $48 = $\frac{1}{6}$ = 16$\frac{2}{3}$% New Discount Rate

In neither case was the list price changed.

Example 3. Another article is listed at $76, with discounts of 25%–10%, so it is selling for $51.30. What additional discount would reduce the price to $48.74? The third discount is based on the price *after* the first two discounts have been applied; in this case, $51.30:

$51.30 − $48.74 = $2.56 Additional Discount

$2.56 ÷ $51.30 = .05 = 5% Additional Discount Percent

Example 4. If the original selling price of $51.30 in Example 3 is to be increased to $55.29, what should the second discount be?

$76	List Price
.25 × $76 = $19	First Discount
$76 − $19 = $57	Price After First Discount
$57 − $55.29 = $1.71	Additional Discount Needed
$1.71 ÷ $57 = .03 = 3%	Additional Discount Percent

The discounts become 25%–3%. The discounts have changed, but not the list price.

Problems

1. The Empire Sales Company had been selling CB sets for $380 less 20%, to give a selling price of $304. What should the *single* discount be if they want to reduce the selling price to $292.60

    _____%

2. In Problem 1, what *additional* discount might be added to achieve the same result without changing the first discount?

    _____%

3. Automobile parts listed in a catalog at $242 are sold at discounts of 20%–15%, thus giving a selling price of $164.56. If the selling price is increased to $178.11 and the first discount stays the same, what should the second discount be?

    _____%

16.6   CASH DISCOUNTS

Manufacturers, wholesalers, and other business establishments often give discounts for prompt payment. The purchaser gains from this, of course, and the seller gains, in that funds are acquired to pay debts and to expand the business. *Cash discount terms* are shown on the invoice along with the other details of sales on account. Cash discount terms are expressed as follows:

2/10, n/30	The total debt is due 30 days from the date of the invoice. If the bill is paid within 10 days, 2% can be deducted.
3/10, 2/20, n/60	The debt is due in 60 days. If the bill is paid within 10 days, 3% may be subtracted; if it is paid within between 10 and 20 days, 2% may be deducted.
2/10, n/30 e.o.m.	This is like the first example, but as a further inducement to purchase goods, the supplier has extended the cash discount period by starting the period at the end of the month (e.o.m.), rather than on the date of the invoice.
3/10, n/60 r.o.g.	This form is often used if the date of delivery of the purchases is questionable or likely to be delayed; the terms of the invoice start with the date of the receipt of the goods (r.o.g.).

Example. The Dombrosky Furniture Store receives an invoice dated March 6 for $2,418.60. The terms are 3/10, n/60. a. What is the last date on which the cash discount can be taken? b. If the discount is not taken, what is the date on which the payment is due? c. What is the dollar amount of the discount? d. Suppose Dombrosky borrowed enough to pay the invoice less the discount on the last day of the discount period, paying back the loan at the end of the invoice period. At 8% interest, what would be the charge? e. How much would be gained by borrowing funds in this way, to take advantage of the cash discount?

a. March 6 + 10 days = March 16 Last Discount Date
b. March 6 + 60 days = May 5 Net Amount Due Date
c. .03 × $2,418.60 = $72.56 Discount Available
d. $2,418.60 − $72.56 = $2,346.04 Amount to Be Borrowed
    .08 × $2,346.04 × $^{50}/_{365}$ = $25.71 Charge for Loan
e. $72.56 − $25.71 = $46.85 Amount Gained

Problems

Determine the last date on which the discounts can be taken:

1. April 15   2/15, n/30   _____

2. May 25   3/10, n/60   _____

3. June 25   2/10, n/30 e.o.m.   _____

Find the amount due for each of the following:

	Amount of Invoice	Invoice Date	Term	Payment Date	
4.	$2,680.15	July 6	3/10, n/30	July 16	$_____
5.	$1,817.50	Aug. 7	2/10, n/60 e.o.m.	Sept. 10	$_____
6.	$3,228.70	Sept. 4	4/15, n/30	Sept. 20	$_____
7.	$1,677.29	Oct. 24	5/10, n/60	Nov. 4	$_____
8.	$4,650.10	Nov. 21	2/10, 1/30, n/60	Dec. 21	$_____
9.	$882.40	Dec. 5	3/10, n/60 e.o.m.	Jan. 9	$_____

10. An invoice dated January 15 for $3,280 was paid on January 25. The payment terms were 3/10, n/30, so the discount was taken. a. What was the amount of the discount? b. What was the net amount paid? c. If funds to pay the invoice were borrowed at 9% on the last day of the discount period and paid back at the end of the invoice period, what was the charge for interest?

a. $_____

b. $_____

c. $_____

Chapter Review

1. The Alpha Music Company lists a piano at $1,475. Discounts of 15% and 7% are offered to prospective customers. What is the selling price?

$_____

2. A jobber buys wood stoves from a manufacturer. The stoves are priced at $385. Trade discounts of 10%–10%–5% are available to the jobber. What is the actual price?

$_____

3. What is the single equivalent discount for the chain discounts 15%–10%–5%?

_____%

4. In Problem 3, what is the net selling price equivalent?

_____%

5. Using Table 16-1, what is the selling price of an item listed at $89.50, less 25%–10%–5%?

$_____

6. Compute the list price of a fireplace set which sells for $76.80 after discounts of 10% and 5% have been subtracted.

$_____

7. After the chain discounts of 10%–5%–3% were applied to the list price of a table, the discount amounted to $59.59. a. What was the list price? b. What was the selling price?

a. $_____

b. $_____

8. If an article to be sold for $125 is listed at $150, what single discount should be given?

_____%

9. If the selling price of the article in Problem 8 is to be reduced to $100, what additional discount will need to be given?

_____%

10. The Castro Company receives an invoice dated July 8 for $4,270.50. Terms of payment are 3/15, n/30 e.o.m. a. When is the invoice due? b. What is the last date of the discount period? c. What is the amount of the discount available? d. On the last day of the discount period, the Castro Company borrows funds at 9% interest to pay the invoice. The period from the last day of the discount period to the due date of the invoice is the term of the loan. What is the interest charge?

a. _____

b. _____

c. $_____

d. $_____

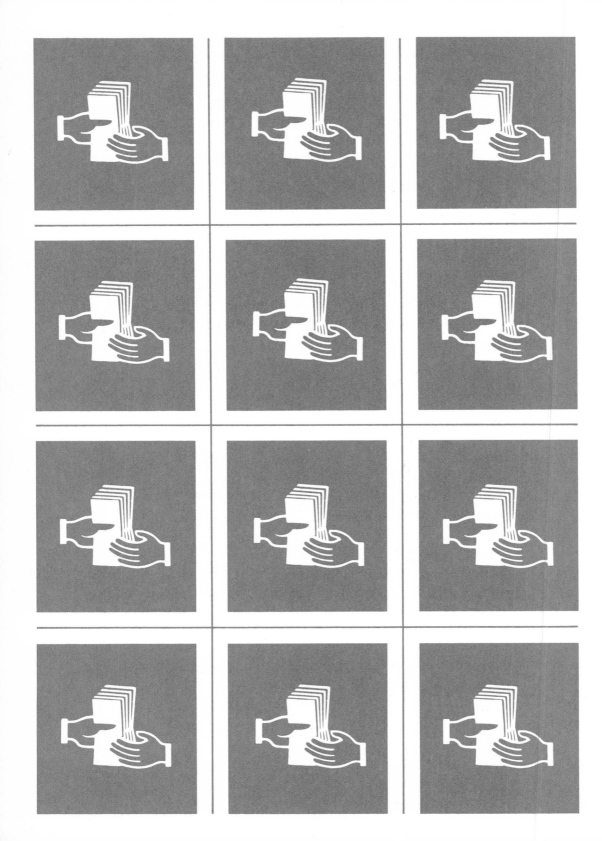

17

Discounting Notes

A business or individual needing funds for a relatively short period of time—from a few days up to a year—may obtain a loan from a commercial or all-purpose bank or from other financial institutions. In this process, a *promissory note* is issued and is often discounted.

17.1 BANK DISCOUNT

A promissory note represents a promise by the *maker* of the note to pay a certain amount of money at a specified time. Such a note is *negotiable;* that is, the note can be sold and the holder of the note on the due date is entitled to the payment. The amount for which payment is promised is the *face* of the note, and the length of time until payment must be made is the *term* of the note.

A promissory note may be *interest bearing* or *non-interest bearing;* in either case, the borrower must pay a charge for the use of the funds.

The sample note in Fig. 17-1 is an example of an interest-bearing note. The face of the note is $800, and the term is 30 days. The maker, Joseph Ingles, is promising to pay the *maturity value:* $800 plus interest at an annual rate of 8% for 30 days.

With a non-interest-bearing note, the maturity value is the same as the face of the note, but the borrower does not receive the full amount. Instead, a *discount* is computed on the face value, at the *discount rate* for the *term of discount.* The discount is subtracted from the face to find the *proceeds,* the amount the borrower actually receives. At the end of the term, the full face value is due.

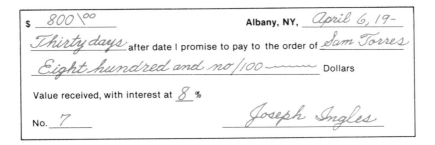

Fig. 17-1   Promissory Note

When a note is sold by the *payee* (Sam Torres in the Fig. 17-1 sample note), the maturity value is discounted. In this case, the term of discount may be the same as the original term or it may be less, since time may have elapsed between the date when the note was signed by the maker and the date when it is discounted. When a note is sold by any holder, it must be endorsed on the back, just as a check would be.

Example 1. J. Jilson signs a non-interest-bearing note for $400, due in 90 days. If the bank's discount rate is 8%, what are the proceeds of the note?

$$\$400 \times .08 \times {}^{90}/_{365} = \$7.89 \text{ Discount}$$
$$\$400 - \$7.89 = \$392.11 \text{ Proceeds}$$

Example 2. F. Fowler signs a note for $400, with interest at 7%, due in 90 days. If the payee discounts the note at 9% on the day it is signed, what are the proceeds to the payee?

$$\$400 + (.07 \times \$400 \times {}^{90}/_{365}) = \$400 + \$6.90 = \$406.90 \text{ Maturity Value}$$
$$\$406.90 \times .09 \times {}^{90}/_{365} = \$9.03 \text{ Discount}$$
$$\$406.90 - \$9.03 = \$397.87 \text{ Proceeds to Payee}$$

Problems

Group 1

Find the bank discount and the proceeds for the following non-interest-bearing notes:

	Face	Term of Discount	Rate	Discount	Proceeds
1.	$1,000	60 days	6%	$_____	$_____

2.	$800	180 days	7%	$_____	$_____
3.	$500	90 days	8%	$_____	$_____
4.	$2,400	75 days	9%	$_____	$_____
5.	$3,000	30 days	5%	$_____	$_____

Group 2

Find the maturity values, bank discounts, and proceeds of the following 6% notes. The terms of the notes and of the discounts are the same.

	Face	Term	Maturity Value	Discount Rate	Discount	Proceeds
1.	$600	90 days	$_____	7%	$_____	$_____
2.	$740	40 days	$_____	5%	$_____	$_____
3.	$2,800	120 days	$_____	8%	$_____	$_____

4. Jill Adams signs a non-interest-bearing note for $450, due in 210 days. What amount does she receive from her bank if the discount rate is 9%?

   $_____

5. The Ajax Company discounted its 9% note for $3,400 at a bank where the discount rate was 8%. The note was due in 110 days. The term of the note and the term of discount were the same. a. What is the maturity value of the note? b. What is the amount of the discount? c. What are the proceeds?

   a. $_____

   b. $_____

   c. $_____

17.2   DATE OF MATURITY AND TERM OF DISCOUNT

When a note is discounted some time after the date of the note, it is necessary to determine the term of discount.

For instance, a wholesaler may sell merchandise to a retailer on credit, with a sixty-day promissory note signed by the retailer as the credit document. After holding the note for ten days, the wholesaler discounts the note at the bank, receiving the proceeds. When the note falls due, the bank will collect the maturity value from the retailer. Should the retailer fail to pay, the bank will collect from the wholesaler who endorsed the note. The wholesaler in effect has promised to pay the maturity value if the retailer does not. In this case, the term of the note is sixty days and the term of discount is fifty days.

The most accurate way to find the term of discount is to determine the maturity date first. Then count the days between the date of discount and the maturity date to get the term of discount.

If the term of the note is expressed in days, the date of maturity is that number of days after the date of the note. This may be computed by using Table 5-1.

If the term of the note is given in months, the date of maturity is the same day of the month, the given number of months in the future. When such a note falls due in a month with fewer days than the date of the note, the date of maturity is the last day of the month.

Example 1. Find the maturity date of a sixty-day note dated April 14.

$$30 - 14 = \quad 16 \quad \text{Days Left in April}$$
$$\underline{+\ 31} \quad \text{Days in May}$$
$$47$$
$$60 - 47 = \quad 13 \quad \text{June Maturity Date}$$

Or, using Table 5-1:
April 14 is Day 104
104 + 60 = 164
Day 164 is June 13

Example 2. Find the maturity date of a two-month note dated April 14.

April 14 + 2 months = June 14

Example 3. Find the date of maturity of a one-month note dated January 31.

January 31 + 1 month = February 28 or 29 (There is no February 31.)

Example 4. On June 25, the Mart Company discounts a customer's three-month note for $1,000, dated May 1. What is the term of discount?

May 1 + 3 months = August 1 Date of Maturity
The term of discount is from June 25 to August 1.

$$5 \quad \text{Days Left in June}$$
$$31 \quad \text{Days in July}$$
$$\underline{+\ 1} \quad \text{Day in August (Maturity Date)}$$
$$37 \quad \text{Days Term of Discount}$$

When the term of the note is given in days, you can subtract the time between the date of the note and the date of discount from the term of the note to find the term of discount. This method is simpler when the time between the date of the note and the date of discount is short.

Problems

Find the dates of maturity for the following:

1. 60-day note dated March 10 _____

2. 2-month note dated February 16 _____

3. 3-month note dated March 19 _____

4. 30-day note dated April 6 _____

5. 60-day note dated June 10 _____

6. 1-month note dated April 25 _____

7. 90-day note dated May 13 _____

8. 30-day note dated October 19 _____

9. 6-month note dated May 27 _____

10. 90-day note dated November 30 _____

11. 2-month note dated March 31 _____

12. 4-month note dated August 29 _____

13. 45-day note dated September 2 _____

14. 180-day note dated March 10 _____

15. 20-day note dated April 18 _____

16. 2-month note dated December 31 _____

17. 3-month note dated November 27 _____

18. 1-month note dated May 31 _____

19. 70-day note dated August 9 _____

20. 5-month note dated October 31 _____

Find the term of discount:

	Date of Note	Term of Note	Date of Discount	Term of Discount
21.	April 19	3 months	May 3	————
22.	March 14	2 months	April 11	————
23.	May 30	1 month	June 11	————
24.	June 16	4 months	August 22	————
25.	November 20	6 months	April 14	————
26.	December 15	60 days	January 19	————
27.	March 17	30 days	April 4	————
28.	April 4	60 days	May 20	————
29.	May 10	90 days	July 7	————
30.	June 8	45 days	July 8	————

17.3   PROCEEDS OF NON-INTEREST-BEARING NOTES

To find the proceeds when a note is discounted:
1. Determine the maturity value.
2. Find the term of discount. To do this, you may need to find the date of maturity as well as the date of discount.
3. Find the rate of discount.
4. Compute the bank discount.
5. Find the proceeds by subtracting the bank discount from the maturity value.

Example. A $2,000 90-day non-interest-bearing note dated March 16 is discounted at 8% on May 15. Find the bank discount and the proceeds.
1. The maturity value is $2,000, as the note is non-interest-bearing.
2. The date of maturity is March 16 + 90 days:

$$31 - 16 = 15 \quad \text{Days Left in March}$$
$$30 \quad \text{Days in April}$$
$$\underline{+ \ 31} \quad \text{Days in May}$$
$$76$$
$$90 - 76 = 14 \quad \text{June Maturity Date}$$

The term of discount is May 15 to June 14:

$$31 - 15 = 16 \quad \text{Days Left in May}$$
$$+ \ 14 \quad \text{Days in June to Maturity Date}$$
$$\overline{ \ 30} \quad \text{Days Term of Discount}$$

3. The rate of discount is given at 8%.

4. The bank discount is for $2,000 at 8% for 30 days:
$$\$2,000 \times .08 \times {}^{30}\!/_{365} = \$13.15 \ \text{Bank Discount}$$

5. $2,000 - $13.15 = $1,986.85 Proceeds

Banks use tables similar to Table 17-1 when computing the discount. In step 4 of this example, the computation would be:
$$\$2,000 \times .006575 = \$13.15$$
By combining days, you can determine the discount for periods not shown directly on the table. For example, to get the amount per dollar for 37 days at 6%, add the rates for 30 days and for 7 days:

$$.004932 \quad \text{Rate for 30 Days}$$
$$+ \ .001151 \quad \text{Rate for 7 Days}$$
$$\overline{.006083} \quad \text{Rate for 37 Days}$$

Table 17-1. Bank Discount Schedule at Annual Rates of Interest

Time in Days	6%	7%	8%	9%
1	.000164	.000192	.000219	.000247
2	.000329	.000384	.000438	.000493
3	.000493	.000575	.000658	.000740
4	.000658	.000767	.000877	.000986
5	.000822	.000959	.001096	.001233
6	.000986	.001151	.001315	.001479
7	.001151	.001342	.001534	.001726
8	.001315	.001534	.001753	.001973
9	.001479	.001726	.001973	.002219
10	.001644	.001918	.002192	.002466
20	.003288	.003836	.004384	.004932
30	.004932	.005753	.006575	.007397
40	.006575	.007671	.008767	.009863
50	.008219	.009589	.010959	.012329
60	.009863	.011507	.013151	.014795
70	.011507	.013425	.015343	.017260
80	.013151	.015342	.017534	.019726
90	.014795	.017260	.019726	.022192

Problems

Fill in the form below for each of the following discounted non-interest-bearing notes:

	Face of Note	*Date of Note*	*Term*	*Discount Rate*	*Discount Date*
1.	$ 800	April 14	60 days	7%	June 1
2.	600	March 28	2 months	8%	May 4
3.	1,800	August 31	4 months	6%	November 16
4.	2,500	June 25	90 days	9%	July 31
5.	12,400	October 14	30 days	8%	November 1

	1.	2.	3.	4.	5.
Maturity Value	$_____	$_____	$_____	$_____	$_____
Term of Discount	_____	_____	_____	_____	_____
Rate of Discount	_____	_____	_____	_____	_____
Bank Discount	$_____	$_____	$_____	$_____	$_____
Proceeds	$_____	$_____	$_____	$_____	$_____

6. Find the proceeds of a note for $2,800, payable 4 months after March 16 and discounted at the bank on April 11 at $7\frac{1}{2}\%$.

$_____

7. On September 4 you received a 60-day promissory note for $1,240 from a friend. What will you get for the note if you discount it at your bank on September 25 at 8%?

$_____

8. Grace Henshaw discounts Henry Bly's 60-day note for $1,760 on May 12 at 7%. The date of the note is April 30. How much credit will Grace receive from the bank?

$_____

9. Gerry Goya received a 90-day note for $4,000, dated June 8. He discounted the note on June 22 at $8\frac{1}{2}\%$. Find the proceeds.

    $_____

10. What is the bank discount on a note for $960, dated April 10 and payable in 4 months, if it is discounted on June 1 at 9%?

    $_____

17.4 DISCOUNTING INTEREST-BEARING NOTES

The process for discounting a non-interest-bearing note is also used for discounting an interest-bearing note. The only difference is that the maturity value will need to be computed. This is done by adding the interest on the note to the face value.

Example. Thomas Bacon received the note shown in Fig. 17-2 from Jill Joy, a customer:

If Bacon discounts this note at his bank on April 20 at 9%, what will he receive as proceeds?
1. Maturity Value: $3,000 + (.08 \times \$3,000 \times {}^{90}\!/_{365}) = \$3,059.18$
2. Date of Maturity: March 21 + 90 days

$$31 - 21 = \begin{array}{l} 10 \text{ Days Left in March} \\ 30 \text{ Days in April} \\ \underline{+31} \text{ Days in May} \\ 71 \end{array}$$

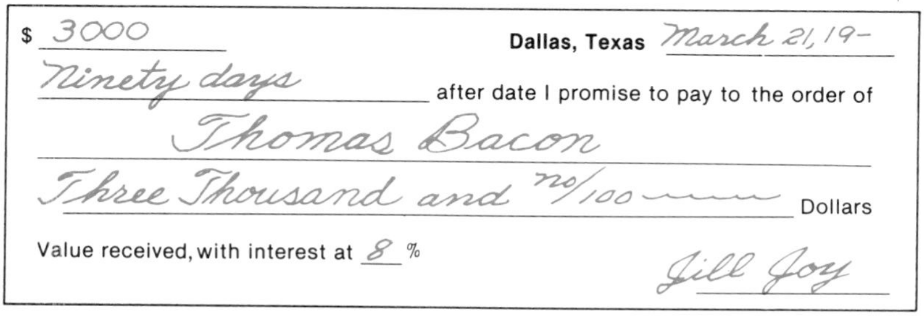

$ _3000_____   Dallas, Texas _March 21, 19-_

_Ninety days_____ after date I promise to pay to the order of

_____ _Thomas Bacon_____

_Three Thousand and ${}^{no}\!/_{100}$_____ Dollars

Value received, with interest at _8_ %

Jill Joy

Fig. 17-2   Promissory Note

$$90 - 71 =$$

19 June Date of Maturity
10 Days Left in April
31 Days in May
+ 19 June Maturity Date
60 Days Term of Discount

3. The rate of discount is given as 9%.
4. .09 × $3,059.18 × $^{60}/_{365}$ = $45.26 Amount of Discount
5. $3,059.18 − $45.26 = $3,013.92 Proceeds

Problems

Find the net proceeds on each of the following interest-bearing notes by using the form given below:

	Date of Note	Face	Term	Interest Rate	Discount Date	Discount Rate
1.	Mar. 5	$ 960	60 days	7%	Apr. 4	8%
2.	Apr. 6	1,500	90 days	8%	May 6	8%
3.	Oct. 8	1,760	60 days	6%	Nov. 8	9%
4.	July 6	1,940	90 days	5%	July 12	7½%
5.	Feb. 14	1,200	30 days	8%	Mar. 1	8½%
6.	May 27	950	90 days	7½%	June 10	9%
7.	Aug. 28	300	45 days	6½%	Sept. 5	10%
8.	Jan. 10	870	60 days	6%	Feb. 3	6%
9.	Dec. 4	2,400	90 days	7%	Jan. 5	8%

	Maturity Value	Term of Discount	Rate of Discount	Amount of Discount	Proceeds
1.	$_____	_____	_____	$_____	$_____
2.	_____	_____	_____	_____	_____
3.	_____	_____	_____	_____	_____
4.	_____	_____	_____	_____	_____
5.	_____	_____	_____	_____	_____
6.	_____	_____	_____	_____	_____
7.	_____	_____	_____	_____	_____

	Maturity Value	Term of Discount	Rate of Discount	Amount of Discount	Proceeds
8.	$_____	_____	_____	$_____	$_____
9.	_____	_____	_____	_____	_____

10. Find the proceeds of the note shown in Fig. 17-3, which was discounted on August 4 at 9%.

$_____

Fig. 17-3   Promissory Note

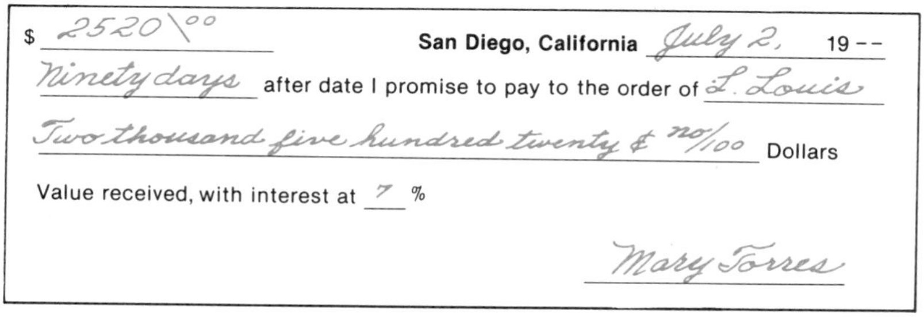

```
$  2520 00                    San Diego, California  July 2,      19 --

Ninety days  after date I promise to pay to the order of  L. Louis

Two thousand five hundred twenty & no/100  Dollars

Value received, with interest at  7  %

                                        Mary Torres
```

Chapter Review

1. May Jenner signs a note for $800, due in 120 days. If the bank's discount rate is 9%, how much does she receive?

$_____

2. Find the maturity value of a $2,500 note due in 90 days, with interest at 7%.

$_____

3. Find the maturity date of a 75-day note dated April 10.

_____

4. Find the maturity date of a 3-month note dated November 30.

_____

5. On May 6, the Sample Company discounts a customer's 4-month note, dated April 7. What is the term of discount?

    _____

6. A $4,000 90-day note dated June 24 is discounted on July 18 at 8%. Find a. the bank discount and b. the proceeds.

    a. $_____

    b. $_____

7. From a customer, the Good Company accepted a 120-day note for $2,000 with interest at 8%. The same day, the note was discounted at the bank at 9%. What were the proceeds?

    $_____

8. The Joy Company receives a note from a customer promising to pay $2,400 in 30 days, with interest at 7%. Ten days later, the company discounts the note at 8%. How much does it receive?

    $_____

18

Partnership Mathematics

A *partnership* is a contractual relationship of two or more persons who join together to operate a business for a profit. The partners generally sign a written contract, called *articles of partnership,* which specifies how profits and losses are to be divided. The partners may want to share profits equally or to adjust the division agreement to take into account the amount of money invested by each partner, the time spent at work, special talents, or length of service. If no written agreement exists, then profits and losses are usually divided equally. Many disagreements between or among partners can be avoided by written agreements. Any method agreed upon for the division of profits may be used. This chapter will explore some of the more common methods.

18.1 DIVISION OF PROFITS AND LOSSES—EQUAL OR RATIO

If the partners agree or if they have no written agreement, each share of net income or loss will be the same. For example, Mary Dunn, Walter Jacobs, and Jane Kolbe divided profits and losses equally. Their income-and-loss history is:

1977	$42,000 Net Income
1978	$21,000 Net Income
1979	$(12,000)[1] Net Loss
1980	$(18,000) Net Loss

[1] Parentheses denote a loss or deduction.

A distribution of net income would be reported as follows:

Net Income Distribution Report

Year	Dunn		Jacobs		Kolbe		Total
	1	+	1	+	1	=	3
1977	$14,000		$14,000		$14,000		$42,000
1978	7,000		7,000		7,000		21,000
1979	(4,000)		(4,000)		(4,000)		(12,000)
1980	(6,000)		(6,000)		(6,000)		(18,000)

Calculations:

$$1 + 1 + 1 = 3 \text{ parts}$$

1977	$42,000 ÷ 3 = $14,000 Each
1978	$21,000 ÷ 3 = $7,000 Each
1979	$(12,000) ÷ 3 = $(4,000) Each
1980	$(18,000) ÷ 3 = $(6,000) Each

Division by a ratio may also be agreed upon. For example, suppose Mary, Walter, and Jane agreed to share profits on the basis of some ratio. A possible reason for this would be that Mary plans to work more hours than Walter and Jane, so they divide profits, giving Mary 2 parts and Walter and Jane 1 part each, or a 2:1:1 ratio. Using the same profit-and-loss history from the example above, the profits and losses would be divided as follows:

Net Income Distribution Report

Year	Dunn		Jacobs		Kolbe		Total
	2	+	1	+	1	=	4
1977	$21,000		$10,500		$10,500		$42,000
1978	10,500		5,250		5,250		21,000
1979	(6,000)		(3,000)		(3,000)		(12,000)
1980	(9,000)		(4,500)		(4,500)		(18,000)

Calculations:

$$2 + 1 + 1 = 4 \text{ parts}$$

1977	$42,000 ÷ 4 = $10,500 per Part
1978	$21,000 ÷ 4 = $5,250 per Part
1979	$(12,000) ÷ 4 = $(3,000) per Part
1980	$(18,000) ÷ 4 = $(4,500) per Part

Dunn

1977	$10,500 × 2 = $21,500
1978	$5,250 × 2 = $10,500
1979	$(3,000) × 2 = $(6,000)
1980	$(4,500) × 2 = $(9,000)

Problems

1. Three partners agree to divide income and loss equally. What will each partner's share be for each of the three years below if there is no written agreement?

		A	B	C
1979	$21,000 Net Income	$_____	$_____	$_____
1980	(18,000) Net Loss	_____	_____	_____
1981	31,000 Net Income	_____	_____	_____

2. In each of the cases listed below, use the ratio provided to determine each partner's share of income or loss.

	Ratio			*Share*		
Income (Loss)	A	B	C	A	B	C
$ 18,000	3 :	2 :	2	$_____	$_____	$_____
(27,000)	4 :	4 :	1	_____	_____	_____
15,000	1 :	1 :	3	_____	_____	_____
(18,000)	3 :	2 :	3	_____	_____	_____

3. Mary Anderson, Delila Day, and Mary Brothers operate The Clothing Shop. During the first year of operations, the partnership had a net loss of $9,000. In the second year, the partnership had net income of $15,000, and in the third year net income was $18,000. What was each partner's total share of income or loss over the three year period?

Year	Anderson	Day	Brothers
1	$_____	$_____	$_____
2	_____	_____	_____
3	_____	_____	_____
Total	_____	_____	_____

4. Five partners agree to share profits according to the following ratio:

Melinda Larson	3 Parts $_____
Rose Espland	3 Parts _____
Jan Wallers	3 Parts _____
Eleanor Mikes	2 Parts _____
Bob Mabbs	2 Parts _____

For the year 1979, net income amounted to $60,000. What was each partner's share?

5. Three partners agree to divide profits and losses according to the ratio of time spent at work. Mark spends three-quarters of his time, Jean spends half her time, and Esther spends a third of her time on the job. What will be the profit share for each partner if net income is $180,000?

Mark $_____

Jean $_____

Esther $_____

18.2   DIVISION OF PROFITS AND LOSSES—INVESTMENT RATIO

Partners may agree to divide profits and losses on the basis of each individual's investment in the partnership. The ratio used to find each partner's share may be determined by using the amount of original investment, annual beginning investments, or average annual investment.

Example 1—Original Investment. Brooks, Brown, and Brabec form a partnership by investing $18,000, $12,000, and $8,000, respectively. The articles of copartnership state that profits and losses are to be divided on the basis of the original investments. The net income for the fiscal period just ended is $9,500. What is each partner's share of net income?

Net Income Distribution Report

	Investment	Fractional Share	Amount
Brooks	$18,000	$18/38$	$4,500
Brown	12,000	$12/38$	3,000
Brabec	8,000	$8/38$	2,000
Totals	$38,000		$9,500

Calculations:
$9,500 ÷ $38,000 = $.25 Income per Dollar, or $250 per $1,000 Invested
Brooks 18 × $250 = $4,500
Brown 12 × $250 = $3,000
Brabec 8 × $250 = $2,000
> *or*

Brooks $^{18}/_{38}$ × $9,500 = $4,500
Brown $^{12}/_{38}$ × $9,500 = $3,000
Brabec $^8/_{38}$ × $9,500 = $2,000

If the agreement allows partners to withdraw from or add to their capital investments, the division ratio may be based upon the relative capital investments at the beginning of each fiscal year.

Example 2—Beginning Investment. A. Johnson and B. Johnson start a partnership with original investments of $30,000 each. The agreement states that profits and losses are to be divided on the basis of annual beginning investments. In the first year of operations, profits amounted to $16,000. A. Johnson withdrew half her share of profits, and B. Johnson withdrew $2,000. Profits for the second year were $21,000.

Net Income Distribution Report—Year 1

	Investment	Fractional Share	Amount
A. Johnson	$30,000	$^1/_2$	$ 8,000
B. Johnson	30,000	$^1/_2$	8,000
Totals	$60,000		$16,000

Capital Changes—Year 1

	A. Johnson	B. Johnson
Profit Share	$ 8,000	$ 8,000
Withdrawals	(− 4,000)	(− 2,000)
Investment Increase	4,000	6,000
Old Beginning Balance	30,000	30,000
New Beginning Balance	$34,000	$36,000

Net Income Distribution Report—Year 2

	Investment	Fractional Share	Amount
A. Johnson	$34,000	$^{34}/_{70}$	$10,200
B. Johnson	36,000	$^{36}/_{70}$	10,800
Totals	$70,000		$21,000

Calculations:

$21,000 ÷ $70,000 = $.30 Income per Dollar, or $300
per $1,000 Investment

A. Johnson 34 × $300 = $10,200
B. Johnson 36 × $300 = $10,800

or

A. Johnson $^{34}/_{70}$ × $21,000 = $10,200
B. Johnson $^{36}/_{70}$ × $21,000 = $10,800

When the agreement allows partners to add to or withdraw from their investments, a more equitable approach to profit sharing is an *average investment ratio*. An average investment amount guards against large withdrawals immediately after a beginning balance ratio has been calculated.

Example 3—Average Investment. Harvey Lee, Cliff Lewis, and Wendy Fisher agree to share profits in the ratio of their average investments. Their 1979 investment and withdrawal transactions are summarized below:

| Partner | Investments | | Withdrawals | |
	Amounts	Date	Amounts	Date
Lee	$60,000	January 1	$10,000	April 1
	20,000	July 1		
Lewis	80,000	January 1	20,000	July 1
Fisher	90,000	January 1	10,000	April 1
			10,000	July 1
			10,000	October 1

Net income for 1979 was $83,000. What was each partner's share?

Net Income Distribution Report

	Average Investment	Fractional Share	Amount
Lee	$ 62,500	$^{62,500}/_{207,500}$	$25,000
Lewis	70,000	$^{70,000}/_{207,500}$	28,000
Fisher	75,000	$^{75,000}/_{207,500}$	30,000
Totals	$207,500		$83,000

Calculations:

Average Investment—Lee

Capital Balance	Dates	Months	Month Dollars
$60,000	Jan. 1–Mar. 31	3	× $60,000 = $180,000
50,000	Apr. 1–June 30	3	× 50,000 = 150,000
70,000	July 1–Dec. 31	6	× 70,000 = 420,000
		12	$750,000

$750,000 ÷ 12 = $62,500 Average Investment

Average Investment—Lewis

Capital Balance	Dates	Months	Month Dollars
$80,000	Jan. 1–June 30	6	× $80,000 = $480,000
60,000	July 1–Dec. 31	6	× 60,000 = 360,000
		12	$840,000

$840,000 ÷ 12 = $70,000 Average Investment

Average Investment—Fisher

Capital Balance	Dates	Months	Month Dollars
$90,000	Jan. 1–Mar. 31	3	× $90,000 = $270,000
80,000	Apr. 1–June 30	3	× 80,000 = 240,000
70,000	July 1–Sept. 30	3	× 70,000 = 210,000
60,000	Oct. 1–Dec. 31	3	× 60,000 = 180,000
		12	$900,000

$900,000 ÷ 12 = $75,000 Average Investment

$62,500 + $70,000 + $75,000 = $207,500 Total Average Investment

Calculations:

$83,000 ÷ $207,500 = $.40 Income per Dollar, or $400 per $1,000 Invested.

$$\text{Lee } 62.5 \times \$400 = \$25,000$$
$$\text{Lewis } 70 \times \$400 = \$28,000$$
$$\text{Fisher } 75 \times \$400 = \$30,000$$

or

$$\$62,500/\$207,500 \times \$83,000 = \$25,000$$
$$\$70,000/\$207,500 \times \$83,000 = \$28,000$$
$$\$75,000/\$207,500 \times \$83,000 = \$30,000$$

Problems

1. Anderson, Armstrong, and Bails invest $15,000, $20,000, and $25,000, respectively, in a partnership. The partnership's net income for the year is $36,300. Profits are to be shared in the ratio of the original investments. What portion of the profits will be allocated to each partner?

   Anderson $_____

   Armstrong $_____

   Bails $_____

   Total $_____

2. Dee, DeBoer, and Dobson agreed to divide profits in the ratio of their capital balances at the beginning of each year. The partnership had net income of $12,000 the first year and a loss of ($4,000) the second. Assume that Dee invested $25,000; DeBoer, $15,000; and Dobson, $20,000. No withdrawals were made. Prepare a report of profit and/or loss allocations for the two years of operations.

Year	Dee	DeBoer	Dobson	Total
1	$_____	$_____	$_____	$_____
2	_____	_____	_____	_____

3. Cramer and Curtis are partners with respective investment balances of $53,000 and $65,000 on January 1, 1979. On March 1, Cramer withdrew $3,000, and on August 1 she invested $6,000. Curtis invested $3,000 on March 1, July 1, and September 1. They agree to share profits in the ratio of their average investment. Prepare a report showing the division of $18,000 net income.

   Cramer $_____

   Curtis $_____

   Total $_____

4. A. Larson and B. Larson form a partnership on July 1, 1981, by investing $12,000 and $15,000, respectively. The articles of copartnership state that profits and losses are to be allocated in the ratio of the average

investments. A. Larson invests an additional $2,000 on October 1, and B. Larson invests an additional $2,000 on the same day. If net income for the six months of operations is $21,750, how much will be allocated to each partner?

A. Larson $_____

B. Larson $_____

Total $_____

5. Continuing with the facts of Problem 4, assume that for the twelve months ending December 31, 1982, the partnership earns $23,000. A Larson withdraws $3,750 on July 1, 1982, and B. Larson withdraws $3,000 on March 1, July 1, and October 1, 1982. What amounts of net income would be allocated to each partner for 1982?

A. Larson $_____

B. Larson $_____

Total $_____

18.3   DIVISION OF PROFITS AND LOSSES—INTEREST ON INVESTMENTS

Partners may choose to recognize investment-amount differences by agreeing to an interest allowance on investment. An agreed-to rate, say 6%, is multiplied by either the beginning or the average investment. The interest-allowance amounts are then deducted from net income, with the balance divided equally or according to some agreed-upon ratio. Using an interest allowance is just another way to provide for differences in each partner's invested capital.

Example 1—Interest on Investment. On January 1, 1980, Williams had a balance in his capital account of $100,000, and Johnson had a balance of $150,000 in her account on the same date. Their agreement provides that each partner is to be allowed 10% on the beginning investment, with the balance allocated in a 3:2 ratio. If net income for 1980 is $36,000, what will be each partner's share?

Net Income Distribution Report

	Williams	Johnson	Total
Interest Allowance	$10,000	$15,000	$25,000
Balance 3:2 Ratio	6,600	4,400	11,000
Totals	$16,600	$19,400	$36,000

Calculations:

Interest Allowance

	Net Income		$36,000
Williams	$100,000 × 10% =	$10,000	
Johnson	$150,000 × 10% =	$15,000	
		$25,000	(25,000)
	Unallocated Balance		$11,000

3:2 Ratio

	$11,000 ÷ 5 = $ 2,200 per Part
Williams	3 × $2,200 = $ 6,600
Johnson	2 × $2,200 = $ 4,400
Total	$11,000

Example 2—Interest on Investment. Assume the same facts as in Example 1, except that the net income for the year amounts to $15,000.

Net Income Distribution Report

	Williams	Johnson	Total
Interest Allowance	$10,000	$15,000	$25,000
Deficiency Deduction 3:2 ratio	(6,000)	(4,000)	(10,000)
Totals	$ 4,000	$11,000	$15,000

Calculations:

Interest Allowance

	Net Income		$15,000
Williams	$100,000 × 10% =	$10,000	
Johnson	$150,000 × 10% =	$15,000	
		$25,000	(25,000)

Deficiency (Excess Interest Allowance) $(10,000)

The sum of the interest allowance exceeds net income by $10,000; therefore, the *deficiency* is divided in the ratio of 3:2 and subtracted from each partner's interest allowance, to arrive at each partner's share of net income.

3:2 Ratio

	$(10,000) \div 5 = $(2,000)$ Deficiency per Part
Williams	$3 \times$(2,000) = $(6,000)$
Johnson	$2 \times$(2,000) = \underline{(4,000)}$
Total	$(10,000)$

Example 3—Interest on Investment. Assume the same facts as in Example 1, except that for 1980 the firm has a *loss* of $10,000.

Net Loss Distribution Report

	Williams	Johnson	Total
Interest Allowance	$ 10,000	$15,000	$25,000
Deficiency Deduction 3:2 Ratio	(21,000)	(14,000)	(35,000)
Totals	$(11,000)	$ 1,000	$(10,000)

Note: Johnson's capital increases by $1,000, while Williams's decreases by $11,000.

Calculations:

Interest Allowance

	Net Loss		$(10,000)
Williams	$100,000 \times 10\% = $10,000		
Johnson	$150,000 \times 10\% = $15,000		
	$25,000	(25,000)	
	Total Deficiency	$(35,000)	

The sum of the interest allowance is added to the net loss to arrive at a total *deficiency* figure. The deficiency is divided in the ratio of 3:2 and subtracted from each partner's interest allowance to arrive at each partner's share of net loss:

3:2 Ratio

	$(35,000) \div 5 = $(7,000)$ Deficiency per Part
Williams	$3 \times$(7,000) = $(21,000)$
Johnson	$2 \times$(7,000) = \underline{(14,000)}$
Total	$(35,000)$

Problems

1. Scott and Stevens formed a partnership. Scott invested $15,000, and Stevens $20,000. What was each partner's share of net income or loss in each case, if 6% was allowed on investment and the balance was divided equally?

	Scott	Stevens	Total
a. Net Income $6,000	$_____	$_____	$_____
b. Net Income $2,000	_____	_____	_____
c. Net Loss $(3,000)	_____	_____	_____

2. E. Olson and K. Perkins are partners, with capital balances of $97,000 and $108,000, respectively. The interest allowance is 8% on investment, with remaining net income or loss divided in a ratio of 7:3. What is each partner's share in each case below?

	Olson	Perkins	Total
a. Net Income $36,400	$_____	$_____	$_____
b. Net Income $15,400	_____	_____	_____
c. Net Loss $(7,400)	_____	_____	_____

3. Stewart and Stone formed a partnership on January 1, 1979. Stewart invested $20,000, and Stone $35,000. Stewart withdrew $3,000 on April 1 and $2,000 on September 1, 1979. Stone withdrew $2,000 on May 1 and $3,000 on November 1, 1979. The partnership agreement called for interest at 6% on the average investment, with the balance of income or loss divided equally. What was each partner's share if net income amounted to $12,000 for 1979?

Stewart $_____

Stone $_____

Total $_____

4. In their partnership, Hay begins the fiscal year with a capital balance of $15,000, and Hill starts with $12,000. Hay invests $2,000 for the year and withdraws $150 a week, while Hill adds $2,000 during the year and

withdraws $200 a week. The agreement allows for an 8% interest allowance on ending capital balances before profits. The remainder is to be divided equally. What is each partner's share of $16,000 net income?

Hay $_____

Hill $_____

Total $_____

5. Abigail, Berniece, and Catherine Fisher, sisters, formed a partnership on July 1, 1979, by investing $12,000 each. On August 1, Catherine withdrew $2,000. On September 1, Abigail and Berniece each withdrew $2,000. Abigail and Berniece invested $2,000 each on December 1, 1979, and Catherine invested $1,000 on the same date. The written agreement stated that profits and losses were to be divided on the basis of average capital invested, after allowing 3% interest on average investment. If their 1979 six-month net income was $1,800, what was each sister's share?

Abigail $_____

Berniece $_____

Catherine $_____

Total $_____

18.4   DIVISION OF PROFITS AND LOSSES—SALARY ALLOWANCES

Talents and time worked may vary with each partner. The partnership agreement may provide for differences in talent or time by providing a different salary allowance to each partner.

Example 1—Salary Allowance. Gowan and Gull enter into a partnership. Gowan is allowed a salary of $5,000, and Gull, a salary of $8,500. The balance of net income after salary allowances is to be divided equally. Net income for the year is $21,500.

Net Income Distribution Report

	Gowan	*Gull*	*Total*
Salary Allowance	$5,000	$8,500	$13,500
Balance ½ Each	4,000	4,000	8,000
Total	$9,000	$12,500	$21,500

Calculation:

Salary Allowance

Net Income		$21,500
Gowan Salary Allowance	$5,000	
Gull Salary Allowance	8,000	
	$13,500	(13,500)
Unallocated Balance		$ 8,000

$8,000 \div 2 = $4,000$ Each Partner

As with the case of interest allowances, the salary allowance may exceed the net income for the year or the partnership may experience a loss. The steps in the calculation of each partner's share are the same as with interest allowances.

Example 2—Salary Allowance. On January 1, 1979, Eddy had a balance of $100,000 in his capital account, Erickson had a balance of $150,000, and James had a balance of $75,000. The profit-and-loss agreement allowed for a salary of $20,000 to Eddy, $15,000 to Erickson, and $10,000 to James. Any remaining profits or losses were to be divided equally. For the year ended 1979, the firm experienced a ($21,000) net loss. What was each partner's share of the loss?

Net Loss Distribution Report

	Eddy	Erickson	James	Total
Salary Allowance	$20,000	$15,000	$ 10,000	$ 45,000
Deficiency Deduction	(22,000)	(22,000)	(22,000)	(66,000)
Totals	$(2,000)	$(7,000)	$(12,000)	$(21,000)

Calculations:

Salary Allowance

Net Loss		$(21,000)
Eddy Salary Allowance	$20,000	
Erickson Salary Allowance	15,000	
James Salary Allowance	10,000	
	$45,000	(45,000)
Total Deficiency		$(66,000)

$(66,000) \div 3 = $(22,000)$ Each

Problems

1. Lew, Lear, and Luff form a partnership. Lew invests $15,000, Lear $20,000, and Luff $25,000. What is each partner's share of net income in each case below, if the agreement calls for a salary allowance of $6,000, $4,000, and $4,000, respectively and the balance is to be shared equally?

	Lew	Lear	Luff	Total
a. Net Income $38,000	$_____	$_____	$_____	$_____
b. Net Income $25,300	_____	_____	_____	_____
c. Net Income $18,200	_____	_____	_____	_____

2. A. and B. are partners with original capital balances of $75,000 and $50,000, respectively. A. is allowed a salary of $6,000, and B. is allowed a salary of $8,000. The remaining net income or loss is divided in the ratio of their original capital balances. Find each partner's share in each case below:

	A.	B.	Total
a. Net Income $18,000	$_____	$_____	$_____
b. Net Income $12,000	_____	_____	_____
c. Net Loss ($11,000)	_____	_____	_____

3. Nelson and McDonald share profits in the ratio of their average monthly capital balances with allowances of a $5,000 salary to Nelson and a $3,000 salary to McDonald. Nelson starts the year with a capital balance of $36,000 and invests an additional $6,000 on July 1. McDonald begins the year with a capital balance of $42,000 and invests an additional $2,000 on March 1. What is each partner's share a. if the firm experiences a profit of $18,000 and b. if the firm experiences a loss of ($4,000)?

	Nelson	McDonald	Total
a.	$_____	$_____	$_____
b.	_____	_____	_____

4. X and Y form a partnership. X invests $41,000, and Y invests $82,000. The agreement provides for salary allowances of $1,000 a month to X and $1,200 a month to Y. Any balance of net income is to be shared equally. Each partner withdraws $1,000 per month. If profits for the year amount to $78,000, find each partner's share of net income.

    X $_____

    Y $_____

    Total $_____

5. Mutch and Moore begin the year with capital balances of $130,000 and $140,000, respectively. The agreement provides for 3% investment return on beginning capital balances, a salary allowance of $3,000 per month to Mutch and $4,000 per month to Moore. The balance of profits is to be divided in the ratio of the annual salary allowances. Find each partner's share if net income for the year is $134,000.

    Mutch $_____

    Moore $_____

    Total $_____

Chapter Review

1. For each of the cases below, show the division of net income or net loss among investors A, B, and C. Use the ratio of investment for the division.

	Investments			Net Profit	Net Loss		A	B	C	Total
	A	B	C							
a.	$4,000	$4,000	$4,000	$10,000			$____	$____	$____	$____
b.	5,000	3,000	2,000		($10,000)		____	____	____	____
c.	2,000	3,500	2,500	1,400			____	____	____	____
d.	3,500	2,500	1,500	750			____	____	____	____
e.	1,000	2,000	3,000		(1,000)		____	____	____	____

2. Sanchez and Tally own a garden shop. Their first year of operations showed a profit of $8,357.01. They had agreed to share profits and losses equally, after allowing 6% interest on average investment. Their investments and withdrawals for the year were:

Sanchez:	January 1	Investment	$30,000
	July 1	Withdrawal	5,000
	September 1	Investment	5,000
Tally:	January 1	Investment	$25,000
	July 1	Investment	2,500
	September 1	Withdrawal	2,500

Find each partner's share of net income.

Sanchez $_____

Tally $_____

Total $_____

3. Find each partner's share of income or loss in each of the following cases:

	Investment			Profit or Loss for Year		Rate of Interest Allowance	Balance Divided
	X	Y	Z				
a.	$10,000	$ 7,500	$ 5,000	Profit	$1,000	6%	Equally
b.	15,000	10,000	15,000	Profit	4,000	6%	15:10:15
c.	8,000	4,000	4,000	Loss	(200)	6%	Equally
d.	5,000	7,000	12,000	Profit	3,000	6%	5:7:12
e.	4,000	7,000	9,000	Profit	1,500	6%	4:7:9

	X	Y	Z	Total
a.	$_____	$_____	$_____	$_____
b.	_____	_____	_____	_____
c.	_____	_____	_____	_____
d.	_____	_____	_____	_____
e.	_____	_____	_____	_____

4. A and B agreed to start a business with a total investment of $40,000. Each partner was to invest one-half of the needed capital. A was to receive 40% of the profit, and B was to receive 60%. A was short of funds, so he invested only $15,000. B made up A's shortage by investing the additional amount needed to bring the firm's capital to $40,000. B is to be allowed 6% on the excess investment over the agreed amount. Profits for the year were $1,200. What was each partner's share of profits?

A $_____

B $_____

Total $_____

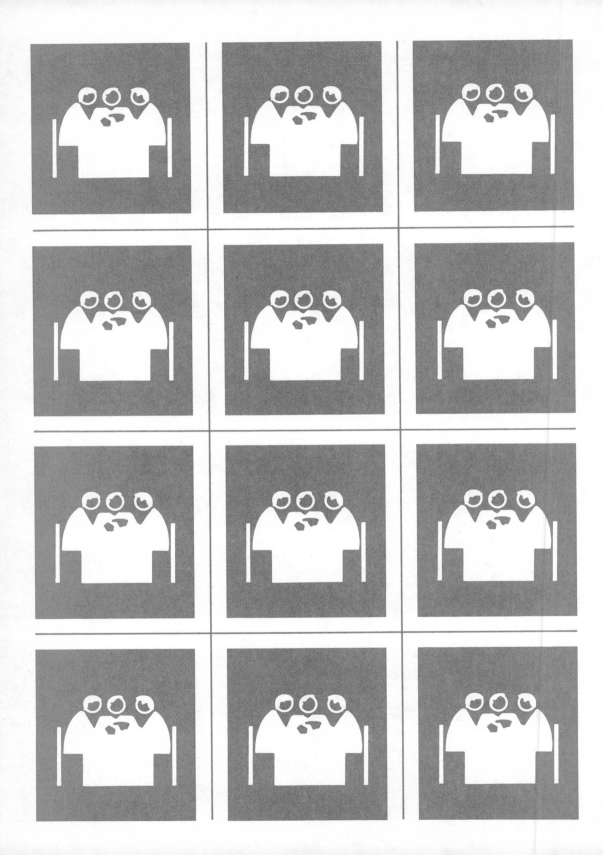

19

Corporations and Cooperatives

19.1 BUYING AND SELLING STOCK

Ownership interests in a corporation are represented by the number of shares of *capital stock* held by each owner. Each share of stock represents a portion of ownership in the corporation's assets. The maximum number of ownership shares that a corporation may issue to the public is set by its charter. Once the shares have been issued, the individual owners may transfer their ownership by selling their stock. The sale and purchase of capital stock is usually done through a formal *securities exchange*.

Two of the major securities exchanges in the United States are located in New York City: the New York Stock Exchange and the American Stock Exchange. These provide a marketplace for about 90 percent of the stock and bond sales in this country. The prices of securities traded on the exchange are published daily in major newspapers throughout the United States.

Stock price quotations, a sample of which is shown in Table 19-1, are based upon exchange transactions. These are governed by supply and demand.

The table is read as follows:
52 Weeks—High and Low: This shows the highest and lowest prices for the stock during the past 52 weeks; for example, AMF traded in a range from a high of $23.65 to a low of $15.50.

Table 19-1. Stock Quotations

52 Weeks High	52 Weeks Low	Stock	Dividend	Sales in 100s	High	Low	Close	Net Change
$23^5/_8$	$15^1/_2$	AMF	1.24	968	$17^7/_8$	17	$17^1/_8$	$- {}^3/_4$
$40^5/_8$	$27^1/_2$	AmExp	1.60	5623	$31^1/_2$	$29^1/_8$	$29^3/_8$	$- 2^3/_4$
$23^3/_8$	$14^3/_8$	BellHow	.96	408	$15^1/_2$	$15^1/_4$	$15^3/_8$	$- {}^1/_8$
$316^1/_4$	$234^3/_4$	IBM	13.76	4693	$314^1/_2$	$307^5/_8$	$308^1/_4$	$- 4^3/_4$
$32^3/_4$	$23^3/_4$	Lenox	1.12	93	29	$28^5/_8$	$28^3/_4$	$+ {}^1/_2$
14	9	MaryK	.48	203	$11^1/_2$	$10^3/_4$	$11^1/_2$	$+ {}^3/_4$
$73^7/_8$	$58^1/_8$	Mobil	4.80	6769	$73^7/_8$	$71^1/_4$	$71^1/_4$	—
$32^3/_4$	$6^1/_8$	Playboy	.12	514	$17^5/_8$	$15^5/_8$	$16^1/_2$	-1
59	$37^7/_8$	Revlon	1.30	4388	$53^5/_8$	$50^1/_8$	$50^5/_8$	$+ 2^7/_8$
$37^3/_8$	$28^1/_2$	ShellOil	2	1172	$33^3/_8$	$31^3/_4$	$32^1/_8$	—
$92^1/_2$	$61^3/_8$	Texinst	2	687	$87^1/_4$	83	$83^1/_8$	$- 4^3/_8$
64	$40^1/_2$	Xerox	2	5006	$59^3/_4$	57	57	$- 2^3/_4$

Stock: The name of the company is abbreviated; "AmExp" stands for the American Express Company.

Dividend: This expresses the last quarterly or semiannual dividend declaration as an annual rate; BellHow paid dividends at an annual rate of $.96 per share.

Sales in 100s: The total shares are shown in 100-share lots; IBM, 439, 300 shares were traded.

High—Low: This shows the highest and lowest price for the stocks during the past trading day; Lenox stock sold as high as 29 and as low as $28^5/_8$ dollars a share.

Close: This is closing price for the stock the past day; Mary K closed at $11^1/_2$ on the day shown.

Net Change: This shows the difference between the closing price and the closing price of the preceding day; Playboy was *down* 1, Revlon up $2^7/_8$, and Mobil showed no change.

Notice that stock prices are quoted in dollars and fractions of dollars. Eighths, fourths, and halves are the fractions used. For example, Texinst (Texas Instruments) sold 68,700 shares, with a closing price of $83^1/_8$, or $83.125.

Most stocks traded on the major securities exchanges are sold and purchased in *round lots,* usually 100-share units. (A round lot for infrequently traded shares may be smaller.) Stock sales in units less than a round lot are called *odd lots.* For example, a sale of 35 shares would be an odd-lot sale. Sales may be in round lots, odd lots, or some combination.

Securities are usually bought or sold through a *brokerage firm* by a broker. A fee or *commission* is charged for these services. These charges vary, depending somewhat on the service rendered by the broker in the way of research and advice. One broker's fee schedule shows the following commission rates:

Up to $100	10%
$100 to $1,000	3.3%
$1,000 to $10,000	2.5%
$10,000 to $30,000	2.0%
Over $30,000	1.75%

In addition, on sales (not purchases), the Securities Exchange Commission (SEC) charges special fees, and states where exchanges are listed may levy a transfer tax on each share traded. New York State transfer taxes are:

	Residents	*Nonresidents*
Per share, under $5	$.0125	$.0078
$5 to $9.99	.025	.0156
$10 to $19.99	.0375	.0234
$20 or over	.05	.0313

The total *cost basis* for stock purchases includes the price per share, together with any fees.

Example 1. Stock Purchase—Round Lot. An investor purchased 100 shares of Lenox at $29^5/_8$. What was the total cost of the purchase, including a commission of 2.5%?

100 Shares × $29.625 per share	=	$2,962.50
Commission: 2.5% × $2,962.50	=	74.06
Total Cost		$3,036.56

Cost per Share $3,036.56 ÷ 100 = $30.37

When odd-lot purchases are made, the broker must buy the stock through an odd-lot dealer. For the extra service, the odd-lot dealer charges a fee, called the *odd-lot differential fee*. The usual fee is $^1/_8$ ($12^1/_2$¢) per share.

Example 2. Stock Purchase—Odd Lot. An investor purchased 23 shares of BellHow, listed at $15^1/_2$. What was the total cost of the purchase, including the commission of 3.3%?

Price per Share	$15.50
Odd-Lot Differential	+ .125
Cost per Share, Before Commission	$15.625
23 Shares × $15.625 =	$359.38
Commission: .033 × $359.38 =	11.86
Total Cost	$371.24

Cost per Share $371.24 ÷ 23 = $16.14

Example 3. Stock Purchase—Combination: Round + Odd Lot. An investor purchased 412 shares of Xerox, listed at $59^3/_8$. What was the total cost of the purchase, including the commission of 2%?

Round-Lot: 400 Shares × $59.375 =	$23,750.00
Odd-Lot: 12 Shares × ($59.375 + $.125) =	+ 714.00
	$24,464.00
Commission: .02 × $24,464 =	+ 489.28
Total Cost	$24.953.28

Cost per Share = $24,953.28 ÷ 412 = $60.57

Example 4. Sale of Stock. Mary Churchill sold 75 shares of Shell Oil at $33^3/_8$. In addition to the 2.5% commission, she paid a New York State transfer tax of $.0313 per share. The Securities Exchange Commission also levies a fee of $.01 per $300 (or fractional part thereof) on stock sales. What are Ms. Churchill's total proceeds from the sale. What are the proceeds per share?

Price per Share	$33.375	
Odd-Lot Differential	− .125	
Total per Share	$33.250	
75 Shares × Gross Proceeds	$33.250 =	$2,493.75

Commission: 2.5% × $2,493.75 = $62.34
NYS Transfer Fee: 3.13¢ × 75 =   2.35
SEC Fee: $.01 × 9   =   .09
Total Fees $64.78
Net proceeds: $2,493.75 − 64.78   = $2,428.97
        Receipts per Share: $2,428.97 ÷ 75 = $32.39

Problems

1. Use the price quotations found in Table 19-1 and the broker's schedule shown to complete the following:

Stocks	Purchases	Price	Total	Commission	Total Cost
A. AMF	200	$ _____	$ _____	$ _____	$ _____
B. IBM	175	_____	_____	_____	_____
C. MaryK	153	_____	_____	_____	_____
D. Playboy	500	_____	_____	_____	_____
E. Xerox	35	_____	_____	_____	_____

    What is the cost per share for the 153 shares of MaryK purchased?

    $ _____

2. According to the schedule shown, what is the commission on the purchase of 38 shares of Avon, listed at $51^3/_4$? What is the cost per share?

    Total Commission $ _____

    Cost per Share $ _____

3. At the rates listed, what is the commission on 135 shares of GM, if the current price is $56^3/_8$? What is the cost per share?

    Total Commission $ _____

    Cost per Share $ _____

4. What are the proceeds from a sale of 121 shares of KMart, listed at $24^1/_8$, if the commission is 2.5%, the New York State transfer tax is 5¢ per share, and SEC fees are 1¢ per $300 or fraction thereof?

    $ _____

5. What are the proceeds from a sale of 57 shares of Mobil, if the stock is sold at the high for the day, the commission rate is 2.5%, the SEC levies a fee of $.01 per $300 or fractional part thereof, and the New York State transfer tax is 3.13¢ per share. (Use Table 19-1.)

$ —————

19.2 BUYING AND SELLING BONDS

When a corporation needs large amounts of additional capital and does not wish to expand ownership interest, it may borrow money by issuing *bonds*. A bond is a written agreement to pay a principal amount (*face*), usually in multiples of $1,000, at a future maturity date. The corporation generally pays a stated rate of interest, based on the face, semiannually.

Some bond price quotations are shown in Table 19-2.

Table 19-2. Bond Quotations

Bonds			Current Yield	Volume	High	Low	Close	Net Change
AAir	11	88	11	3	$104^3/_8$	$104^3/_8$	$104^3/_8$	—
ATT	$7^1/_8$	03	8.8	28	81	$80^3/_4$	$80^3/_4$	$- \frac{1}{4}$
Chrysl	$8^7/_8$	95	12	18	77	76	76	—
MGM	$10^1/_2$	96	11	2	100	100	100	—
Mobil	$8^1/_2$	01	9.2	69	$92^1/_2$	92	$92^1/_8$	$- \frac{3}{8}$
RCA	$4^1/_4$	90	9.4	5	$98^1/_8$	$98^1/_8$	$98^1/_8$	$- 1^7/_8$
Sears	$4^3/_4$	83	5.5	65	$86^1/_2$	$85^3/_4$	$85^3/_4$	$- \frac{1}{8}$
ShellO	8	07	9	6	89	89	89	-1
TVA	8.05	99	8.8	5	$91^1/_4$	$91^1/_4$	$91^1/_4$	—
TWA	10	85	10	15	$98^1/_4$	$98^1/_4$	$98^1/_4$	$+ \frac{1}{8}$
USSt	$4^1/_2$	86	5.9	2	$76^1/_2$	$76^1/_8$	$76^1/_8$	$+ \frac{1}{8}$
Xerox	8.2	82	8.5	22	$96^1/_8$	96	96	$+ \frac{1}{4}$

The table is read as follows:

Bonds: This shows the name of the corporation, the rate of interest, and the year of maturity; "AAir 11 88" means "American Airlines bonds at 11%, due in 1988."

Current Yield: This is the interest rate actually earned if the bond is purchased at the current price.

Volume: This is the current sales, in units of $1,000. (Bonds usually have a face value of $1,000.)

High—Low: This gives the highest and lowest price for the day, as a percentage of face value; for example, Sears ranged from a high of $865 to a low of $857.50 per bond.

Net Change: This is the difference between the closing price and the closing price for the preceding day.

Note that prices of bonds are quoted in percentages of face value. For example, Mobil Oil $8^{1}/_{2}$ 01 had a closing price of $92^{1}/_{8}$, or $92^{1}/_{8}\%$. This is equal to $92.125 per $100, or $921.25 per $1,000.

Like stocks, bonds are purchased and sold on major securities exchanges; as with stocks, the commission on bonds increases the purchase cost and decreases the sale proceeds. Broker's fees vary on bond sales, but they generally are a set fee on each bond purchased or sold, $7.50 per bond, for example.

Example 1. Sale of Bonds. Calculate the commission and the proceeds from the sale of 15 TWA 10s bonds sold at the closing price, if the commission is $7.50 per bond.

15 Bonds × $982.50	=	$14,737.50
Commission: $7.50 × 15	=	112.50
Net Proceeds		$14,625.00

The calculations in Example 1 assume that the sale occurred on an interest payment date, and so it was not necessary to take into account any interest that might have accrued on the bonds since the previous interest payment date. When bonds are sold between interest payment dates, the interest due the seller must be calculated and added to the proceeds. Interest is paid to the seller for the time from the last interest payment until the sale. Note that accrued interest on bonds being sold or bought is figured on whole months counted as 30 days each plus any additional days. The year is considered to have 360 days for computation purposes. For example, if the last semiannual interest date on a bond was March 31 and the sale date was June 20, the accrued interest period would be:

March 31 to May 31: 2 Months = 60 days
May 31 to June 20: 20 days
Period of Accrued Interest 80 days

If the bond sale was for twenty $1,000 bonds bearing interest at 12%, the amount of interest due the seller would be

$$\$20,000 \times .12 \times {}^{80}/_{360} = \$533.33$$

Example 2. If the sale just shown was for twenty bonds at $105^{1}/_{8}$ and the seller had to pay a commission of $7.50 per bond, what would be the net sales price and the proceeds?

Market Value: 20 Bonds × $1,051.25	=	$21,025.00
Commission: $7.50 × 20	=	− 150.00
Net Sales Price		$20,875.00
Accrued Interest		+ 533.33
Proceeds:		$21,408.33

The cost to the purchaser would be:

Market Price	$21,025.00
Commission	+ 150.00
Cost of Bonds	$21,175.00
Accrued Interest	+ 533.33
Total Expenditure	$21,708.33

The net price per bond to the seller is calculated on the net sales price:

$$\$20,875 \div 20 = \$1,043.75$$

The cost per bond to the buyer is calculated on the cost of the bonds:

$$\$21,175.00 \div 20 = \$1,058.75$$

Note that accrued interest does not enter into either of these calculations.

Problems

1. Use the price quotations in Table 19-2 to complete the following:

	Bonds	Number	Closing Price	Total	Commission ($7.50 per Bond)	Total Cost
a.	ATT	20	$ _____	$ _____	$ _____	$ _____
b.	RCA	12	_____	_____	_____	_____
c.	TVA	31	_____	_____	_____	_____

	Bonds	Number	Closing Price	Total	Commission ($7.50 per Bond)	Total Cost
d.	USSt	4	$_____	$_____	$_____	$_____
e.	Xerox	17	_____	_____	_____	_____

2. For each case below, determine the number of days that would be used for accrued interest calculations and the interest on a $1,000 bond.

	Interest Dates	Purchase Date	Interest Rate	Days Accrued Int.	Interest
a.	Jan. 1 and July 1	May 25	8%	_____	$_____
b.	May 1 and Nov. 1	Feb. 5	$4\frac{1}{2}\%$	_____	$_____
c.	June 1 and Dec. 1	Mar. 14	9%	_____	$_____
d.	Mar. 1 and Sept. 1	Dec. 27	7%	_____	$_____
e.	Jan. 1 and July 1	Apr. 10	$5\frac{3}{4}\%$	_____	$_____

3. What is the amount of accrued interest due the seller of three $1,000 bonds if the interest rate is 8%, the interest is payable on August 1 and February 1, and the sale is transacted on October 23?

$ _____

4. Jim Brokenleg sold seven Shell Oil 8s bonds at 89 on April 25. The commission was $6.50 per bond, and the interest was payable on November 30. a. What was the net sale price? b. What were the proceeds?

a. $ _____

b. $ _____

5. Mary Montoya purchased thirty TVA 8.05s bonds at $91\frac{1}{4}$ on August 6. The interest dates for TVA 8.05s are July 1 and January 1, and she pays a commission of $7.50 per bond. a. What is the net cost? b. What is the cost per bond? c. What is the amount of accrued interest she must pay the seller?

a. $ _____

b. $ _____

c. $ _____

19.3 RETURN ON INVESTMENT—STOCK

Investors in stocks expect to benefit from their investments. They expect to receive annual returns on capital invested, in the form of dividends; they also hope to gain by someday selling the stock at an amount above the cost. The dividend return is called the *rate of yield* on stock. The gain or loss on stock sales is called *capital gain or loss*. The dividends received combined with the gain or loss on the sale represent a stockholder's *total return* from the capital invested.

Stock yield or rate of yield is the dividend on stock expressed as a percentage of the cost of the stock.

Example 1. An investor purchases 55 shares of stock at a cost per share, including the odd-lot differential, of $37^{1}/_{8}$. The annual dividend per share is $1.25. What is the rate of yield on the stock purchased?

$$\frac{\$1.25}{\$37.125} = 3.37\% \text{ Rate of Yield}$$

The yield may also be determined on the basis of total dividend and total investment:

Total Dividend 55 × $1.25 = $68.75
Total Cost 55 × $37.125 = $2,041.88

$$\frac{\$68.75}{\$2,041.88} = 3.37\%$$

The *capital gain or loss* on stock is the difference between the net proceeds (selling price less commission and fees) and the total cost (purchase price plus commission and fees).

Example 2. The purchase in Example 1 was for 55 shares costing $2,041.88, plus a $51.05 commission. After six months the stock is sold at $41^{3}/_{4}$, including the odd-lot differential, less a commission of $57.41, a tax of $.0313 a share, and an SEC fee of 8¢. What is the gain or loss on the sale of the stock?

Cost	Price: 55 × $37.125	=	$2,041.88
	Commission		+ 51.05
	Total Cost		$2,092.93

Net Proceeds Price: 55 × $41.75   = $2,296.25
           Commission   − 57.41
           Tax: 55 × $.0313   =   −1.72
           Fees   − .08
           Net Proceeds $2,237.04

Capital Gain Net Proceeds $2,237.04
           Cost   − 2,092.93
           Capital Gain $ 144.11

Example 3. If the investor in the previous examples had held the stock for four years and then sold it, what would the total percent of gain or loss have been? What would be the annual percent of gain or loss?

           Total Dividends: $1.25 × 55 × 4   = $275.00
           Capital Gain from Sale   + 144.11
           Total Return over 4 Years $419.11

$$\frac{\$\ 419.11}{\$2,092.93} = 20.025\%\ \text{Gain}$$

20.025% ÷ 4 = 5.10% Annual Percent of Return

Problems

1. Calculate the ratio of yield on each of the following purchases:

	Cost per Share	Dividends per Share	Rate of Yield
a.	$ 29.05	$1.10	_____ %
b.	37.88	1.85	_____ %
c.	43.91	2.00	_____ %
d.	101.50	8.50	_____ %
e.	237.90	6.00	_____ %

2. Determine the total gain or loss and the annual percent of gain or loss for each of the following:

	Number of Shares	Cost per Share	Net Proceeds per Share	Annual Dividend	Number of Years Held	Total Gain or Loss	Annual Gain or Loss
a.	21	$ 83.71	$ 95.00	$2.05	4	$_____	___%
b.	24	91.78	92.00	5.00	4	$_____	___%
c.	75	141.70	150.00	2.50	7	$_____	___%
d.	81	302.25	187.50	1.00	10	$_____	___%
e.	32	78.91	121.75	.50	2	$_____	___%

5. Josephine Gomako sold 75 shares of Penn Central at an odd-lot price of $71^5/_8$. The broker's fee was $115, the tax was .0313 per share, and the SEC fee was 1¢ per $300 unit. She had purchased the stock seven years earlier at a cost per share, after commission, of $65^1/_8$. The annual dividend was $1.50. a. What were the net proceeds from the sale? b. What was the capital gain? c. What was the annual dividend yield? d. The percent gain from investment? e. The annual percent of gain.

a. $_____

b. $_____

c. _____%

d. _____%

e. _____%

19.4 RETURN ON INVESTMENT—BONDS

Investors in bonds also expect to benefit from their investments, by receiving an annual return on the capital invested, in the form of interest.

The rate of *annual yield* from an investment in bonds is the relationship, expressed as a percent, between the annual interest and the net cost of the bond.

Example 1. May Wallace purchased five $1,000 Goodyear 7s bonds at $97^1/_4$. The commission was $37.50. What was the rate of annual yield on the bonds?

Annual Interest

$$\$1,000 \times 7\% = \$70 \text{ Annual Interest per Bond}$$
$$5 \times \$70 = \$350 \text{ Total Interest}$$

Net Cost

5 × $972.50	= $4,862.50
Commission	+37.50
Net Cost	$4,900.00

Annual Yield

$$\frac{\$350}{\$4,900} = 7.14\% \text{ Rate of Annual Yield}$$

Notice that the yield of 7.14% exceeds the stated interest rate of 7% on the bonds and that the bonds sold at *less than face*, or at a *discount* of $27.50 under the $1,000 face.

Example 2. Suppose the bonds were purchased for 102¹/₂. What was the rate of annual yield on the bonds?

Annual Interest

$$\$1,000 \times 7\% = \$70 \text{ Interest per Bond}$$
$$5 \times \$70 = \$350 \text{ Total Interest}$$

Net Cost

5 × $1,025.00	= $5,125.00
Commission	+37.50
Net Cost	$5,162.50

Annual Yield

$$\frac{\$350}{\$5,162.50} = 6.78\% \text{ Rate of Annual Yield}$$

Notice that the yield of 6.78% is less than the stated interest rate of 7% on the bonds and that the bonds sold at *more than face*, or at a *premium* of $25 over the $1,000 face.

The market price for bonds is influenced by a corporation's credit rating, by the maturity date, and by current interest rates. For example, if current market rates of interest for similar investments are higher than the rate stated on the bond, the bond will sell for less than face, or at a *discount*. When bonds sell at a discount (Example 1) the yield is higher than the stated rate and therefore closer to current market rates. If, however, current market rates for interest are lower than that stated on the bond, the bond will sell for more than face, or at a *premium*. When bonds sell at a premium (Example 2) the yield is lower than the stated rate and therefore closer to current market rates.

The annual-yield calculation is acceptable if bonds are to be held for a relatively short period of time, say, one or two years. The wise investor, however, is interested in the *yield-to-maturity rate,* the yield rate over the entire life of the bond. When an investment in bonds is made for a number of years, the discount or premium is spread over the life of the bond, starting from the date of purchase and ending with the date of maturity. This allocation of discount or premium influences the calculated bond yield.

Example 1. Assume that the five Goodyear 7s bonds were purchased at $97^{1}/_{4}$ ten years before the date of maturity. The $27.50 discount would be divided by 10, resulting in an annual allocation of $2.75.

The formula for calculating the yield to maturity for bonds selling at a discount is

$$\text{Yield to Maturity} = \frac{\text{Annual Interest} + \text{Annual Discount}}{\text{Average Investment}}$$

The average investment is the average of the original investment and the face value. In this case,

$$\frac{\$70 + \$2.75}{(\$972.50 + \$1,000) \div 2} = \frac{\$72.75}{\$986.25} = 7.38\% \text{ Yield to Maturity}$$

Note that the discount is *added to* the interest. Assuming that the Goodyear 7s bonds were purchased 10 years before the date of maturity at $102^{1}/_{2}$, the $25 premium would be divided by 10, resulting in an annual allocation amount of $2.50.

The formula for calculating the yield to maturity for bonds selling at a premium is

$$\text{Yield to Maturity} = \frac{\text{Annual Interest} - \text{Annual Premium}}{\text{Average Investment}}$$

In this case,

$$\frac{\$70 - \$2.50}{(\$1,025 + \$1,000) \div 2} = \frac{\$67.50}{\$1,012.50} = 6.67\% \text{ Yield to Maturity}$$

Note that the premium is *deducted from* the interest.

Problems

1. Harry Graber purchased a $1,000 Ford Motor Company 8% bond. He held the bond for one year. The purchase price was 97. What was his annual yield?

   _____ %

2. Genevieve Sievers purchased a $1,000 General Motors 11% bond. She held the bond for one year. The purchase price was 107. What was her annual yield?

   _____ %

3. Mr. & Mrs. Jerald Ollerich purchased 17 Gillette $9^3/_8$s bonds at $98^3/_4$. The bonds mature in ten years. What is the yield to maturity?

   _____ %

4. Connie O'Gorman purchased 21 Aetn $11^1/_2$s bonds at $103^1/_4$. The bonds mature in eight years. What is the yield to maturity?

   _____ %

5. North Central Airlines purchased 210 ALCOA $8^3/_4$s bonds at $96^1/_4$. The bonds mature in fifteen years. a. What was the total cost of the bond purchase? b. What is the yield to maturity?

   a. $_____

   b. _____ %

19.5 COOPERATIVES

A cooperative is a type of business organization formed to provide goods or services for its *patron-owners* or to sell their products. While farmers' cooperatives are the principal type of cooperative association, there are other cooperatives in the country. These include urban consumer cooperatives, cooperative wholesaling businesses owned by retailers, cooperative housing corporations, and others.

In addition to enjoying savings through membership in a cooperative, the members are frequently paid dividends, called *patronage dividends.* Patronage dividends are paid on the basis of the quantity or value of business done with the cooperative by the member (patron) and are determined by reference to the net income earned from business done through patrons.

Example. A small local cooperative of 135 farmers operates a number of departments, including a grain marketing department. Patrons bring in a total 7,000 bushels of grain, which is purchased and marketed by the co-op, for an income of $1,400. One grain farmer had brought in 800 bushels of grain. What is the farmer's share of net income?

$$\$14,000 \times \frac{800}{7,000} = \$1,600 \text{ Potential Patronage Dividend Earned}$$

Problem

Farmer A sold 50 hogs, 1,000 cattle, and 1,500 bushels of corn to the cooperative. Farmer B sold 25 hogs, 300 cattle, and 2,500 bushels of corn. Farmer C sold 75 hogs, 1,500 cattle and 7,500 bushels of corn. All the livestock and corn were sold by the co-op. What was each farmer's potential patronage dividend, if net profit on the sales was

Hogs	$ 1,050.00
Cattle	36,316.00
Corn	12,937.50

Patronage Dividends

Farmer	Hogs	Cattle	Corn	Total
A	$_____	$_____	$_____	$_____
B	_____	_____	_____	_____
C	_____	_____	_____	_____

Chapter Review

1. What are the proceeds from the sale of 37 shares of Bulova if they are sold at $9^7/_8$, less a commission of $12.50, an SEC fee of 1¢ per $300 or fractional part thereof, and a transfer tax of $2^1/_2$¢ per share?

   $_____

2. For each case below, determine the number of days that would be used for accrued-interest calculations on bonds.

Interest Date	Purchase Date	Days Accrued Interest
a. Jan. 1 and July 1	Oct. 7	_____
b. June 1 and Dec. 1	Nov. 3	_____
c. Mar. 1 and Sept. 1	May 4	_____
d. Jan. 1 and July 1	Feb. 2	_____
e. May 1 and Nov. 1	May 15	_____

3. Rae Flower purchased eighty-five duPont $8^1/_2$s bonds at $95^1/_8$. The purchase took place on March 5. Interest dates for duPont $8^1/_2$s bonds are June 1 and December 1. Rae pays a commission of $87.50 on the transaction. a. What is the cost to Rae? b. What is the cost per bond purchased? c. What amount of accrued interest is due the seller?

   a. $_____

   b. $_____

   c. $_____

4. Calculate the rate of yield on each of the following purchases:

	Cost per Share	Dividend per Share	Rate of Yield
a.	$37.12	$1.37	_____%
b.	47.12	2.21	_____%
c.	18.12	.87	_____%

5. Kim Tanaka purchased 21 shares of Honda at $24^3/_4$, plus a commission of
    $18.50. The annual stock dividend was $1.25 during the four years she
    held the stock. She sold the stock of $37^1/_8$, including differential, fees and
    commission. a. What was the rate of stock yield? b. What was the amount
    of her capital gain or loss? c. What was the total percent of gain or loss on
    her investment?

    a. _____ %

    b. $_____

    c. _____ %

6. Mr. and Mrs. Martin Bird purchased three $1,000 Kmart 6s bonds at $90^1/_2$.
    They held the bonds for a year. What was the annual yield?

    _____ %

7. An investor purchased 87 Ozark $6^3/_4$s bonds at $85^1/_2$. The bonds mature in
    fifteen years. What is the yield to maturity?

    $_____

8. An investor purchased 27 ElPaso $8^1/_2$s bonds at $103^1/_4$. The bonds mature in
    6 years. What is the yield to maturity?

    $_____

9. Explain in your own words why a bond might sell at a discount or at a
    premium._____

    _____

    _____

10. Seventy-five dairy farmers form a cooperative for the purpose of
    processing milk products. During the year, the cooperative processes
    135,000 gallons of milk at a net profit of $12,853. If you had sold the
    cooperative 18,000 gallons of milk during the year, what would your share
    of net income be?

    $_____

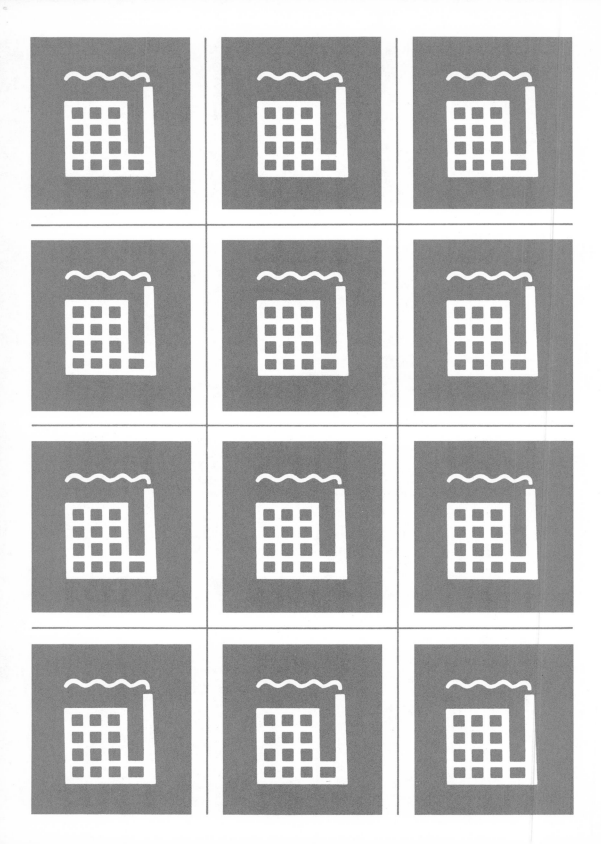

20

Mathematics of Depreciation and Depletion

Such tangible assets as equipment, trucks, and buildings that have a relatively long life and provide economic benefits to the firm over more than one accounting period are called *long-lived* assets, *fixed* assets, or *property, plant, and equipment*. With the passage of time, however, long-lived assets lose the capacity to provide economic benefits either because of wear and tear or because they become inadequate or obsolete. The reduction in asset value is called *depreciation*. Depreciation may also be viewed as a *cost allocation* process, that is, the cost of the long-lived asset is charged (subtracted) against present and future revenues in some systematic manner.

Depreciation methods of determining the dollar amount used in the cost allocation process vary. However, the methods generally fall into three groups: the *straight-line method,* in which equal amounts of asset cost are allocated each year; the *accelerated method,* in which more cost is charged in the early years and less in the later years; and *activity,* in which cost is charged against revenue, based upon the amount of actual use.

Four decisions must be made before the depreciation charge can be determined. The accountant must:

First—Decide on the depreciation method to be used in the cost allocation process: straight-line, accelerated, or activity.
Second—Determine the asset cost. In the case of equipment purchases, the asset cost includes the purchase price, less any cash discounts, plus transportation and set-up costs.
Third—Estimate the service life of the asset. The estimated life may be stated in units, in time, such as number of years, or in units of production, such as number of miles.

Fourth—Estimate the *scrap* or *salvage* value expected at the end of the asset service life. Final values are sometimes referred to as *residual values*.

In many instances the Internal Revenue Service provides guidelines for estimating the life and residual values of long-lived assets.

20.1 DEPRECIATION—STRAIGHT-LINE (SL)

When asset cost is allocated using the SL method of depreciation, the dollar amount charged as depreciation is the same each year and the depreciation rate is therefore uniform throughout the asset life.

Example. The accountant wants to determine a certain machine's annual rate of depreciation, using the SL method. The purchase price of the machine is $11,000. Transportation amounts to $150, and set-up costs are $250. The machine has an estimated five-year service life and a residual value of $1,000. Find the annual depreciation charge. Prepare a depreciation schedule.

Asset Cost: $11,000 + $150 + $250 = $11,400
Residual Value   − 1,000
Depreciable Cost $10,400

The annual depreciation charge is found by dividing the depreciable cost by the estimated serivce life. Since the total depreciable cost is allowed in five years, the annual rate is $1/_5$, or 20%, of the depreciable cost.

Annual Depreciation $10,400 ÷ 5 = $2,080 per Year

If monthly depreciation estimates are needed, divide the annual amount by 12. In this case, $2,080 ÷ 12 = $173.33.

A five-year depreciation schedule for this machine is illustrated in Table 20-1.

Table 20-1. Depreciation Schedule

Asset: Machine #187523	*Estimated Service Life:* 5 years
Cost: $11,400	*Depreciation Method:* SL (Straight-Line)
Residual Value: $1,000	*Depreciation Rate:* 20%
Depreciable Cost: $10,400	*Annual Depreciation Charge:* $2,080

Year	A Annual Depreciation	B Accumulated Depreciation	C Book Value
0	$ 0	$ 0	$11,400
1	2,080	2,080	9,320
2	2,080	4,160	7,240
3	2,080	6,240	5,160
4	2,080	8,320	3,080
5	2,080	10,400	1,000 (R)

(R) = Residual Value

The original cost less the accumulated depreciation is called the *book value*. After the first year in the example, the book value is $11,400 − $2,080 = $9,320. After the second year, the book value is $11,400 − $4,160 = $7,240. This same result can be obtained by subtracting the annual depreciation amount from the book value at the end of the previous year: $9,320 − $2,080 = $7,240.

Problems

1. Find the annual SL depreciation rate for each of the following:

	Service Life	Annual SL Rate
a.	4	_____%
b.	7	_____%
c.	30	_____%
d.	40	_____%

2. Find the annual SL depreciation amount for assets with a. a cost of $8,400, an estimated life of 8 years, and a scrap value at the end of 8 years of $400; b. a cost of $72,000, an estimated life of 35 years, and a salvage value at the end of 35 years of $16,000.

   a. $_____

   b. $_____

3. Find the annual SL depreciation charge for a truck purchased for $6,500 with a life of 5 years, and a scrap value of $500.

   $_____

4. An item of machinery had a retail purchase price of $10,000, less a 2% discount. The cost of transportation to the plant was $1,200, and the materials and labor required to install the machine amounted to $1,000. The estimated service life was 15 years, and the salvage value at that time was set at $500. a. What was the annual depreciation charge? b. What was the monthly charge?

    a. $_____

    b. $_____

5. Walt's and Mary's, Inc. bought dry-cleaning equipment with a purchase price of $12,600 on July 1, 1973. The equipment life was estimated at 10 years, and no residual value was expected. The cleaning equipment was sold on January 1, 1980, for $4,000. Determine the book value of the equipment on that date. Did the equipment sell for more or less than the book value? How much more or less?

    $_____

    _____

    $_____

6. The Ham Company purchased the following long-lived assets:

Item	Date Acquired	Purchase Price	Discount	Transportation and Set-Up Costs	Salvage Value	Service Life
752	1/1/1980	$70,000	———	$7,000	$5,000	10 years
753	1/1/1980	22,000	2%	2,440	3,000	5 years
754	1/1/1980	25,000	2%	1,000	1,500	6 years
755	3/1/1980	21,000	———	1,000	———	20 years

Find the 1980 depreciation charge for each item. What percentage of depreciable cost is the annual depreciation charge?

Item	1980 Depreciation Charge	Annual Depreciation Rate
752	$_____	_____%
753	$_____	_____%
754	$_____	_____%
755	$_____	_____%

7. An asset acquired by the Day Corporation had a purchase price of $5,000, with a 4% discount given. The estimated residual value was $400. The estimated useful life was four years. Prepare a depreciation schedule covering the life of the asset.

20.2 DEPRECIATON—DOUBLE-DECLINING BALANCE (DDB)

Two commonly used accelerated depreciation methods are *double-declining balance* (DDB) and *sum-of-the-years-digits* (SYD). Both methods are reducing-charge methods, in that a larger amount of depreciation is charged in the first years, with progressively smaller amounts charged each year after the first.

With the DDB method, the fixed percentage used to determine the depreciation charge is usually *double* the straight-line rate. This fixed rate is applied the *first year* to *asset cost* and each year thereafter to the *previous year's book value* of the asset. Residual value is ignored in the DDB calculation. The asset should not be depreciated below a reasonable or estimated residual value, however.

Example. Using the same data from the previous SL example, apply the DDB method to find the annual rate of depreciation, find the annual depreciation charge, and prepare a depreciation schedule.

The annual depreciation rate is found by multiplying the SL depreciation rate by 2:

$$\text{SL Depreciation Rate: } 20\%$$
$$\text{DDB Rate: } 2 \times \text{SL} = 2 \times 20\% = 40\%$$

The annual depreciation charge is found by applying the 40% DDB rate to the asset cost and thereafter to the declining book values.

Year			Book Value		Rate		Depreciation Charge
1.	Asset Cost	=	$11,400	×	40%	=	$4,560
2.	$11,400 − $4,560	=	6,840	×	40%	=	2,736
3.	6,840 − 2,736	=	4,104	×	40%	=	1,642
4.	4,104 − 1,642	=	2,462	×	40%	=	985
5.	2,462 − 985	=	1,477	×	40%	=	591

The five-year schedule based on these calculations is illustrated in Table 20-2.

Table 20-2. Depreciation Schedule

Asset: Machine #187523	*Estimated Service Life:* 5 years	
Cost: $11,400	*Depreciation Method:* DDB	
Residual Value: $1,000	*Depreciation Rate:* 40% = 2 × SL	
Depreciable Cost: $10,400	*Annual Depreciation Charge:* varies	

Year	A Annual Depreciation	B Accumulated Depreciation	C Book Value
0	$ 0	$ 0	$11,400
1	4,560	4,560	6,840
2	2,736	7,296	4,104
3	1,642	8,938	2,462
4	985	9,923	1,477
5	477[1]	10,400	1,000 (R)

(R) = Residual Value

[1] The table assumes a residual value of $1,000, so the depreciation charge for the fifth year is $477, rather than the $591 computed, in order to keep the residual value from going below $1,000. Depreciation charges should not be made after the estimated residual amount is reached. There are techniques that can be used to adjust the DDB method to keep this problem from developing, but these are beyond the scope of this text.

Problems

1. Find the SL and DDB depreciation rates for the following:

	Service Life	SL Rate	DDB Rate
a.	8 years	_____%	_____%
b.	12 years	_____%	_____%
c.	15 years	_____%	_____%
d.	16 years	_____%	_____%

2. Compute the first-year DDB depreciation amounts for the following:

	Cost	Estimated Life	Scrap Value	First-Year DDB Depreciation
a.	$ 9,600	5 years	$ 600	$_____
b.	1,450	3 years	50	$_____
c.	8,950	6 years	450	$_____
d.	36,000	7 years	5,000	$_____

3. Margaret's Market, Inc. has purchased a truck for $18,500. The estimated life is five years, and the trade-in value is estimated at $1,750. a. Compute the annual depreciation charges, using the DDB method. Do not depreciate the truck below the estimated trade-in amount. Prepare a depreciation schedule for this truck.

    a. 1st year $_____

       2nd year $_____

       3rd year $_____

       4th year $_____

       5th year $_____

4. Prepare a depreciation schedule, using the DDB method, for printing press #17848, which has a purchase price of $17,391, less a 1% discount. Its estimated service life is ten years, at which time it will have an estimated scrap value of $950.

5. Use the information in Problem 4 to answer the following: a. How much depreciation was taken during the first 3 years? b. How much depreciation was taken during the last 3 years?

    $_____

    $_____

20.3   DEPRECIATION—SUM-OF-THE-YEARS DIGITS (SYD)

The SYD method provides larger amounts of depreciation in the first few years by use of a series of fractions: larger fractions in the early years, smaller fractions in later years. The fractions' denominator is found by adding together all of the service-life periods. For example, an asset with a service life of 5 years would have a fraction denominator (sum-of-the-years digits) of $1 + 2 + 3 + 4 + 5 = 15$. The annual reducing fraction for depreciation charges would be calculated as follows:

Years	Reducing Fraction
1	$^5/_{15}$
2	$^4/_{15}$
3	$^3/_{15}$
4	$^2/_{15}$
+ 5	$^1/_{15}$
15	Sum of Digits (Denominator)

The largest fraction ($^5/_{15}$) is used in the first year, thus providing a larger first-year charge.

The short way to find the digits sum is by this formula:

$$\text{Sum of Digits} = \frac{N\,(N + 1)}{2}$$

N is the number of periods. If N is 5, as in the example, then

$$\text{Sum of Digits} = \frac{5\,(5 + 1)}{2} = \frac{5 \times 6}{2} = \frac{30}{2} = 15$$

If N is 10, for example, the sum of the digits is

$$\frac{10\,(10 + 1)}{2} = \frac{10 \times 11}{2} = \frac{110}{2} = 55$$

Once the fractions have been determined, they are multiplied by the depreciable cost (asset cost *less* residual value).

Example. Using the SYD method, find the annual depreciation charge and prepare a depreciation schedule for a machine costing $14,100, with an estimated life of 6 years and a salvage value of $1,500.

Asset Cost	$14,100
Less Salvage	− 1,500
Depreciable Cost	$12,600

Sum of Digits $= \ ^6/_2\,(6 + 1) = 3 \times 7 = 21$ (denominator)

$$\frac{\text{Depreciable Cost}}{\text{Sum of digits}} = \frac{\$12,600}{21} = \ \$600 \text{ (Each 21st Part)}$$

Year	Fraction (SYD)	Annual Depreciation Charge	Asset Book Value
1	$6/21$	$3,600	$14,100 − $3,600 = $10,500
2	$5/21$	3,000	10,500 − 3,000 = 7,500
3	$4/21$	2,400	7,500 − 2,400 = 5,100
4	$3/21$	1,800	5,100 − 1,800 = 3,300
5	$2/21$	1,200	3,300 − 1,200 = 2,100
6	$1/21$	600	2,100 − 600 = 1,500

A depreciation schedule should be prepared from these calculations. Table 20-3 shows such a schedule.

Table 20-3. Depreciation Schedule

Asset: Machine #73281	Estimated Service Life: 6 Years
Cost: $14,100	Depreciation Method: SYD
Residual Value: $1,500	Depreciation Rate: Fraction
Depreciable Cost: $12,600	Annual Depreciation Charge: Varies

Year	A Annual Depreciation	B Accumulated Depreciation	C Book Value
0	$ 0	$ 0	$14,100
1	3,600	3,600	10,500
2	3,000	6,600	7,500
3	2,400	9,000	5,100
4	1,800	10,800	3,300
5	1,200	12,000	2,100
6	600	12,600	1,500 (R)

(R) = Residual Value

Problems

1. Find the SYD denominator and first year fraction for the following:

	Service Life	SYD Denominator	First Year Fraction
a.	8	_____	/
b.	12	_____	/
c.	15	_____	/
d.	16	_____	/

2. Find the first year SYD depreciation charge for the following:

	Cost	Estimated Life	Trade-in Value or Salvage	First Year Depreciation
a.	$ 9,600	3 years	$ 600	$_____
b.	9,750	10 years	none	$_____
c.	875	3 years	75	$_____
d.	72,000	20 years	12,000	$_____

3. Pete's Florist Shop purchased a cooler for $7,800. The cooler was expected to last 15 years and then have a scrap value of $600. Compute the annual depreciation charges, using the SYD method. Prepare a depreciation schedule.

Year		Year		Year	
1	$_____	6	$_____	11	$_____
2	$_____	7	$_____	12	$_____
3	$_____	8	$_____	13	$_____
4	$_____	9	$_____	14	$_____
5	$_____	10	$_____	15	$_____

4. Prepare a depreciation schedule, using the SYD method, for copy machine #8321, which cost $7,650. It has an estimated service life of 8 years and an estimated trade-in value of $300.

5. Answer the following questions, using the data from Problem 4. a How much depreciation was taken the first 3 years? b. How much depreciation was taken the last 3 years? c. If the DDB method had been used, what would be the depreciation for the first 3 years? d. Which method, SYD or DDB, gives the largest depreciation charges in the early years? e. Would the total depreciation charge for the service life differ with SL, DDB, or SYD methods? f. What advantage, if any, is there in using an accelerated depreciation method, as opposed to the SL method?

a. $_____   d. _____

b. $_____   e. _____

c. $_____   f. _____

20.4   DEPRECIATION—ACTIVITY

An *activity* approach to allocating asset cost over the service life is supported by the assumption that depreciation charges should match asset productive output or use. The activity method requires an estimate of the total asset productive capacity (the units it produces) or service hours (use). The depreciable cost is divided by the total estimated productive output units or hours, to arrive at a per-unit-of-activity cost. The production or use for each accounting period is multiplied by the per-unit-of-activity cost.

Example. The Roberts Company purchased a printing press for $19,900. The company estimates the press to have a total printing capacity of 935,000 reams of paper. The scrap value is estimated at $1,200.

The press provided this annual output over its 5-year life:

1st Year	100,000	Reams
2nd Year	120,000	Reams
3rd Year	250,000	Reams
4th Year	300,000	Reams
5th Year	165,000	Reams

a. Find the cost per estimated unit of production (ream).
b. Find the annual depreciation charge.
c. Prepare a depreciation schedule.

a. The cost per unit of output is found by dividing the depreciable cost by the total estimated output:

Asset Cost	$19,900
Scrap Value	− 1,200
Depreciable Cost	$18,700

$$\text{Depreciation per Unit} = \frac{\$18,700}{935,000} = \$.02 \text{ per Ream}$$

b. The annual depreciation charge is found by multiplying the annual output by the unit rate (.02).

1st Year 100,000 × $.02 = $2,000 Depreciation Charge
2nd Year 120,000 × .02 = 2,400 Depreciation Charge
3rd Year 250,000 × .02 = 5,000 Depreciation Charge
4th Year 300,000 × .02 = 6,000 Depreciation Charge
5th Year 165,000 × .02 = 3,300 Depreciation Charge

c. The depreciation schedule prepared from these calculations is shown in Table 20-4.

Table 20-4.   Depreciation Schedule

Asset: Printing Press #12111	Estimated Service Life: 935,000 Reams
Cost: $19,900	Depreciation Method: UP
Residual Value: $1,200	Depreciation Rate: .02¢ per Ream
Depreciable Cost: $18,700	Annual Depreciation Charge: Varies

Year	Units Produced	A Annual Depreciation	B Accumulated Depreciation	C Book Value
0	——	$ 0	$ 0	$19,900
1	100,000	2,000	2,000	17,900
2	120,000	2,400	4,400	15,500
3	250,000	5,000	9,400	10,500
4	300,000	6,000	15,400	4,500
5	165,000	3,300	18,700	1,200 (R)

(R) = Residual Value

Problems

1. The Clock Factory uses the activity method for charging depreciation on a parts-stamping machine. The stamping machine cost $31,000, scrap is estimated at $700, and the maximum service time is expected to be 1,150,000 hours. Find the annual depreciation charge, using the units of production method. The production schedule shows:

    1975 175,000 Hours of Use $_____

    1976 178,000 Hours of Use $_____

    1977 179,000 Hours of Use $_____

    1978 173,000 Hours of Use $_____

    1979 170,000 Hours of Use $_____

    1980 174,000 Hours of Use $_____

2. A truck costing $18,700, with an estimated trade-in value of $1,500 and a life of 150,000 miles, was driven as follows:

1976	31,200 Miles
1977	35,000 Miles
1978	28,000 Miles
1979	23,000 Miles
1980	31,000 Miles

What was the annual depreciation charge for the five years?

1976 $_____

1977 $_____

1978 $_____

1979 $_____

1980 $_____

How much of the truck remains undepreciated?

$_____

3. Prepare a depreciation schedule for the truck in Problem 2.

20.5 DEPLETION

The reduction in the value of natural resources through such processes as the mining of ore, the cutting of timber, or the withdrawal of natural gas is called *depletion*. Because the natural resources will be used up, or depleted, the cost can be shown in the same way as depreciation.

To find the per-unit depletion cost, add the costs of acquiring and developing the resource, including the costs of restoring the land. Subtract the value of any permanent assets or residual values, then divide by the estimated quantity of the resource. To determine the depletion charge, multiply the per-unit cost by the number of units extracted in each accounting period.

Example. A tract of timberland with an estimated yield of 900,000,000 board feet was purchased for $10,000,000. What is the depletion charge for a year in which 110,000,000 board feet were cut?

$$\frac{\text{Cost of Timberland}}{\text{Estimated Board Feet}} = \frac{\$10,000,000}{900,000,000} = \$.011 \text{ per Board Foot}$$

$$110,000,000 \times \$.011 = \$1,210,000 \text{ Depletion Charge}$$

Problems

1. The Wirk Timber Company purchased a tract of land for $800,000 at the beginning of the year. The tract had on it a building valued at $50,000. The timber on the land was estimated at 12,500,000 board feet. What would be the depletion charge if 1,250,000 board feet were cut and sold?

   $_____

2. A coal mine with an estimated tonnage of 8,450,235 tons was discovered by the Lie Mining Company. The mining area cost the company $2,353,232. If 53,230 tons of coal were mined in one year, what would the depletion charge be?

   $_____

3. Sioux Steel Co., Inc. purchased an iron-ore deposit at a cost of $1,200,000. Additional development costs amounted to $150,000. The company estimated that the land would sell for $90,000 after the ore was exhausted. The total potential tonnage was estimated at 750,000 tons. What would be the depletion charge in a year when 77,000 tons of ore were extracted?

   $_____

4. The Redstone Gravel Corporation acquired land at a price of $250,000. The land should sell for $25,000 after the gravel has been removed. Restoration costs are expected to amount to $10,000. An access road will cost $1,000. It is expected that the land will produce 750,000 cubic yards of gravel. What was the depletion charge in a year when 47,000 cubic yards were dug?

   $_____

5. Crossroads, Inc. constructed a pipeline to a newly discovered oil well, at a cost of $25,000. The drilling costs were $150,000. The total oil reserve was estimated at 1,250,000 barrels. Production in one year was 85,000 barrels. What was the depletion cost for that year?

   $_____

Chapter Review

1. A delivery truck was purchased by Vans, Inc. for $50,000 on January 1, 1980. The truck had a 6-year life and an expected trade-in value of $5,000. The following depreciation methods were being considered: a. Straight-line, b. Sum-of-the-years-digits, and c. Double-declining balance. Find the depreciation charges, using each method, for the first year; find which method provides the largest depreciation charge.

   a. $_____   Method _____

   b. $_____

   c. $_____
       _____

2. The Bajema and Armstrong Partnership purchased a machine for $60,000. They estimated that the machine would have a 10-year life and a scrap value of $6,000. The machine's life was also expressed in service hours, estimated at 33,000 hours, and units of production, estimated at 600,000. During the year, the machine operated 4,000 hours and produced 69,000 units. Compute the depreciation charge for the year, using a. the straight-line method, b. the service-hours method, and c. the unit-production method. Which method provides the largest depreciation charge?

   a. $_____   Method _____

   b. $_____

   c. $_____
       _____

3. For $480,000, the XXX Mining Company acquired a parcel of land containing an iron-ore deposit. The company estimated that the ore-deposit amounts to 1,600,000 tons. A road to the mine cost $50,000. a. What was the depletion cost per ton? b. What would be the depletion charge for the first year if 80,000 tons of ore were extracted?

   a. $_____

   b. $_____

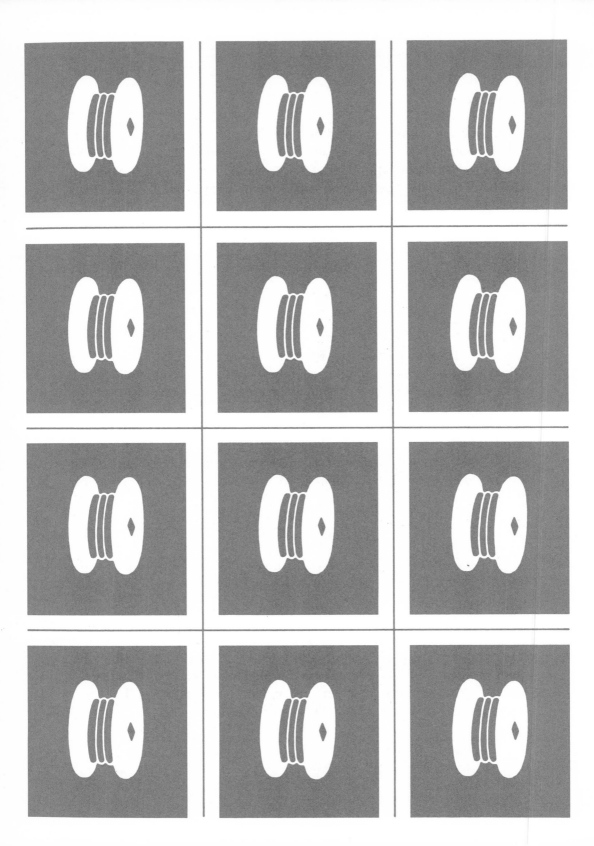

21

Inventory Valuation

Many businesses invest large dollar amounts in goods held for resale or in materials to be used in the production of goods for sale. The goods on hand in a retail or wholesale business are usually called *merchandise inventory*. In a manufacturing concern, inventories consist of *raw materials, goods in process*, and *finished goods*. Inventories are often the largest single asset owned by a firm. The calculation of inventory dollar values requires great care and is extremely important. Errors in inventory calculation and valuation may have a major effect on the amount of net income reported by a firm.

The goods or materials in inventories may be evaluated by one of four commonly accepted costing methods: *specific identification; weighted average; first-in, first-out* (FIFO); and *last-in, first-out* (LIFO). The costing method used need not actually relate to the physical flow of goods or materials on or off a shelf or in and out of a bin. A business may use any of these four accepted methods of assigning costs, so long as that method is applied consistently. Regardless of the costing method, the system should provide the cost of purchases, the inventory at cost, and the cost of sales. Inventories may be kept either on a "perpetual" basis or by periods.

21.1 SPECIFIC-IDENTIFICATION COSTING

The specific-identification costing method shows the actual cost of each individual item; it is usually used for inventories with small unit volumes and large unit prices. An example of a perpetual inventory record, with costs assigned by applying the specific-identification method, is outlined in Table 21-1.

Table 21-1. Inventory Record

Item and Code Number: Door (7321)	Costing Method: Specific Identification
Location: Warehouse No. 3	Reorder Point: 15
Inventory System: Perpetual	Maximum Inventory: 50

Invoice Number and Date 1981	Purchases			Sales (at Cost)			Inventory on Hand		
	Number of Units	Unit Cost $	Total Cost $	Number of Units	Unit Cost $	Total Cost $	Number of Units	Unit Cost $	Total Cost $
Balance 1/1		—			—		15	$60	$ 900
#368 1/18	25	$80	$2,000		—		25	80	2,000
#501 3/7				10	$60	$ 600	5	60	300
				12	80	960	13	80	1,040
#497 4/12	25	90	2,250		—		25	90	2,250
#570 8/15				10	90	900	5	60	300
							13	80	1,040
							15	90	1,350
Totals 12/31	50		4,250	32		2,460	33		2,690
1982 Balance 1/1		—			—		5	60	300
							13	80	1,040
							15	90	1,350

Note: After each sale (3/7, 8/15), the inventory on hand is adjusted to reflect specific items remaining and a line is drawn above this point to separate previous inventory unit × cost extensions from new unit × cost extensions.

A close review of Table 21-1 reveals what has occurred:

1/1: Fifteen units at a cost of $60 each were on hand, for a total value of $900.

1/18: Twenty-five units at a cost of $80 each were purchased, at a total cost of $2,000. Total inventory is:

 Units on Hand 15 + 25 = 40

 Cost: $900 + $2,000 = $2,900

3/7: Twenty-two units were sold. Ten units sold were $60 items, and twelve units sold were $80 items. Total inventory is now:

 Units on hand: 5 + 13 = 18

 Cost: $300 + $1,040 = $1,340

The line drawn above this entry separates it from what went before.

4/12: Twenty-five units were purchased at $90, for a total cost of $2,250. The inventory is now:

 Units on Hand: 5 + 13 + 25 = 45

 Cost: $300 + 1,040 + 2,250 = $3,590

8/15: Ten units were sold and identified as $90 items. The inventory is now:
Units on Hand: 5 + 13 + 15 = 33
Cost: $300 + 1,040 + 1,350 = $2,690
On December 31, the year-end totals are:

	Units	Total Cost
Purchases	50	$4,250
Sales	32	2,460
Inventory	33	2,690 (same as 8/15)

In the periodic inventory system, the calculation of inventory values and cost of sales is deferred (delayed) until the end of each accounting period. To illustrate the periodic inventory system, the cost data summarized in Table 21-2 will be used.

Table 21-2. Inventory, Purchases, and Cost of Sales Summary

Item #85				
Invoice Number and Date	Transactions	Number of Units	Unit Cost $	Totals $
1981 1/1	Inventory Purchases	50	$ 7	$ 350
P12 1/7		50	8	400
P20 3/7		25	9	225
P43 6/2		75	9	675
P49 8/4		25	10	250
Totals		175		$1,550
	Cost of Sales			
S15 1/24	(Sales Price $10)	35	_____	_____
S29 3/18	(Sales Price $10)	50	_____	_____
S51 6/8	(Sales Price $11)	50	_____	_____
S69 9/18	(Sales Price $12)	50	_____	_____
Totals		185	_____	_____
	Inventory			
12/31	175 + 50 (−) 185	40	_____	_____

The 40 units on hand at the end of the accounting period are identified with the actual purchase price (cost) paid for the unit. If, of the 40 units on hand, 15 were from 1/7 purchases and 25 were from 8/4 purchases, the calculation of purchases, inventory value, and cost of sales is:

Purchases	175 Units	$1,550
Inventory Value 12/31		
1/7 15 Units at $8		$ 120
8/4 +25 Units at 10		+ 250
Total 40		$ 370
Cost of Sales		
1/1 Inventory		$ 350
Purchases		+1,550
Goods Available at Cost		$1,900
Inventory 12/31		− 370
Cost of Sales		$1,530

Problems

1. Lear Parts, Inc. uses a perpetual inventory system. The July transaction record for part #4W31 is presented below:

	Units	Unit Cost
Beginning Inventory 7/1	100	$19
Purchases: 7/8	20	22
7/15	60	23
7/28	25	23
Sales: 7/10	40	
7/16	50	
7/30	30	

a. What would be the cost of goods sold, if the 7/10 sale came from 7/1 items, the 7/16 sale from 7/15 items, and the 7/30 sale from 7/1 items? b. What would be the value of the 7/31 inventory?

a. $ ———————

b. $ ———————

2. The Yates Auto Sales Company uses the specific-identification costing method. A record of the inventory, purchases, and sales at cost of truck 81-3C showed the following:

	Units	Unit Cost
Inventory 3/1	3	$5,700
Purchase 4/9	3	5,900
Sales: (January–June)		
1 of 3/1	1	5,700
2 of 4/9	2	5,900
Purchases 7/8	3	6,000
Sales: (July–December)		
2 of 3/1	2	5,700
2 of 7/8	2	6,000

Determine a. The value of the ending inventory and b. the cost of sales.

a. $ _____

b. $ _____

21.2 WEIGHTED-AVERAGE COSTING

The weighted-average costing method applied to a perpetual inventory system requires a new average unit-cost calculation *after each purchase.* Since average unit costs change with each purchase, the costing method is usually called a *moving* weighted average.

Example.

	Units	Unit Price	Total Cost
Inventory 1/1	25	$10	$250
Purchases 1/12	50	11	550
Total Units	75		
Total Cost			$800

Weighted Average Cost: $800 ÷ 75 = $10.67

The $11 units "carry more weight" than the $10 units, because there are twice as many $11 units as $10 units.

An example of a perpetual inventory record, with costs assigned by applying the moving weighted-average method, is outlined in Table 21-3.

Table 21-3. Inventory Record

Item and Code Number: Door (7321)			Costing Method: Weighted Average					
Location: Warehouse No. 3			Reorder Point: 15					
Inventory System: Perpetual			Maximum Inventory: 50					

Invoice Number and Date 1981	Purchases			Sales (at Cost)			Inventory on Hand		
	Number of Units	Unit Cost $	Total Cost $	Number of Units	Unit Cost $	Total Cost $	Number of Units	Unit Cost $	Total Cost $
Balance 1/1	—			—			15	$60.00	$ 900.00
#368 1/18	25	$80	$2,000				40	72.50*	2,900.00
#501 3/7				22	$72.50	$1,595.00	18	72.50	1,305.00
#497 4/12	25	90	2,250				43	82.67*	3,554.81
#570 8/15				10	82.67	826.70	33	82.67	2,728.11
Totals 12/31	50		4,250	32		2,421.70	33		2,728.11
1982 Balance 1/1		—			—		33	82.67	2,728.11

*Calculation: New Average

$$1/18 \quad \frac{\$2,000 + \$900}{15 + 25} = \frac{\$2,900}{40} = \$72.50$$

3/7 Sold 22 at New Average Cost

$$4/12 \quad \frac{\$2,250 + \$1,305.00}{18 + 25} = \frac{\$3,555}{43} = \$82.67$$

8/15 Sold 10 at New Average Cost

From the inventory record:

Purchases	$4,250.00
Cost of Sales	2,421.70
Ending Inventory	2,728.11

To calculate the weighted-average unit cost using a periodic inventory system, add together the beginning inventory (units and cost) and purchases (units and cost) and then average them. The calculation from Table 21-2 for the purchases, inventory value, and cost of sales, applying the weighted-average method would be:

Weighted Average

	Units	Costs
1/1 Beginning Inventory	50	$ 350
1/7 Purchases	50	400
3/7 Purchases	25	225
6/2 Purchases	75	675
8/4 Purchases	25	250
	225	$1,900

$$\text{Weighted Average: } \frac{\text{Total Cost}}{\text{Total Units}} = \frac{\$1,900}{225} = \$8.44 \text{ per Unit}$$

Purchases	$1,550.00
Inventory Value 12/31: 40 × $8.44 =	337.60
Cost of Sales	
Goods Available	$1,900.00
Inventory 12/31	− 337.60
Cost of Sales	$1,562.40

Problems

1. The White Retailers store uses a perpetual inventory system and a weighted moving-average costing method. The company's computer printout shows the following cost information for product #17A:

		Units	Unit Cost
Beginning Inventory 1/1		30	$10
Purchases:	3/11	50	11
	4/15	50	13
	6/12	50	13
	8/7	50	14
Sales:	2/7	10	
	3/17	50	
	5/12	30	
	7/15	40	
	11/21	50	

Prepare an inventory record and then find a. the number of units on hand, b. the total cost of purchases, c. the cost of goods available for sale, d. the cost of 12/31 inventory, and e. the cost of goods sold.

a. $ _____

b. $ _____

c. $ _____

d. $ _____

e. $ _____

2. Using the data in Problem 1, 21.1, for Lear Parts, Inc., prepare an inventory record and calculate a. the cost of the purchases, b. the cost of the 7/31 inventory on hand, and c. the cost of the goods sold, applying the moving weighted-average method, as in Table 21-3.

a. $ _____

b. $ _____

c. $ _____

3. The Harvey Parts Company uses a periodic inventory system and has the record below for part #47A:

	Units	Unit Cost
Beginning Inventory 1/1	100	$17
Purchases	35	22
	55	24
	20	20
Total Sales	110	

Compute a. the value of the ending inventory and b. the cost of the goods sold, using weighted-average costing methods.

a. $ _____

b. $ _____

21.3   FIRST-IN, FIRST-OUT COSTING (FIFO)

The FIFO costing method assumes that the first items purchased are the first items sold. The last items purchased are assumed to be in the inventory on hand. An example of a perpetual inventory record with costs assigned by applying the first-in, first-out method is outlined in Table 21-4.

From the inventory record:

Purchases	$4,250
Cost of Sales	2,260
Ending Inventory	2,890

Table 21-4. Inventory Record

Item and Code Number: Door (7321)	Costing Method: FIFO
Location: Warehouse No. 3	Reorder Point: 10
Inventory System: Perpetual	Maximum Inventory: 50

Invoice Number and Date 1981	Purchases			Sales (at Cost)			Inventory on Hand		
	Number of Units	Unit Cost $	Total Cost $	Number of Units	Unit Cost $	Total Cost $	Number of Units	Unit Cost $	Total Cost $
Balance 1/1		—			—		15	$60	$ 900
#368 1/18	25	$80	$2,000		—		25	80	2,000
#501 3/7				15	$60	$ 900			
				7	80	560	18	80	1,440
#497 4/12	25	90	2,250		—		25	90	2,250
#570 8/15				10	80	800	8	80	640
							25	90	2,250
Totals 8/31	50		4,250	32		2,260	33		2,890
1982 Balance 1/1		—			—		8	80	640
							25	90	2,250

Calculations: 3/7   Sold 22

First in 15 @ $60 (1/1)   First out   15 @ $60
Next in 25 @ $80 (1/18) First out + 7 @ $80 (22 − 15 = 7)
8/15   Sold 10
First in 18 @ $80 (1/18) First out   10 @ $80

To calculate the inventory value in a periodic system, using FIFO, assume that the first purchases were sold first and that the inventory is made up of the last purchase, then the next-to-last purchase, and so on, until all the units have been extended at a cost price. The calculation from Table 21-2 for purchases, inventory value, and cost of sales, applying the FIFO method, would be:

Purchases	$1,550
Inventory Value 12/31	
8/4 25 @ $10	$ 250
6/2 +15 @ $ 9	+ 135
Total 40	$ 385
Cost of Sales	
Goods Available	$1,900
Inventory 12/31	− 385
Cost of Sales	$1,515

Problems

1. Jones Wholesale Company uses a perpetual inventory system and FIFO costing. Inventory records reveal the following for April:

	Unit	Unit Cost
Beginning Inventory 4/1	100	$1.00
Purchase 4/6	200	1.15
Sale 4/15 @ $2.50	107	
Purchase 4/21	100	1.25
Sale 4/28 @ $2.50	150	

    Prepare an inventory record for the month; a. determine the value of the 4/30 inventory, b. determine the cost of sales; and c. determine the gross profit.

    a. $————   b. $————   c. $————

2. Use the data for Lear Parts, Inc. in Problem 1, 21.1, to prepare an inventory record, applying the FIFO method. Calculate a. the cost of the purchases, b. the cost of the 7/31 inventory on hand, and c. the cost of the goods sold.

    a. $————   b. $————   c. $————

3. Using the data provided in Problem 1, 21.2, and assuming that White Retailers uses the FIFO method; find a. the purchases, b. the inventory, and c. the cost of the goods sold.

    a. $————   b. $————   c. $————

4. The HyVee Company records inventory, using FIFO costing and a periodic inventory system. At the beginning of the year, the company had 210 units on hand, at a total cost of $472.50. The following purchases were made during the year:

Date	Units	Unit Cost
1/15	200	$2.35
3/11	150	2.55
6/21	300	2.70
8/27	400	2.25
11/12	100	2.75

a. Determine the cost of the ending inventory, if the physical count reveals 300 units on hand at the end of the year. b. Determine the cost of goods sold.

a. $———————   b. $———————

21.4 LAST-IN, FIRST-OUT COSTING (LIFO)

The LIFO costing method assumes that the last item purchased is the first item sold. The first item purchased is assumed to be in the inventory on hand. An example of a perpetual inventory record, with costs assigned by applying this method, is outlined in Table 21-5.

Table 21-5. Inventory Record

Item and Code Number: Door (7321)				Costing Method: LIFO					
Location: Warehouse No. 3				Reorder Point: 15					
Inventory System: Perpetual				Maximum Inventory: 50					

Invoice Number and Date 1981	Purchases			Sales (at Cost)			Inventory on Hand		
	Number of Units	Unit Cost $	Total Cost $	Number of Units	Unit Cost $	Total Cost $	Number of Units	Unit Cost $	Total Cost $
Balance 1/1		—			—		15	$60 $	$ 900
#368 1/18	25	$80	$2,000		—		25	80	2,000
#501 1/7				22	$80	$1,760	15	60	900
							3	80	240
#497 4/12	25	90	2,250		—		25	90	2,250
#570 8/15				10	90	900	15	60	900
							3	80	240
							15	90	1,350
Totals 8/31	50		4,250	32		2,660	33		2,490
1982 Balance 1/1		—			—		15	60	900
							3	80	240
							15	90	1,350

Calculations: 3/7   Sold 22
              Last in 25 @ $80 (1/18) First out   22 @ $80
          8/15   Sold 10
              Last in 25 @ $90 (4/12) First out   10 @ $90

From the inventory record:

Purchases	$4,250
Cost of Sales	2,660
Ending Inventory	2,490

In a periodic system, as shown in Table 21-2, to calculate the inventory value using LIFO, assume that the last item purchased was the first item sold. The inventory on hand (40 units) therefore would be made up of the old (first-in) items. The calculation for purchases, inventory value, and cost of sales, applying the LIFO method, would be:

Purchases		$1,550
Inventory Value 12/31: 40 @ $7	$ 280	
Cost of Sales		
Goods Available	$1,900	
Inventory 12/31	− 280	
Cost of Sales	$1,620	

Problems

1. Assume that Jones Wholesale Company (Problem 1, 21.3) uses a perpetual inventory system and LIFO costing. Prepare an inventory record for the month; a. determine the value of the 4/30 inventory, b. determine the cost of sales, and c. find the gross profit.

   a. $ _____

   b. $ _____

   c. $ _____

2. Use the data for Lear Parts, Inc. in Problem 1, 21.1. Prepare an inventory record similar to Table 21-5 and calculate a. the cost of purchases, b. the cost of the 7/31 inventory on hand, and c. the cost of goods sold, using LIFO.

   a. $ _____

   b. $ _____

   c. $ _____

3. If White Retailers in Problem 1, 21.2, used LIFO, what would be a. the cost of the 12/31 inventory and b. the cost of the goods sold?

a. $ _____

b. $ _____

4. The Waters Corporation records inventory, using LIFO costing and a periodic inventory system. At the beginning of the year, the corporation had 175 units on hand, at a total cost of $962.50. The following purchases were made during the year:

Date	Units	Unit Cost
1/18	174	$5.50
2/21	125	5.65
4/18	250	5.75
7/30	300	5.65
12/13	100	5.80

a. Determine the cost of the ending inventory if the physical count reveals 200 units on hand at the end of the year. b. Determine the cost of goods sold.

a. $ _____

b. $ _____

21.5   ESTIMATING THE VALUE OF ENDING INVENTORY

There are many reasons why estimating inventories may be useful. For example, it may be impractical to take a physical count for interim accounting statements, or a firm may need verification of inventory values for tax purposes, for valuation for insurance coverage, or for valuation of destroyed merchandise.

Gross-Profit Method of Estimating

To estimate the value of the inventory using the gross-profit method, the gross profit margin (markup percent) should be clearly established by company policy. Records should provide the cost of beginning inventory, the cost of purchases, the net sales, and the gross margin percent. With these four items of information, the value of the ending inventory can be estimated by subtracting the cost of goods sold from the cost of goods available for sale.

Example 1. If the beginning inventory was $45,000, the purchases were $90,000, the net sales were $120,000 at sales price, and the gross margin was 30%, estimate the ending inventory.

Determine the cost of the goods available for sale:

Beginning Inventory	$ 45,000
Net Purchases	+90,000
Goods Available at Cost	$135,000

Determine the cost of goods sold:

Net Sales	$120,000
Markup: 30% × $120,000	− 36,000
Cost of Goods Sold	$ 84,000

3. Deduct what was sold at cost from what was available at cost:

Goods Available at Cost	$135,000
Cost of Goods Sold	− 84,000
Estimated Ending Inventory	$ 51,000

Retail Method of Estimating

The retail method is similar to the gross-profit method except that a cost percent (the relationship between cost and retail prices) must be determined from the records, which must provide retail as well as cost prices for all goods purchased. The ending inventory at retail can be estimated by subtracting the retail price of the goods sold from that of the goods available at the retail price.

Example 2. From the information in Example 1, estimate the ending inventory at retail.

Determine the goods available for sale at cost and retail:

	Cost	Retail
Beginning Inventory	$ 45,000	$ 64,286
Purchases	+90,000	+128,571
Goods Available During Period	$135,000	$192,857

Divide the goods available at cost by the goods available at retail to determine the cost percent:

$$\frac{\$135,000}{\$192,857} = 70\%$$

Determine the ending inventory at retail:

Goods Available at Retail	$192,857
Net Retail Sales	−120,000
Inventory at Retail	$ 72,857

Multiply the cost percent by the ending inventory at retail to find the ending inventory at cost:

$$70\% \times \$72,857 = \$50,999 \text{ at Cost}$$

Problems

1. The average gross profit margin of the Young Retail Store for the past three years has been 45% of sales. Calculate the ending inventory value from the data given below:

	Cost	Selling Price
Beginning Inventory	$ 40,000	
Net Purchases	100,000	
Net Sales		$175,000
	$ _____	

2. From the following facts, find the inventory as of December 31:

	Cost	Selling Price
Inventory 1/1	$16,000	
Purchases	25,000	
Purchase Returns	(3,000)	
Sales		$32,000
Sales Returns		(2,500)
Gross Margin: 25%		

$ _____

3. You have been employed by the Kids Department Store to estimate the inventory in the sporting goods department. The department had an opening inventory of $40,000 at cost and $65,000 at retail. Net purchases for the month had a billed cost of $49,000 and were valued at $80,000 at retail. Net sales were $100,000.

$ _____

4. The inventory of the F. Barry Company was destroyed by fire on March 15, 1980. The accounting records showed:

	Cost	Retail
January 1 Inventory	$22,500	$29,250
January 1–March 15 Net Purchases	15,750	20,475
Net Sales		30,000

Estimate the cost of the destroyed inventory $ _____

5. From the following facts, find the inventory as of December 31:

	Cost	Selling Price
Inventory 1/1	$ 76,000	
Purchases	155,000	
Purchase Returns	(2,300)	
Sales		$219,000
Sales Returns		(3,000)
Gross Margin: 30%		

$ _____

Chapter Review

1. The March 1 inventory of item XX317-B and information on purchases and sales for three months are presented below:

	Sales Price	Units	Unit Cost	Total Cost
March 1 Inventory		5	$14.25	
March 6 Purchase		10	16.50	
March 15 Sale	$25	7		
March 29 Sale	25	3		
April 11 Purchase		8	16.50	
April 20 Sale	25	5		
April 23 Sale	26	3		
April 29 Purchase		7	17.00	
May 3 Sale	26	6		
May 15 Sale	26	3		
May 21 Purchase		10	17.00	
May 30 Sale	26	6		

a. Prepare a perpetual inventory record, using the specific-identification costing system if the sales of 3/15 were from the purchase of 3/6, those of 3/29 from the 3/1 inventory, those of 4/20 and 4/23 from the purchase of 4/11, those of 5/3 from the purchase of 4/29, those of 5/15 from the purchase of 3/6, and those of 5/30 from the purchase of 5/21. b. Prepare a perpetual inventory record, using the weighted-average costing method. c. Record the inventory, the purchases, and the cost of goods sold in a perpetual inventory record, using the FIFO costing method. d. Record the inventory, the purchases, and the cost of goods sold in a perpetual inventory record, using the LIFO costing method.

2. The Lewis Corporation uses a periodic inventory system. The listing of plumbing fixtures purchased during the first year of operation reflected the following information:

Month	Units	Cost per Unit	Total Cost
January	400	$35	$ 14,000
February	200	37	7,400
April	600	38	22,800
June	200	40	8,000

August	300	40	12,000
September	400	42	16,800
October	500	43	21,500
December	200	45	9,000
Totals	2,800		$111,500

During the year, 2,300 fixtures were sold. Calculate the inventory value and the costs of goods sold for the year, assuming a. Weighted average, b. FIFO, and c. LIFO. Assuming that the fixtures in the ending inventory were identified as April purchases, what would be d. the value of the inventory and e. the cost of goods sold?

	Inventory Value	Costs of Goods
a.	$ _____	$ _____
b.	$ _____	$ _____
c.	$ _____	$ _____
d.	$ _____	
e.	$ _____	

3. From the information given below, find a. the cost of goods sold and b. the estimated value of the ending inventory:

A.   Beginning Inventory $ 5,000   Cost
     Net Purchases   15,000   Cost
     Net Sales   20,000   Selling Price
     Markup on Sales   25%

                                            a. $ _____
                                            b. $ _____

B.   Beginning Inventory $ 6,500   Cost
     Net Purchases   27,000   Cost
     Net Sales   41,000   Selling Price
     Markup on Sales   30%

                                            a. $ _____
                                            b. $ _____

C.

Beginning Inventory	$15,000	Cost
Purchases	75,000	Cost
Purchases Returns	(3,500)	Cost
Sales	80,000	Selling Price
Sales Returns	(3,000)	Selling Price
Markup on Sales	40%	

a. $ _____

b. $ _____

4. Determine the Adams Company inventory for departments A and B at the end of the month by using the retail inventory method:

Department A

	Cost	Retail
Inventory 3/1	$30,000	$45,000
March Purchases	20,000	35,000
March Sales		25,000

$ _____

Department B

	Cost	Retail
Inventory 3/1	$25,000	$43,000
March Purchases	30,000	47,000
March Sales		35,000

$ _____

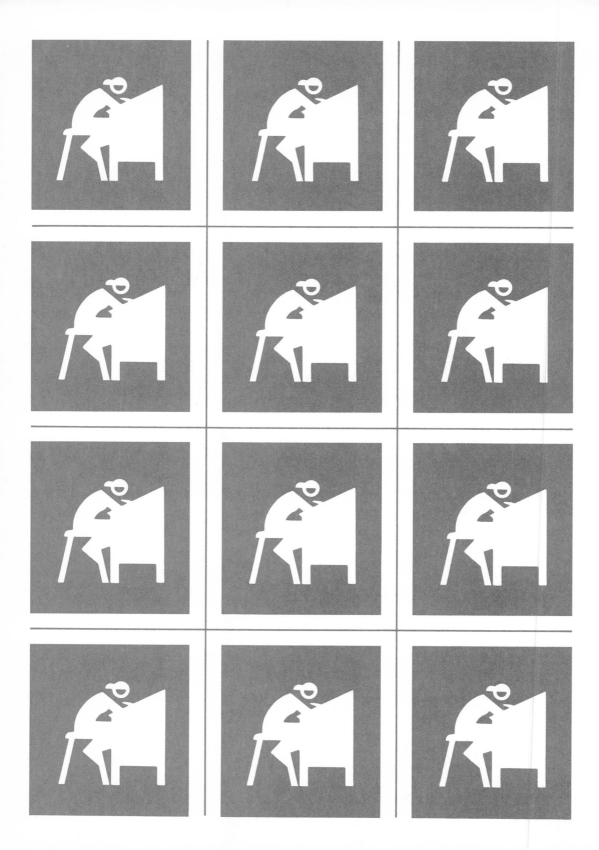

22

Analysis of Financial Statements

22.1 THE BALANCE SHEET

Almost every business must report the values of its assets (property), liabilities (debts), and owner's equity (capital). Such a report is called a *balance sheet*. The balance sheet, along with other reports, is used for making management decisions. Assets, liabilities, and corporate owner's equity are usually classified like this:

Assets	*Description*
Current Assets (CA)	Intended to be converted to cash or consumed within a short period of time (usually one fiscal year)
Investments (I)	Not intended to be used as a ready source of cash
Property–Plant–Equipment (P) (Fixed Assets)	Long-lived assets used but not usually to be converted to cash
Other Assets (OA)	Assets not falling within the above classifications

Liabilities	
Current Liabilities (CL)	Debts that will be paid within a short period either with cash or by converting current assets to cash
Long-Term Liabilities (L-TL)	Debts not due within next accounting period (12 months)

Other Liabilities (OL)	Liabilities not falling within the above classifications

Owners' Equity

Capital Stock (CS)	Par value of stock, multiplied by the number of shares issued
Paid-in Capital in Excess of Par (PIC)	Selling price of stock issued, multiplied by the number of shares sold, less the par value amount
Retained Earnings (RE)	Earnings of the firm that have not been distributed as dividends

Table 22–1 is an example of a classified balance sheet:

Table 22–1.
Classified, Inc.
Balance Sheet
December 31, 1981

Assets		Liabilities	
Current Assets		*Current Liabilities*	
Cash	$ 10,000	Note Payable	$ 4,000
Accounts Receivable	12,000	Accounts Payable	10,000
Inventory	15,000	Other Short-Term Liab.	2,000
Total Current Assets	37,000	Total Current Liab.	16,000
Investments		*Long-Term Liabilities*	
Stock of H, Inc.	7,000	Mortgage	20,000
Property-Plant-Equipment		Total Liabilities	36,000
Land	15,000	Owner's Equity	
Building (Net)	39,000	*Capital Stock* ($20 Par,	
Equipment (Net)	8,000	$1,000 Shares Issued)	20,000
Total Property–Plant–		Paid-in Capital in Excess	
Equipment	62,000	of Par	5,000
		Retained Earnings	45,000
		Total Owner's Equity	70,000
		Total Liabilities and	
Total Assets	$106,000	Owner's Equity	$106,000

Note: Total assets are the same as total liabilities added to owner's equity, because the value of the assets is the same as the value of the claims on those same assets by the creditors and owners. A balance sheet must always balance. Assets equal claims to assets.

$$(\text{Assets}) \ \$106,000 \ = \ (\text{Claims}) \ \$106,000$$
$$\text{or}$$
$$\text{Assets} \ = \ \text{Liabilities} \ + \ \text{Owner's Equity}$$
$$\$106,000 \ = \ \$36,000 \ + \ \$70,000$$

Problems

1. Classify the following list of assets, liabilities, and owner's equity accounts, using the abbreviations given in the text.

Account Title	Classification	Amount
Cash	———	$ 8,590
Accounts Receivable	———	6,880
Salaries Payable	———	296
Note Payable (Next Month)	———	5,500
Office Supplies	———	1,480
Land	———	20,000
Taxes Payable	———	500
Long-Term Bond Payable (5 Years Ahead)	———	20,000
Merchandise Inventory	———	12,150
Patent	———	1,809
Marketable Securities	———	3,200
Investment in Y Corporation	———	5,000
Capital in Excess of Par	———	20,000
Common Stock, $40 Par, 1,000 Shares	———	———
Store Equipment (Net)	———	27,350
Building	———	39,100
Accounts Payable	———	9,420
Retained Earnings	———	29,843

2. From the accounts and amounts in Problem 1, prepare a classified Balance Sheet on this form:

Midtown, Inc.
Balance Sheet
December 31, 1981

Assets		*Liabilities*	
Current Assets		Current Liabilities	
_____	_____	_____	_____
_____	_____	_____	_____
_____	_____	_____	_____
_____	_____	_____	_____
_____	_____	_____	_____
_____	_____	_____	_____
Total Current Assets	_____	Total Current Liabilities	_____
Investments		Long-Term Liabilities	
_____		_____	_____
Property–Plant–Equipment		_____	_____
_____	_____	Total L-T Liabilities	
		Total Liabilities	_____
		Owner's Equity	
	_____	_____	_____
Total Property–Plant–		_____	_____
Equipment	_____	_____	_____
Other Assets			
		Total Owner's Equity	_____
_____	_____	Total Liabilities and	
Total Assets	_____	Owner's Equity	_____

22.2   THE INCOME STATEMENT

Owners and managers need to know the results of the operations of their businesses. The *income statement,* which shows the revenues (sales or fees), costs, and expenses for a certain period of time, provides this information. Revenues less costs and expenses equals net income (profit) or loss. The income statement is frequently set up with the following classifications:

Item	*Description*
Revenues (R)	Amounts charged to customers (selling price) for goods and/or services (sales or fees) (Returns of sales are revenue reductions (RR).)
Cost of Sales (C)	Amount paid (cost) for goods sold to customers

Operating Expenses
  Selling (S)
  General (G)
	Costs incurred or assets consumed in the production of revenues (selling and general expenses)

Other Revenues and Expenses (ORE)	Revenues earned and expenses incurred unrelated to the general operation of the business (financial)
Income Taxes (T)	Amounts paid to the U.S. or state government, based upon income
Net Income	Revenues less costs, expenses, and income taxes (profit after taxes)

An example of a classified income statement is shown in Table 22–2:

Table 22-2.
Classified, Inc.
Income Statement
For the Year Ended December 31, 1981

Net Sales (Sales Less Sales Returns, $5,000)		$305,000
Cost of Goods Sold		− 208,000
Gross Margin on Sales		97,000
Operating Expenses		
Selling Expenses		
Sales Salaries	$38,000	
Advertising	10,000	
Depreciation—Equipment	1,550	
Insurance	1,100	
Miscellaneous	400	
Total Selling Expenses	51,050	

General Expenses		
Office Salaries	19,000	
Depreciation—Equipment	1,050	
Rent	2,400	
Insurance	300	
Miscellaneous	100	
Total General Expenses	22,850	
Total Operating Expenses		− 73,900
Income from Operations		23,100
Other Expenses—Interest		− 600
Income Before Taxes		22,500
Income Taxes		− 4,950
Net Income		$ 17,550

Problems

1. Classify the following list of revenues, costs, and expenses, using the abbreviations given in the text.

Account Title	Classification	Amount
Cost of Goods Sold	————	$133,900
Sales	————	210,000
Advertising	————	2,310
Insurance Expense—Store	————	530
Depreciation Expense—Office	————	950
Sales Salaries	————	22,320
Office Salaries	————	7,310
Rent Expense—Store	————	8,400
Insurance Expense—Office	————	600
Depreciation Expense—Store Equipment	————	1,000
Loss on Disposal of Equipment	————	230
Delivery Expense	————	1,600
Miscellaneous Expense—General	————	650
Miscellaneous Expense—Selling	————	1,000
Income Taxes	————	22%
Sales Return	————	200

2. From the accounts and amounts in Problem 1, prepare an income statement on the form provided below:

Midtown, Inc.
Income Statement
For the Year Ended December 31, 1981

Revenue

  Sales   _____

  Less: _____   _____

  Net Sales   _____

Less: _____   _____

Gross Margin on Sales   _____

Operating Expenses

  Selling Expenses

    _____   _____

    _____   _____

    _____   _____

    _____   _____

    _____   _____

    _____   _____

  Total Selling Expenses   _____

General Expenses

    _____   _____

    _____   _____

    _____   _____

    _____   _____

    _____   _____

  Total General Expenses   _____

Total _____   _____

Net Income from Operations   _____
Less: Other Expenses   _____

    _____   _____   _____

Income Before Taxes   _____
Less: _____   _____

Net Income   _____

The balance sheet reports a firm's financial position at a *point in time,* and the income statement reports operations over a *period of time.* Analysis of these statements aids management in making decisions which will predict and affect the future operation of the business. Predicting the future is important from the viewpoint of investors (owners), creditors, and unions, as well as managers. Investors and creditors want to protect their equity, unions want a fair return for their efforts, and managers have responsibility for planning the future activities of the business. Comparative statements, percentage, and financial ratios are helpful ways of analyzing the reports.

22.3 COMPARATIVE ANALYSIS—HORIZONTAL

Financial statements are frequently shown and analyzed by comparing a current year with as many as five preceding years. *Horizontal analysis* is the comparison of an amount on one statement with the same item on a preceding statement.

Income Statement—Horizontal Analyses

This shows increases or decreases from one year to the next, with the earlier year used as the base for converting increases and decreases to percentages. See Table 22–3.

Note that the amount of each item in the income statement is compared with the corresponding item on the earlier statement. The increase or decrease in the amount of the item is then listed. Decreases are shown by enclosing the figure in parentheses. Each increase or decrease is then converted to a percentage.

Example. From the income statement shown in Table 22–3:

	1980	1979	Increase
Net Sales	$563,064	$556,848	$6,216

$6,216 ÷ $556,848 = 1.12% Increase

Comparisons are made in two ways: by absolute amounts ($6,216) and by percent changes (1.12%). Absolute differences are easier to compute, but percent differences frequently are more revealing. In the example given, the delivery expense increased by $200, or 5.65%, while taxes increased the same amount, $200, but this was 3.31%. Although the absolute increase is the same for delivery expense and taxes, the percentage of increase is different.

Table 22–3.
Ram's, Incorporated
Comparative Income Statement
For the Years Ended December 31, 1980 and 1979

	Years Ended		Increase (Decrease) 1980 over 1979	
	1980	1979	Amount	Percent
Gross Sales	$566,764	$559,798	$6,966	1.24
Returns	−3,700	−2,950	−750	25.42
Net Sales	563,064	556,848	6,216	1.12
Cost of Goods Sold	−371,506	−371,201	−305	.08
Gross Margin on Sales	191,558	185,647	5,911	3.18
Operating Expenses				
Selling				
Sales Salaries	35,611	35,973	(362)	(1.01)
Advertising	4,200	4,700	(500)	(10.64)
Travel & Entertainment	1,800	1,900	(100)	(5.26)
Delivery	3,740	3,540	200	5.65
Utilities	3,040	2,700	340	12.59
Depreciation	13,009	12,732	277	2.18
Total—Selling	61,400	61,545	(145)	(0.24)
General				
Officer's Salaries	22,800	22,800	——	——
Office Salaries	19,169	18,721	448	2.39
Bad Debts Expense	2,350	2,500	(150)	(6.00)
Taxes—Payroll & Property	6,250	6,050	200	3.31
Insurance	3,000	2,900	100	3.45
Utilities	5,900	5,830	70	1.20
Depreciation	10,980	10,980	——	——
Total—General	70,449	69,781	668	.96
Total Operation Expenses	131,849	131,326	523	.40
Income from Operations	59,709	54,321	5,388	9.92
Financial Income (Expenses)				
Interest Expense	(7,508)	(4,797)	2,711	56.51
Investment Income	1,210	2,833	(1,623)	(57.29)
Net Financial	(6,298)	(1,964)	4,334	220.67
Income Before Taxes	53,411	52,357	1,054	2.01
Income Taxes	26,224	25,655	569	2.22
Net Income	$27,187	$26,702	$485	1.82

1979—Base Year

Problem

1. Complete the following comparative income statement worksheet, using horizontal analysis. Find the absolute differences and the percentage differences for each item on the statement. (Round the percents to two decimal places.)

Sweetwater Plumbing, Inc.
Comparative Income Statement
For the Years Ended December 31, 1980 and 1979

| | Year Ended | | Increase (Decrease) 1980 over 1979 | |
	1980	1979	Amount	Percent
Gross Sales	$153,050	$123,400	_____	_____
Returns & Allowances	−3,250	−3,400	_____	_____
Net Sales	149,800	120,000	_____	_____
Cost of Sales	104,300	82,000	_____	_____
Gross Margin on Sales	45,500	38,000	_____	_____
Operating Expenses				
Selling Expenses				
Sales Salaries	10,500	8,600	_____	_____
Delivery	2,300	2,100	_____	_____
Travel	500	350	_____	_____
Advertising	3,600	3,450	_____	_____
Depreciation	2,200	2,200	_____	_____
Total Selling	19,100	16,700	_____	_____
General Expenses				
Office Salary	3,000	3,000	_____	_____
Rent	3,500	3,000	_____	_____
Bad Debts	1,900	1,790	_____	_____
Insurance	350	350	_____	_____
Taxes—Payroll & Property	750	750	_____	_____
Depreciation	900	900	_____	_____

Total General Expenses	10,400	9,740		
Total Operating Expenses	29,500	26,440		
Net Income from Operations	16,000	11,560		
Other Income	850	1,100		
Other Expenses	(600)	(1,200)		
Net Income Before Taxes	16,250	11,460		
Income Taxes	7,150	5,810		
Net Income	$ 9,100	$ 5,650		

Balance Sheet—Horizontal Analysis

As with the income statement, the amount of each item on the most recent balance sheet is compared with the corresponding item on an earlier statement. The increase or decrease in the amount of the item is then listed. Each increase or decrease is converted to a percentage as shown in the comparative balance sheet for Ram's, Incorporated, Table 22–4.

Example. From the balance sheet:

	1980	1979	Decrease
Accounts Receivable	$97,079	$112,905	$(15,826)

$15,826 ÷ $112,905 = (14.02%)

Table 22–4.
Ram's, Incorporated
Comparative Balance Sheet
December 31, 1980 and 1979

	December 31		Increase (Decrease) 1980 over 1979	
	1980	*1979*	*Amount*	*Percent*
Assets				
Current Assets				
Cash	$ 16,111	$ 11,723	$ 4,338	37.43
Marketable Securities	64,153	5,010	59,143	1,180.50
Accounts Receivable (Net)	97,079	112,905	(15,826)	(14.02)
Inventories	90,817	108,383	(17,566)	(16.21)
Prepaid Expenses	18,351	11,659	6,692	57.40
Total Current Assets	286,511	249,680	36,831	14.75
Investments	32,359	28,885	3,474	12.02

| | December 31 | | Increase (Decrease) 1980 over 1979 | |
	1980	1979	Amount	Percent
Property, Plant, and Equipment				
Land	4,965	4,965	—	—
Buildings	89,474	85,069	4,405	5.18
Equipment	220,486	199,614	20,872	10.46
Total Prop., Plant, & Equip.	314,925	289,648	25,277	8.73
Depreciation	− 163,078	− 151,782	− 11,296	7.44
Total Prop., Plant, & Equip. (Net)	151,847	137,866	13,981	10.14
Total Assets	$470,717	$416,431	$54,286	13.04
Liabilities				
Current Liabilities				
Note Payable	5,298	13,364	(8,066)	(60.36)
Current Portion L-T Debt	3,503	1,398	2,105	150.57
Accounts Payable	51,649	52,367	(718)	(0.14)
Salaries Payable	14,682	7,425	(2,743)	(15.74)
Taxes Payable	19,281	21,063	(1,782)	(8.46)
Interest & Other Liabilities	21,373	19,016	2,357	12.39
Total Current Liabilities	115,786	124,633	(8,847)	(7.10)
Long-Term Debt	106,864	67,270	39,594	58.86
Total Liabilities	222,650	191,903	30,747	16.02
Shareholder's Equity				
Common Stock, $3 Par	11,925	11,730	195	1.66
Capital in Excess of Par	22,523	19,767	2,756	13.94
Retained Earnings	213,619	193,031	20,588	10.67
Total Shareholder's Equity	248,067	224,528	23,539	10.48
Total Liabilities & Shareholder's Equity	$470,717	$416,431	$54,286	13.04

*1979—Base Year

Note once again that comparisons are made in two ways: dollar amount differences and percentage changes.

Problem

2. Complete the following comparative balance sheet, using horizontal analysis. Find the absolute difference and the percentage difference for each item on the statement. (Round the percents to two decimal places.)

Sweetwater Plumbing, Inc.
Comparative Balance Sheet
December 31, 1980 and 1979

	December 31		Increase (Decrease) 1980 over 1979	
	1980	1979	Amount	Percent
Assets				
Current Assets				
Cash	$ 9,050	$ 6,470		
Marketable Securities	7,500	6,000		
Accounts Receivable (Net)	11,500	12,000		
Inventories	26,400	23,530		
Prepaid Expenses	550	5,300		
Total Current Assets	55,000	53,300		
Investments	9,500	17,750		
Property and Equipment				
Land	5,000	5,000		
Equipment (Net)	44,450	47,000		
Total Prop. and Equip.	49,450	52,000		
Total Assets	$113,950	$123,050		
Liabilities				
Current Liabilities				
Notes Payable	10,000	12,000		
Accounts Payable	10,100	10,910		
Wages Payable	650	590		
Other Current Liabilities	250	800		
Total Current Liabilities	21,000	24,300		
Long-Term Debt	10,000	20,000		
Total Liabilities	31,000	44,300		

	December 31		Increase (Decrease) 1980 over 1979	
	1980	1979	Amount	Percent
Shareholder's Equity				
Common Stock, $10 Par	50,000	50,000		
Contributed Capital in Excess of Par	15,000	15,000		
Retained Earnings	17,950	13,750		
Total Shareholder's Equity	82,950	78,750		
Total Liabilities and Shareholder's Equity	$113,950	$123,050		

22.4 COMPONENT ANALYSIS—VERTICAL

A financial statement is frequently analyzed by relating each item on it to another item on that same statement. *Vertical analysis* expresses each item as a percentage of a *base item* on the same statement.

Income Statement—Vertical Analyses

The base item on the income statement is net sales. All other items on the income statement are reported as percentages of net sales. These may then be compared with past periods, with figures from similar firms, or may be used to construct future budgets. Examine the example in Table 22–5 and note its ratio of total operating expenses to net:

$$\frac{\text{Total Operating Expense}}{\text{Net Sales (Base)}} \quad \frac{1980}{\$563,074} = 23.42\% \quad \frac{1979}{\$556,848} = 23.58\%$$

Total operating expenses as a percentage of sales and as an absolute amount have changed very little.

Table 22–5.
Ram's, Incorporated
Comparative Income Statement
For Years Ended December 31, 1980 and 1979

| | Year Ended | | | |
| | 1980 | | 1979 | |
	Amount	Percent	Amount	Percent
Gross Sales	$566,764	100.66	$559,798	100.53
Returns and Allowances	− 3,700	− .66	− 2,950	− .53
Net Sales*	563,064	100.00	556,848	100.00
Cost of Goods Sold	− 371,506	− 65.98	− 371,201	− 66.66
Gross Margin on Sales	191,558	34.02	185,647	33.34
Operating Expenses				
Selling and Distribution				
Sales Salaries	35,611	6.32	35,973	6.46
Advertising	4,200	.75	4,700	.84
Travel and Entertainment	1,800	.32	1,900	.34
Delivery	3,740	.66	3,540	.64
Utilities	3,040	.54	2,700	.48
Depreciation	13,009	2.31	12,732	2.29
Total—Selling & Dist.	61,400	10.90	61.545	11.05
General and Administrative				
Officers' Salaries	22,800	4.05	22,800	4.09
Office Salaries	19,169	3.40	18,721	3.36
Bad Debts Expense	2,350	.42	2,500	.45
Taxes—Payroll & Property	6,250	1.11	6,050	1.09
Insurance	3,000	.53	2,900	.52
Utilities	5,900	1.05	5,830	1.05
Depreciation	10,980	1.95	10,980	1.97
Total—General & Admin.	70,449	12.51	69,781	12.53
Total Operating Expenses	131,849	23.42	131,326	23.58
Income from Operations	59,709	10.60	54,321	9.76
Financial Income (Expense)				
Interest Expense	(7,508)	1.33	(4,797)	.86
Investment Income	1,210	.21	2,833	.51
Net Financial Income (Exp.)	(6,298)	1.12	(1,964)	.35
Income Before Taxes	53,411	9.49	52,357	9.40
Income Taxes	26,224	4.66	25,655	4.61
Net Income	$ 27,187	4.83	$ 26,702	4.79

*Base

Problem

1. Complete the following income statement, using vertical analysis. Convert each item to a percentage of net sales. (Round the percents to two decimal places.)

Sweetwater Plumbing, Inc.
Income Statement
For Years Ended December 31, 1980 and 1979

| | Year Ended | | | |
| | 1980 | | 1979 | |
	Amount	Percent	Amount	Percent
Gross Sales	$153,050		$123,400	
Returns and Allowances	3,250		3,400	
Net Sales	149,800		120,000	
Cost of Sales	104,300		82,000	
Gross Margin on Sales	45,000		38,000	
Operating Expenses				
Selling Expenses				
Sales Salaries	10,500		8,600	
Delivery	2,300		2,100	
Travel	500		350	
Advertising	3,600		3,450	
Depreciation	2,200		2,200	
Total Selling Expenses	19,100		16,700	
General Expenses				
Office Salary	3,000		3,000	
Rent	3,500		3,000	
Bad Debts	1,900		1,790	
Insurance	350		350	
Taxes—Payroll & Prop.	750		700	
Depreciation	900		900	
Total General Expenses	10,400		9,740	
Total Operating Expenses	29,500		26,440	
Net Income from Operations	16,000		11,560	
Other Income	850		1,100	
Other Expenses	(600)		(1,200)	
Net Income Before Taxes	16,250		11,460	
Income Taxes	7,150		5,810	
Net Income	$ 9,100		$ 5,650	

Balance Sheet—Vertical Analyses

As with the income statement, the balance sheet can be subjected to vertical analysis. On the balance sheet, the base is total assets. All items on the balance sheet are reported as percentages of total assets. These percentages may then be compared with past periods, with figures for similar firms, or may be used to construct future budgets. Examine the example in Table 22–6 and note particularly the ratio of notes payable to total assets:

$$\frac{\text{Notes Payable}}{\text{Total Assets (Base)}} \quad \frac{\overset{1980}{\$\ 5,298}}{\$470,717} = 1.13\% \quad \frac{\overset{1979}{\$\ 13,364}}{\$416,431} = 3.21\%$$

Observe that notes payable as a percent of total assets have decreased considerably, from 3.21% to 1.13%.

Table 22–6.
Ram's, Incorporated
Comparative Balance Sheet
December 31, 1980 and 1979

	December 31, 1980		December 31, 1979	
	Amount	*Percent*	*Amount*	*Percent*
Assets				
Current Assets				
Cash	$ 16,111	3.42	$ 11,723	2.82
Marketable Securities	64,153	13.63	5,010	1.20
Accounts Receivable (Net)	97,079	20.62	112,905	27.11
Inventories	90,817	19.29	108,383	26.03
Prepaid Expenses	18,351	3.90	11,659	2.80
Total Current Assets	286,511	60.87	249,680	59.96
Investments	32,359	6.87	28,885	6.94
Property, Plant, and Equipment				
Land	4,965	1.05	4,965	1.19
Buildings	89,474	19.01	85,069	20.43
Equipment	220,486	46.84	199,614	47.93
Total Prop., Plant, & Equip.	314,925	66.90	289,648	69.55
Depreciation	− 163,078	− 34.64	− 151,782	− 36.45
Total Prop., Plant, & Equip. (Net)	151,847	32.26	137,866	33.11
Total Assets*	$470,717*	100.00[1]	$416.431*	100.00[1]

	December 31, 1980		December 31, 1979	
	Amount	Percent	Amount	Percent
Liabilities				
Current Liabilities				
Note Payable	5,298	1.13	13,364	3.21
Current portion L-T Debt	3,503	.74	1,398	.34
Accounts Payable	51,649	10.97	52,367	12.58
Salaries Payable	14,682	3.12	17,425	4.18
Taxes Payable	19,281	4.10	21,063	5.06
Interest & Other Liabilities	21,373	4.54	19,016	4.57
Total Current Liabilites	115,786	24.60	124,633	29.93
Long-Term Debt	106,864	22.70	67,270	16.15
Total Liabilities	222,650	47.30	191,903	46.08
Shareholder's Equity				
Common Stock, $3 Par	11,925	2.53	11,730	2.82
Capital in Excess of Par	22,523	4.78	19,767	4.75
Retained Earnings	213,619	45.38	193,031	46.35
Total Shareholder's Equity	248,067	52.70	224,528	53.92
Total Liabilities & Shareholder's Equity	$470,717*	100.00[1]	$416,431*	100.00[1]

*Base
[1]Columns may not total, because of rounding.

Problem

2.   Complete the following balance sheet, using vertical analyses. (Round the percentages to two places.)

Sweetwater Plumbing, Inc.
Balance Sheet
December 31, 1980 and 1979

	December 31, 1980		December 31, 1979	
	Amount	Percent	Amount	Percent
Assets				
Current Assets				
Cash	$ 9,050	_____	$ 6,470	_____
Marketable Securities	7,500	_____	6,000	_____
Accounts Receivable (Net)	11,500	_____	12,000	_____
Inventories	26,400	_____	23,530	_____
Prepaid Expenses	550	_____	5,300	_____
Total Current Assets	55,000	_____	53,300	_____

	December 31, 1980		December 31, 1979	
	Amount	Percent	Amount	Percent
Investments	9,500	_____	17,750	_____
Property and Equipment				
Land	5,000	_____	5,000	_____
Equipment (Net)	44,450	_____	47,000	_____
Total Property and Equipment	49,450	_____	52,000	_____
Total Assets	$113,950	_____	$123,050	_____
Liabilities				
Current Liabilities				
Notes Payable	10,000	_____	12,000	_____
Accounts Payable	10,100	_____	10,910	_____
Wages Payable	650	_____	590	_____
Other Current Liabilities	250	_____	800	_____
Total Current Liabilities	21,000	_____	24,300	_____
Long-Term Debt	10,000	_____	20,000	_____
Total Liabilities	31,000	_____	44,300	_____
Stockholder's Equity				
Common Stock, $10 Par	50,000	_____	50,000	_____
Contributed Capital in Excess of Par	15,000	_____	15,000	_____
Retained Earnings	17,950	_____	13,750	_____
Total Shareholder's Equity	82,950	_____	78,750	_____
Total Liabilities and Shareholder's Equity	$113,950	_____	$123,050	_____

22.5 OTHER ANALYTICAL MEASURES—RATIOS AND PERCENTAGES

In addition to comparative and component analyses, a number of relationships within and between these financial reports may be expressed as ratios or percentages. To be useful, the results must express meaningful relationships. Numerous financial measures can be computed from a single set of financial statements; a common procedure is to compute certain widely used ratios and percentages. Financial measures can be grouped loosely into three broad categories: *liquidity ratios, profitability ratios,* and *equity ratios.*

All ratios calculated in the following examples are based upon the financial data reported in the two general purpose statements of Ram's, Incorporated, Tables 22–4 and 22–6.

Liquidity Ratios

These are designed to measure the ability of the firm to meet its short-term obligations and current liabilities. Included among these ratios are

Current Ratio, a popular measure of overall liquidity. The current ratio is computed by dividing current assets by current liabilities. A widely employed rule of thumb is that the current ratio should be at least two. This provides for a shrinkage in current asset values of fifty percent before the firm is unable to meet current short-term obligations:

$$1980 \quad \frac{\text{Current Assets}}{\text{Current Liabilities}} = \frac{\$286,511}{\$115,786} = 2.47$$

Quick Ratio, another measure of overall ability to pay current debts. It is a ratio of the sum of cash, receivables, and marketable securities, called *quick assets,* to current liabilities. Inventories and prepaid items are deducted from current assets. This takes into account the uncertainty of the length of time required to convert inventory to cash; prepaid expenses generally are not converted to cash.

$$1980 \quad \frac{\text{Current Assets} - (\text{Inventories} + \text{Prepaid Items})}{\text{Current Liabilities}}$$

$$= \frac{\$286,511 - (\$90,817 + \$18,351)}{\$115,786} = \frac{\$286,511 - \$109,168}{\$115,786}$$

$$= \frac{\$117,343}{\$115,786} = 1.53$$

Inventory Turnover, a measure of how quickly the inventory is sold. The ratio is computed by dividing the cost of goods sold by the average inventory. The higher the ratio, the more quickly cash is generated.

$$\frac{\text{Cost of Goods Sold (1980)}}{\text{Average Inventory}} = \frac{\$371,506}{(\$90,817 + \$108,383)/2} = \frac{\$371,506}{\$99,600} = 3.73$$

Dividing the days in a year by the turnover ratio provides a measure of the inventory supply:

$$\text{Average Number of Days Supply}$$

$$= \frac{\text{Days in Year}}{\text{Inventory Turnover}} = \frac{365}{3.73} = 97.86 = \text{about 98 Days}$$

Trade Receivable Turnover, a measure of the effectiveness of the granting of credit and the collection practices of the firm. The ratio is determined by dividing the credit sales by the average trade accounts and notes receivable. The ratio reflects how many times receivables were recorded and collected, again recorded and collected, etc., during the period:

$$\frac{\text{Net Sales}}{\text{Average Net Receivables}} = \frac{\$563,064}{(\$97,079 + \$112,905)/2} = \frac{\$563,064}{\$104,992} = 5.36$$

Dividing the days in a year by the turnover ratio provides a measure of how long it takes to collect trade receivables:

$$\text{Average Collection Period} = \frac{\text{Days in Year}}{\text{Receivable Turnover}} = \frac{365}{5.36} = 68.10$$

$$= \text{About 68 Days}$$

Problem

1. The following financial data were taken from Brands, Inc.:

	1980
Cash	$105,000
Marketable Securities	35,000
Accounts and Notes Receivable (Net) (1979, $146,000)	140,000
Merchandise Inventory (1979, $183,000)	175,000
Prepaid Expenses	7,500
Accounts and Notes Payable (1979, $195,000)	190,000
Other Liabilities	40,000
Cost of Sales	1,400,000
Net Sales (Credit)	1,460,000

Calculate a. the current ratio, b. the quick ratio, c. the inventory turnover, and d. the trade receivable turnover. Also compute e. the number of days of inventory and f. the average collection period.

a. ————

b. ————

c. ————

d. ————

e. ————

f. ————

Profitability Ratios
These indicate the general overall success of the firm and focus on measuring the adequacy of income.

Net Operating Margin measures the effectiveness of production and sales in generating pretax profits. Operation income excludes costs associated with financing sources and ordinary (nonoperating) items. The margin is calculated by dividing income from operations by net sales.

$$1980 \quad \frac{\text{Income from Operations}}{\text{Net Sales}} = \frac{\$ 59,709}{\$563,064} = 10.60\%$$

Return on Owner's Investment shows the earning power of the common stockholders' investment. This ratio looks at profitability from the viewpoint of the investor. Investors commit their dollars to an enterprise and need to be able to compare the value of that investment with alternative investments. The rate of return is determined by dividing net income (before any extraordinary items) by the average owners' investment:

$$1980 \quad \frac{\text{Net Income}}{\text{Average Owners' Equity}} = \frac{\$27,187}{\$248,067 + \$224,528/2} = 11.51\%$$

Return on Assets is the rate of return earned by the firm for all its investors, including debt holders. It represents an overall measure of management's performance in using all the firm's resources available during the year. The rate of return is determined by dividing net income (before extraordinary items) plus interest on debt by average total assets:

$$1980 \; \frac{\text{Net Income + Interest}}{\text{Average Total Assets}} = \frac{\$27,187 + \$7,508}{\$470,717 + \$416,431/2} = \frac{\$ \; 34,695}{\$443,574}$$

$$= 7.82\%$$

Leverage is the advantage or disadvantage that a firm derives from borrowed funds. Positive leverage exists if the firm earns more on total assets than on owners' investment or if the net interest cost of borrowed funds is less than the company's earnings rate overall. Leverage can be computed by finding the difference between return on owners' investment and the return on total assets.

Return on Owners' Investment (1980)	11.51%
− Return on Total Assets (1980)	−7.82%
(Positive) Leverage	3.69%

Problem

2. The following financial data were taken from Brands, Inc.:

	1980	1979
Net Income from Operations	310,000	328,200
Net Income	146,000	160,000
Interest Expense (Net)	46,000	36,000
Total Assets	3,200,000	2,800,000
Common Stock	1,000,000	1,000,000
Retained Earnings	780,000	700,000
Net Sales	3,075,000	2,652,000

Calculate a. net operating margin, b. return on owners' investment, c. return on assets, and d. leverage.

a. _____ %

b. _____ %

c. _____ %

d. _____ %

Equity Ratios

These are a set of measures designed to reflect the extent to which a firm's expansion has been financed by debt.

Debt to Total Assets is a measure designed to highlight the percentage of total assets to which all kinds of creditors have a claim:

$$1980 \quad \frac{\text{Total Liabilities}}{\text{Total Assets}} = \frac{\$222,650}{\$470,717} = 47.30\%$$

The debt to total assets is sometimes referred to as the *leverage ratio*.

Owners' Equity to Total Assets is really the complement of the total debt to total assets ratio. Some analysts prefer two ratios, which measure the same relationship; they always add to 1, or 100%:

$$1980 \quad \frac{\text{Total Owners' Equity}}{\text{Total Assets}} = \frac{\$248,067}{\$470,717} = 52.70\%$$

Note that 47.30% (debt to total assets) plus 52.70% equals 100%. Taken together, the two ratios indicate the total amount of resources contributed to the firm by each group of capital suppliers.

Debt to Owners' Equity is a popular measure designed to reflect the capital structure of the firm. It expresses the direct proportion between debt and owners' equity:

$$1980 \quad \frac{\text{Total Debt}}{\text{Owners' Equity}} = \frac{\$222,650}{\$248,067} = 89.75\%$$

For every $1 invested by owners, there is 90¢ invested by creditors.

Problems

3. The following financial data were taken from Brands, Inc.:

Total Debt	$1,420,000
Total Assets	3,200,000
Total Owners' Equity	1,780,000

    Calculate a. The debt–to–asset ratio, b. the owners'–equity–to–asset ratio, and c. the debt–to–owners'–equity ratio.

    a. _____ %

    b. _____ %

    c. _____ %

4. The following financial data were taken from Investor Unlimited, Inc.:

	1980	1979
Cash	$ 38,000	$ 40,000
Receivables (Net)	117,000	86,000
Inventory	180,000	120,000
Prepaid Items	55,000	42,000
Notes Payable—Current	50,000	10,000
Accounts Payable	66,000	30,000
Other Current Liabilities	31,400	54,000
Plant & Equipment (Net)	500,000	467,000
Long-Term Liabilities	200,000	250,000
Common Stock	350,000	300,000
Capital in Excess of Par	70,000	40,000
Retained Earnings	182,600	176,000
Net Sales	900,000	750,000
Cost of Goods	585,000	468,000
Operating Expense	243,000	169,500
Interest Expense	12,000	15,000
Income Taxes	23,400	44,200
Net Income	36,600	52,500

Calculate:

a. Current Ratio _____
b. Quick Ratio _____
c. Inventory Turnover _____
d. Number of Days Supply _____
e. Trade Receivable Turnover _____
f. Average Collection Period _____
g. Net Operating Margin _____%
h. Return on Owners' Investment _____%
i. Return on Assets _____%
j. Leverage _____%
k. Debt–to–Assets Percentage _____%
l. Debt–to–Owners'–Equity Percentage _____%
m. Owners'–Equity–to–Asset Percentage _____%

Chapter Review

The financial information presented below is for Projects, Inc.:

	1981	1980
Balance Sheet Items:		
Cash	$ 35,000	$ 25,000
Accounts Receivable	91,000	90,000
Inventory	160,000	140,000
Prepaid Expenses	4,000	5,000
Investment in X, Inc.	90,000	100,000
Equipment (Net)	220,000	140,000
Building (Net)	400,000	300,000
Total	$1,000,000	$ 800,000
Acounts Payable	$ 105,000	$ 46,000
Other Liabilities—Short-Term	40,000	25,000
Long-Term Debt—Note	283,600	284,000
Capital Stock, $5 Par	165,000	110,000
Retained Earnings	406,400	335,000
Total	$1,000,000	$ 800,000
Income Statement Items:		
Net Sales	$2,200,000	$1,600,000
Cost of Sales	1,606,000	1,120,000
Gross Margin	594,000	480,000
Operating Expenses	(307,600)	(329,600)
Interest Expense	(22,400)	(22,400)
Income Taxes	(91,000)	(48,000)
Extraordinary Loss	(6,600)	-0-
Net Income	$ 166,400	$ 80,000

1. Balance Sheet: Prepare a horizontal analysis and a vertical analysis.
2. Income Statement: Prepare a horizontal analysis and a vertical analysis.
3. Calculate the following ratios and percentages:

    a. Current Ratio   _____

    b. Quick Ratio   _____

    c. Inventory Turnover   _____

    d. Number of days supply   _____

    e.   Trade Receivable Turnover   _____

    f.   Average Collection Period   _____

    g.   Net Operating Margin   _____%

    h.   Return on Owners' Investment   _____%

    i.   Return on Assets   _____%

    j.   Leverage   _____%

    k.   Debt–to–Assets–Percentage   _____%

    l.   Debt–to–Owners'–Equity Percentage   _____%

    m.   Owners'–Equity–to–Asset Percentage   _____%

4.   For the management of Projects, Inc., prepare a general overview of the company's strengths and weaknesses revealed by your financial analysis.

23

Capital Expenditures

A *capital expenditure* is the payment for an asset which will be used for more than a year. Examples include money spent for land, buildings, and equipment. Proposals for the purchase of these long-lived assets are called *capital-project proposals*. Planning for and selecting capital projects from among these proposals is called *capital budgeting*.

The capital budget serves as the basis for deciding whether or not to purchase the capital asset being considered. Decisions are made on the basis of the benefits received versus the costs involved. This boils down to comparing the *cash inflows* (cash received) with the *cash outflows* (cash payments) over a period of time.

23.1 CASH-FLOW ANALYSIS

Only those cash inflows and outflows which occur as the result of a particular capital proposal should be considered in the evaluation of a project.

Cash inflows are generated by increasing revenues, reducing costs, or both. Cash outflows occur when payment is made for the capital item purchased plus any additional costs associated with the project. A reasonably accurate forecast of the cash flows in an uncertain future is basic to the analysis of a proposal. Economists, marketing experts, and other people who specialize in forecasting business conditions are used in this process.

The techniques of forecast analysis are varied and complex, but they generally involve probabilities and expected values. Here, we are concerned not with determining the probability that something will occur, but rather with applying the probabilities developed by others to particular situations. For example, assume that you are told that the chances of next year's being a boom year for business are one in ten; for being a moderate boom year, three in ten; for being a normal or average year, three in ten; for being a recession year, two in ten; and for being a dismal depression year, one in ten. These probabilities can be expressed as .1, .3, .3, .2, and .1; these add up to 1.0. By assigning a sales volume developed by the marketing expert to each of these probabilities, we can develop an expected sales volume as shown in Table 23-1.

Table 23-1.
1981—Expected Value of Sales—Capital Project #A-3

A *Possible Sales Volumes*	B *Probable States of Economy*		A × B *Weighted Sales Volumes*
$60,000	0.1	Boom	$ 6,000
40,000	0.3	Moderate Boom	12,000
30,000	0.3	Normal	9,000
20,000	0.2	Recession	4,000
5,000	0.1	Depression	500
	1.0	Expected Sales Level	$31,500

Note that each projected possible sales volume is multiplied by the probability of achieving that volume to determine the weighted sales volume. The sum of these then gives the expected sales level.

The next step in the analysis is to prepare a projected cash-flow statement, using estimates of expected expenses, in addition to the estimates of income from sales. Table 23-2 is such a statement, covering a five-year period, using $60,000 as the initial cost of the capital expenditure.

Table 23-2. *Project #A-3*
Projected Annual Cash Flows for the Years 1980–1984

	1980	1981	1982	1983	1984
Expected Sales—					
Cash Inflow	$31,500	$31,500	$35,000	$40,000	$40,000
Expected Expenses—					
Cash Outflow	(15,000)	(15,000)	(15,000)	(15,000)	(15,000)
Depreciation Exp.	(10,000)	(10,000)	(10,000)	(10,000)	(10,000)
Increased Income					
Before Tax	6,500	6,500	10,000	15,000	15,000
Tax at 46%—Outflow	(2,990)	(2,990)	(4,600)	(6,900)	(6,900)
Net Income—After Tax	3,510	3,510	5,400	8,100	8,100
Depreciation Add back	10,000	10,000	10,000	10,000	10,000
	13,510	13,510	15,400	18,100	18,100
Expected Salvage					
Value—Cash Inflow					10,000
Expected Annual After-					
Tax Cash Flows—					
Net Cash Flow	$13,510	$13,510	$15,400	$18,100	$28,100

Project Initial Investment	$60,000
Salvage Value	− 10,000
Amount to Be Depreciated	$50,000
Economic Life	5 Years
Depreciation per Year—S-L	$50,000 ÷ 5 = $10,000

Notice that depreciation is separated from other expenses in the cash-flow analysis. Depreciation represents the decrease in the value of the capital asset through use; it is not a cash-flow item. Depreciation is deductible as an expense for tax purposes, however. Because depreciation is not a cash outflow item, the amount deducted must be added back to give the final annual *after-tax* cash-flow estimates.

Problems

1. Given the following projected sales values and associated probabilities, what sales should be expected?

1982 Projections

Sales	Probability
$5,000	0.05
10,000	0.10
15,000	0.20
25,000	0.30
30,000	0.20
35,000	0.10
40,000	0.50
	1.00

$_____

2. Mary Packer purchased an antique car last year for $8,000. Today she received an offer of $12,000 for the car. She plans to attend an antique-car auction next month. If she estimates possible selling prices at the auction as follows, should Ms. Packer sell now or wait until the antique sale?

Possible Price	Probability of Price
$18,000	0.1
15,000	0.2
14,000	0.3
12,000	0.3
8,000	0.1
	1.0

3. Your school is planning a rock concert next month. Concerts are held in a local hall with a variable seating capacity of 1,000 to 1,500. The minimum charge for the hall is $3,000. The rate for seating over 1,000 is $200 for each block of 100 additional seats. The concert committee chairperson has provided you with the data below. At what price would you recommend the tickets be sold?

Ticket Price	Attendance	Probability
$3.25	1,800	0.1
	1,600	0.1
	1,200	0.2
	1,000	0.6
		1.0
$3.00	1,800	0.2
	1,600	0.4
	1,200	0.3
	1,000	0.1
		1.0
$2.75	1,800	0.5
	1,600	0.3
	1,200	0.1
	1,000	0.1
		1.0

$_____

4. XYZ, Inc. installed a machine with these expected first-year results:

Increase in revenue	$8,000
Labor savings	2,000
Increase power costs	1,000
Increase maintenance costs	600
Depreciation	200

If the tax rate is 46% and expectations are realized, what will be the first-year net cash-flow amount?

$_____

5. A corporation wants to acquire new equipment with which to make a new product. The equipment will cost $37,000, and it will have an economic life of three years and a salvage value of $1,000. The additions to sales each year will be $20,000. The additional cash outflow will be $2,500 for the first year, $1,700 for the second, and $900 for the third. The tax rate is 46%. Calculate the annual after-tax cash flow for each of the three years.

1st $_____

2nd $_____

3rd $_____

23.2   PAY-BACK METHOD

The *pay-back method* of evaluating capital projects shows how long it will take to recover the initial capital investment amount, in the form of net cash flows. The amount of time it takes to recover the initial investment is called the *pay-back period*. For example, assume that $15,000 is needed to invest in a new machine, the machine has an economic life of six years, and the estimated uniform *after-tax* cash flow for each year is $3,000. The pay-back calculation is:

$$\frac{\text{Investment}}{\text{After-Tax Cash-Flow Amount}} = \frac{\$15,000}{\$3,000} = \text{5-Year Pay-Back Period}$$

Management assumes that the initial investment will be recovered in five years, one year before the end of the economic life of the machine.

When after-tax cash flows are not uniform, the pay-back calculation must include cumulative after-tax cash-flow totals. For example:

Investment $30,000
After-Tax Cash Flows

Year	Each Year	Cumulative Amount	Unrecovered Investment
1	$12,000	$12,000	$18,000
2	8,000	20,000	10,000
3	6,000	26,000	4,000
4	6,000	32,000	0

To recover the $4,000 needed at the end of the third year would require $4,000 ÷ $6,000, or two-thirds of the year, or eight months. The pay-back period is approximately three years and eight months, assuming the cash flows are uniform throughout the year in which the final $4,000 is recovered.

If a firm has a policy of rejecting capital projects that require more than four years to recover costs, then the first example (five-year recovery) would be rejected and the second example (three years, eight months) would be accepted. When a four-year pay-back policy is used to compare one capital project with another, the one with the shorter acceptable pay-back period is selected.

Problems

1. A company is considering the purchase of a new machine, at a cost of $33,000. The machine is expected to reduce costs by $6,000 each year for seven years. a. What is the payback period? b. If the company accepts only projects with a pay-back period of five years or less, will it accept or reject the proposal?

   a. _____

   b. _____

2. Compute the pay-back period for the following capital projects:

   Cash Flows

Year	Project A	Project B
1	$10,000	$24,000
2	15,000	24,000
3	20,000	18,000
4	24,000	12,000
5	36,000	12,000
6	12,000	6,000
7	12,000	6,000
Investment:	$67,000	$93,000

   Project A _____

   Project B _____

3. A company uses a five-year pay-back evaluation measure. Within the pay-back period, the company should recover the initial investment, plus a 15% reutrn on invested capital for the period of the investment. Using the following data, which project would you rank as first priority in the capital budget?

	Project 1	Project 2
Investment	$10,000	$10,000
Salvage Value	0	0
Economic Life	5 Years	5 Years
Expected Annual After-Tax Cash Flows		
Year 1	$ 2,000	$ 2,000
2	4,500	4,000
3	2,000	5,000
4	6,000	6,000
5	2,000	5,000

4. The financial information below was collected for three cost-saving capital projects:

Project	Cost	Economic Life	Annual After-Tax Cash Flow
I	$12,000	4	$2,000
II	20,000	5	5,000
III	35,000	10	5,000

Complete the pay-back period for each project. a. If you are willing to accept a pay-back period of six years, which projects would you go ahead with?

b. If you had to choose only one project, which one would you select?

a. —————

b. —————

23.3 ACCOUNTANTS' METHOD

As the standard for capital project acceptance, some firms apply a company-established rate of return per year on investments. The approach is called the *accountants' method* because it uses the accounting definition of net income. Each capital project is evaluated to determine the rate of return on the invested dollars. If the project meets the company standard for an acceptable rate of return on investments, then the project is considered acceptable. If more than one project is being evaluated, the project with the highest rate of return is assigned the highest priority.

In the accountants' method, net income rather than after-tax cash flow is considered the benefit derived from the project. To arrive at net income in the cash-flow analysis, calculate depreciation and subtract it from the after-tax cash-flow amounts. (Recall that in 23.1 depreciation was added to net income to arrive at after-tax cash flow.) The accountants' rate of return *based upon initial investment* may be calculated as follows:

$$\text{Accountants' Rate of Return} = \frac{\text{Average Annual Net Income}}{\text{Initial Investment}}$$

Example. The average annual after-tax cash flow for a proposed capital expenditure of $12,000 is expected to be approximately $3,500 a year. The project has a four-year economic life.

Average Annual After-Tax Cash Flow: $3,500
Salvage Value: $2,000
Straight-Line Depreciation: $12,000 − $2,000 = $10,000
$10,000 ÷ 4 Years = $2,500 Annual Depreciation

Cash Flow	$3,500
Depreciation	− 2,500
Estimated Average Annual Net Income	$1,000

Accountants' Rate of Return: $1,000 ÷ $12,000 = 8.333%

A modification of the above method uses an average-investment figure as the denominator in the calculation. This technique, referred to as the *Average-Rate-of-Return Method,* is:

$$\text{Average Rate of Return} = \frac{\text{Average Annual Net Income}}{\text{Average Investment}}$$

Example. Using the data provided below, calculate the average rate of return:

Project Cost:	$25,000	Cost	$25,000
Salvage Value:	$5,000	Salvage Value	− 5,000
Economic Life: 5 Years		Amount to Be Depreciated	$20,000

$20,000 ÷ 5 Years = $4,000 Annual Depreciation

	Estimated Annual Net Income		
End of Year	After Tax Cash Flow	Annual Depreciation	Annual Net Income
1	$8,000	$4,000	$ 4,000
2	8,000	4,000	4,000
3	6,000	4,000	2,000
4	6,000	4,000	2,000
5	4,000	4,000	0
		Total	$12,000

Average Annual Net Income: $12,000 ÷ 5 = $2.400

Estimated Average Investment

End of Year	Assumed Annual Remaining Investment
0	$25,000
1	21,000
2	17,000
3	13,000
4	9,000
5 6 periods	5,000
Sum of the Values	$90,000

"Assumed annual remaining investment" is the depreciated value of the investment at the end of each investment period (year).

Using the sum of the investment values ($90,000) and the number of investment periods (6), the calculation of the average investment is:
$90,000 ÷ 6 Years = $15,000 Annual Average Investment

A short method of calculating average investment *when straight-line depreciation is used* is to add together the beginning and ending investment values, then divide by 2:
$25,000 + $5,000 = $30,000
$30,000 ÷ 2 = $15,000
$2,400 ÷ $15,000 = 16% Average Rate of Return

The average investment method is supported by the argument that a portion of an investment is recovered each year through depreciation; therefore the rate of return should be based upon the average-investment amount.

Problems

1. Compute the rate of return from the following data, using the accountants' method:

Project Investment	$23,000
Salvage Value	3,000
Economic Life	5 Years
Annual After-Tax Cash Flow	6,000

_____%

2. From the data in Problem 1, compute the rate of return, using the average-rate-of-return method: _____%

3. Your staff has developed for you the financial information given below. You are planning to provide the controller with the rate-of-return computation for the two proposed projects. As part of the preparation of your report, you need to complete the forms provided. Fill in the blanks for Project I and Project II.

Project I

Initial Investment	$55,000
Salvage Value	5,000
Depreciation	S-L
Economic Life	5 Years
Annual Depreciation	_____
Average Annual Net Income	_____
Estimated Average Investment	_____

End of Year	After-Tax Cash Flow	Annual Depreciation	Annual Net Income	Assumed Annual Remaining Investment
0	—	—	—	$55,000
1	$ 8,000	_____	_____	_____
2	13,000	_____	_____	_____
3	18,000	_____	_____	_____
4	21,000	_____	_____	_____
5	21,000	_____	_____	_____

Project II

Initial Investment	$60,000
Salvage Value	0
Depreciation	S-L
Economic Life	5 Years
Annual Depreciation	_____
Average Annual Net Income	_____
Estimated Average Investment	_____

End of Year	After-Tax Cash Flow	Annual Depreciation	Annual Net Income	Assumed Annual Remaining Investment
0	—	—	—	$60,000
1	$15,000	_____	_____	_____
2	15,000	_____	_____	_____
3	20,000	_____	_____	_____
4	20,000	_____	_____	_____
5	20,000	_____	_____	_____

4. a. Compute the rate of return for Projects I and II above, using the accountants' method. If you had to select one project, which project would you select, assuming unlimited funding? b. Compute the rate of return for Projects I and II, using the average-rate-of-return method. If you had to select one project, which project would you select, assuming unlimited funding?

a. _____

b. _____

5. Compute the pay-back period for each project. Which project would you select, using the pay-back method? (Remember to use after-tax cash flow.)

_____

23.4   NET-PRESENT-VALUE METHOD

Of the several methods used by business firms to make capital investment decisions, the *net present value* (NPV) approach is generally preferred. The NPV method takes into account the time value of money: a dollar received today is preferable to a dollar received at some future date. It makes possible an *accept-reject decision* for the selection of capital projects.

The NPV method includes the following steps some of which are included in 23.1, 23.2, 23.3, and Chapter 6.

First, estimate after-tax net cash flows for each capital project.

Second, assess the amount of risk or uncertainty associated with the net cash flows.

Select a *cost-of-capital rate* for discounting the net cash flow. The cost of capital depends on the amount of risk associated with the project, the current interest rates, and other financial factors. (For problems in this unit, cost of capital will be assumed to be 12%.)

Discount future after-tax net cash flows, to determine the sum of their present values. (See Chapter 6.)

Decide whether to accept or reject the project, on the basis of whether the NPV of future after-tax cash flows exceeds the cost of the project. If the NPV is positive (exceeds cost), the project would be beneficial to the firm's growth and would be accepted.

The calculations for the NPV of two capital projects are presented in Table 23-3.

The NPV of both projects is positive: the Project L-1 NPV is $192, and the Project L-2 NPV is $618. On the basis of their NPV, both projects would be considered acceptable. However, if you had to choose between Projects L-1 and L-2, then Project L-2, with the higher NPV of $618, compared to the Project L-1 NPV of $192, would clearly be the better choice. L-2 provides $426 greater value to the firm.

Table 23-3.
Net-Present-Value Calculation
Initial Cost $2,000
Cost of Capital 12%

	Project L-1				Project L-2		
Year	A After-Tax Cash Flow	B 12% PV¹ of $1	A × B PV of Cash Flows	Year	A After-Tax Cash Flow	B 12% PV¹ of $1	A × B PV of Cash Flows
1	$1,000	.89	$ 890	1	$ 200	.89	$ 178
2	800	.80	640	2	400	.80	320
3	600	.71	426	3	600	.71	426
4	200	.64	128	4	800	.64	512
5	100	.57	57	5	1,000	.57	570
6	100	.51	51	6	1,200	.51	612
	PV of Cash Flows		$2,192		PV of Cash Flows		$2,618
	Cost		− 2,000		Cost		− 2,000
	NPV (+)		$ 192		NPV (+)		$ 618

¹ From Table 23-4: Present Values of $1

Table 23-4.
Present values of $1.

Year	10%	12%	15%
1	.91	.89	.87
2	.83	.80	.76
3	.75	.71	.66
4	.68	.64	.57
5	.62	.57	.50
6	.56	.51	.43

Problems

1. A firm is considering two possible capital projects, at a cost of capital of 12%. Each project requires a capital expenditure of $20,000. The two projects provide the following cash flows:

Year	A	B
1	$10,000	$ 5,000
2	10,000	5,000
3	10,000	20,000

a. Calculate the NPV for each project. b. Which project should be accepted if you have $40,000 to invest? c. If you have only $20,000 to invest?

a. A_____

    B_____

b. _____

c. _____

2. A project costing $12,500 was expected to produce the following cash flow:

Year	Cash Flow
1	$5,000
2	4,000
3	3,000
4	2,000
5	2,000
6	1,000

a. Should the project be accepted if capital costs 10%? b. If capital costs 15%?

a. _____

b. _____

3. A corporation is considering the purchase of a new machine which will reduce operating costs $2,000 annually for the next five years. The machine costs $8,000. The corporation rejects projects with a rate of return of less than 12%. Should this project be rejected? (Hint: $2,000 for five years is the same as an equal series of payments.) The present value of an annuity of $1 for 5 periods at 12% is $3.605.

_____

4. A local theater manager has asked for your advice. He has a concession stand which is losing $1,000 per year. He is considering installing a popcorn machine at a cost of $8,000. The machine will produce a net income of $2,000 per year for the next five years. Should he install the

machine? Use the NPV method. The manager requires at least a 12% rate of return on investments.

_____

5. Two projects are being considered by a firm. Each project requires an investment of $2,000. The firm's cost of capital is 12%. The after-tax net cash flows for the two projects are:

	Project	
Year	X	Y
1	$1,000	$600
2	800	600
3	600	800
4	200	800
5	0	100
6	0	100

a. Calculate the pay-back period for each project. b. Calculate the NPV for each project. c. Which project would you select if you used the pay-back method for project evaluation? d. Which project would you select, using the NPV method for project evaluation? e. Which project do you recommend for investment considering both the pay-back and the NPV methods? Why?

a. X_____

    Y_____

b. X_____

    Y_____

c. _____

d. _____

e. _____

_____

Chapter Review

_____

The Capital City Market is considering an investment in three possible projects. The president asks for your recommendation for project selection. Each project is expected to require a $30,000 initial cost; the projects have different economic lives. Development programs of the firm are evaluated using a 12% cost of capital. Your analysis of future benefits and costs associated with the three projects reveals:

	Project		
Annual Amounts	#1	#2	#3
Increase in Revenues (Cash)	$12,000	$15,000	$18,000
Increase in Costs (Cash)		1,000	2,000
Decrease in Costs (Cash)	2,000		
Depreciation	6,000	7,500	7,500
Salvage Value	0	0	0
Economic Life	5 Years	4 Years	4 Years

(The tax rate for Capital City Markets is 25%.)

For each project determine a. the net income, b. the after-tax cash flow, c. the pay-back period, d. the average rate of return, and e. the net present value. The present value of an annuity of $1 for four periods at 12% is $3.037. See problem 3 for 5-year annuity factor. f. Which project would you recommend to the president as the best investment?

a.   #1 $_____   c.   #1 _____   e.   #1 $_____

    #2 $_____   #2 _____   #2 $_____

    #3 $_____   #3 _____   #3 $_____

b.   #1 $_____   d.   #1 _____% f.   _____

    #2 $_____   #2 _____%

    #3 $_____   #3 _____%

Appendices

Answers to pretest:

1.	$39.43	18.	52	35.	$1/40$
2.	359.59	19.	$63.75	36.	24
3.	42.95	20.	$1/8$	37.	$25/83$
4.	$7 1/8$	21.	15	38.	$1/5$; $1/4$; $1/3$; $1/2$
5.	$9.16$2/3$	22.	$1,704.60	39.	$1/3$; $3/8$; $2/5$
6.	317.1	23.	$4,495.10(4)	40.	.07; .107; $7/10$; .71
7.	$141.97	24.	$.46526718	41.	54,000
8.	$7.15	25.	$47.25	42.	53,600
9.	$1/8$	26.	26.067$1/9$	43.	53,570
10.	461.7	27.	1250	44.	20¢
11.	$1.14	28.	28	45.	28¢
12.	1.104	29.	3577.6	46.	4¢
13.	1.904	30.	52.143	47.	14¢
14.	.126759	31.	.004	48.	7¢
15.	1.25	32.	1.725	49.	100 lb.
16.	1,000,000,000	33.	.085	50.	2¢
17.	.00000001	34.	89.583		

This test is not as easy as it looks. Very few people will avoid all errors. If you have only one or two, remember their cause so that you can avoid similar errors as you go on in the course.

If you have more errors—perhaps up to ten—you will need to proceed carefully, paying particular attention to the areas where you have proved weakest. If you have more than ten errors, it will be to your advantage in the long run to take time, before going on, to review the basic mathematics on the pages that follow. If you can pinpoint the causes of errors and concentrate on them, do so. Otherwise, be careful to go over every part until you are sure you understand it.

Where did you go wrong? If you missed Problems 5, 6, 10, 28, and 29 and very few others, concentrate on Section V, on notation. If most of the problems you missed were from 30 to 34 and from 41 to 48, be sure you understand rounding, Section IV. If you have trouble with fractions, check Section II. If your errors are spread over the whole test, you may especially need to review the use of decimals in Section III.

When you are sure of your understanding and skill, go ahead in the study of mathematics applied to business.

I. Whole Numbers

A. Addition. The addition of whole numbers is basic to almost every kind of computation. The standard method of addition is to add the ones column first, carrying over any tens into the tens column, and so on.

In adding a long column of figures, it is important to align the columns clearly to avoid mixing them. There is nothing wrong in writing a figure to be carried from one column at the top of the next column. Another way of avoiding confusion is the "accountants' method," by which each column is totaled separately and the sum of the columns is found later:

```
2 33
1,398          Accountants' Method:
6,579                    ones       35
8,768                    tens      310
7,046                hundreds     1,700
2,254               thousands    24,000
26,045                           26,045
```

The most common method of checking addition is to add each column in the opposite direction—from top to bottom, if the first addition was from bottom to top:

Practice: 1.   7,437   2.   149,624   3.   58,724
                   4,608   617   567
                   3,942   3,289   9,423
                                   73   74,872

              4.   67,782   5.   9,243   6.   377
                  248,729   80,741   1,608
                  146,710   2,080   38,700
                      298   342,673   2,985

Sometimes it is useful to add numbers horizontally—from left to right, instead of from top to bottom. This is usually harder, because it is not so easy to separate tens from hundreds, for example, when they are not in a column. With numbers of one or two digits, it is not difficult to add each number as a whole, adding first the ones digit and then the tens digit to the cumulative total.

$$36 + \quad 43 + \quad 29 + \quad 18 + \quad 8 + \quad 16$$
$$= 36 + 3 + 40 + 9 + 20 + 8 + 10 + 8 + 6 + 10$$
$$= 36, \quad 39, \quad 79, \quad 88, \quad 108, \quad 116, \quad 126, \quad 134, \quad 140, \quad 150$$

With larger numbers, it is better to add each place separately:

Practice:
1. $24 + 71 + 23 + 61 + 22 + 41 + 73 = $ _____
2. $7 + 91 + 5 + 71 + 3 + 16 + 8 = $ _____
3. $849 + 983 + 874 + 102 + 127 + 185 = $ _____
4. $2,851 + 8,392 + 36,512 + 18,143 = $ _____
5. $10,726 + 1,918 + 12,685 + 6,851 + 4,513 = $ _____

Again, a good way of checking is to add in the opposite direction.

In some cases it is necessary to add both vertically and horizontally—for example, to find a production total for each day of the week and also for each worker. When these subtotals are added, the results should be the same, providing a check on both processes:

Practice:

1.	Mon.	Tue.	Wed.	Thu.	Fri.	Sat.	Totals
A	122	121	104	121	76	108	_____
B	113	82	99	95	108	122	_____
C	97	124	103	116	97	134	_____
D	127	122	116	86	116	102	_____
E	132	96	109	132	96	113	_____
Totals	_____	_____	_____	_____	_____	_____	_____

2.	July	August	September	Totals
F	26,451	25,401	20,432	_____
G	21,023	26,114	25,124	_____
H	13,511	33,045	34,415	_____
I	21,026	22,321	26,412	_____
J	23,143	21,014	31,941	_____
K	20,315	25,310	27,919	_____
Totals	_____	_____	_____	_____

When a calculator is used, mistakes are less likely, but all results should be checked. If you need more practice, make up your own problems and check them.

B. Subtraction. Subtraction, the reverse of addition, is always done with only two figures at a time. For instance, if we buy items for $1.29, $3.75, and $2.84, paying for them with a $10 bill, we do not subtract $1.29 from $10, then $3.75, and then $2.84. Rather we first add $1.29, $3.75, and $2.84 together, then subtract that sum from $10:

$$\$1.29 \ + \ \$3.75 \ + \ \$2.84 \ = \ \$7.88$$
$$\$10.00 \ - \ \$7.88 \ = \ \$2.12$$

In subtracting, we are asking ourselves, "What must we add to $7.88 to make $10.00?" Subtraction is always checked by adding upwards.

Practice:

1.	980	2.	1,000	3.	739	4.	1,238
	− 403		− 478		− 86		− 789

5.	27,628	6.	52,062	7.	876,994	8.	430,781
	− 19,789		− 1,973		− 548,792		− 278,936

C. Multiplication. Multiplication is a quick way of adding. If we pay $255 a month for rent for a year, we could add up twelve $255s to get the annual figure, but it is much easier to multiply:

$$\$255 \ \times \ 12 \ = \ \$3,060$$

A person who is not sure of the multiples of 12 could do this multiplication in two steps, first by the ones and then by the tens:

$$
\begin{array}{r}
\$255 \\
\times \quad 12 \\
\hline
510 \\
255 \quad \\
\hline
\$3,060
\end{array}
$$

If we wanted to know how much would be paid at that rate in 15 years, we could either a. multiply the annual rate by 15, or b. first multiply 15 by 12 to find the total number of months and then multiply the result by the monthly rate:

a.	b.	
$3,060	15	$255
× 15	× 12	× 180
15300	30	20400
3060	15	255
$45,900 Total	180 Months	$45,900

We have checked this result by using another method. The most common way to check multiplication is by switching the multiplicand and the multiplier, and then multiplying, which would give the same result.

Notice that in the second part of b. the 0 in the ones place of the multiplier 180 is placed to the right of the multiplicand $255. This is one of the shortcuts we can take in multiplying. The final 0 is not forgotten, but since the result of multiplying 255 by 0 is 0, we simply put 0 in the ones place and go on. What we are doing is multiplying 255 by 18 tens. The same sort of shortcut could have been used in a. by writing:

$$
\begin{array}{r}
3060 \\
\times\quad 15 \\
\hline
15300 \\
306 \\
\hline
45{,}900
\end{array}
$$

If you are comfortable with such a shortcut, by all means use it; but you need not use it if you do not feel comfortable with it.

There are other shortcuts in multiplication, all of which may be used but need not be:

We have just observed that, to multiply by ten, we simply move the multiplicand to the tens place and put a zero in the ones place (familiarly we say we "add a zero"). Since five is half of ten, to multiply by five, we can multiply by ten and divide by two:
$$3{,}486 \times 5 = 34{,}860 \div 2 = 17{,}430$$
Or, since twenty-five is one-fourth of one hundred, to multiply by twenty-five, we may multiply by one hundred (by "adding two zeroes") and then divide by four:
$$3{,}486 \times 25 = 348{,}600 \div 4 = 87{,}150$$

Many prices are set at figures just under an even number of dollars—$1.98 or $6.99, for example. To find the price of seven such articles, we could multiply:

$$
\begin{array}{r}
\$1.98 \\
\times\quad 7 \\
\hline
\$13.86
\end{array}
\qquad
\begin{array}{r}
\$6.99 \\
\times\quad 7 \\
\hline
\$48.93
\end{array}
$$

However, the quickest way to find the total price is to decide what it would be in whole dollars and then subtract the odd cents:

$$
\begin{array}{rcr}
\$2 \times 7 = & \$14.00 \\
-.02 \times 7 = & -\ .14 \\
\hline
& \$13.86
\end{array}
\qquad
\begin{array}{rcr}
\$7 \times 7 = & \$49.00 \\
-.01 \times 7 = & -\ .07 \\
\hline
& \$48.93
\end{array}
$$

Using such shortcuts will often save time, but may also increase the chances for error. Use them if you feel secure with them.

Practice:

1.	48 ×27	2.	528 × 63	3.	694 × 87	4.	8,061 × 49
5.	396,493 × 73	6.	76,081 × 807	7.	26,492 × 23	8.	4,783 × 654
9.	4,672 × 700	10.	1,325 × 250	11.	899 × 3	12.	498 × 99

D. Division. Dividing is the reverse of multiplying, and just as multiplying is a quick way of adding, dividing is a quick way of subtracting. When we divide a dividend by a divisor, we are really asking how many times the divisor could be subtracted from the dividend.

Because there may be some "remainder" left in the dividend after the divisor has been subtracted as many whole times as possible, division is the only one of the four fundamental operations that may *not* result in a whole number. We may show what is left as a remainder, round the quotient to the nearest whole number (see Section IV), express the remainder as a decimal fraction (see Section III), or express the remainder as a common fraction (see Section II).

"Short" division, where the divisor is a small number, may usually be done mentally: $4,782 \div 3 = 1,594$, although it is always a good idea to check immediately by multiplying the quotient by the divisor, also mentally: $1,594 \times 3 = 4,782$.

"Long" division, by a larger number, is more complicated and requires the use of multiplication and subtraction:

```
            184
256)47,293     256 will go once but not twice into 472.
    256        256 × 1 = 256.
    2169       472 − 256 = 216. Add 9 in tens place. 256 will go into 2,169 eight times.
    2048       256 × 8 = 2,048
    1213       2,169 − 2,048 = 121. Add 3 in ones place. 256 will go into 1,213 four times.
    1024       256 × 4 = 1,024
     189       1,213 − 1,024 = 189, the Remainder
```

To check division, multiply the quotient by the divisor and add the remainder. The result should be the dividend:

```
        184    Quotient
      × 256    Divisor
       1104
        920
        368
     47,104
   +    189    Remainder
     47,293    Dividend
```

When the divisor has factors (smaller numbers that can be multiplied together to make the divisor) division may sometimes be done by two "short" division steps instead of one "long" division. For instance, to divide 1,288 by 56, we see that 56 is 7×8. We may divide first by 7:

$1,288 \div 7 = 184$

and then by 8:

$184 \div 8 = 23,$

so $1,288 \div 56 = 23$

Suppose we had divided first by 8: $1,288 \div 8 = 161$
and then by 7: $161 \div 7 = 23$, the same result.
This *factor method* of dividing is quicker and easier when there is no remainder.

Practice: 1. $23\overline{)2,472}$ 2. $38\overline{)12,844}$ 3. $685\overline{)73,041}$

4. $9,648 \div 72 =$ 5. $4,116 \div 49 =$ 6. $2,072 \div 56 =$

7. $3,600 \div 25 =$ 8. $19,376 \div 28 =$

II. Common Fractions

The value of a common fraction, such as $\frac{2}{3}$ or $\frac{12}{16}$, is not changed if both the numerator (top number) and the denominator (bottom number) are multiplied or divided by the same number.

To reduce a fraction to its simplest terms, divide both numerator and denominator by any factor contained in both:

$$\frac{12}{16} \quad \frac{12 \div 4}{16 \div 4} = \frac{3}{4} \qquad \frac{45}{75} = \frac{45 \div 3}{75 \div 3} = \frac{15}{25} = \frac{15 \div 5}{25 \div 5} = \frac{3}{5}$$

To change to higher terms, multiply both numerator and denominator by any desired number. In order for two fractions to be added or subtracted, they must first have the same denominator.

$$\frac{2}{3} = \frac{4}{6} = \frac{12}{18} = \frac{84}{126} \qquad \frac{1}{6} = \frac{3}{18} = \frac{6}{36} = \frac{18}{108}$$

Practice: 1. $\frac{1}{3} = \frac{3}{9}$ 2. $\frac{3}{5} = \frac{12}{20}$ 3. $\frac{2}{7} = \frac{8}{28}$

4. $\frac{1}{2} = \frac{6}{12}$ 5. $\frac{5}{6} = \frac{10}{12}$ 6. $\frac{1}{4} = \frac{3}{12}$

In adding or subtracting fractions, it is best to use the smallest denominator that will contain the original denominators. Once two or more fractions have the same denominator, the numerators are added or subtracted and placed over the denominator to show the sum or difference. The result should be shown in simplest terms:

$$\frac{1}{6} + \frac{2}{3} + \frac{3}{4} = \frac{2}{12} + \frac{8}{12} + \frac{9}{12} = \frac{19}{12} = 1\frac{7}{12}$$

$$\frac{5}{6} - \frac{2}{5} = \frac{25}{30} - \frac{12}{30} = \frac{13}{30}$$

Practice: 1. $\frac{1}{4} + \frac{2}{3} = $ —— $+$ —— $=$ ——   2. $\frac{2}{3} - \frac{1}{4} = $ —— $-$ —— $=$ ——

3. $\frac{7}{8} + \frac{5}{6} + \frac{1}{3} = $ —— $+$ —— $+$ —— $=$ ——   4. $\frac{7}{8} - \frac{1}{3} = \frac{}{24} - \frac{}{24} = $ ——

5. $\frac{1}{3} + \frac{1}{4} + \frac{1}{5} = $ —— $+$ —— $+$ —— $=$ ——   6. $\frac{1}{4} - \frac{1}{5} = $ —— $-$ —— $=$ ——

7. $\frac{3}{7} + \frac{1}{2} + \frac{3}{4} = $ —— $+$ —— $+$ —— $=$ ——   8. $\frac{3}{4} - \frac{3}{7} = $ ——

To multiply or divide fractions, it is not necessary to change to other terms. Fractions are multiplied by placing the product of the numerators over the product of the denominators and reducing to simplest terms:

$$\frac{1}{3} \times \frac{4}{5} = \frac{1 \times 4}{3 \times 5} = \frac{4}{15} \qquad \frac{5}{6} \times \frac{1}{2} = \frac{5 \times 1}{6 \times 2} = \frac{5}{12} \qquad \frac{7}{8} \times \frac{2}{9} = \frac{7 \times 2}{8 \times 9} = \frac{14}{72} = \frac{7}{36}$$

Often the work can be made easier by canceling common factors in any numerator and any denominator before multiplying:

$$\frac{7}{\overset{}{\underset{4}{8}}} \times \frac{\overset{1}{2}}{9} = \frac{7}{36} \qquad \frac{1}{\overset{}{2}} \times \frac{\overset{}{2}}{\overset{}{3}} \times \frac{\overset{3}{9}}{13} = \frac{3}{13}$$

Since division is the reverse of multiplication, fractions are divided by multiplying the first fraction by the *reciprocal* of the second—that is, by the second fraction turned upside down:

$$\frac{1}{3} \div \frac{4}{5} = \frac{1}{3} \times \frac{5}{4} = \frac{5}{12} \qquad \frac{5}{6} \div \frac{1}{2} = \frac{5}{\underset{3}{6}} \times \frac{\overset{1}{2}}{1} = \frac{5}{3} = 1\frac{2}{3}$$

Practice: 1. $\frac{3}{4} \times \frac{1}{7} =$ 2. $\frac{1}{2} \times \frac{4}{5} =$ 3. $\frac{1}{5} \times \frac{3}{4} \times \frac{5}{12} =$

4. $\frac{3}{4} \div \frac{1}{7} = \frac{3}{4} \times \frac{7}{1} =$ 5. $\frac{1}{2} \div \frac{4}{5} = \frac{}{2} \times \frac{5}{4} = \frac{5}{8}$

6. $\frac{3}{7} \times \frac{4}{9} \times \frac{21}{24} =$ 7. $\frac{13}{17} \times \frac{34}{39} =$ 8. $\frac{2}{3} \div \frac{13}{17} = $ —— $\times$ —— $=$

In the introductory pretest, Problem 38 asks you to arrange $\frac{1}{5}, \frac{1}{2}, \frac{1}{3},$ and $\frac{1}{4},$ in order of size. Since each fraction shows a whole divided into 5, 2, 3, or 4 parts, you can see that the more parts there are, the smaller each part will be. In order, they are $\frac{1}{5}, \frac{1}{4}, \frac{1}{3}, \frac{1}{2}.$

Problem 39 asks the same about $\frac{2}{5}, \frac{3}{8},$ and $\frac{1}{3}.$ This can be solved by finding a common denominator so that the numerators can be compared: $\frac{2}{5}, \frac{3}{8}, \frac{1}{3} = \frac{48}{120}, \frac{45}{120}, \frac{40}{120}$. In order, the original fractions are $\frac{1}{3}, \frac{3}{8}, \frac{2}{5}$.

Instead, you might compare two fractions at a time: $\frac{1}{3} = \frac{8}{24}$ and $\frac{3}{8} = \frac{9}{24}$, so $\frac{3}{8}$ is larger than $\frac{1}{3}$. Similarly, $\frac{3}{8} = \frac{15}{40}$ and $\frac{2}{5} = \frac{16}{40}$, so $\frac{2}{5}$ is larger than $\frac{3}{8}$. The result is the same; in order, they are $\frac{1}{3}, \frac{3}{8}, \frac{2}{5}$.

III. Decimal Fractions

By using only fractions with denominators of 10, 100 or other multiples of ten, we can often simplify our work, because we can use the same arithmetic processes as for whole numbers. Digits to the-right of the decimal point denote tenths, hundredths, thousandths, etc., just as those to the left of the one's place in whole numbers denote tens, hundreds, thousands, etc.

While the arithmetic is the same, there are more opportunities for error. In adding or subtracting, it is necessary to be very sure that decimal points are carefully aligned:

$$
\begin{array}{r} 12.346 \\ -\ 1.28 \\ \hline 11.066 \end{array} \qquad
\begin{array}{r} 101.65 \\ -\ 23. \\ \hline 78.65 \end{array} \qquad
\begin{array}{r} 101.65 \\ -\ 2.30 \\ \hline 99.35 \end{array} \qquad
\begin{array}{r} 101.65 \\ -\ .23 \\ \hline 101.42 \end{array}
$$

In multiplying decimals, there should be as many places to the right of the decimal point in the product as there are in the multiplicand and the multiplier combined:

$$
\begin{array}{r} 101.65\ \ [2] \\ \times\ 23\ \ [0] \\ \hline 30495 \\ 20330\ \ \\ \hline 2337.95\ \ [2] \end{array} \qquad
\begin{array}{r} 10.165\ \ [3] \\ \times\ 2.3\ \ [1] \\ \hline 30495 \\ 20330\ \ \\ \hline 23.3795\ \ [4] \end{array} \qquad
\begin{array}{r} .10165\ \ [5] \\ \times\ .23\ \ [2] \\ \hline 30495 \\ 20330\ \ \\ \hline .0233795\ \ [7] \end{array}
$$

In dividing one decimal by another, note the number of places to the right of the decimal place in the divisor, then mark off the same number of places in the dividend and place the decimal point in the quotient directly above:

$$
\begin{array}{r}
101.65 \\
23\overline{)2337.95} \\
\underline{23} \\
37 \\
\underline{23} \\
149 \\
\underline{138} \\
115 \\
\underline{115}
\end{array}
\qquad
\begin{array}{r}
10.165 \\
2.3\overline{)23.3795} \\
\underline{23} \\
37 \\
\underline{23} \\
149 \\
\underline{138} \\
115 \\
\underline{115}
\end{array}
\qquad
\begin{array}{r}
.10165 \\
.23\overline{).0233795} \\
\underline{23} \\
37 \\
\underline{23} \\
149 \\
\underline{138} \\
115 \\
\underline{115}
\end{array}
$$

In the first example, the divisor has nothing to the right of the decimal point, so the decimal point of the dividend is left where it is. In the second, the divisor has one place to the right of the decimal point, so the decimal points of the divisor and the dividend are both moved one place to the right. In the third example, both are moved two places to the right.

Practice: Add: 1.   14.63 + 201.095 + 1.689 + 100 + 2.0695 =
            2.   .0005 + 1.001 + 21 + 3.02 + 79.15 =

       Subtract: 3.   260.15 − 29.1 =
                   4.   37.216 − 2.89 =
                   5.   .07653 − .0007 =
       Multiply: 6.   469.55   7.   .004   8.   5.8   9.   .036
                        × 7.3   × 3.7   × .63   × .071

Divide: 10. 15.5)534.75   11. 5.37)37.6437   12. 123)84.132

IV. Rounding

Rounding is a way of eliminating the parts of numbers in which we are, at least for the time being, not interested. If a home is purchased for $75,200.23, for example, the twenty-three cents is insignificant. Even the two-hundred dollars might not seem important, compared to $75,000. However, if the cost were $75,900, it would be more nearly correct to call it $76,000 than $75,000. Even $75,600, $75,550, or $75,501 is closer to $76,000 than to $75,000. By convention, $75,500, which is exactly halfway between $75,000 and $76,000, is rounded to the next higher figure, $76,000. At $75,499, the $499 would be dropped, and the price rounded to $75,000.

It is important to remember which *place* in a numeral is to be considered. In the case of the house, we were rounding to thousands of dollars. At a price of $75,494, rounding to the nearest thousand dollars gives $75,000; to the nearest hundred, $75,500; and to the nearest ten, $75,490. To the nearest ten thousand dollars, the price is $80,000.

The rule for rounding is to find the significant place and replace all subsequent digits by zeroes, except that if the first digit to be replaced is 5 or more, the digit in the significant place is increased by one.

If the significant place (the place we are rounding to) is 10,000,
487,458 is rounded to 490,000
to the nearest 1,000:   487,000
to the nearest 100:   487,500
to the nearest 10:   487,460

Decimal fractions are rounded in the same way, except that places beyond the significant place may be dropped, rather than replaced with zeroes. It is customary to speak of "rounding to so many places," meaning "places after the decimal point."

53.9684 rounded to three places is 53.968
rounded to two places is 53.97
rounded to one place is 54.0
rounded to the nearest whole number is 54.

Practice: Round to the nearest 10,000; the nearest 1,000; the nearest 100; and the nearest 10:

1. 529,684   _____   _____   _____   _____

2. 1,358,496   _____   _____   _____   _____

3. 49,494   _____   _____   _____   _____

4. 23,672,357   _____   _____   _____   _____

5. 835,549   _____   _____   _____   _____

Round to four places; to three places; to two places; and to one place:

6. .53257   _____   _____   _____   _____

7. .49163   _____   _____   _____   _____

8. .254869   _____   _____   _____   _____

9. 2.828947   _____   _____   _____   _____

10. 5.365459   _____   _____   _____   _____

V. Notation

There are some ways of writing mathematical material that can be confusing at first, although they are not really difficult.

Parentheses () in mathematical expressions mean that the operations inside them are to be done first, before other indicated procedures outside them.
In the expression $3,273 + (.28 \times 1,356)$
  First, multiply what is inside the parentheses: $.28 \times 1,356 = 379.68$
  Then add: $3,273 + 379.68 = 3,652.68$
In the expression $(3,273 + .28) \times 1,356$
  First, add: $3,273 + .28 = 3,273.28$
  Then multiply: $3,273.28 \times 1,356 = 4,438,567.68$
As you can see, the results are quite different.
Expressions shown as fractions mean that the part above the line is to be divided by the part under the line. (Each part should first be expressed as a single number.)

$$\frac{2,250 + 1,305}{18 + 25} = \frac{3,555}{43} = 3,555 \div 43 = 82^{29}/_{43}$$

With a result like this, if money is involved, the division ordinarily should be continued to two decimal places and then rounded:
$$\$3,555 \div 43 = \$82.67$$

Practice: 1. $4,215 - (.62 \times 1.241) =$
2. $(.15 \times 489) + (376 \times .29) =$
3. $(\$3,499 + \$4,692 + \$591 - \$2,872) \div (16 \times 31) =$
4. $\dfrac{\$5,639 + \$4,398 + \$6,873}{28 + 57} =$
5. $15 + \dfrac{283 + 9.65}{3} =$

VI. Word Problems

Word problems often seem harder than they really are. They may be complicated, calling for several different operations, and the student may be afraid of choosing the wrong procedure. In most cases, there may be different ways of approaching the problem, all of them right, although one way may be easiest.

Consider this problem. Beets are priced at two bunches for 37¢. What should a customer be charged for six bunches?

We could divide 37¢ by two to find the price of one bunch:

$$37¢ \div 2 = 18\frac{1}{2}¢ \text{ a Bunch,}$$

and then multiply by six the (number of bunches):

$$18\frac{1}{2} ¢ \times 6 = \frac{37}{2} \times 6 = \$1.11$$

Most people find it easier to ask how many groups of two bunches, at 37¢, were bought:

6 Bunches = 3 Groups of 2 Bunches, at 37¢

3 × 37¢ = $1.11 for 6 Bunches

Both methods solve the problem. Either method is good.

In Problem 50 in the pretest, a case of 24 cans of peaches costs $7.20, and one can sold separately costs 32¢. We are asked to find the saving on each can when buying a case.

One method would be to first multiply 32¢ × 24 = $7.68, the cost of 24 cans if sold separately:

$7.68 − $7.20 = $.48 Total Saving

$.48 ÷ 24 = $.02 Saving per Can

Another way is to find the cost per can when they are bought by the case:

$7.20 ÷ 24 = $.30 Cost per Can

32¢ − 30¢ = 2¢ Saving per Can

Again, the results are the same, and either method is good.

Sometimes extraneous figures are included in a problem and must be disregarded. For instance, we might have been told the number of beets in a bunch or the weight of a case of peaches. Neither would have any effect on the result.

Practice: 1. A bus made five round trips a week, each trip totaling 376 miles. How far would the bus travel in twenty-one weeks?

_____miles

2. At one baseball game, 924 tickets were sold at $5.85 each and 326 tickets were sold at $7.35 each. What were the total receipts?

$_____

3. In one class, two students received grades of 95, four 90, six 85, five 80, three 75, four 70, and two 65. What was the class average?

_____

Answers to Practice Problems

I. Whole Numbers   A. Addition   1.   15,987   2.   153,603   3.   143,586
     4.   463,519   5.   434,737   6.   43,670
     1.   315   2.   201   3.   3120   4.   65,898   5.   36,693
     1.   Total   3,289   2.   Total 444,917
     B. Subtraction   1.   577   2.   522   3.   653   4.   449   5.   7,839
        6.   50,089   7.   328,202   8.   151,845
     C. Multiplication   1.   1,296   2.   33,264   3.   60,378   4.   394,989
        5.   28,943,989   6.   61,397,367   7.   609,316
     8.   3,128,082   9.   3,270,400   10.   331,250   11.   2,697
     12.   49,302
     D. Division   1.   107, remainder 11   2.   338   3.   106, remainder 431
        4.   134   5.   84   6.   37   7.   144   8.   692

II. Common Fractions   1. $^3/_9$ 2. $^{12}/_{20}$ 3. $^8/_{28}$ 4. $^6/_{12}$ 5. $^{10}/_{12}$ 6. $^3/_{12}$

   1. $^3/_{12} + ^8/_{12} = ^{11}/_{12}$ 2. $^8/_{12} - ^3/_{12} = ^5/_{12}$ 3. $^{21}/_{24} + ^{20}/_{24} + ^8/_{24} = ^{49}/_{24} = 2^1/_{24}$
   4. $^{21}/_{24} - ^8/_{24} = ^{13}/_{24}$ 5. $^{20}/_{60} + ^{15}/_{60} + ^{12}/_{60} = ^{47}/_{60}$ 6. $^5/_{20} - ^4/_{20} = ^1/_{20}$
   7. $^{12}/_{28} + ^{14}/_{28} + ^{21}/_{28} = ^{47}/_{28} = 1^{19}/_{28}$ 8. $^{21}/_{28} - ^{12}/_{28} = ^9/_{28}$

   1. $^3/_{28}$ 2. $^2/_5$ 3. $^1/_{16}$ 4. $5^1/_4$ 5. $^5/_8$ 6. $^1/_6$ 7. $^2/_3$
   8. $^2/_3 \times ^{17}/_{13} = ^{34}/_{39}$

III. Decimal Fractions
     1.   319.4835
     2.   104.1715
     3.   231.05
     4.   34.326
     5.   .07583
     6.   3,427.715
     7.   .0148
     8.   3.654
     9.   .002556
     10.   34.5
     11.   7.01
     12.   .684

IV. Rounding
     1.   530,000 530,000 529,700 529,680
     2.   1,360,000 1,358,000 1,358,500 1,358,500

3. 50,000 49,000 49,500 49,490
4. 23,670,000 23,672,000 23,672,400 23,672,360
5. 840,000 836,000 835,500 835,550
6. .5326 .533 .53 .5
7. .4916 .492 .49 .5
8. .2549 .255 .25 .3
9. 2.8289 2.829 2.83 2.8
10. 5.3655 5.365 5.37 5.4

V. Notation
1. 4,214.23058   2. 182.39   3. $11.92   4. $198.94   5. 112.55

VI. Word Problems
1. 39,480 mi.   2. $7,801.50   3. 80.57692 or $80^{15}/_{26}$

B   USE OF ELECTRONIC CALCULATORS

The development and availability of hand electronic calculators at reasonable prices raises the question of how much arithmetic a person needs to know. In no way does the calculator eliminate the need for understanding the fundamental processes of addition, subtraction, multiplication, and division. Understanding common fractions, decimal fractions, and percentages is also important. Giving meaning to the figures is something the calculator cannot do.

The degree of skill needed in handling the processes may be affected by the availability of calculators, however. Everyone should understand and be able to perform the fundamental processes, given sufficient time. But to develop a high degree of skill in long division of six-digit numbers or multiplication of five-digit decimals may be a waste of time if calculators are available.

The Process

Using an electronic calculator is reasonably easy. Directions given with the machines are explicit and clear; all you need do is press the proper buttons. The problem is knowing what should be done and in what order for a particular situation. The procedures for arriving at the solution of a problem must be thought through carefully before turning to the machine. For example, 400 (300 + 55) is 400 times 355, or 142,000, not 400 × 300 + 55, or 120,055.

In working with common fractions, decimal fractions, and percentages, the ability to shift from one to another is extremely useful. For example, to find 25 percent of a number, you can multiply by .25 or divide by 4. To find $16\frac{2}{3}$ percent of a number, you can multiply by .166667 or simply divide by 6, because $16\frac{2}{3}\% = \frac{1}{6}$.

Checking for Accuracy

The use of a calculator does not diminish the need for checking the work. In fact, it may increase the need, as the use of a machine somehow gives the impression of accuracy, whether the impression is correct or not. How thoroughly the checking needs to be done depends on the situation, of course.

The easiest method of checking is to do the work over in the same way it was done originally. The problem with this method is that the same error may easily be repeated. It is better to do the work in a somewhat different way; adding from the bottom to the top of a column, for example, or reversing the order of the numbers you have multiplied together: 25×35 rather than 35×25. You can check a division problem by multiplying your answer by the divisor to get the dividend. In all cases, you should at least check the answer by applying the "test of reasonableness." Does the answer make sense? Is it reasonable?

Rounding the Answer

Using calculators may compound the problem of rounding answers appropriately. After deciding on the decimal place to be rounded, a digit of five or more in the next place calls for adding one to the place to be rounded. A digit of four or less is ignored. The problem, then, is one of deciding which place is to be used for rounding. This depends on the situation. On a Federal income tax report, for example, you are permitted to round to the dollar place. In determining property tax rates, you need to use five decimal places. In some Social Security problems, the rounding is to the nearest ten cents. Care must be taken in rounding at the intermediate stages of solving a problem. If the final answer is to be accurate through two decimal places, the intermediate answers usually should be carried out to five decimal places.

C BINARY AND OCTONAL SYSTEMS

A digital computer completes a complicated program by making a great many decisions, one at a time. Each of these decisions is a yes-no, either-or choice, with only two alternatives. In other words, the computer has only two digits, and operates by means of the *binary* system.

Unlike our customary decimal number system, with its ten digits—1, 2, 3, 4, 5, 6, 7, 8, 9, 0—the binary system has only two digits—1 and 0. Like the decimal system, it uses place value so that any number, however large, can be represented. In the decimal system, digits to the *left* of the decimal point represent:

. . . millions, hundred thousands, ten thousands, thousands, hundreds, tens, ones

. . . 10^6 10^5 10^4 10^3 10^2 10^1 10^0

The superscript, as you know, denotes the *power* of ten; for example, $10^2 = 10 \times 10 = 100$; $10^4 = 10 \times 10 \times 10 \times 10 = 10,000$; $10^1 = 10$.

Any digit in a certain position represents the value of the position times the value of the digit itself, for example:

$20 = 2 \times 10^1 = 2 \times 10$; $600 = 6 \times 10^2 = 6 \times 100$; $40,000 = 4 \times 10^4 = 4 \times 10,000$.

Similarly:

$526 = (5 \times 10^2) + (2 \times 10^1) + (6 \times 10^0) = (5 \times 100) + (2 \times 10) + (6 \times 1)$

In the binary system, the digits in those places represent:

. . . sixty-fours, thirty-twos, sixteens, eights, fours, twos, ones

. . . 2^6 2^5 2^4 2^3 2^2 2^1 2^0

In the binary system, the places and the superscripts in the lines above indicate powers of two, rather than of ten. Since the binary system has only two digits, each place is filled with either 1 or 0. Note that 1 means the same in either system; so does 0; and any number to the zero power equals one.

Binary numbers may be written with a subscript $_2$ to distinguish them from decimal numbers; when both are used together, the decimal numbers can also have a subscript$_{10}$. So $1,000_2$ means 1×2^3, or eight (8_{10}). Similarly, 111_2 means 7_{10}: $111_2 = (1 \times 2^2) + (1 \times 2^1) + (1 \times 2^0) = (1 \times 4_{10}) + (1 \times 2_{10}) + (1 \times 1) = 4_{10} + 2_{10} + 1 = 7_{10}$. Binary numbers such as $1,000_2$ and 111_2 should always be read "one, zero, zero, zero" and "one, one, one," even to yourself—never in such a way as to confuse them with decimal numbers.

Any decimal number can be written as a binary number by considering it as the sum of powers of two, and placing a 1 in the appropriate positions. For example, the decimal number 99 may be written as a binary number:

$99_{10} = (1 \times 64) + (1 \times 32) + (0 \times 16) + (0 \times 8) + (0 \times 4) + (1 \times 2) + (1 \times 1)$

$99_{10} = 1,100,011_2$

Similarly, $100_{10} = (1 \times 64) + (1 \times 32) + (1 \times 4) = 1,100,100_2$. The powers of two that make up the number are represented by a 1 in the appropriate position; the powers of two that do *not* make up the number are represented by zeroes (the sixteens, eights, twos, and ones places in the last example).

Although the binary system can show any number, a large number can be very cumbersome. One way to shorten the numerals without sacrificing the advantages of the binary system is to translate them to octonal (sometimes called octal) numbers, which are based on eight, using the digits, 1, 2, 3, 4. 5, 6, 7, and 0.

In the octonal system, the places to the left of the octonal point denote the powers of eight: ones, eights, sixty-fours, five hundred twelves, etc. This means that each octonal digit is the equivalent of a group of three binary digits: $10_8 = 1{,}000_2$; $53_8 = 101{,}011_2$; $111_8 = 1{,}001{,}001_2$.

To make the translation, it is only necessary to remember the equivalents of any group of three binary digits:

$001_2 = 1_8$
$010_2 = 2_8$
$011_2 = 3_8$
$100_2 = 4_8$
$101_2 = 5_8$
$110_2 = 6_8$
$111_2 = 7_8$

Exercise I. Show each number in the decimal system, the binary system, and the octonal system:

	Decimal	*Binary*	*Octonal*
1. Twenty-three	_____	$10{,}111_2$	_____
2. Seventeen	_____	_____	21_8
3. Fifty	_____	_____	_____
4. Eighty-six	86_{10}	_____	_____
5. One hundred nine	_____	_____	_____

Do you find it easier to go from the binary to the octonal system or from the octonal to the binary? Which is easier to translate from the decimal system?

Digits to the *right* of the point (called a "decimal point," a "binary point," or an "octonal point") represent *fractions* in tenths, in halves, or in eighths. These fractions may also be marked off in groups of three digits.

Decimal System: tenths, hundredths, thousandths; ten-thousandths, . . .

Binary System: halves, fourths, eighths; sixteenths, thirty-secondths, . . .

Octonal System: eighths, sixty-fourths, five-hundred-twelfths; . . .

Fractions in tenths are convenient for performing computations in the decimal system, but halves, fourths, etc. often seem more understandable, and are readily translated to octonal fractions.

In the case of buying and selling securities (see Chapter 19), in which prices are given in eighths of a dollar, only one place is ever needed in octonal fractions, instead of as many as three places in decimal fractions. On the other hand, when fractions are in thirds, fifths, and other parts not easily related to eight, finding octonal fractions is not easy. Rounding may be a problem, since it must be kept in mind that the next place represents either $\frac{1}{8}$ or $\frac{1}{2}$ of the place being rounded.

To convert a binary fraction to a decimal fraction, express each digit as a common decimal fraction and add:

$$.011,01_2 = \frac{0}{2_{10}} + \frac{1}{4_{10}} + \frac{1}{8_{10}} + \frac{0}{16_{10}} + \frac{1}{32_{10}} = \frac{1}{4_{10}} + \frac{1}{8_{10}} + \frac{1}{32_{10}} =$$

$$\frac{8 + 4 + 1}{32_{10}} = \frac{13}{32_{10}} = .40625_{10}$$

To convert a decimal fraction to a binary fraction, multiply the decimal fraction by two. Any whole number in the product is the first digit of the binary fraction; if there is no whole number, 0 is the first digit. Then multiply the fractional part of the product by two; any whole number in the result is the second digit in the binary fraction. The process may be repeated as far as needed:

$.40625 \times 2 = .8125$	The first binary digit is 0.
$.8125 \times 2 = 1.625$	The second binary digit is 1.
$.625 \times 2 = 1.25$	The third binary digit is 1.
$.25 \times 2 = .5$	The fourth binary digit is 0.
$.5 \times 2 = 1.0$	The fifth binary digit is 1.

$$.40625_{10} = .01101_2$$

A similar process can be used with octonal fractions, multiplying by eight:

$.40625 \times 8 = 3.25$	The first octonal digit is 3.
$.25 \times 8 = 2$	The second octonal digit is 2.

$$.40625_{10} = .32_8$$

A common fraction may itself be multiplied by eight (or by two) in the same manner, when that is easier. To convert $\frac{7}{12}$ to an octonal fraction:

$\frac{7}{12} \times 8 = \frac{56}{12} = 4\frac{2}{3}$	The first octonal digit is 4.
$\frac{2}{3} \times 8 = \frac{16}{3} = 5\frac{1}{3}$	The second octonal digit is 5.
$\frac{1}{3} \times 8 = \frac{8}{3} = 2\frac{2}{3}$	The third octonal digit is 2.

The last two digits will repeat; the octonal fraction will be .4525252 . . .,
which may be written as .4$\overline{52}$, meaning that the digits under the line will be repeated
indefinitely.

Exercise II. Show each fraction in the decimal system, the binary system, and the
octonal system:

		Decimal	Binary	Octonal
1.	One sixteenth	. _____	.000,1$_2$	. _____
2.	Two thirds	. _____	. _____	. _____
3.	Three eighths	. _____	. _____	.3$_8$ _____
4.	One fifth	.2$_{10}$ _____	. _____	. _____
5.	Five twelfths	. _____	. _____	. _____

Arithmetic in binary or octonal numbers follows all the rules for decimal numbers. The
only caution is that, in adding binary numbers, it is best to add only two numbers at a
time, since three or more numbers will often carry over two or more places.

To add: $1,101_2 + 10,111_2 + 1,110_2$,

First add: $1,101_2$
                    $10,111_2$
                    $\overline{100,100_2}$ (Remember that $1_2 + 1_2 = 10_2$.)

Then add: $+\ \ 1,110_2$
              $\overline{110,010_2}$

In octonal numbers, this would be 15_8
                                        27_8
                                $+\ \ 16_8$ $(6_8 + 7_8 = 15_8)$
                                $\overline{62_8}$

In decimal numbers, 13_{10}
                          23_{10}
                  $+\ \ 14_{10}$
                  $\overline{50_{10}}$

Exercise III. Make the indicated binary calculations, then convert the binary numbers
to octonal and then to decimal numbers and make the same calculations:

1. Add: $11,011_2$ _____ $_8$ _____ $_{10}$

     $+\ 10,111_2$ $+$ _____ $_8$ $+$ _____ $_{10}$

     _____ $_2$ _____ $_8$ _____ $_{10}$

2. Subtract: $110,110_2$ _____$_8$ _____$_{10}$

                      $-\ \ 11,011_2$ $-$ _____$_8$ $-$ _____$_{10}$

                      _____$_2$ _____$_8$ _____$_{10}$

3. Multiply: $1,111_2$ _____$_8$ _____$_{10}$

                      $\times\ \ \ \ 101_2$ $\times$ _____$_8$ $\times$ _____$_{10}$

                      _____$_2$ _____$_8$ _____$_{10}$

4. Divide: $11_2\overline{)101,101_2}$ $_8\overline{)\ \ \ \ \ \ \ \ }_8$ $_{10}\overline{)\ \ \ \ \ \ \ \ }_{10}$

Answers for the three exercises are shown below. Do you agree?

I. 1. 23_{10} $10,111_2$ 27_8
    2. 17_{10} $10,001_2$ 21_8
    3. 50_{10} $110,010_2$ 62_8
    4. 86_{10} $1,010,110_2$ 126_8
    5. 109_{10} $1,101,101_2$ 155_8

II. 1. $.0625_{10}$ $.0001_2$ $.04_8$
    2. $.\overline{6}_{10}$ $.\overline{10}_2$ $.\overline{52}_8$
    3. $.375_{10}$ $.011_2$ $.3_8$
    4. $.2_{10}$ $.\overline{0011}_2$ $.\overline{1463}_8$
    5. $.41\overline{6}_{10}$ $.01\overline{10}_2$ $.32\overline{5}_8$

III. 1. $110,010_2;$ $33_8 + 27_8 = 62_8;$ $27_{10} + 23_{10} = 50_{10}$
     2. $11,011_2;$ $66_8 - 33_8 = 33_8;$ $54_{10} - 27_{10} = 27_{10}$
     3. $1,001,011_2;$ $17_8 \times 5_8 = 113_8;$ $15_{10} \times 5_{10} = 75_{10}$
     4. $1,111_2;$ $55_8 \div 3_8 = 17_8;$ $45_{10} \div 3_{10} = 15_{10}$

D   ANSWERS TO ODD-NUMBERED PROBLEMS

1.1

A. 1. 15%   3. 18%   5. 7.53%   7. 82.6%   9. 15.26%
11. 51%
B. 1. 1,450%   3. 337.5%   5. 587.5%   7. 212.5%   9. 70%
C. 1. .36   3. .048   5. 1.2   7. .0002   9. .006   11. .00268

1.2, Group 1

1. 15   3. 30.1   5. 13.6   7. .7335   9. 560   11. .432
13. 19.5   15. 81.25

Group 2

1. Food $4,508; Housing $4,704; Clothing $1,568; Savings $980; Car $2,548; Gifts $980; Recreation $784; Income Taxes $3,528; Total $19,600 3. Motor Vehicles $37,666,816,-000; Home Furnishings $8,132,608,000; Groceries $44,301,312,000; Mail Order Sales $1,712,128,000 5. 3rd year sales $203,212.80

1.3, Group 1

1. $33^1/_3\%$ 3. $16^2/_3\%$ 5. 60%   7. $33^1/_3\%$ 9. 50%
11. 35.56%   13. 29.31%   15. 24.24%   17. 18%   19. 555.56%

Group 2

1. 63.6%   3. 5.47%   5. 75.3%   7. Anderson 48%; Peterson 20%; Carlson 32%

1.4, Group 1

1. 342.86   3. 200   5. 6,400   7. 50   9. 20   11. 960
13. 500   15. 640   17. 53.64   19. 1,640

Group 2.

1. $28,666.67   3. $1,500   5. 1,300

1.5, Group 1

1. 60%   3. $33^1/_3\%$ 5. 20%

Group 2

1. 25%   3. $12^1/_2\%$ 5. Totals: 82,784.40; 87,403.55; Increase $4,619.15; Percent of Increase 5.6

Chapter Review, Group 1

1. 26%
3. 40%
5. 4.61%
7. .14
9. 2.4
11. 37.5%
13. 18.75%
15. 800
17. .41
19. 67.2
21. 300%
23. .11
25. 1,000
27. 265
29. 80

Group 2

1. $4,780   3. Farm Workers 3.59%; Managers 10.24%; Clerical Workers 17.24%; Sales Workers 6.42%   5. 1930: 17,064,426 16.1%; 1940: 8,894,229 7.2%; 1950: 19,028,086 14.4%; 1960: 28,625,814 19.0%; 1970: `23,912,123 13.3%.

2.1, Group 1

1. 12 ft. 9 in.
3. 151 in.
5. 5,184 sq. in.
7. 21,780 sq. ft.
9. 1,320 ft; $\frac{1}{4}$ mi.

Group 2

1. $8\frac{1}{2}$ qt.   3. 25,000 lb.   5. 4 oz.   7. 48 qt.   9. 16 servings

2.2.

1. 1 000 mg
3. 10 mm; .01 m
5. .153L
7. 100 cm; 1 000 mm
9. .0001 m²
11. 1 000 000 m²
13. .424 kg
15. .003684 m³

2.3

1. 12 lb. 2 oz.   3. 7 c. 7 tbsp.   5. The opposing side's 43 yd. line
7. 942 g or .942 kg   9. 177 cL or 1.77 L

2.4

1. 56 gal. 1 qt.   3. 1,917 lb. 8 oz.   5. 143 mi. 940 yd.   7. 65.2904 m²
9. 40.0024 m³

2.5

1. 4 lb. 2 oz.   3. 3 ft. 10 in.   5. 6′ 5.6″   7. 81 cL or .81L
9. $.0177

2.6

1. 2 hr. 5 min.   3. 9′   5. 8°C; 8°F   7. 22 hr. 25 min.   9. 33 hr. 45 min.

2.7

1. 4.191 m   3. 11.355 L   5. 11.811 in.   7. 1,058.4 oz.
9. $^9/_5 = 1.8$ 11. 15.613 gal.

2.8

1. $5.12   3. $24.25   5. $.31 = £.179; £.12 = $.208 U.S. more: 10¢ or 6 pence

Chapter Review

1. 192 qt.   3. 10,392 cu. in.   5. 12 oz.   7. 12 T 258 lb.
9. A $8^1/_8$¢; B $13^4/_7$¢; C $17^2/_3$¢   11. 3,456 cu. in; .056 633 472 m³ (approx.)

3.1

1. 8:1   3. a. 1:50; b. $^1/_{50}$; c. .02; d. 2% 5. 4:5   7. 5:46; 16:161; 32:35
9. 1:400; 5:4

3.2

1. 12:5 = 60.25   3. 4.36 c.   5. 3.57 lb.   7. $7.50

3.3

1. 12 and 24   3. $945; $1,260; $1,575   5. 35; 49; 21

3.4

1. $^1/_6$ 3. $^1/_{13}$ 5. $^1/_9$; $2.25; 9 to 1   7. $^1/_7$; $3.50; 7 to 2

Chapter Review

1. 1 to 40   3. 24 to 1   5. 10 to 30   7. $3^1/_2$:42 = 7:84
9. 65:13 = 75:15   11. $1,000; $750; $1,250   13. 5 minutes   15. $^1/_6$

4.1

3. Total populations: New England 11,841,663; Middle Atlantic 37,199,040; East North Central 40,252,476; West North Central 16,319,187; South Atlantic 30,671,337; East South Central 12,803,470; West South Central 19,320,560; Mountain 8,281,562; Pacific 26,522,631.
5. 1790: 4.42; 1810: 4.22; 1830: 7.20; 1850: 7.75; 1870: 13.17; 1890: 20.83; 1910: 30.43; 1930: 40.62; 1950: 41.86; 1970: 56.21

4.2

1. Number of degrees of circle to be measured off for:

	Men	Women	Total
White-Collar Workers	143.42°	218.38°	172.26°
Blue-Collar Workers	170.60	58.18	127.40
Service Workers	28.55	77.76	47.45
Farm Workers	17.42	5.69	12.92

3. Degrees of circle to be shown for: Africa 72.00; Antarctica 34.42; Asia 106.31; Australia 18.58; Europe 23.44; North America 58.75; South America 42.52; Misc. 3.96.

4.3

1. The graph would show the changes more clearly if the range were limited to 250,000–460,000.

4.4

1. Mean 54.53; median 54; mode 57.
3. Mean $2,520.25 million; median $1,569 million; mode $500 million. The figures have no real meaning.
5. Average area 8,127,429 sq. mi. North America is closest.
7. Mean 140.380. No definitive mode. Grouped by fives, estimated average, 139.969 is only .411 less than true mean.

4.5

1. 157.2; 236.9; 309.0; 413.8; 519.8; 604.1; 650.8; 649.4; 672.2.
3. Decreases: Durable Goods 1.97%; Mining 2.46%. Increases: Utilities 4.21%; Non-Durable Goods 2.62%; Res. Const. 41.74%; Other Construction 3.08%; Consumer Prices 4.30%; Wholesale Prices 3.17%; Total .19%.
5. All Items 155; Food 163; Housing 154; Transportation 143, Med. Care 188

Chapter Review

3. Index numbers: Mercury 39.24; Venus 96.20; Earth 100.0; Mars 53.16; Jupiter 1,101.27; Saturn 911.39; Uranus 392.41; Neptune 417.72; Pluto 96.20

5.

	1967		1980	
Hydropower	222.2	18.57%	372.2	13%
Coal	630.2	52.68	1,345.6	47
Nuclear	7.3	.61	544.0	19
Oil	89.9	7.51	114.5	4
Gas	246.7	20.62	486.7	17
	1,196.3	99.99%	2,863.0	100%

7. Averages: Bismarck 42.2°; Honolulu 75.9°; Nashville 60.0°.
9. Mean 55.28. Mean by grouping by fives, 55.33; by threes, 55.08. Median is 56. Mode by fives, 57; by threes, 55.

5.1, Group 1

1. $ 450
      2,950

3.   60
        260
5.   52
        377
7.   87.10
        757.10
9.   84
        564
11.   114.19
        839.19
13.   99.18
        925.68
15.   142.46
        1,046.96
17.   14
        714
19.   1.20
        81.20

Group 2

1. $72; $90; $2,862   3. $123.20   5. $339   7. a. $202.50, b. $168.75
9. $6,487

5.2, Group 1

1. 459 days   3. 1,382 days   5. 439 days   7. 232 days   9. 989
days

Group 2

1. 155 days   3. 234   5. 92   7. 185   9. 27

5.3, Group 1

1. 6.0%   3. 7.0%   5. 9.25%   7. 8.56%   9. 9.2%

Group 2

1. 6.92%   3. 8.33%   5. a. 7.16%; b. 6.73%

5.4, Group 1

1. $7,000   3. $9,523.81   5. $3,000   7. $5,679.61   9. $4,909.09

Group 2

1. $12,000   3. $26,666.66   5. $13,052.63

5.5

1. $18.49   3. $36.44   5. $6.18   7. $3.95   9. $10.36

5.6

1. $3.25   3. $2.13   5. $1.73   7. $21.00   9. $15.00
11. $20   13. $35   15. $12.50   17. $9.07   19. $19.80

Chapter Review, Group 1

1. $1,292
3. $56.05
5. $176.40
7. 86 days
9. 336 days
11. 115 days
13. 6%
15. 8.5%
17. 8.75%
19. $10,000
21. $10,037.88
23. $8,985.51
25. $42.74 (65 da.)
27. $198.25 (30 da.)
29. $18.31 (67 da.)
31. $4.45
33. $84
35. $8.74

Group 2

1. $3,670.40   3. 8.9%   5. Estimate $8.63, Actual $8.51

6.1

1. $2,778.30, $378.30
3. $2,040.73, $540.73
5. $1,562.71, $362.71
7. $4,507.29, $507.29
9. $1,900.15, $400.15

6.2, Group 1

1. $5,049.91, $1,049.91
3. $2,638.96, $638.96
5. $6,760.95, $760.95
7. $450.60, $50.60
9. $2,536.48, $536.48

Group 2

1. $7,401.22, $2,401.22   3. $3,958.44   5. Account $9,564.94, Inflation Value $9,261.

6.4, Group 1

1. $2,484.35, $915.65
3. $6,855.34, $1,344.66
5. $6,855.53, $2,944.47
7. $1,588.21, $771.79
9. $3,826.66, $3,873.34

Group 2

1. $9127.74

6.5

1. Amount of Annuity $1,216.65, Interest $216.65

Group 1

1. $792.44   3. $19,200.91   5. $5,859.47

Group 2

1. $1,667.94, $167.94   3. $4,956.66

6.6, Group 1

1. $3,270.29   3. $17,204.88   5. $11,305.01   7. $17,852.97
9. $32,115.78

Group 2

1. $10,183.28   3. $48,561.25   5. $16,308.39; Annuity $3,691.61 Less Costly

6.7, Group 1

1. $271.85   3. $351.96   5. $294.75

Group 2

Deposits $14,126.63

Chapter Review

1. Amount $5,858.30, Interest $858.30
3. $4,860.70; $2,939.30   5. $950.60   7. $3,793.40

Group 2

1. $14,347.42; more if compounded daily.   3. $7,813.42
5. $17,739.60

10.4

1. $143

	a.	b.	c.	d.	e.	f.
3.	$38,400	91.15%	$8,645.58	$4,940.33	$3,705.25	
5.	97,076	92.71	23,577.08	15,718.05	5,239.35	$2,619.68
7.	91,556	96.12	12,358.15	5,617.34	5,617.34	1,123.47
9.	67,320.80	90.61	6,958.85	5,703.98	1,140.80	114.08

Chapter Review

1. a. $55; $43; $28; $21; $17; $48; b. $1,000 Deductible; c. Full window-glass coverage; d. $50-deductible
3. a. $2,478; b. $496; c. $638
5. a. $20,413.75; b. $6,471.25; c. $8,562.63

11.1

1. Monthly $38, Semiannually $580   3. $52.80, $1,056

11.2

1. $17.22, $249.40   3. a. 91.17%;   b. 90.49%;   c. 89.64%; d. 88.72%;   e. 87.95%   5. $1,740

11.3

1. $4,622, Total, 20-Payment Life; $3,713.60, Total, Paid-Up-At 65
3. 3,971 to 7,542 or .5265; 3,571 to 7,042 or .5071; 3,521 to 6,992 or .5036
5. a. $10,640; b. $7,132; c. $10,305

11.4

1. $1,179.30, $416.40, 35.31%
3. $1,196.40, $614.40, 51.35%
5. $1,260.00, $991.80, 78.71%
7. $1,431.60, $1,876.50, 131.08%
9. $401.30, $797.60

11.5

1. $11,804.10   3. $8,886, $10,217.40, 114.98%, $9,706.53   5. $20,000, $6,592.40, $10,926

11.6

1. $434   **3.** $338.26   **5.** $13,920, $36,815, $4,185.60, $1,096.40, $56,017

Chapter Review

1. Age 20: $17.75, $30.50, $56.00
   Age 25: 18.50, 32.00, 59.00
   Age 30: 19.80, 34.60, 64.20
   Age 35: 22.75, 40.50, 76.00
   Age 40: 29.65, 54.30, 103.60
   Age 45: 41.00, 77.00, 149.00
3. $1,000: $15.39, 17.22, 19.56; 22.59, 26.53, 31.66
   $20,000: $212.80, 249.40, 296.20, 356.80, 435.60, 538.20
5. Age 20: $22.58, $16.20, $534.90, $343.50
   Age 25: 24.89, 18.43, 604.20, 410.40
   Age 30: 27.61, 21.38, 685.80, 498.90
   Age 35: 30.89, 25.44, 784.20, 620.70
   Age 40: 34.87, 31.19, 903.60, 793.20
   Age 45: 39.71, 39.71, 1048.80, 1048.80
   Age 50: 45.75, 53.50, 1230.00, 1462.50
   Age 55: 53.58, 79.83, 1464.90, 2252.40
7. 20-Year Decreasing Term: $43.00, $11.18, $3.87
   5-Year Term: 59.00, 15.34, 5.31
   Straight Life: 249.40, 64.84, 22.45
   Life Paid-up-At 65:   273.60, 71.14, 24.62
   Endowment At 65:   334.20, 86.89, 30.08
   20-Payment Life: 402.80, 104.73, 36.25
   20-Year Endowment: 790.00, 205.40, 71.10
9. a. $2,771.50, $810.00; b. $1,648.10, $818.65; c. $1,565.70, $777.72; d. $3,434.30, $4,222.28

12.1

1. a. $12.20, $7.79;   b. $57.70, $24.60;   c. $30.90, $18.86;   d. $1.90, $9.58
3. 5. Adjusted Gross Income $23,900.50; Taxable Income $19,900.50, Tax $3,201.12
7. Tax Table Income $18,837, Taxable Income $15,837, Tax $2,228, Refund $772.40, Delaware Refund $120.34
9. Taxable Income $17,113, Georgia Liability $766.78

12.2, Group 1

1. $12,950, $310.80
3. $28,900, $687.82
5. $112,500, $2,677.50
7. $91,000, $955.50
9. $98,000, $2,450.00

Group 2

1. a. $1,354,000; b. .02630; c. $26.30; d. $1,049.61   3. $914.20
    5. $6.38 per $100

12.3

1. a. .24; b. .54; c. 1.64; d. 2.41; e. .36   **3.** .50   5. .04,
.07, .18, .13, .37

12.4

1. $20.64   3. a. —   b. $15, .15; c. $20, .20; d. $5, .05; e. $35, .35;
f. $10, .10; g. $12.50, .13; Totals $97.50, .98

Chapter Review
1. Refund $61   3. $1,314.60   5. Federal $2,796.84; Delaware $1,289.01
7. 6   9. Taxable Income $14,375.24, Georgia Tax $602.51

13.1

1. $84,597.65   3. $182,145.23

13.2

1. $843.29, $121,433.76, $39,433.76   3. $689.33   5. $415.67

13.3

1. $4,180   3. $508.74   5. $81.65, $584.11

13.4

1. $9,658.33   3. $10,700   5. 1951 through 1957 $6,800

13.5

1. $443.50   3. Hooper $300.30, Wife $150.20   5. Approximately 50% at
65, Approximately 47% at 62   7. His Account $322.50, Her Account $182.30,
After Wife's Death $364.50.

Chapter Review

1. $57,200.76   3. $366.67   5. $2,097.90   7. $14,417.
9. Angela's Account $35.85 Better

14.1, Group 1
a. 1. $230.95;   3. $254.70;   5. $290.66   b. 1. $237.15;
3. $267.30;   5. $290.66

Group 2

1. $205.80   3. $5.17   5. $7.18

14.2

1. $325.92   3. $247.31   5. $208.02

14.3

1. $272   3. $8,000, $2,000   5. $1,320

14.4

1. $29.10   3. $18.80   5. $55.80   7. $39.60   9. $62.30
1. $7.85   3. $1,403.77   5. $1,403.77   7. $352.48   9. $16.86

14.5

Totals of Payroll Register Columns:
$1,501.20 $92.03 $231.50 $102.70 $426.23 $1,074.97

14.6

Change Memorandum and Payroll Slip Should Show:
Twenties 121, Tens 3, Fives 4, Ones 12, Halves 2, Quarters 5,
Dimes 7, Nickels 4, Pennies 10

Chapter Review

1. $195.53   3. $328.79   5. $41.60   7. $1,403.77
9. Change Memorandum and Payroll Slip Should Show:
Twenties 36, Tens 2, Fives 2, Ones 6, Halves 2, Quarters 3, Dimes 2, Nickels 1, Pennies 5

15.1

1. $21.60   3. $10.49   5. $457.52   7. $90.77   9. $161.79
11. $60.00

15.2

1. $192   3. $9.43   5. $4.22   7. $32   9. $182   11. $373.75

15.3

Group 1:   1. 100%   3. 25%   5. 13.6%   7. 9.1%   9.   23.1%
Group 2:   1. $16^2/_3\%$ 3. 25%   5. 28.6%   7. $66^2/_3\%$

15.4

1. 24.69%   3. 29.24%

15.5

1. OP.SZ   3. C.MS   5. CI.LS   7. P.ZS   9. PT.SZ
11. $13.89   13. $470.03   15. $38.60

Chapter Review

1. $9.35   3. $9.87   5. $64.37   7.   14.29%   9.   26.15%

16.1, Group 1

1. $9.84   3. $137.44   5. $59.70   7. $720   9. $307.80

Group 2

1. $1,828.96   3.   a. $60.75;   b. $59.85   5. $288.56, $288.56

16.2, Group 1

1. 33.5%   3.   46%   5.   40%   7.   54.1%   9.   36.825%

Group 2

1. 28.75%   3.   43.6%   5.   40.57%   7.   21.34%   9.   a.   44.56%;
b.   45.19%

16.3

1. 76.5%   3.   68%   5.   73.8%   7.   51.3%   9.   69.55%
11. $201.60   13. $598.50   15. $4,570.83

16.4, Group 1

1. $400   3. $1,260   5. $6,400   7. $3,037.04   9. $2,222.22
11. $90 List, $72 Net   13. $2,700 List, Net $2,430   15. $2,000 List $1,008
Net

Group 2

1. $5,680   3. $33^{1}/_{3}$%   5. $520.20

16.5

1. 23%   3.   8%

16.6

1. April 30   3.   July 10   5. $1,781.15   7. $1,677.20   9. $855.93

Chapter Review

1. $1,165.99   3.   27.325%   5. $57.39   7. $349.19, $289.60
9.   20%

17.1, Group 1

1. $9.86 Discount, $990.14 Proceeds   3. $9.86 Discount, $490.14 Proceeds
5. $12.33 Discount, $2,987.67 Proceeds

Group 2

1. $608.88 Maturity Value, $10.51 Discount, $598.37 Proceeds   3. $2,855.23 Maturity Value, $75.10 Discount, $2,780.13 Proceeds   5. $3,492.22 Maturity Value, $84.20 Discount, $3,408.02 Proceeds

17.2

1. May 9   3. June 19   5. August 9   7. August 11   9. November 27   11. May 31   13. October 17   15. May 8   17. February 27   19. October 18   21. 77 days   23. 19 days   25. 36 days   27. 12 days   29. 32 days

17.3

	1	3	5
Maturity Value	$800	$1,800	$12,400
Term of Discount	12 da.	45 da.	12 da.
Rate of Discount	7%	6%	8%
Bank Discount	1.84	13.32	32.61
Proceeds	798.16	1,786.68	12,367.39

7. $1,229.40   9. $3,929.21

17.4

	Maturity Value	Term of Discount	Rate of Discount	Amount of Discount	Proceeds
1.	$971.05	30 da.	8%	$6.38	$964.67
3.	1,777.36	29 da.	9%	12.71	1,764.65
5.	1,207.89	15 da.	$8^{1}/_{2}\%$	4.22	1,203.67
7.	302.40	37 da.	10%	3.07	299.33
9.	2,441.42	58 da.	8%	31.04	2,410.38

Chapter Review

1. $776.33   3. 75 days   5. June 24   7. $1,991.87

18.1

1. $7,000, ($6,000); $10,333.33

3.

	1st Year	2nd Year	3rd Year	Total
M. Anderson	($3,000)	$5000	$6000	$8,000
D. Day	($3,000)	5,000	6,000	8,000
M. Brothers	($3,000)	5,000	6,000	8,000

5. $85,263.12; $56,842.08; $37,894.72

18.2

1. Anderson $9,075;   Armstrong $12,100;   Bails $15,125   3. Cramer $7,756.02; Curtis $10,243.98   5. Larson $10,907.86;   B. Larson $12,092.14

18.3

1. a. Scott $2,850; Stevens $3,150;   b. Scott $850;   Stevens $1,150;   c. Scott ($1,650); Stevens ($1,350)   3. Stewart $5,517.50;   Stone $6,482.50
5. a. Fisher $609.23;   b. Fisher $609.23;   c. Fisher $581.54

18.4

1. A. Lew $14,000;   Lear $12,000;   Luff $12,000;   B. Lew $9766.67;   Lear $7,766.67;   Luff $7,766.66;   C. Lew $7,400;   Lear $5,400;   Luff $5,400
3. Net Income Distribution: Nelson $9,718;   McDonald $8,282
Net Loss Distribution: Nelson ($662);   McDonald ($3,338)
5. Mutch $57,900;   Moore $76,200

Chapter Review

1. A. Each gets $3,333.33;   B. A ($5,000);   B ($3,000);   C ($2,000);
C. A $350;   B $612.50;   C 437.50;   D. A $350;   B $250;   C $150;
E. A ($166.67);   B ($333.33)   C ($500.00)

3.

		X	Y	Z
	A.	$483.33	$333.33	$183.34
	B.	1,500.00	1,000.00	1,500.00
	C.	93.33	(146.67)	(146.66)
	D.	625.00	875.00	1,500.00
	E.	300.00	525.00	675.00

19.1

		Price	Total	Commission	Total Cost
1.	A.	$17^1/_8$	$3,425.00	$85.63	$3,510.63
	B.	$308^1/_4$	53,953.13	944.18	54,897.31
	C.	$11^1/_2$	1,766.13	44.15	1,810.28
	D.	$16^1/_2$	8,250.00	206.25	8,456.25
	E.	57	1,999.38	49.98	·2,049.36

3. Commission $190.38, Cost per Share $57.82
5. $4,096.73

19.2

		Closing Price	Total	Commission	Total Cost
1.	A	$80^3/_4$	$16,150.00	$150	$16,300.00
	B	$98^1/_8$	11,775.00	90	11,865.00
	C	$91^1/_4$	28,287.50	232.50	28,520.00
	D	$76^1/_8$	3,045.00	30.00	3,075.00
	E	96	16,320.00	127.50	16,447.50

3. $54.67   5. $27,600; $920, $234.79

19.3

1. a. 3.73%;   b. 4.88%;   c. 4.55%,   d. 8.37%;   e. 2.52%
3. Stock Yield 4.12%; Capital Gain $62.28; Percent of Gain 22.80%; Annual Percent of Gain 7.60%   5.   Net Proceeds $5,254.35; Gain on Sale $369.97; Dividend Yield 23.03%; Total Percent of Gain 23.697%, Annual Percent of Gain 3.39%

19.4

1. 8.25%   3. 9.56%   5. Cost $202,125, Yield 9.13%

19.5

Problem: Totals: a. $15,007.50;   b. $6878.50;   c. $28,417.50

Chapter Review

1. $351.94   3. Cost $80,943.75; Cost per Bond $952.28; Accrued Interest $1,886.53   5.   Yield 5.05%; Capital Gain $241.38; Total Percent of Gain 64.35%; Annual Percent of Gain 16.09%   7. 8.32%

20.1

1. a. 25%;   b. 14.29%;   c. 3.33%;   d. 2.5%   3. $1,200
5. Book Value $4,410, Sold for $410 Less   7. Annual Depreciation $1,100

20.2

1 SL Rates: a. 12.5%;   b. 8.33%;   c. 6.67%;   d. 6.25%
DDB Rates: a. 25%;   b. 16.67%;   c. 13.33%;   d. 12.5%
3. DDB Rate: 40%, Annual Depreciation Amounts: $7,400, $4,400, $2,664, $1,598, and $648
5. a. $8,402;   b. $1,762

20.3

1. SYD denominators: a. 36;   b. 78;   c. 120;   d. 136
First Year Fractions: a. $8/_{36}$;   b. $12/_{78}$;   c. $15/_{120}$;   d. $16/_{136}$ 3. The annual depreciation begins with $900 for the first year and decreases $60 each year from then on.   5. a. $4,287;   b. $1,225;   c. $1,913, $1,434, $1,076;
d. DDB;   e. No;   f. Takes more expenses earlier

20.4

1.   1975: $4,611;   1976: $4,690;   1977: $4,717;   1978: $4,559;   1979: $4,480;   1980: $4,585

3.

Year	Miles	Annual Dep.	Accum. Dep.	Book Value
1976	31,200	$3,588	$3,588	$15,112
1977	35,000	4,025	7,613	11,087
1978	28,000	3,220	10,833	7,867
1979	23,000	2,645	13,478	5,222
1980	31,000	3,565	17,043	1,657

20.5

1. $75,000   3. $129,360   5. $11,900

Chapter Review

1. Straight-Line $7,500; Sum-of-the-Years Digits $12,857; DDB $16,667
3. Depletion Cost per Ton: .33125; First-Year Charge: $26,500

21.1

1. Cost of Goods Sold $2,480, 7/31 Inventory $1,815

21.2

1. a. 50;   b. $2,550.00;   c. $2,850.00;   d. $667.50;
   e. $2,181.60
3. Value of Inventory $1,995, Cost of Goods Sold $2,195

21.3

1. Value of 4/30 Inventory $174.45, Cost of Sales $280.55, Gross Profit $361.95
3. Purchases $2,550; Inventory $700; Cost of Goods Sold $2,150

21.4

1. Value of 4/30 Inventory $149.45, Cost of Sales $305.55, Gross Profit $336.95
3. 12/31 Inventory $590; Cost of Goods Sold $2,260

21.5

1. Estimated Inventory $43,750   3. $27,621   5. $77,500

Chapter Review

3. A. Cost of Goods Sold $15,000, Estimated Ending Inventory $5,000
   B. Cost of Goods Sold $28,700, Estimated Ending Inventory $4,800
   C. Cost of Goods Sold $46,200, Estimated Ending Inventory $40,300

22.1

1.	Cash	CA	Marketable Securities	CA
	Accounts Receivable	CA	Investment in Y Corporation	I
	Salaries Payable	CL	Contrib. Cap. in Excess of Par	PIC
	Notes Payable	CL	Common Stock, $40 Par	CS
	Office Supplies	CA	Store Equipment	P
	Land	P	Building	P
	Taxes Payable	CL	Accounts Payable	CL
	Long-Term Bonds Payable	L-TL	Retained Earnings	RE
	Merchandise Inventory	CA	Patent	OA

22.2

1.	Cost of Goods Sold	RR	Insurance Expense—Office	G
	Sales	R	Deprec. Ex.—Store Equipment	S
	Advertising	S	Loss on Disposal of Equipment	ORE
	Insurance Expense—Store	S	Delivery Expense	S
	Deprec. Ex.—Office	G	Misc. Expense—General	G
	Sales Salaries	S	Misc. Expense—Selling	G
	Office Salaries	G	Income Taxes	T
	Rent Expense—Store	S	Sales Returns	RR

22.3

		Amount	Percent
1.	Gross Sales	$29,650	24.03
	Less: Returns & Allowances	150	4.41
	Net Sales	29,800	24.83
	Cost of Sales	22,300	27.20
	Gross Margin on Sales	7,500	19.74
	Total Selling Expenses	2,400	14.37
	Total General Expenses	660	6.78
	Total Operating Expenses	3,060	11.57
	Net Income from Operations	4,440	38.41
	Other Income	(250)	(22.73)
	Other Expense	600	50.00
	Net Income Before Taxes	4,790	41.80
	Income Taxes	1,340	23.06
	Net Income	3,450	61.06

22.4

		1980 Percent	1979 Percent
1.	Gross Sales	102.17	102.83
	Net Sales	100.0	100.0
	Cost of Sales	69.63	68.33
	Gross Margin on Sales	30.37	31.67
	Total Selling Expenses	12.75	13.92
	Total General Expenses	6.94	8.12
	Total Operating Expenses	19.69	22.0

	1980 Percent	1979 Percent
Net Income from Operations	10.68	9.63
Other Income	.57	.92
Other Expenses	.40	1.00
Net Income before Taxes	10.85	9.55
Income Taxes	4.77	4.84
Net Income	6.07	4.71

22.5

1. a. Current Ratio 2.01;   b.   Quick Ratio 1.22, Inventory Turnover 7.82, Number of Days in Inventory Approx. 47, Trade Receivable Turnover 10.21, Average Collection Period Approx. 36 Days
3. a. Debt-to-Assets Ratio 44.38%;   b.   Owners' Equity-to-Asset Ratio 55.63%;   c.   Debt-to-Owners'-Equity Ratio 79.78%

Chapter Review

A.   Ratios and percentages for 1980:
1.   Current Ratio 2.0   2.   Quick Ratio, .87
3.   Inventory Turnover 10.71, or a 34-day supply
4.   Receivables Turnover 24.31, Average Collection Period 15 Days
5.   Net Operating Margin 13.02%
6.   Return on Owners' Equity 32.74%
7.   Return on Assets 20.98%
8.   Leverage 11.76%
9.   Debt/Assets Ratio 42.86%
10.   Debt/Owners' Equity Percentage 75%
11.   Owners' Equity/Asset Percentage 57.14%

23.1

1. $23,250   3. $3.25   5.   Net Cash Flow, 1st Year $14,970, 2nd Year $15,402, 3rd Year $16,834

23.2

1. Payback period 5.5 Years; Proposal Rejected
3. Project 1 Payback 3 Years and 6 Months, Project 2 Payback 3 Years and 1 Month, Project 2 should have first priority.

23.3

1. 8.70%

3.

Project I

	Depreciation	Net Income	Remaining Investment
1.	$10,000	($2,000)	$45,000
2.	10,000	3,000	35,000
3.	10,000	8,000	25,000
4.	10,000	11,000	15,000
5.	10,000	11,000	5,000
		$31,000	180,000

Annual Depreciation $10,000; Average Annual Income $6,200; Estimated Average Investment $30,000
Project II: Annual Depreciation $12,000; Average Annual Income $6,000; Average Investment $30,000

5.   Project 1 Payback Period 3 Years and 9 months; Project 2 Payback Period 3 Years and 6 Months

23.4

1.   a.   A NPV $4,000; B NPV $2,650;   b.   Accept both projects if $40,000 is available; accept only A if only $20,000 is available.
3.   NPV is negative $780. Reject.
5.   a.   X   Payback, 2 Years and 4 Months, Y   Payback 3 Years;   b.   X   NPV $84, Y NPV $202;   c.   X;   d.   Y;   e.   Y does not pay back as fast but has a higher present value. The longer the payback, the more uncertain the cash flow.

Chapter Review

A.   Net income: 1. $6,000   2. $4,875   3. $6,375
B.   Cash Flow: 1. $12,000   2. $12,375   3. $13,875
C.   Payback Period: 1.   2.5 Years   2.   2.42 Years   3.   2.16 Years
D.   Average Rate of Return: 1.   40%   2.   32.5%   3.   42.5%
E.   Net Present Value: 1. $43,260   2. $37,583   3. $42,138